cinematography
theory and practice

imagemaking for cinematographers & directors

second edition

cinematography
theory and practice

imagemaking for cinematographers and directors

second edition

blain brown

Focal Press
Taylor & Francis Group

NEW YORK AND LONDON

First published 2012
by Focal Press
70 Blanchard Road, Suite 402, Burlington, MA 01803

Simultaneously published in the UK
by Focal Press
2 Park Square, Milton Park, Abingdon, Oxon OX14 4RN

Focal Press is an imprint of the Taylor & Francis Group, an informa business

Library of Congress Cataloging-in-Publication Data
Brown, Blain.
  Cinematography : theory and practice : image making for cinematographers and directors / Blain Brown.
     p. cm.
   ISBN 978-0-240-81209-0
  1. Cinematography. I. Title.
   TR850.B7598 2012
   778.5--dc22   2011010755

ISBN: 9780240812090 (pbk)
ISBN: 9780080958958 (ebk)

contents

INTRODUCTION

To a great extent the knowledge base of the cinematographer overlaps with the knowledge base of the director. The cinematographer must have a solid familiarity with the terms and concepts of directing, and the more a director knows about cinematography the more he or she will be able to utilize these tools and especially be better equipped to fully utilize the knowledge and talent of a good *DP* (*Director of Photography*). Any successful director will tell you that one of the real secrets of directing is being able to recognize and maximize what every member of the team can contribute.

The DP has some duties that are entirely technical, and the director has responsibilities with the script and the actors, but in between those two extremes they are both involved with the same basic task: *storytelling with the camera* — this is what makes the creative collaboration between them so important. In that regard, one of the main purposes of this book is to discuss "what directors need to know about the camera" and "what cinematographers need to know about directing," with the goal of improving communication between them and fostering a more common language for their collaborative efforts.

The primary purpose of this book is to introduce cinematography/filmmaking as we practice it on a professional level, whether it be on film, video, digital, High Def or any other imaging format. Storytelling is storytelling and shooting is shooting, no matter what medium you work in. Except for two specific sections that relate to motion picture emulsions and the laboratory, the information here is universal to any form of shooting — film, video, or digital.

The first three chapters are a basic introduction to the essential concepts of *visual storytelling*. It is absolutely essential to understand that a cinematographer or videographer cannot be just a technician who sets up "good shots." Directors vary in how much input they want from a DP in selecting and setting up shots; but the DP must understand the methods of visual storytelling in either case.

Cinema is a language and within it are the specific vocabularies and sublanguages of the lens, composition, visual design, lighting, image control, continuity, movement, and point-of-view. Learning these languages and vocabularies is a never-ending and a fascinating life-long study. As with any language, you can use it to compose clear and informative prose or to create visual poetry.

While wielding these tools to fully utilize the language of cinema, there are, of course, rigorous technical requirements; it is up the DP to ensure that these requirements are met and that everything works properly. Those requirements are covered here as well, as not only are they an integral part of the job, but many seemingly mechanical requirements can also be used as forms of visual expression as well. This is why it is important for the director to have at least a passing knowledge of these technical issues. Another reason is that less experienced directors can get themselves into trouble by asking for something that is not a good idea in terms of time, budget, equipment, or crew resources.

This is not to suggest that a director should ever demand less than the best or settle for less than their vision. The point is that by knowing more about what is involved on the technical side, the director can make better choices and work with their DP to think of solutions that are better suited to the situation.

We Don't Need No Stinkin' Rules

It is a well-worn saying that you should "know the rules before you break them." This is certainly true in filmmaking. Newcomers often try to do things "the way it's never been done before." Sometimes (rarely) the results are brilliant, even visionary. In film, however, *reshooting* is extremely expensive and sometimes impossible.

All of the basic rules of filmmaking exist for good reasons: they are the result of over 100 years of practical experience and experimentation. Can you break the rules? Absolutely! Great filmmakers do it all the time. Once you not only know the rules but *understand why they exist*, it is possible to use a violation of them as a powerful tool. Our emphasis here is to not only explain the rules but also the underlying reasons that they exist.

The Scope of this Book

What does the cinematographer need to know about filmmaking in order to do the job properly? Almost everything.

The knowledge base encompasses lenses, exposure, composition, continuity, editorial needs, lighting, grip, color, the language of the camera, even the basic elements of story structure. The job is storytelling with the camera, and the more you know about the elements of that art the better you will be able to assist the director in accomplishing those goals. The DP need not command all these techniques at the level of detail of the editor, the writer, or the key grip, but there must be a firm understanding of the basics and more importantly the *possibilities* — the tools and their potential to serve the storytelling and the vision of the director.

This is especially true as the task of directing is more and more accessible to writers, actors, and others who may not have as broad a background in physical production and the visual side of storytelling. In this situation, being a DP who has a thorough command of the entire scope of filmmaking but is able and willing to work as a collaborator without trying to impose their own vision in place of the director's is a strong asset. By the same token, to have a reputation as a director who can utilize the talents of their creative team and get the best from everybody is also a goal to aim for.

In this book we cover the storytelling issues, continuity, and providing what the editor needs as well as optics, special effects, exposure, composition, filters, color control, and all the other aspects of cinematography that go into the job — all of them approached from the point of view of their value as storytelling tools. The craft of lighting is included here, but for a much more in-depth and thorough discussion of lighting, see the first book, *Motion Picture and Video Lighting*. It is also important to note that if you are dedicated to the idea of using the medium of cinema to its fullest extent and employing every tool of the art form to serve your story, then lighting for video or High Def is not essentially different from lighting for film.

Titles and Terminology

Cinematographer refers to someone who shoots film or video. *Director of Photography* refers to a cinematographer on any type of project. *Cameraman/camerawoman/cameraperson* is interchangeable with either of the above. Although a great deal of production is now done on *High Def* (HD) video, and HD is clearly the wave of the future, it has become common practice to still refer to it as *film* and *filmmaking*.

writing with motion

WRITING WITH MOTION

The term *cinematography* is from the Greek roots meaning "writing with motion." At the heart of it, filmmaking is shooting — but cinematography is more than the mere act of photography. It is the process of taking ideas, words, actions, emotional subtext, tone, and all other forms of nonverbal communication and *rendering them in visual terms*. As we will use the term here, *cinematic technique* is the entire range of methods and techniques that we use to add layers of meaning and subtext to the "content" of the film — the dialog and action.

The tools of cinematic technique are used by both the director and DP, either working together or in doing their individual jobs. As mentioned, cinematography is far more than just "photographing" what is in front of the camera — the tools, the techniques and the variations are wide ranging in scope; this is at the heart of the symbiosis of the DP and the director.

Building a Visual World

When we create a film project, one of our primary tasks is to create a visual world for the characters to inhabit. This visual world is an important part of how the audience will perceive the story; how they will understand the characters and their motivations.

Think of great films like *On the Waterfront, Apocalypse Now,* or *The Big Sleep.* They all have a definite, identifiable universe in which they exist: it consists of the locations, the sets, the wardrobe, even the sounds, but to a large extent these visual worlds are created though the cinematography. All these elements work together, of course — everything in visual storytelling is interrelated: the sets might be fantastic, but if the lighting is terrible, then the end result will be substandard.

Let's look at this sequence from early in *Blade Runner*: (Figures 1.2, through 1.5) Without a single line of dialog, we know it is a high-tech, futuristic world; giant electric signs and flying cars tell us this. The extravagant skyscrapers and squalid street life tell us a great deal about the social structure. In addition, it always seems to be raining, hinting at dramatic climate change. Picked up by the police, Deckard (the Harrison Ford character) is taken by flying car to police headquarters, landing on the roof.

Once inside, there is a sudden shift: the interior is not futuristic at all; in fact it is the inside of the Los Angeles train station — it is *Mission Revival* in its architectural style. Why an 18th-century looking building as a location choice? One thing you will learn as a filmmaker is that everything has to be for a reason — for every choice you make, whether in the story, the location, the props, whatever. Random choices do not help you tell your story. These choices may not always be conscious decisions (although all the major ones should be), but to simply "let things happen" will almost never result in a coherent, smooth flowing story that conveys your original intentions in the way you wanted.

The camera cranes down to the roof of an office and we discover... trash. The camera continues down and we find ourselves in the captain's office. Again, its style and set dressing seems completely anachronistic and odd: wood filing cabinets, a desk fan, an old TV. Why is this?

Then Deckard enters and his trench coat with the upturned collar provides the final clue: this could easily be a scene from a *film noir* detective story. The director is sending us a simple message: this may be the future with flying cars and replicants, but at the heart

Figure 1.1. (previous page). A young Orson Welles in preparation.

Figures 1.2 through 1.5. Visual elements carry the story in this early scene from *Blade Runner,* but they also supply important visual cues about the subtext and tone of the narrative. This is the essence of visual storytelling: to convey meaning to the viewer in ways other than words — to add levels of meaning *in addition to* the dialog and action

of it, this is an old-fashioned detective story with the hard-boiled sleuth and the *femme fatale* — and all of this is communicated entirely through visual means.

So how do we do it? As cinematographers, directors, production designers, and editors, how do we accomplish these aims? What are the essential elements we work with and manipulate to create this visual world?

If cinema is a language, then we must ask: what is the structure of that language? What is vocabulary, what are the rules of grammar, the structure of this cinematic language? What are the *tools* of cinematography and filmmaking — the essential techniques, methods, and elements that we can use to tell our story visually?

Figure 1.6. Strong visual elements tell us a great deal of the situation of the character in the opening frame of *Punch Drunk Love*.

THE [CONCEPTUAL] TOOLS OF CINEMATOGRAPHY

What we're talking about here is not the *physical* tools of filmmaking: the camera, dolly, the lights, cranes and camera mounts, we are talking about the *conceptual* tools of the trade.

So what are they? What are the conceptual tools of visual storytelling that we employ in all forms of visual storytelling? There are many, but we can roughly classify them into some general categories.

• The frame
• Light and color
• The lens
• Movement
• Texture
• Establishing
• POV

The Frame

Selecting the frame is the fundamental act of filmmaking; as filmmakers we must direct the audience's attention: "look here, now look at this, now over here..." Choosing the frame is a matter of conveying the story, but it is also a question of composition, rhythm, and perspective.

Take this opening frame from *Punch Drunk Love* (Figure 1.6). It gives us a great deal of information about the situation and the main character. Instantly, we know he is isolated, cut off from most of the world. The wide and distant shot emphasizes his isolation and loneliness reinforced by the color scheme and the lack of wall decoration. The dull shapeless overhead fluorescent lighting underscores the mood and tone of the scene. Finally, the *negative space* on the right not only plays into the isolation and loneliness but into the possibility of something about to happen.

The strong lines of perspective, both horizontal and vertical, converge on him, "pinning" him in his hunched-over position. Without a word being said, we know a great deal about this person, his world, and social situation, all of which are fundamental to the story.

This frame from a beach scene in *Angel Heart* (Figure 1.7) also communicates a great deal: something is odd, out-of-balance. In unconventional framing, most of the frame is sky: negative space, we barely see the beach at all. One man is bundled in a coat, the other in

a T-shirt, even though it hardly seems like good tanning conditions. The viewpoint is distant, observational. We know this is going to be no ordinary everyday conversation. Even when the dialog begins and you would normally expect the director to go in for close-ups, the camera hangs back, reinforcing the strangeness of the situation.

In this scene from *The Verdict* (Figures 1.8 and 1.9) the entire story is at a climactic point: the trial has reached the end, the lawyer (Paul Newman) has had his entire case thrown out, witnesses disqualified, evidence excluded. He has nothing left but his final summation and everything depends on it. Even though the courtroom is crowded, he is surrounded by empty space: isolated and alone visually, this

Figure 1.7. (top) A frame from *Angel Heart*.

Figures 1.8 and 1.9. (middle and bottom) This scene from *The Verdict* starts with a wide shot, then *pushes in* to a close-up.

Figure 1.10. (top) The compression of space created by a very long lens establishes the visual impression of a trap, a spider's web in the final scene of *Seven* — an excellent example of visual metaphor in cinematography.

Figure 1.11. (bottom) An extremely wide lens creates distortion for comic effect in *City of Lost Children*.

reflects his situation — he is utterly on his own at this point. Strong lines of perspective cut him off and lead the eye constantly back to him.

A lamp hangs over his head like the sword of Damocles as if it might come crashing down any instant. All eyes are turned toward him at the almost exact center of the frame; clearly the weight of the world is on him at this instant. Everything about the visuals tells us that this is his do-or-die moment — that everything about the case, and indeed about his entire life, depends on what he is about to say. As the scene builds in a continuous shot, the camera slowly *pushes in* to a medium shot, thus excluding nearly everything else in the courtroom and focusing the viewer's attention on him alone: other people still in the shot are out of focus.

The Lens

Again, we are not talking about the physical lens, what concerns us here is how various lenses *render* images in different ways. This is a powerful tool of visual storytelling — the ability of optics to alter our perception of the physical world. Every lens has a "personality" — a flavor and an inflection it adds to the image. There are many

factors involved: contrast and sharpness, for example, but by far the most influential aspect of a lens is the focal length: how *wide* or *long* it is. A short focal length lens has a wide field of view, and a long focal length lens is like a telescope or binoculars; it has a narrow field of view.

More importantly, a long lens *compresses* space and a wide lens *expands* and distorts space. Look at this frame from *Seven* (Figure 1.10): at the climactic ending of the film, the detectives are taking John Doe to a place only he knows; as a part of their deal they are kept in the dark. The extremely long lens compresses the space and makes the transmission towers seem like they are right on top of each other: the visual metaphor it establishes is a spider's web, a trap — which is exactly what it turns out to be. It is a powerfully graphic and arresting image that precisely reinforces the story point at that moment.

We see the opposite effect in the frame from *City of Lost Children* (Figure 1.11). Here an extremely wide lens, a visual constant in the films of Jean-Pierre Jeunet, expands our perception of space and distorts the face — it has an effect that is both comedic and ominous.

Figure 1.12. (top) Lighting is not only a strong compositional element in *Apocalypse Now*, it also conveys a great deal of emotional tone and tells us something about the mental state of the character.

Figure 1.13. (bottom) A man trapped in a high-tech world, hunted and ensnared: lighting tells the story in this frame from *Blade Runner*.

Figure 1.14. (top) Desaturated sepia-toned color is the key texture element in *O Brother, Where Art Thou*.

Figure 1.15. (bottom) Color and shadows in addition to makeup effects are central to this music video *Come To Daddy* (Aphex Twin) by Chris Cunningham.

Light and Color

Light and color are some of the most powerful tools in the cinematographers arsenal. Lighting and controlling color are what takes up most of the director of photographer's time on most sets and for good reason. They also have a special power that is shared only by a very few art forms such as music and dance: they have the ability to reach people at a gut, emotional level.

This is the very definition of cinematic language as we use the term here: visual tools that add additional layers of meaning to the content of the story. In this frame from *Apocalypse Now* (Figure 1.12), the single shaft of light powerfully communicates the idea of a man alone, isolated in his madness.

In a climactic frame from *Blade Runner* (Figure 1.13), the stabbing shafts of light and silhouetted bars on the window instantly communicate a man ensnared in a high-tech nightmare world from which there is no escape.

Texture

These days, we rarely shoot anything "straight" — meaning a scene where we merely record reality and attempt to reproduce it exactly as it appears in life. In most cases — particularly in feature films, commercials, and certainly in music videos — we manipulate the image in some way, we add some visual *texture* to it; this is not to be confused with the surface texture of objects. There are many devices we use to accomplish this: changing the color and contrast of the picture, desaturating the color of the image, filters, fog and smoke effects, rain, using unusual film stocks, various printing techniques, and of course the whole range of image manipulation that can be accomplished with digital images on the computer — the list goes on and on.

Some of these image manipulations are done with the camera, some are done with lighting, some are mechanical efx, and some are done in *post production*. A particularly dramatic example is *O Brother, Where Art Thou?* (Figure 1.14). Cinematographer Roger Deakins experimented with many camera and filter techniques to create the faded postcard sepia-toned look that he and the director envisioned. None of them proved satisfactory and in the end, he turned to an entirely new process: the *digital intermediate* (*DI*). The DI employs the best of both worlds: the original images are shot on film and ultimately will be projected on film in theaters. But in the intermediate stages, the image is manipulated electronically, in the digital world, with all the vast array of tools for image making that computers afford us — and there are many.

Some similar techniques are used in this music video *Come to Daddy* by English music video director Chris Cunningham (Figure 1.15) for Aphex Twin. In this video, Cunningham uses a wide variety of visual texture devices, including making film look like bad video, stutter frames, slow motion, and many more. Most visible in this frame are the shadowy lighting, contrasty look and the green/cyan shift of the entire image, all of which reinforce the ghastly, surrealistic imagery of the content.

Figure 1.16. This shot from *Angel Heart* is an *insert* — a tighter shot of a detail from the larger scene. Here it is an *informational insert*, it *establishes* some point of information that the filmmaker needs the audience to know, in this case, that the private detective has many different fake identities at the ready.

Figures 1.17 through 1.23. This opening scene from *Working Girl* is not only a dynamic helicopter move, it is also a powerful visual metaphor that introduces us to two main characters, establishes the tone and some key ideas of the film, some of the *backstory*, and even hints at some of the aspirations and destiny of the main character.

Movement

Movement is a powerful tool of filmmaking; in fact, movies are one of the few art forms that employ motion and time; dance obviously being another one. This opening sequence from *Working Girl* (Figures 1.17 through 1.23) is an excellent example of exciting, dynamic motion that serves an important storytelling purpose. It is a kinetic, whirling helicopter shot that begins by circling the head of the Statue of Liberty, then picks up the Staten Island ferry, and then ultimately goes inside (in a dissolve that simulates continuing the single moving shot) to find the main character, played by Melanie Griffith.

This is far more than just a powerfully dynamic motion; it is also a clear *visual metaphor*: the story is about the main characters transition from a working girl secretary trapped in a dreary existence where every day starts with a ride on the ferry; on this day her birthday is celebrated with a single candle in a cupcake. By the end of the film she is transformed into a strong, independent woman with a good haircut who stands proud and tall, not unlike the Statue of Liberty — the image that opens the film.

Establishing

Establishing is the ability of the camera to reveal or conceal information; think of it as a visual equivalent of *exposition*, which in verbal storytelling means conveying important information or background to the audience. It is really at the heart of telling a story visually — letting the camera reveal information is usually a more cinematic way of getting information across to the audience than is dialog or a *voice-over* narrator. In this frame from *Angel Heart* (Figure 1.16), a close-up of Mickey Rourke's wallet as he leafs through it conveys vital story information without words: clearly he carries fake IDs to assist him in his slightly sleazy work as a cut-rate private detective.

Establishing is accomplished primarily by a choice of the frame and the lens, but it can also be done with lighting that conceals or reveals certain details of the scene.

Point-of-View

Point-of-view (POV) is a key tool of visual storytelling. We use the term in many different ways on a film set, but the most often used meaning is to have the camera see something in much the same way as one of the characters would see it: to view the scene from that character's point-of-view. The importance of this concept can be seen in Figure 1.1. A young Orson Welles has drawn a simple diagram: "eye = I" — the camera essentially becomes the perception of the viewer.

This is fundamental to cinema: the camera is the "eye" of the audience; how the camera takes in the scene is how the audience will perceive it. To a great extent, *cinematography consists of showing the audience what we want them to know about the story*; POV shots tend to make the audience more involved in the story for the simple reason that what they see and what the character sees are momentarily the same thing — in a sense, the audience *inhabits* the character's brain and experiences the world as that character is experiencing it.

There are many ways POV is used in filmmaking, and those will be discussed later, but these frames from *Chinatown* show a basic use of the method. In Figures 1.24 through 1.26, we see *over-the-shoulder* as Jake Gittes follows someone he has been hired to investigate. Parking facing away from the subject to remain unseen, he glances into his rear-view mirror. The scene cuts to *what he sees in the mirror* — his *subjective POV*.

Figure 1.24. (top) This scene from *Chinatown* employs POV to establish plot elements. The first shot is an *over-the-shoulder* which establishes the scene and the relationship between the two cars.

Figures 1.25. (middle) We see the detective looking; this establishes that what we see next will be his point-of-view.

Figure 1.26. (bottom) We see his *subjective POV* of what he sees in the mirror; this is the payoff of what has been established in the previous two shots.

Chinatown employs another layer of POV as well — called *detective POV*. A narrative device that is used in novels and stories as well, it simply means that the audience does not know something until the detective know it — we only discover clues when he discovers them. This means that the viewer is even more involved in how the main character is experiencing the events of the story. Polanksi is a master of taking this story technique and he makes it truly visual. For example a very large number of shots in the film are *over-the-shoulders* of Jake Gittes, the detective played by Jack Nicholson.

PUTTING IT ALL TOGETHER

Filmmaking is a strange and mysterious enterprise — it involves mixing and coordinating many different elements, some of them artistic, some of them technical and businesslike. In particular, the cinematographer must be able to bridge that gap — to understand the practical side of dealing with the camera, lenses, digital aspects, file types, workflow, and so on, but also have their minds firmly planted in the artistic side of creating a visual world, visual metaphor, and storytelling. There is a third aspect as well: being an amateur psychologist. On a film set, there is no more fundamental collaboration than that of the cinematographer and director.

Many directors are adept at conveying their vision of the project either verbally or with drawings, metaphors, or photographic references. Some directors are not good at this — they have a visual

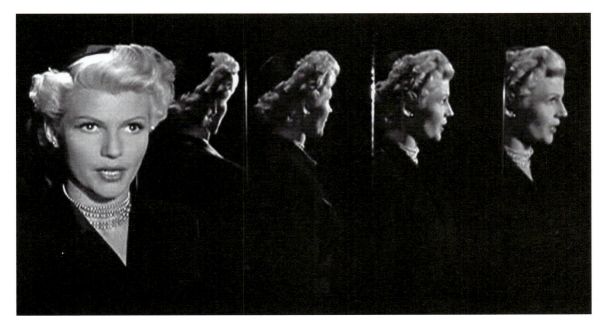

Film is a dream — but whose?
Bruce Kawin

shooting methods

WHAT IS *CINEMATIC*?

It's easy to think of filmmaking as not much more than "We'll put the actors on the set and roll the camera." Obviously there is much more involved, but it's important to understand that even if all you do is record what is in front of the camera, you are still making definite decisions about how the audience is going to perceive the scene.

This is the crucial point: ultimately, filmmaking is about what the audience "gets" from each scene, not only intellectually (such as the plot) but also emotionally. Perhaps just as important, at the end of each scene are they still asking themselves, "I wonder what happens next?" In other words, are they still interested in the story?

A Question of Perception

First of all, we have to recognize that how we perceive the world in a film is fundamentally different from how we perceive the world with our eyes and ears. Film only presents the illusion of the reality.

What do we mean when we say something is *cinematic*? Most of the time, people use the word to mean that a novel or play is fast-paced and visual. Here, we use it in a different way; in this discussion we use the term to mean all the techniques and methods of filmmaking that we use to *add layers of meaning* to the content.

Content means the things we are recording – the sets, the actors, the dialog, the props, and so on. In the theater, there is nothing between the eyes and ears of the audience and what is happening in front of them. In film, we have many methods of altering their perception of that reality.

How It's Different from Theater

In the early days of cinema, many practitioners were theatrical people. When they first saw the movie camera, they conceived it as a tool to extend their audience: they just put the camera where the audience would be and used it to *record* a performance. The upshot of this is that the entire performance is viewed from a single point of view, which is how a theatergoer sees a play. As a result, in early films the camera did not move, there were no close-ups, no shifting point-of-view, and so forth — in other words, practically none of the tools and techniques of cinema as we know them now.

In short, these early films depend almost entirely on their content, just as theater does, but they lack the immediacy and personal experience of a live theater performance. The history of cinema can easily be studied as the introduction and addition of various techniques and methods that we call "cinematic" — in other words, the conceptual tools we referred to in the previous chapter: the frame, the lens, light and color, texture, movement, establishing, and point-of-view. In this chapter we will deal primarily with the frame and another important tool: editing. While editing is not the cinematographer's job, it is critical to understand that the job of the cinematographer and director working on the set is to provide the editor with footage that he or she can use creatively and effectively.

Visual Subtext and Visual Metaphor

So cinematography has many purposes, some of them far beyond the simple act of "photographing" the action. In fact, if you are a filmmaker who only wants the camera to record "reality," you are ignoring some of the most powerful jobs cinematography can do for you. Many of these methods are all about adding *visual subtext* to your scenes. In addition to visual subtext, *visual metaphor* can be a powerful tool as well.

Figure 2.1. (previous page) *The Lady from Shanghai.*

Figure 2.2. To convey the sense of the rigid, hierarchical social structure of 18th century Europe, Stanley Kubrick uses formal, geometric composition throughout most of *Barry Lyndon*.

Deconstructing Reality and Putting It Back Together

Let's say we have a typical scene: two people sitting at a table talking and having coffee. We do a wide shoot, of course, but we also get close-ups of the two characters, a tight shot of the coffee cups, a close shot of the clock on the wall, perhaps a shot of the waitress as she pours, and so on. Think of it this way: every time we do a shot we are taking a slice, a piece of that scene — we are dividing up the scene into small parts; to use a fancy term, we are *deconstructing* it.

We have taken the "real reality" (the actors, the set, the props, the dialog) and broken it up into pieces: the shots that are "in the can." Now comes the second step: we put it back together. This is editing. The magic is that we can reassemble this reality in a any way we choose. We can move things around in time and in physical relation to each other: changing the pace, the tone, the mood, even the events. We create a new reality which can be a fairly accurate representation of what really happened or can be very different — in the viewer's perception.

THE FRAME

Setting the frame is a series of choices that decide what the viewer will see and not see. The first of these decisions is where to place the camera in relation to the scene. After that, there are choices concerning the field of vision and movement, all of which work together to influence how the audience will perceive the shot: both in outright content and in emotional undercurrent and subtext to the action and the dialog.

Static Frame

A static frame is a proscenium. The action of the scene is presented as a stage show: we are a third person observer. There is a proscenium wall between us and the action. This is especially true if everything else about the frame is also normal — that is, level, normal lens, no movement, and so on. This does not mean, however, that a static frame is not without value. It can be a useful tool that carries its own baggage and implications of POV and world view.

In Stanley Kubrick's film *Barry Lyndon*, the fixed, well-composed, balanced frames reflect the static, hierarchical society of the time (Figure 2.2). Everyone has his place, every social interaction is governed by well-defined rules. The actors move within this frame without being able to alter it. It is a reflection of the world they live in, and while it strongly implies a sense of order and tranquility, it also carries an overpowering lack of mobility: both social and physi-

Figure 2.3. The *perspectival appa-ratus* from Peter Greenaway's *The Draughtsman's Contract* — the fun-damental idea of selecting a view-point and defining a frame.

cal. The world is static: the characters try to find their place in it. Each scene is played out completely within this fixed frame: without movement, cuts, or changes in perspective. This use of the frame conveys a wealth of information independent of the script or the actions of the characters. It adds layers of meaning. A similar use of the static frame is the Swedish film *Songs from the Second Floor* (Figure 2.24) which also plays out every scene, with one exception, as a single long take within a completely immobile frame. Jim Jarmusch used the same technique in his second film, *Stranger Than Paradise*. Jarmusch claims that shooting scenes as a single shot was done to save film, but it is also an important stylistic element of the film.

In both the examples, the distancing nature of the frame is used for its own purpose. The filmmakers are deliberately putting the audience in the position of the impersonal observer. This can either lend an observational, judgmental tone or much like objects in the foreground of the frame, make the audience work harder to put themselves into the scene, or a combination of both. As with almost all cinematic techniques they can be used in reverse to achieve a completely different effect than normal.

CINEMA AS A LANGUAGE

You have probably heard interviews with directors where at some point they lean forward with great gravitas and pronounce, "You know, cinema is a language." The first time you hear this your reaction might was likely, "Wow, what an insight. That's deep." Perhaps sometime later you hear an interview with a different director who also announces solemnly, "Cinema is a language all it's own," and the reaction might be "Hey, he's hip to it too."

By the time you hear the fifth or sixth filmmaker grandly say, "Film is a language," your response might be "Yeah, yeah, I know that… now tell me something I can use." What is the structure of this language? What is the vocabulary, the syntax, how does it work?" This is why it is important to study cinematography as more than merely the technical aspects of motion picture photography.

The Shots: Building Blocks of a Scene

It is useful to think of "building" a scene. Since we make scenes one shot at a time, we can consider that we are assembling the elements that will make the scene. If we think of a language of cinema, these shots are the *vocabulary*; how we edit them together would be the *syntax* of this language. These are the visual aspects of the language of film; there are, of course, other properties of this language that relate more to plot structure and narrative, but here we are concerned only with the visual side of this subject.

There are a number of shots that are basic building blocks of film grammar (Figure 2.14). In a by no means exhaustive list, they are:

- Wide shot (or long shot)
- Establishing shots
- Full shot
- Cowboy
- Two shot
- Medium
- Close-ups
- Clean single
- Dirty single
- ECU
- Over-the-shoulder
- Cutaway
- Insert
- Connecting Shot
- Transitional Shot

With a few exceptions, most of these shots apply to the human form, but the terminology carries over to any subject. As they appear in the script they are called stage directions. Let's look at them individually. As with many film terms, the definitions are somewhat loose and different people have slight variations in how they apply them, particularly as you travel from city to city or work in another country; they are just general guidelines. It is only when you are lining it up through the lens that the exact frame can be decided on and all the factors that go into a shot can be fully assessed.

As they appear in the script, stage directions are completely non-binding — it is entirely up to the director to decide what shots will be used to put the scene together. The screenwriter really has no say over what shots will be used, but they are helpful in visualizing the story as you read the script — especially if you are giving the script to people in order to secure financing for the project or to actors so they can decide if they want to be involved. These shots are the basic vocabulary we deal with — both in terms of editing and also in terms of the director communicating to the DP what it is they are trying to do. These basic elements and how they are combined in editorial continuity are the grammar of cinema.

Wide Shot

The wide shot is any frame that encompasses the entire scene. This makes it all relative to the subject. For example, if the script says "Wide shot — the English Countryside" we are clearly talking about a big panoramic scene done with a short focal length lens taking in all the eye can see. On the other hand, if the description is "Wide shot — Leo's room" this is clearly a much smaller shot but it still encompasses all or most of the room.

Figure 2.4. An *establishing shot* from *The Shining*. It gives a great deal of information about the size, location and layout of the hotel — which is essentially a main character in the film. This is also an example of a *wide shot*.

Establishing Shots

The establishing shot is usually a wide shot. It is the opening shot of a scene that tells us where we are. A typical one might be "Establishing shot — Helen's office." This might consist of a wide shot of an office building, so when we cut to a shot of Helen at her desk, we know where we are: in her office building. We've seen that it is a big, modern building, very upscale and expensive and that it is located in midtown Manhattan, and the bustling activity of streets indicate it's another hectic workday in New York. The establishing shot has given us a great deal of information.

Laying Out the Scene — Establishing the Geography

A phrase that is often used is that we have to "establish the geography." In other words we have to give the audience some idea of where they are, what kind of place it is, where objects and people are in relation to each other. Other aspects of this are discussed in the chapter *Cinematic Continuity*.

Establishing the geography is helpful to the audience to let them know the "lay of the land" within a scene. It helps them orient themselves and prevents confusion that might divert their attention from the story. There are times when you want to keep the layout a mystery, of course. As we will see throughout the discussion of film grammar and editing, one of the primary purposes is to not confuse the audience. There will be times of course where you will want to confuse them, but if you don't give them information and they have to spend time trying to figure something out, however subconsciously, you have taken their minds away from the characters and the story. Kurosawa is a master of this type of establishing, as in these shots from *Seven Samurai* (Figures 2.5 and 2.6). He uses it as a way to make abstract ideas concrete and visible.

An establishing shot, such as our office building example, might also include a *tilt up* to an upper floor. This indicates to the audience that we are not just seeing an office building, but that we are going

Figures 2.5 and 2.6. Ever the master of making the abstract concrete, in this scene from *Seven Samurai*, Kurosawa cuts directly from the map of the village to a shot of the samurai walking in the location he was pointing to.

inside. A further variation is to end with a *zoom in* to a particular window, a more obvious cue as to where we are headed. Shots of this type are sometimes considered old-fashioned and prosaic, but they can still be effective. Even though they do give us a good deal of information, they are still a complete stop in the dramatic action.

Many filmmakers consider it more effective if the establishing shot can be combined with a piece of the story. One example: say we are looking down that same bustling street and our character Helen comes into view, rushing frantically and holding a big stack of documents; we pan or dolly with her as she runs into the lobby and dashes to catch a departing elevator. The same information has been conveyed, but we have told a piece of the story as well. Something is up with Helen; all those documents are obviously something important that has put her under a great deal of stress.

Of course, in the story, Helen may already be in her office. One of the classic solutions has been to combine a bit of foreground action with the establishing shot. For example, we start with a medium shot of a sidewalk newsstand. An anonymous man buys a paper and we can read the headline "Scandal Disclosed," and we then tilt to the building. What we have done here is keep the audience in the story and combined it with showing the building and the context.

shooting methods

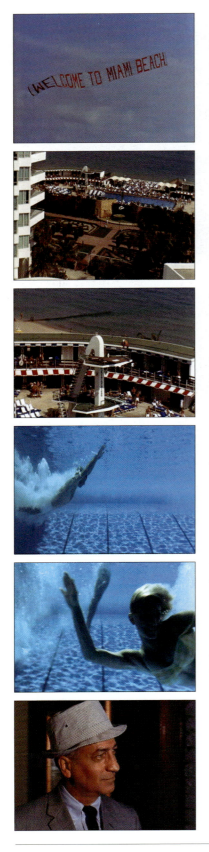

In a sense it is a bit of distraction such as a stage magician might use, but in another sense it does convey some useful information. Certainly it's a lot better than just cutting to Helen and have her do some hackneyed "on the nose" dialog such as, "Oh my god, what am I going to do about the big financial scandal?" Of course, there is one more level you can add: the guy who buys the newspaper is not an anonymous man, but turns out to be the reporter who is going to uncover the real story. These are just examples, of course, but the point is to convey the location information in combination with a piece of the story or something that conveys a visual idea, a sound track inflection or anything that increases our understanding of the place, the mood, or anything that is useful to you as the storyteller.

A more elaborate, but effective establishing sequence is this one from *Goldfinger* (Figures 2.8 to 2.13). The opening shot is a flying banner that tells the audience they are in Miami Beach, and the helicopter shot closes in on a beach hotel and then into a tighter shot of a diver. We follow him down into the water and then cut to under the water where he swims away. A crossing female swimmer carries us back in the opposite direction where we discover Felix Leiter, who walks away to find... *Bond, James Bond*. The sequence elegantly establishes not only the location and circumstance but carries us in a continuous sweep of motion and action.

Character Shots

There are a number of terms for different shots of a single character. Most movies and short films are about people, so shots of people are one of the fundamental building blocks of cinema. The same applies to most commercials and even many music videos. For illustrations of all types of character shots, see Figure 2.14.

Full Shot

Full shot indicates that we see the character from head to toe. It can refer to objects as well: a full shot of a car includes all of the car. A shot that only includes the door and the driver would be more of a medium shot. A variation on this is the *cowboy,* which is from the top of the head to midthigh, originally in order to see the six-guns on his belt. In non-English speaking countries, terms such as *plán americain* or *plano americano* refers to a shot framed from mid-leg up.

Two Shot

The *two shot* is any frame that includes two characters. The interaction between two characters in a scene is one of the most fundamental pieces of storytelling; thus the two shot is one you will use frequently. The two characters don't have to be arranged symmetrically in the frame. They might be facing each other, both facing forward, both facing away from the camera, and so on, but the methods you use for dealing with this type of scene will be the same in any case. You might also occasionally hear the term *three-shot* for a shot of three characters.

Medium Shot

The *medium shot*, like the wide shot, is relative to the subject. Obviously, it is closer than a full shot. Medium shots might be people at a table in a restaurant, or someone buying a soda, shown from the waist up. By being closer in to the action, we can see people's expressions, details of how they are dressed, and so on. We thus become more involved in what they are saying and doing, without focusing on one specific character or any particular detail.

Close-ups

Close-ups are one of the most important shots in the vocabulary. There are a number of variations: *a medium close-up* would generally be considered as something like from top of head to waist or something in that area.

A *close-up (CU)* would generally be from the top of the head to somewhere just below the shirt pockets. If the shot is cut just above the shirt pocket area, it is often called a *head and shoulders*. A *choker* would be from the top of the head down to just below the chin. A *tight close-up* would be slightly less: losing some of the forehead and perhaps some of the chin, framing the eyes, nose, and mouth. An *extreme close-up* or *ECU* might include the eyes only; this is sometimes called a *Sergio Leone* after the Italian director who used it frequently. Just as often, an ECU is an object: perhaps just a ring lying on a desktop, a watch, and so on. Any shot that includes only one character is called a *single*. Terminology for close-ups includes:

- *Medium CU.* Midchest up.
- *Choker*: from the throat up.
- *Big Head CU* or "tight CU": from just under the chin and giving a bit of "haircut." That is cutting off just a little bit of the head.
- *ECU*: Varies, but usually just mouth and eyes.

A close-up, medium or full shot might also be called a *clean single* whenever it's a shot of one actor alone. If we are shooting someone's CU and don't include any piece of the other actor, this is called a *clean single*. If we do include a little bit of the actor in front, it's often called a *dirty single*. This is not to be confused with an *over-the-shoulder* (see below), which includes more of the foreground actor.

Figure 2.7. A classic medium shot from *Shanghai Express*. Note also how the lighting is very specific for this shot and for her pose. If her head were not in just the right position, the lighting would not achieve such an elegant and powerful effect.

Figures 2.8 through 2.13. (opposite page) An *establishing sequence* from *Goldfinger*. This series of shots tells the viewer what city they are in, what hotel, where Bond is situated, and by following a swimmer from the diving board to an underwater view and pan over to find Felix Lighter, it introduces a key character.

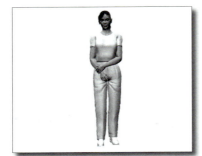

Full shot or *head-to-toe.*

Cowboy. Outside the US, sometimes called the *American shot.*

Medium. Also, any shot that shows a person alone is a *single.*

Three T's or *Medium Close-up.*

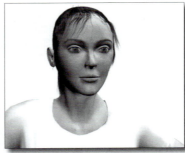

Close-up or *head and shoulders.*

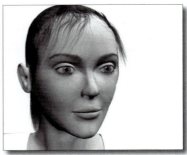

Choker or *big head close-up.*

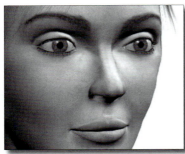

Extreme close-up (*ECU*). It's OK to give them a "haircut."

Two shot. Any shot of two people is a two shot.

Three shot. 'nuff said.

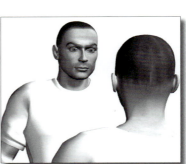

A *50-50.* Don't use it as a cheap substitute for getting proper coverage.

An *over-the-shoulder* (*OTS*). A very important shot in filmmaking.

The *answering shot* for the OTS at left.

Figure 2.14. There is a fairly standard repertoire of shots that are commonly used in film. You are not by any means limited to these shot. It's just that these are the most common ones that have names. There are some variations in the names from place to place, but overall they are fairly consistent.

Figure 2.15. (above) An atmospheric *cutaway* from *Nine and 1/2 Weeks*.

Figure 2.16. (left) A *50-50* shot from *Casablanca*.

Over-the-Shoulder

A variation of the close-up is the *over-the-shoulder* or *OTS*, looking over the shoulder of one actor to a medium or CU of the other actor. It ties the two characters together and helps put us in the position of the person being addressed. The OTS is a useful part of the vocabulary of narrative filmmaking. Even when we are in close shot of the person talking, the OTS keeps the other actor in the scene. An OTS contains more of the foreground actor than a dirty single and their position in the frame is more deliberate.

Cutaways

A *cutaway* is any shot of some person or thing in the scene other than the main characters we are covering but that is still related to the scene. The definition of a cutaway is that it is something we did not see previously in the scene, particularly in the master or any wide shots. Examples would be a cutaway to a view out the window or to the cat sleeping on the floor. Cutaways may emphasize some action in the scene, provide additional information, or be something that the character looks at or points to. If it is a shot of an entirely different location or something unrelated to the scene, then it is not a cutaway, but is a different scene and should have its own scene number in the script. An important use of cutaways is as safeties for the editor. If the editor is somehow having trouble cutting the scene, a cutaway to something else can be used to solve the problem. A good rule of thumb is in almost every scene you shoot, get some cutaways as editorial safety, even if they are not called for in the script or essential to the scene — a cutaway might save the scene in editing.

Reaction Shots

A specific type of close-up or medium is the *reaction shot*. Something happens or a character says something and we cut to another person *reacting* to what happened or what was said; it can be the other person in the dialog or someone elsewhere in the scene. Generally, the term refers to a facial expression or body language, not dialog. A reaction shot is a good way to get a safety cutaway for the editor. Sometimes the term just refers to the other side of the dialog, which is part of our normal coverage. Reaction shots are very important and many beginning filmmakers fail to shoot enough of them. Silent films

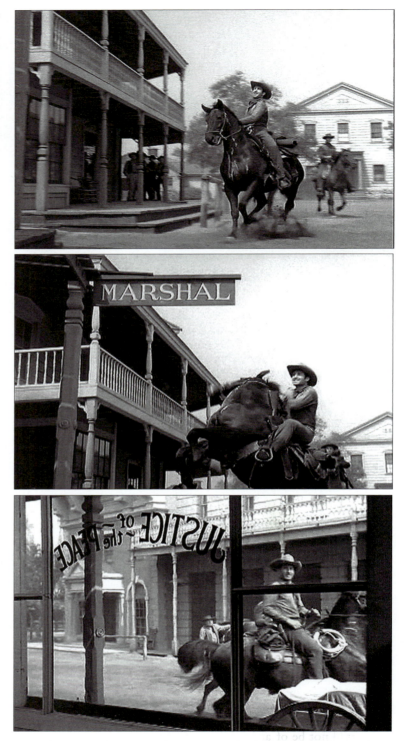

Figures 2.17 through 2.19. An elegantly executed triple *reveal* from *High Noon*. In one shot, the bad guys ride into town; as the horse rears up we see the sign that reads *Marshal*. The bad guys ride on and then from behind we see the sign that reads *Justice of the Peace*, and the camera pulls back to show the marshal in the process of getting "hitched." This shot also clearly tells us *where* we are (in town outside the marshal's office) and starts to establish the geography of the place. It also establishes the main characters and conflicts.

were the apex of reaction shots as a method: you can only watch so much of someone talking without hearing them; even with *title cards*, it doesn't tell the whole story. It is when you see the facial and body language reactions of the listener that you get the entire emotional content of the scene. Reaction shots may not seem important when you are shooting the scene, but they are invaluable in editing.

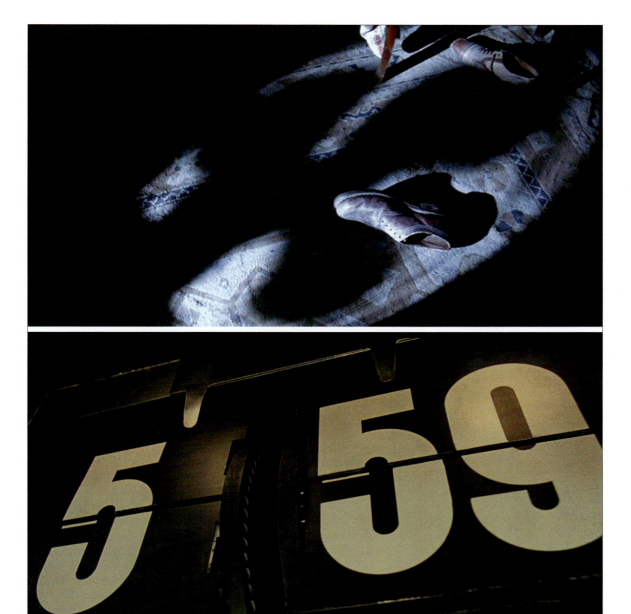

Inserts

An *insert* is an isolated, self-contained piece of a larger scene. To be an insert instead of a cutaway, it has to be something we saw in the wider shots. Example: she is reading a book. We could just shoot the book over her shoulder, but it is usually hard to read from that distance. A closer shot will make it easy to read. Unlike cutaways, many inserts will not be of any help to the editor. The reason for this is that since an insert is a closer shot of the larger scene, its continuity must match the overall action. For example, if we see a wide shot of the cowboy going for his gun, a tight insert of the gun coming out the holster must match the action and timing of the wider shot; this means it can be used only in one place in the scene and won't help the editor if they need to solve a problem elsewhere in the scene.

Figure 2.20. (top) A moody atmospheric cutaway from *Angel Heart*.

Figure 2.21. (bottom) An insert from *Groundhog Day*.

shooting methods

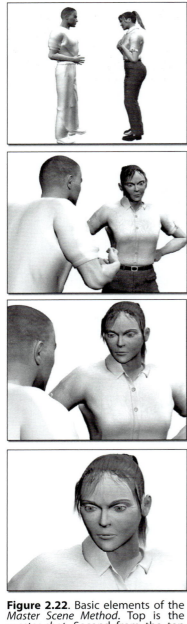

Figure 2.22. Basic elements of the *Master Scene Method*. Top is the *master shot*. Second from the top is a loose *over-the-shoulder* of her. Third down is a tighter medium *over-the-shoulder*. Fourth down is her *close-up* — in this case a *choker*.

When you *turn around* to get the coverage on him, these are the *answering shots*. It is very important that the answering shots match the coverage on her as closely as possible. Using the same focal length lens and the same focus distance will ensure that they are both the same image size, which will make the edits much smoother and less jarring.

There is no need to be specific about the terminology when setting up a shot; it's enough to just say, "let's get an insert of that" however, inserts tend to fit into a few general categories:

- *Informational inserts*. A shot of a clock on the wall is a practical insert, as is reading the headlines on the newspaper or the name of the file being pulled from the drawer. These are mostly about giving the audience some essential piece of information we want them to know.
- *Emphasis inserts*: the tires skid to a halt. The coffee cup jolts as he pounds the table. The windows rattle in the wind. Emphasis inserts are usually closely connected to the main action but not absolutely essential to it.
- *Atmosphere inserts*: these are little touches that contribute to the mood, pacing, or tone of a scene (Figures 2.15 and 2.20).

Atmosphere inserts may have almost no connection to the scene other than mood, tone, or a sort of symbolism or visual allegory. They are generally reserved for more stylized filmmaking. They should be used with caution; such shots can easily be arch, heavy-handed and obvious.

Connecting Shots

Most scenes involving two people can be adequately edited with *singles* of each person; whether are talking to each other or one is viewing the other from a distance, such as a shot of a sniper taking aim at someone. This is sometimes called *separation*. There is always a danger, however, that it will seem a bit cheap and easy and the fact that it is an editing trick might somehow undermine the scene. Any time the scene includes people or objects that cannot be framed in the same shot at some point in the scene, a *connecting shot* is called for. This applies especially to point-of-view shots where the character looks at something, then in a separate shot, we see what she is looking at; but it also applies to any scene where two or more people are in the same general space, whether they are aware of each other or not. A connecting shot is one that shows both of the characters in one shot, often it is in the form of an over-the-shoulder or wide angle that includes both of them (Figure 6.57).

Connecting shots just make a scene feel more complete and whole. The fragmentation of doing it all with POVs and reaction shots is after all a cheat that calls upon movie magic to piece together the whole scene. It works, but may not be as involving or emotionally satisfying to the audience, especially if overused. A connecting shot is a way to tie things together in a way that clarifies and emphasizes the physical, which are usually story relationships as well — clearly, one of the prime objectives of good directing and good shooting is to have the *visual elements* reinforce the *narrative elements*.

Pickups

A *pickup* can be any type of shot, master or coverage, where you are starting in middle of the scene (different from previous takes where you started at the beginning as it is written in the script). You can *pick it up* only if you are sure you have coverage to cut to along the way. Usually a *PU* is added to the scene number on the slate so the editor will know why they don't have a complete take of the shot.

Another use of the term is a *pickup day*. This is one or several days of shooting after the film is already in editing. At this point the director and editor may realize that there are just a few shots here and there that they have absolutely must have in order to make a good edit.

Figure 2.23. A *master shot* from *Ronin*. Once the master has established the basic layout of the scene and the physical relationships of the characters, the editor can easily cut to *medium shots, over-the-shoulders, close-ups, reaction shots,* and so on without confusing the audience.

Transitional Shots

Some shots are not parts of a scene themselves but instead serve to connect two scenes together. We can think of these as *transitional shots.* They might come at the end of a scene, at the beginning, or between scenes. Some are simple cutaways: a scene ends, cut to a shot of a sunset and then into the next scene. There are many other types of transitional shots as well, they are a sort of visual code to the audience that the scene is ending. Scenes of the city or landscape are frequently used as transitional devices as they also add to the mood or pace and are generically visual — meaning they don't need to make a specific point in order to be interesting.

Invisible Technique

In almost all cases, we want our methods to be transparent — we don't want the audience to be aware of them. We are striving for *invisible technique.*

THE SHOOTING METHODS

There are many different ways to shoot a scene, but some basic methods are used most often. The following summaries are some of the most fundamental and frequently used techniques for shooting a scene. The *master scene method* is by far the most frequently used method of shooting a scene, especially for dialog scenes. Actions sequences are an exception to this. It seldom makes sense to use the master scene method for these, as it depends entirely on repeating the action of the scene many times.

The Master Scene Method

In principal, the master scene method is quite simple: first you shoot the entire scene as one shot from beginning to end — this is the *master*. Once you have the master, you move on to the *coverage*. Except in rare cases, it is always best to shoot the master first, as all the rest of the shots must *match* what was done in the master. Not shooting the master first will frequently lead to continuity problems.

The master does not have to be a wide shot but it usually is. Nor does it have to be static; a *moving master* is fine too. The important thing is that it is the entire scene from beginning to end. For complex scenes, we sometimes break it into *mini-masters* within the scene , just use common sense to plan how to best get the scene covered.

Figure 2.24. *Plan-scene*, an *in-one* or *developing master* all mean the same thing: an entire scene played out in one continuous shot. These scenes can be shot with a panning camera, dolly shot, *Steadicam* or hand-held but in the case of *Songs from the Second Floor* (above) every scene in the film plays out as a static single shot. In some countries this method of shooting a scene is called a *plan-sequence*.

Coverage

The *coverage* consists of the over-the-shoulders, medium shots and close-ups that will be used to complete the scene. Think of the master as a *framework* for the whole scene — coverage is the pieces that fit into that framework to make it all work together. This is why you should always shoot the master first. It establishes the *continuity* for the scene — everything you shoot after that has to match what was *established* in the master. After you have shot the master you will have to pick one side (one of the actors) to begin with. It is important to do all of their shots before you *turn around* and do the coverage of the other actor, because changing the camera position from one side to another often involves changing the lighting and moving other equipment. It is a huge waste of time to do some shots of one side, move to the other side and then come back to the original side. The shots you do on the second actor are called the *answering shots,* and it is important for editing that they match the coverage of the first actor in their *lens size* and *focus distance*: this is to keep them a consistent size as you cut back and forth between them. Some basic common sense principals apply when shooting with the master scene method:

- Shoot the master *first*; if you try to shoot coverage first and the master later, it will likely cause problems in continuity.
- Get the whole scene from beginning to end.
- If characters enter, start with a *clean frame* and have them enter.
- If characters leave, make sure they exit entirely, leaving a clean frame. Continue to shoot for a beat after that.
- You might want to use transitional devices to get into or out of the scene.
- Shoot all the shots on one side before moving to the other side of the scene. This is called *shooting out* that side.

If you know you are going to use mostly the coverage when you edit, you may be able to live with some minor mistakes in a master. It is easy to get carried away with dozens of takes of the master.

Overlapping or Triple-Take Method

The *overlapping* method is also called the *triple-take* method. Say you are filming the manufacture of a large axle on a big industrial lathe. It's a real factory and you are doing an industrial video for the company. The metal piece is expensive and they are only making one today. The point is that you are not going to be able to repeat the action. You can ask the machinist to pause for a few minutes but there is no going back to repeat.

On the other hand, you don't want to show a 5 or 10-minute process all from the same angle — that would be incredibly boring. You need different angles. If you were using the master scene method, you would film the scene from one angle, then set up the camera for a different angle and *repeat* the scene, and so on for over-the-shoulders, close-ups, and so on. The triple-take method is useful for scenes where the action cannot be repeated.

Overlapping

So here's what we do: as they bring in the metal piece to be cut, you shoot that in a wide shot to establish the scene; at that point you ask the workmen to pause for a moment. Then as they put the piece on the lathe, you quickly move in for a close-up. The machinists back up a few steps and bring the metal piece in again and carry on with the action, all the way up to securing it in the lathe. You then quickly move to another angle and get more of the action. In the end you will different angles that should cut together smoothly.

Let's take another example: a lecturer walks into a room, sets his notes on the lectern, then pulls up a chair and sits down. This is where the *overlapping* part comes in. You could get a wide shot of him coming in, then ask him to freeze while you set up for a closer shot of him putting the notes on the lectern, then have him freeze again while you set up another shot of him pulling up the chair.

Figure 2.25. (top) Examples of *Hitchcock's rule* in *Touch of Evil*. Hitchcock said that the size of an object in the frame should equal its importance in the story. In this frame and in Figure 2.26, the gun is what is important at that moment in the story.

Figure 2.26. (above) A similar example from *The Lady from Shanghai*.

What you will discover is that the shots probably won't cut together smoothly. The chance of finding a good, clean *cutting point* is a long shot. It is the overlapping that helps you find smooth cut points. Here is what will work much better: you get a wide shot of him walking in and let him take the action all the way through to putting the notes on the lectern. Then set up a different angle and ask the actor to back up a few steps. Once you roll the camera, the actor comes up to the lectern again (repeating the last part of his walk). You then shoot the action all the way through to pulling up the chair.

Again you halt to set up a different angle, and have the actor back up from the lectern, and repeat the action of putting down the notes and then carrying it on through to the end of the scene. All this overlappping will enable you to cut the action together smoothly with good continuity cuts. The most important principal to take from this is to always overlap all action, no matter what shooting method you are using. Giving the editor some extra overlap at the beginning or end of any shot will prevent many potential problems when editing the scene.

In-One

Of all the methods of shooting a scene, by far the simplest is the *in-one*, sometimes called a *oner* or a *developing master,* or the French term *plan-scene* or *plan-sequence*. This just means the entire scene in one continuous shot. A scene might be simple as "she picks up the phone and talks" in which case a single shot is probably plenty. Some in-ones can be vastly more complicated: such as the famous four-minute opening shot of *Touch of Evil* or the long *Steadicam* shot of entering the Copacabana in Martin Scorsese's *Goodfellas*.

A caution, however: when these shots work, they can be magnificent, but if they don't work — for example, if you find in editing that the scene drags on much too slowly — your choices are limited. If all you did was several takes of the long in-one, you really don't have much choice in editing. Play it safe — shoot some coverage and cutaways just in case.

Freeform Method

Many scenes theses days (and even entire movies) are shot in what is commonly called *documentary style*. Think of movies like *Cloverfield* or *The Hurt Locker;* the camera is handheld, loose, and the actor's movements don't seem preplanned.

It seems like documentary style but it is not really. When shooting a real documentary, we can almost never do second takes, or have them repeat an action. Our aim in shooting fiction scenes like this is to make it *seem* like a documentary. In most cases, scenes like this are shot several times with the actors repeating the scene for several takes. Since the camera is hand-held, the *camera operator* usually does their best to *follow the dialog*: they pan the camera back and forth to always be on the person who is speaking. This can be a disaster for the editor. Imagine that you shoot a scene three times like this. You end up with three takes that are almost the same and the camera is only on the actor who is talking.

Imagine trying to edit these three takes together — almost impossible. What you really have are three takes that are mostly the same, which is a nightmare for editors. Editing is all about having different angles to cut to. If all you have is three very similar takes, there are not really any different angles to cut to. Also, you have no reaction shots of the person listening; as we discussed before, reaction shots are important to the storytelling and the editing. So what to do?

Shooting the Freeform Method

Here's a method that works well; we call it the *freeform method*:

- On the first take, follow the dialog. Do your best to stay with the actor who is speaking. This is the *dialog pass*.
- On the next take, pan back and forth to stay with the person who is *not* talking. This will give you lots of good *reaction shots*, which are important. It will also give the editor lots of things to cut away to. This is the *reaction pass*.
- For the third take (if you do one) *improvise*: follow the dialog sometimes, go to the nonspeaking actor sometimes, occasionally back up to get a wide shots — whatever seems appropriate. This is the *freeform pass*.

All these together will give you a scene you can cut together smoothly and give the editor lots of flexibility to cut the scene in various ways and to tighten up parts that seem to be dragging.

shooting methods

Figure 2.29. (top) *The Lady in the Lake* is one of the very rare examples of truly subjective point of view sustained throughout the entire film. Although the entire film is seen through the detective's subjective POV, the director cheats a bit to get a few shots of the detective as in this mirror shot. It's a cheat because that is not how the scene would actually appear to the character as he is looking in a mirror.

Figure 2.30. (bottom) The reaction shot of the crowd as the detective enters is very awkward because all of the actors need to look directly into the lens, which makes the audience aware of the camera.

Montage

There is a special form of editing used in dramatic narrative film-making that does not aim for continuity at all; this is called *montage*. A montage is simply a series of shots related by theme. Say the theme is "Springtime in the city" — you might have a series of shots of the flowers blooming, gentle rain showers, the sun breaking through the clouds, that sort of thing.

Some kinds of montage advance the story but without linear continuity. For example, *Rocky* prepares for the big fight: we see him working out, punching the bag, running on the streets of Philly, then finally running up the stairs to triumph. It is not real-time continuity — it takes place over months — but we see the story develop. It's a series of *related* shots, not scenes with *linear continuity*.

All of these methods share one common goal: to be invisible. We don't want the audience to be aware they are a movie because this would distract them from the story. There are some exceptions to this of course, such as when Ferris Bueller addresses the audience directly; at times such as this all conventions of fiction are tossed aside, generally for comic effect (Figure 2.31).

Figure 2.31. *Ferris Buehler's Day Off* contains several examples of *breaking the fourth wall* as the character looks straight into the lens to address the audience directly. In most films, this technique is used as a comic device.

INVOLVING THE AUDIENCE: POV

Recall the three forms of literary voice: first person, second person, and third person. In first person storytelling (whether in a short story, novel, or in film), a character in the story is describing the events. He can only describe things that he himself sees. First person speaks as "I." Such as "I went to the zoo." Second person speaks as "you," as in "You went to the zoo." It is someone who is not the speaker but who is part of the conversation. Third person, on the other hand, speaks about "they," as in "They go to the zoo sometimes." Third person is completely *objective*, and first person is completely *subjective*.

In this context, objective means merely showing or stating what is happening without getting involved. Imagine we are watching some people arguing from 20 feet away. In this case we are just watching "those people over there" and we can see them arguing — there is not much motivation for us to get deeply involved physically or emotionally. The complete opposite is when we are one of the people involved in the argument: we are completely engaged in every way.

Second person is somewhere in between. Let's think of it as if we are standing right behind one of the people arguing, right over their shoulder. We are not directly in the argument, but clearly it is much more involving and engaging than viewing it from a distance.

There are few clear-cut lines of delineation between subjective and objective — only gradations. We have previously talked about giving the scene a point-of-view (or even several points-of-view). Each camera angle has a point-of-view as well, and there are several variations to that meaning. Our two people are talking; the camera stands off to one side of them. The camera is essentially part of the scene, since it sees the people but it is not involved in the scene in any way. It is a neutral observer. It is completely objective — third person (Figure 2.38).

This is like the *omniscient narrator* in a novel or story. An omniscient narrator or POV is a voice that tells the story but is not a character in the story and can "see" everything that is going on. The voice can tell us what each and every character is doing at any time. What is a completely *subjective shot*? It is when the camera takes the place of one of the characters. In the case of our two people talking, if the other character is talking, she would look directly into the lens as if she were looking into the eyes of the man. In actual practice this is almost never done in narrative filmmaking, although it is used

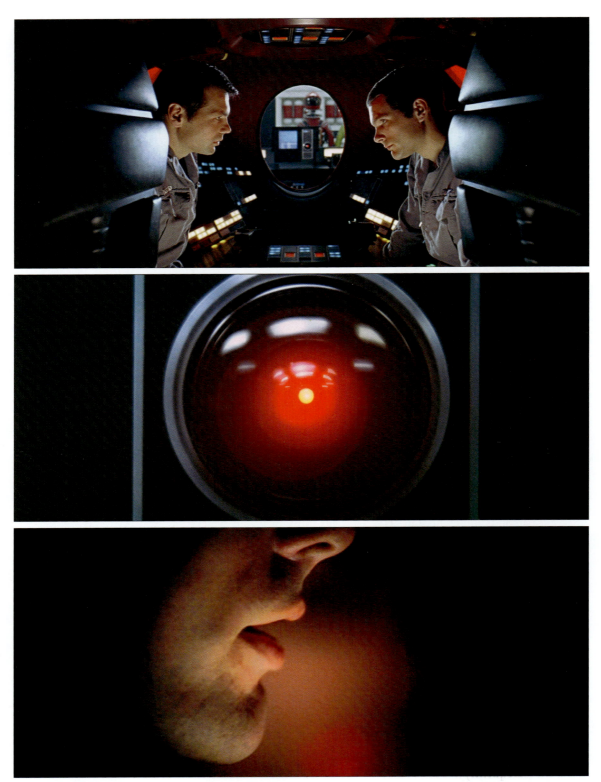

Figure 2.32. (top) In *2001: A Space Odyssey*, Kubrick establishes that the astronauts are safe from being overheard by the ship's computer HAL.

Figure 2.33. (middle)The close-of HAL's red eye establishes that the next shot will be his POV.

Figure 2.34. (bottom) Kubrick then uses a POV shot to show that HAL can read lips; a dramatic and chilling moment.

cinematography

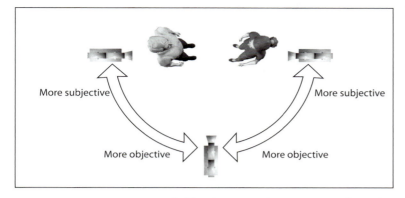

on very rare occasions. Probably the most famous example is the *noir* film *The Lady in the Lake* (Figures 2.29 and 2.30). In this case the story is seen in an entirely first person, purely subjective fashion as if the camera is the detective. When other characters speak to the detective they look directly into the lens. As a result we can never see the detective because the camera *is* the detective — the lens becomes his eyes. The only time we see him is when he looks into a mirror. A fascinating and very successful modern variation of this is a film titled *84 Charlie Mopic*, a Vietnam war film (Figure 2.40). The premise is that a cameraman along with a journalist/interviewer are sent along with a long-range reconnaissance team to record everything they do. Throughout the entire film everything we see is only what is photographed by Mopic's camera. It's a terrific conceit and is executed beautifully. We see Mopic only three time in the entire film. At the very end they are under fire and are being evacuated by helicopter. Mopic is just about to get into the chopper and he is shot. He tosses the camera into the chopper and it lands on the floor facing him. It records his death as the chopper takes off without him. The fact that his death affects us so much illustrates the power of subjective POV as a device to involve the audience both visually and emotionally. Similar devices have been used in *Cloverfield* and a number of other films.

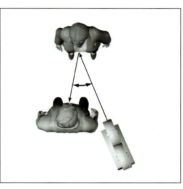

Other forms of POV are things like *doggie cam*. If there is a dog in the scene and the camera is placed low to the ground and moves along in a fashion resembling how a dog moves, we are seeing the scene from a dog's point of view.

The Fourth Wall and POV

Subjective POV is often used to represent someone observing a scene from hiding, however, it is rarely carried all the way through. For example, if the "victim" were to see the stalker and walk over to confront him, logically he would look directly into the camera. There are two problems with this. First it would break the illusion of the film. The audience would be made jarringly aware that they are watching the movie. In the theater it would be called *breaking the fourth wall*. This is when an actor in the play talks directly to the audience (Figures 2.30 and 2.31). To take it to its most extreme and ridiculous logical end, if the man were to ask the stalker a question and he agreed, we would have to nod the camera up and down.

The most frequently used type of character POV is the *POV look*. An example of this is when we see someone looks up, and then the next shot is a view of an airplane (Figure 6.57) The proper execution is discussed in more detail in the chapter *Cinematic Continuity*. It is often used as a device to cheat a location or establish a physical rela-

Figure 2.35. (top) An over-the-shoulder medium shot.

Figure 2.36. (middle) When moving to a tighter shot, the same angle will seem too far off axis and the eyeline will seem wrong.

Figure 2.37. (bottom) As the camera moves in for tighter coverage, the lens must be closer to the eyeline axis.

Figure 2.38. (above, left) In general, the closer the camera gets to the performer's perspective, the more subjective the shot becomes. The ultimate example of this is a subjective POV where the camera becomes the eyes of the character; this puts the audience into the character's head.

Figure 2.39 (above). Top: eyeline too far from the lens. Middle: correct eyeline. Bottom: eyeline on wrong side of lens.

Figure 2.40. (above, right) Even the titles are cleverly done in POV style in *84 Charlie Mopic:* here they are written in the sand with a knife.

tionship that didn't really exist on the set or location. For example if we want to establish that the character has a view of the city, but the location you are using doesn't really have one, it is a simple matter to get a shot of the character looking and then cut to a long shot of the city. To take it to the next step, it would also be possible to take the actor (or even a stand-in) to another location and get an over-the-shoulder of a view of the city. This is a cheated connecting shot and only requires that the two windows (or at least what they see of them) match visually.

In their book *Film Art —An Introduction*, David Bordwell and Kristin Thomson call this the *Kuleshov effect*. This is named for Lev Kuleshov, one of the early Russian formalist filmmakers in the 1920's. He performed an experiment in which is used the same shot of a famous Russian actor with a completely neutral look intercut (at various times) with shots of nature, some soup, a baby and, a dead woman. When asked about what emotions the actor was expressing, the audience said he was either showing tranquility, hunger, joy, or great sorrow.

This illustrates the storytelling power of simply putting two shots together. When we show someone tilt his head up and his eyes turn toward something off-screen, then cut to a clock tower or an airplane, the audience will always make the connection that our character is looking at that tower or plane.

This demonstrates not only the usefulness of subjective POVs for storytelling and emotional subtext, but also hints at the importance of the off-screen space as part of our narrative. It also reminds us that we are almost never doing shots that will be used in isolation: ultimately shots are used in combination with other shots. This is really the essence of filmmaking: doing shots that are good on their own is important, but in the end what really counts is how the shots work when they are put together in editing.

visual language

Figure 3.1. (previous page) A visually strong and expressive frame from *The Conformist,* shot by Vittorio Storaro.

Figure 3.2. (above) This frame from the finale of *The Big Combo* is not only graphically strong in composition, but the many visual elements all work together to reinforce and add subtext to the story content of the scene.

MORE THAN JUST A PICTURE

Let's think of the frame as more than just a *picture* — it is information. Clearly some parts of the information are more important than others, and we want this information to be perceived by the viewer in a certain order — we want the information organized in a particular way. Composition (and lighting, which can be part of composition) is how this is accomplished. Through composition we are telling the audience where to look, what to look at and in what order to look at it. The frame is fundamentally two-dimensional design. 2-D design is about guiding the eye and directing the attention of the viewer in an organized manner that conveys the meaning that you wish to impart. It is how we impose a point of view on the material that may be different from how others see it.

If all we did was simply photograph what is there in exactly the same way everyone else sees it, the job could be done by a robot camera; there would be no need for the cinematographer or editor. An image should convey meaning, mode, tone, atmosphere, and subtext on its own — without regard to voice-over, dialog, audio, or other explanation. This was in its purest essence in silent film, but the principle still applies: the images must stand on their own.

Good composition reinforces the way in which the mind organizes information. In some cases it may deliberately run counter to how the eye/brain combination works in order to add a new layer of meaning or ironic comment. Composition selects and emphasizes elements such as size, shape, order, dominance, hierarchy, pattern, resonance, and discordance in ways that give meaning to the things being photographed that goes beyond the simple: "here they are." We will start with the very basic rules of visual organization then move on to more sophisticated concepts of design and visual language. The principles of design and visual communication are a vast subject; here we will just touch on the basics in order to lay the foundation for discussion.

Figure 3.3. (top) Balance plays a role in this film noir frame.

Figure 3.4. (bottom) Visual rhythm with an ironic twist in this shot from Stanley Kubrick's *Killer's Kiss*, his first feature.

Design Principles

Certain basic principles pertain to all types of visual design, whether in film, photography, painting, or drawing. These principles work interactively in various combinations to add depth, movement, and visual force to the elements of the frame.

- Unity
- Balance
- Visual tension
- Rhythm
- Proportion
- Contrast
- Texture
- Directionality

Unity

Unity is the principle that the visual organization be a "whole," self-contained and complete. This is true even if it is a deliberately chaotic or unorganized composition. In Figure 3.2, this climactic final shot from *The Big Combo* uses frame-within-a-frame composition to tell the story visually: having defeated the bad guys, the hero and femme fatal emerge from the darkness into the light of morning.

visual language

Figure 3.5. Lighting, perspective, choice of lens, and camera position combine to give this Gregg Toland shot tremendous depth and three-dimensionality in *The Long Voyage Home.*

Balance

Visual balance (or lack of balance) is an important part of composition. Every element in a visual composition has a visual weight. These may be organized into a balanced or unbalanced composition. The visual weight of an object is primarily determined by its size but is also affected by its position in the frame, its color, movement, and the subject matter itself.

Visual Tension

The interplay of balanced and unbalanced elements and their placement in the frame can create visual tension, which is important in any composition that seeks to avoid boring complacency.

Rhythm

Rhythm of repetitive or similar elements can create patterns of organization. Rhythm plays a key role in the visual field, sometimes in a very subtle way as in Figures 3.4, a frame from *Killer's Kiss.*

Proportion

Classical Greek philosophy expressed the idea that mathematics was the controlling force of the universe and that it was expressed in visual forces in the *Golden Mean.* The Golden Mean is just one way of looking at proportion and size relationships in general.

Contrast

We know a thing by its opposite. Contrast is a function of the light/dark value, the color and texture of the objects in the frame and the lighting. It is an important visual component in defining depth, spatial relationships, and of course carries considerable emotional and storytelling weight as well.

Figure 3.6. Visual texture in a scene from *The Conformist*.

Texture

Based on our associations with physical objects and cultural factors, texture gives perceptual clues. Texture be can a function of the objects themselves, but usually requires lighting to bring it out, as in Figure 3.6. We also add texture in many different ways in filmmaking; see the chapter *Lighting Basics* where we will discuss adding visual texture to lighting as a way of shaping the light.

Directionality

One of the most fundamental of visual principles is directionality. With a few exceptions, everything has some element of directionality. This directionality is a key element of its visual weight, which determines how it will act in a visual field and how it will affect other elements. Anything that is not symmetrical is directional.

The Three-Dimensional Field

In any form of photography, we are taking a three-dimensional world and projecting it onto a two-dimensional frame (although this is less true of 3-D filmmaking). A very big part of our work in directing and shooting visual stories is this essential idea of creating a three-dimensional world out of two-dimensional images. It calls into play a vast array of techniques and methods, not all of them purely design oriented: the lens, blocking of actors, lighting, and camera movement all come into play. In reality, 3-D filmmaking is still two-dimensional, it just has an extra feature that makes it appear to be three-dimensional — all the basic design principals still apply whether you are shooting 2-D or 3-D.

There are, of course, times when we wish to make the frame more two-dimensional, even replicating the *flat space* of an animated cartoon, for example; in that case the same visual design principles apply, they are just used in a different fashion to create that visual effect. Many visual forces contribute to the illusion of depth and dimension. For the most part, they relate to how the human eye/brain combination perceive space, but some of them are cultural and historical as well — as film viewers we all have a long history of visual education from everything we have seen before.

Depth

In working toward establishing this sense of depth and three-dimensionality, there are a number of ways to create the illusion: Figure 3.5 is a deep focus shot from *The Long Voyage Home*, photographed by Gregg Toland; it shows a great sense of depth in a visual field. In terms of the editing, it is useful to view a scene from more than one angle — shooting a scene entirely from a single angle creates what we call *flat space*. Elements that create a sense of visual depth include:

- Overlap
- Size change
- Vertical location
- Horizontal location
- Linear perspective
- Foreshortening
- Chiaroscuro
- Atmospheric perspective

Overlap

Overlap clearly establishes front/back relationships; something "in front of" another thing is clearly closer to the observer; as in this frame from the noir classic *The Big Combo* (Figure 3.7).

Relative Size

Although the eye can be fooled, the relative size of an object is an important visual clue to depth, as in Figure 3.8. Relative size is a component of many optical illusions and a key compositional element in manipulating the viewer's perception of the subject; it can be used to focus the viewers attention on important elements. There are many ways to manipulate relative size in the frame, using position or different lenses.

Vertical Location

Gravity is a factor is visual organization; the relative vertical position of objects is a depth cue. This is particularly important in the art of Asia, which has not traditionally relied on linear perspective as it is practiced in Western art. See the chapter *Lens Language* for an example of how Kurosawa translates this concept in his use of lenses distinctive to the visual tradition in which he operated.

Left/Right

Largely a result of cultural conditioning, the eye tends to scan from left to right. This has an ordering effect on the visual weight of elements in the field. It is also critical to how the eye scans a frame and thus the order of perception and movement in the composition. It can also relate to the staging of actors within the frame. In theater the downstage (nearest the audience) right corner is considered to be the "hot" area of the stage.

Figure 3.8. (top) *Relative size* is key in this shot from *High Noon*, but clearly *linear perspective* and *overlap* also play a role.

Figure 3.9. (bottom) Kubrick uses *linear perspective* to convey a sense of the rigid military and social structure in *Paths of Glory*.

Figure 3.10. *Chiaroscuro* lighting uses light and shadow to create depth and focus the attention of the audience, such as this frame from *Apocalypse Now*.

Linear Perspective

Linear perspective was an invention of the Renaissance artist Brunelleschi. In film and video photography, it is not necessary to know the rules of perspective, but it is important to recognize its importance in visual organization. Director Stanley Kubrick uses it to reinforce the rigid nature of French society in Figure 3.9, a frame from *Paths of Glory*; he uses similar geometry in *Barry Lyndon* (Figure 2.2) and *Dr. Strangelove* (Figure 3.21) for similar storytelling purposes.

Foreshortening

Foreshortening is a phenomenon of the optics of the eye. Since things that are closer to the eye appear larger than those farther away, when part of an object is much closer than the rest of it, the visual distortion gives us clues as to depth and size.

Chiaroscuro

Italian for light (*chiara*) and shadow (*scouro*, same Latin root as obscure), *chiaroscuro*, or gradations of light and dark (Figure 3.10), establishes depth perception and creates visual focus. Since dealing with lighting is one of our major tasks, this is an important consideration in our work. Figure 3.10 is a shot from *Apocalypse Now*. See also Figure 5.1 at the beginning of the chapter *Visual Storytelling*: a masterpiece by the painter Caravaggio, one of the great old masters of chiaroscuro.

Atmospheric Perspective

Atmospheric perspective (sometimes called aerial perspective) is something of a special case as it is an entirely "real world" phenomenon. The term was coined by Leonardo da Vinci, who used it in his paintings. Objects that are a great distance away will have less detail, less saturated colors, and generally be less defined than those that are closer. This is a result of the image being filtered through more atmosphere and haze. Haze in the air filters out some of the long (warmer) wavelengths, leaving more of the shorter, bluer wavelengths. It can be recreated on set with haze effects, scrims and lighting (Figure 3.11).

FORCES OF VISUAL ORGANIZATION

All of these basic elements can then be deployed in various combinations to create a hierarchy of perception: they can create an organization of the visual field that makes the composition coherent and guides the eye and the brain as it puts the information together. The visual elements that help the eye/brain combination organize the scene include:

The Line

The line, either explicit or implied, is a constant in visual design. It is powerful in effect and multifaceted in its use. Just a few simple lines can organize a two-dimensional space in a way that is comprehensible by the eye/brain.

The Sinuous Line

The *sinuous line*, which is sometimes referred to as the *reverse S*, (Figure 3.12) was used extensively as a compositional principle by Renaissance artists; it has a distinctive harmony and balance all its own, as seen in these examples from *The Black Stallion* and *Seven Samurai* (Figures 3.15 and 3.16).

Compositional Triangles

Triangles are a powerful compositional tool. Once you start looking for them, you will see compositional triangles everywhere. Figure 3.17 is a frame from *Citizen Kane*, an outstanding example of the strong visuals in filmmaking. The compositional triangles keep the frame active even through a fairly long expositional scene.

Horizontals, Verticals and Diagonals

The basic lines are always a factor in almost any type of compositions. Nearly infinite in variety, they always come back to the basics: horizontal, vertical, and diagonal. Lines may be explicit, as in these shots from *Seven Samurai* (Figures 3.14) and *The Conformist* (Figures 3.1 and 3.18) or implied in the arrangement of objects and spaces.

Figure 3.11. *Atmospheric perspective* in the form of a heavy fog effect is an important element of this shot from *City of Lost Children*; not only for the sense of sadness and isolation but also because it is a set built in a studio. Without the sense of atmospheric perspective added by the smoke and backlight, it is doubtful the illusion would hold up so well.

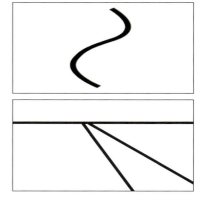

3.12. (top) The sinuous reverse S; a specialized type of line that has a long history in visual art.

Figure 3.13. (bottom) Even a few simple lines can imply linear perspective.

visual language

Figure 3.14. (top) Line as form and movement in this frame from *Seven Samurai*.

Figure 3.15. (bottom) The classic *sinuous S* in this shot from *The Black Stallion*.

The Horizon Line and Vanishing Point

Our innate understanding of perspective lends a special association to lines that are perceived as horizon lines, lines of perspective and, vanishing point. Figure 3.13 shows how ingrained the horizon line is in our perception: three simple lines on white space are enough to suggest it.

The Power of the Edge: the Frame

As we visually identify an object or group of objects in a frame, we are also subconsciously aware of the frame itself. The four edges of the frame have a visual force all their own. Objects that are close to the frame are visually associated with it and viewed in relation to it more than if they are farther away. The frame also plays an important role in making us aware of those spaces off-frame: left/right,

Figure 3.16. (top) The sinuous S and its use in Kurosawa's *Seven Samurai*.
Figure 3.17. (bottom) Compositional triangles in *Citizen Kane*.

Figure 3.18. (above) Strong diagonal lines are crucial to this shot from *The Conformist* and also in Figure 3.1 at the beginning of this chapter.

Figure 3.19. (right, middle) Diagonals in the noir film *Out Of The Past*.

Figure 3.20. (right, bottom) Verticals and horizontals in this shot from *JFK* are especially strong given the widescreen aspect ratio. Notice also how the unbalanced frame and negative space on the right side are especially important to the composition. Imagine if they had framed only the important elements on the left. It would not be nearly as strong a composition and would not work nearly so well for wide screen.

up/down, and even the space behind the camera — all part of the filmspace of the entire composition and crucial to making the visual experience more three-dimensional. This power of the frame itself is also important in our choice of aspect ratio — which is shape of the frame. It has changed over the history of film, generally from an almost square shape (Figure 3.19) to a wider, more horizontal rectangle (Figure 3.18) to an extreme wide frame as in this frame from *JFK* (Figure 3.20).

Open and Closed Frame

An open frame is one in which one or more of the elements either pushes the edge or actually crosses the edge (Figure 3.21). A closed frame is one in which the elements are comfortably contained within the frame (Figure 3.22), which is associated with more formal composition. Although we look at the frames here as still photographs, most frames of a motion picture are dynamic, even to the point of blurring, which you can see if you pause a DVD or Blu-Ray — we normally don't perceive the blurring but it affects our perception.

Figure 3.21. (top) An open frame composition from *Seven Samurai*.

Figure 3.22. (bottom) A closed frame composition from *Dr. Strangelove*.

Figure 3.23. (above) Negative space and unbalanced composition in *The Black Stallion*.

Figure 3.24. (right) Frame within a frame in the Kubrick film *Killer's Kiss*.

Frame within a Frame

Sometimes the composition demands a frame that is different from the aspect ratio of the film. A solution is to use a *frame within a frame* — which means using framing elements within the shot. Figure 3.24 is an example from Kubrick's *Killer's Kiss*. It is particularly useful with very widescreen formats. Frame within a frame can be used not only to alter the aspect ratio of the shot but also to focus attention on important story elements.

Balanced and Unbalanced Frame

We touched on balance before; now let's look at it in the context of the frame. Any composition may be balanced or unbalanced. This shot from *Dr. Strangelove* (Figure 3.22) is both a closed frame and also a formal/balanced composition. Using formal geometry in the composition of the frame to comment on social structure is a constant in Kubrick's work. See also Figure 3.9. The frame from *JFK* (Figure 3.20) is also an unbalanced frame. This is more than just composition: the graphic design of the frame also conveys story information about the situation.

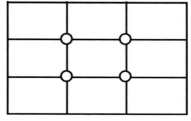

Figure 3.25. (above) The *rule of thirds* is a means of helping you organize any visual field (such as a film or video frame).

Figure 3.26. (left) Strong visual movement in the frame reinforces character relationships and subtext in this shot from *Seven Samurai*.

Positive and Negative Space

The visual weight of objects or lines of force can create positive space, but their absence can create negative space, as in this frame from *The Black Stallion* (Figure 3.23). The elements that are "not there" have a visual weight as well. It is important to remember that the space off-screen can be important also, especially if the character looks off-screen to the left, right, up, down, or even past the camera.

Movement in the Visual Field

All of these forces work in combination, of course — in ways that interact to create a sense of movement in the visual field. These factors combine to create a visual movement (eye scan) from front to back in a circular fashion (Figure 3.26). This movement in the frame is important not only for the composition but also plays an important role in what order the viewer perceives and assimilates the subjects in the frame. This influences their perception of content. In analyzing frames in this way, remember that we are talking about the movement of the eye, not movement of the camera or movement of the actor or object within a shot.

The Rule of Thirds

The *rule of thirds* starts by dividing the frame into thirds (Figure 3.25). The rule of thirds proposes that a useful approximate starting point for any compositional grouping is to place major points of interest in the scene on any of the four intersections of the interior lines. It is a simple but effective rough guideline for any frame composition. The rule of thirds has been used by artists for centuries.

MISCELLANEOUS RULES OF COMPOSITION

If ever there were rules made to be broken, they are the rules of composition, but it is important to understand them before deviating or using them in a contrary style.

Don't cut off their feet. Generally, a frame should end somewhere around the knees or include the feet. Cutting them off at the ankles will look awkward; likewise, don't cut off their hands at the wrist. Naturally, a character's hand will often dart in and out of the frame as the actor moves and gestures, but for a long static shot, they should be clearly in or out. Watch out for *TV Safe* — as video is currently broadcast, there is considerable variation in the size of the picture on the home screen. For this reason, most ground glass markings

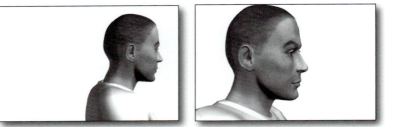

Figure 3.27. (top) Too much headroom.

Figure 3.28. (middle) Too little headroom.

Figure 3.29. (bottom) About the right amount of headroom.

Figure 3.30. (above, near right) Not enough noseroom.

Figure 3.31. (above, far right) Enough noseroom.

include both the entire video frame (either Standard Def or High Def) and a marking that is 10% less, called TV Safe. All important compositional elements should be kept inside TV Safe.

Pay attention to the heads of people standing in the background. When framing for our important foreground subjects, whether or not to include the heads of background people is a judgment call. If they are prominent enough, it is best to include them compositionally. If there is enough emphasis on the foreground subjects and the background people are strictly incidental or perhaps largely out of focus, it is OK to cut them off wherever is necessary.

If the situation does call for not showing their heads, you will probably want to avoid cutting through their heads at nose level. For example, in a scene where two people are dining, if the waiter approaches and asks them a question, you clearly want to show all of the waiter. If the waiter is not a speaking role and he is merely pouring some water, it would be acceptable just to show him from the shoulders down, as the action with his arm and hands is what is relevant to the scene.

Basic Composition Rules for People

When it comes to people there are some other framing principals that are important to observe.

Headroom

Certain principles apply particularly to photographing people, particularly in a medium shot or close-up. First is *headroom* — the amount of space above the head. Too much headroom makes the figure seem to be lost in the frame (Figure 3.27). Headroom is also wasted compositionally as it is often just sky or empty wall. It adds no information to the shot and may draw the eye away from the central subject. The convention is to leave the least amount of headroom that doesn't make the head seem to be crammed against the top of the frame (Figure 3.29). As the close-up gets bigger, it becomes permissible to leave even less headroom. Once the shot becomes a choker, you can even give the character a "haircut," and bring the top of the frame down to the forehead but not as in Figure 3.28, which is too wide a shot for a haircut. The idea is simply that the forehead and hair convey less information than the lower part of the face and neck. A head shot cut off above the eyebrows seems perfectly normal. A shot that shows the top of the head but cuts off the chin and mouth would seem very odd.

Noseroom

Next is *noseroom*, also called *looking room* (Figures 3.30 and 3.31). If a character is turned to the side, it's as if the gaze has a certain visual weight. As a result, we rarely position the head in the exact middle of the frame, except when the actor is looking more or less straight toward or away from the camera. Generally, the more the head is turned to the side, the more noseroom is allowed. Think of it this way: the *look* has visual weight, which must be balanced.

language of the lens

Figure 4.1. (previous page) Deliberately flaring the lens is an essential element of this shot from *Nine and 1/2 Weeks*.

Figure 4.2. (right) A well-composed, balanced frame from *Barry Lyndon* implies static formalism. The static camera position and the centered "head on" viewpoint all add up to reinforce the story content of a rigid social structure and a highly formalized social milieu in which the story takes place.

THE LENS AND THE FRAME

As we use the term in this book, cinematic technique means the methods and practices we use to add additional layers of meaning, nuance, and emotional context to shots and scenes in addition to their objective content. The lens is one of the prime tools in achieving these means. Together with selecting the frame, it is also the area of cinematography in which the director is most heavily involved.

Foreground/Midground/Background

As we discussed in *Shooting Methods*, one of the key elements of film is that we are projecting 3-dimensional space onto a 2-dimensional plane. Except where we want this flatness, it is a goal to recreate the depth that existed in the scene. A big part of this is to create shots with a foreground, midground, and background.

In the book *Hitchcock/Truffaut*, Hitchcock makes the point that a basic rule of camera position and staging is that the importance of an object in the story should equal its size in frame. We see that principle employed in the shots from *Lady from Shanghai* (Figure 2.26) and *Touch of Evil* (Figure 2.25). The gun is what is important in the scene, so Welles uses a low camera angle and positioning to feature it prominently in the frame — the choice of lens is also important.

Lens Perspective

As we discussed in the previous chapters, the fundamental aspect of the frame is that it constitutes a selection of what the audience is going to see. Some things are included and some are excluded. The first decision is always where the camera goes in relation to the subject. But this is only half of the job. Once the camera position is set, there is still a decision to be made as to how much of that view is to be included. This is the job of lens selection.

Human vision, including peripheral, extends to around 180°. Foveal (or central) vision, which is more able to perceive detail, is around 40°. In 35mm film, the 50mm is generally considered the normal lens. In fact, something around a 40mm is closer to typical vision. In video, the "normal" lens varies depending on the size of the video receptor. A normal lens is considered to be one where the focal length equals the diagonal of the receptor. The focal length is significant in another way in addition to its field of view. Remember that all optics (including the human eye) work by projecting the three-dimensional world onto a two-dimensional plane. Lenses in the normal range portray the depth relationships of objects in a way fairly close to human vision.

Figure 4.3. The wide lens creates a palpable space between the characters in this climactic scene in *The Lady from Shanghai*; he is heading out toward the light and she is in complete silhouette, all of which precisely underpin the story point at this moment in the film.

Wide Lenses and Expansion of Space

With a wider than normal lens, depth perception is exaggerated: objects appear to be farther apart (front to back) than they are in reality. This exaggerated sense of depth has psychological implications. The perception of movement towards or away from the lens is heightened; space is expanded and distant objects become much smaller. All this can give the viewer a greater sense of presence —a greater feeling of being *in* the scene — which is often a goal of the filmmaker. As the lens gets even wider, there is distortion of objects, particularly those near the lens. This is the fundamental reason why a longer focal length lens is considered essential for a portrait or head shot. It's a simple matter of perspective. If you are shooting a close-up and you want to fill the frame, the wider the lens, the closer the camera will have to be. As the camera gets closer, the percentage difference in distance from the nose to the eyes increases dramatically, which causes distortion.

For example, if the tip of the nose is 30 cm (centimeters) from the lens, then the eyes may be at 33 cm, a 10% difference. With a wide lens, this is enough to cause a mismatch in size: the nose is exaggerated in size compared to the face at the plane of the eyes. With a longer than normal lens, the camera will be much farther back to achieve the same image size. In this case, the tip of the nose might be at 300 cm, with the eyes at 303 cm. This is a percentage difference of only 1%: the nose would appear normal in relation to the rest of the face. The same fundamental principle applies to the perception of all objects with very wide lenses (Figure 1.11).

Another aspect of wide lenses is that at a given distance and f/stop, they have greater depth-of-field. Not to get too technical here (we'll do that in the chapter *Optics & Focus*), but suffice it to say that the depth-of-field of a lens is inversely proportional to the square of its focal length. We'll get into the details in later chapters, but perceptual ramifications are very much a part of the psychology of the lens. This greater depth-of-field allows more of the scene to be in focus. This was used to great effect by master cinematographers of the 30's and 40's such as Gregg Toland, who used it to develop an entire look called deep focus, such as in the frame from *The Long Voyage Home* (Figure 3.5 in *Visual Language*). In this film and in other films he shot in this period (such as *Wuthering Heights*) Toland perfected deep focus as a visual system that he later introduced to Orson Welles (Figures 4.3 and 4.4) when they worked together on *Citize Kane*, which was Welles' first film.

Figure 4.4. A deep focus shot from *Citizen Kane*. Three levels of the story are shown in the same frame.

Deep Focus

The high point of deep focus as a storytelling tool is *Citizen Kane*. According to David Cook in *A History of Narrative Film*, "Welles planned to construct the film as a series of long takes, or sequence shots, scrupulously composed in depth to eliminate the necessity for narrative cutting within major dramatic scenes. To accomplish this, Toland developed for Welles a method of deep focus photography capable of achieving an unprecedented depth-of-field."

This deep focus facilitates composition in depth to an unprecedented degree. Throughout the film we see action in the background that complements and amplifies what we are seeing in the foreground. For example, early in the film we see Mrs. Kane in the foreground, signing the agreement for Mr. Thatcher to be the young Charles Foster Kane's guardian. Throughout the scene, we see the young man through a window, playing outside with his sled even as his future is being decided (Figure 4.4).

Welles also uses the distortion of wide angle lenses for psychological effect. Frequently in the film we see Kane looming like a giant in the foreground, dwarfing other characters in the scene — a metaphor for his powerful, overbearing personality. Later, Welles uses the exaggerated distances of wide lenses to separate Kane from other characters in the scene, thus emphasizing his alienation (Figure 14.8).

Compression of Space

At the other end of this spectrum are *long focal length lenses*, which you might hear referred to as *telephoto* lenses. They have effects that are opposite of wide lenses: they compress space, have less depth-of-field and de-emphasize movement away from or toward the camera.

This compression of space can be used for many perceptual purposes: claustrophobic tightness of space, making distant objects seem closer and heightening the intensity of action and movement. Their ability to decrease apparent distance has many uses both in composition but also in creating the *psychological space*.

The effect of having objects seem closer together is often used for the very practical purpose of making stunts and fight scenes appear more dramatic and dangerous than they really are. With careful camera placement and a long lens, a speeding bus can seem to miss a child on a bicycle by inches, when in fact, there is a comfortably safe distance between them, a trick frequently used to enhance stunt

shots and action sequences. The limited depth-of-field can be used to isolate a character in space. Even though foreground and background objects may seem closer, if they are drastically out of focus, the sense of separation is the same. This can result in a very detached, third-person point of view for the shot. This detachment is reinforced by the fact that the compression of space makes more tangible the feeling that the real world is being projected onto a flat space. We perceive it more as a two-dimensional representation — more abstract; this is used very effectively in Figure 4.5.

Another use of long lenses for compression of space is for beauty. Most faces are more attractive with longer lenses. This is why the 105mm and the 135mm lenses (long focal lengths) are known as *portrait* lenses for still photographers who do beauty and fashion or portraiture. Movement toward us with a long lens is not as dynamic

Figure 4.5. (top) Very long lens perspective makes this shot from *Rain Man* abstract. It is reduced to the simple idea of beginning a journey into the unknown future; the road seems to rise up into their unknown future. It is no accident that this frame is used on the poster for the film; it elegantly expresses the basic story of the film.

Figure 4.6. (bottom) A wide lens is essential to this shot from a later scene in *Rain Man*. Trapped in the car with his extremely annoying brother, the wide shot in the emptiness of the prairie emphasizes how the car is like a lifeboat from which there is no escape.

Figure 4.7. (top) This wide master from *The Lady from Shanghai* shows a normal perspective.

Figure 4.8. (bottom) In the close-ups, Welles uses projections of the fish at ten times their normal size to introduce menace and a feeling of strangeness to the otherwise pleasant setting of the aquarium. The huge fish and the rippling motivated lighting from the water all work together to suggest that the character is "in over his head and out of his depth."

and therefore is abstracted. It is more of a presentation of the *idea* of movement than perceived as actual movement of the subject. This is especially effective with shots of the actors running directly toward the camera; as they run toward us, there is very little change in their image size. We would normally think of this as decreasing the sense of movement, but in a way, it has the opposite effect. The same is true of slow motion. Although shooting at a high frame rate actually slows the movement down, our perceptual conditioning tells us that the people or objects are actually moving very fast — so fast that only high-speed shooting can capture them on film. Thus shooting something in slow motion and with a long lens has the ultimate effect of making the moving seem faster and more exaggerated than it really is. The brain interprets it in a way that contradicts the visual evidence.

This is an excellent example of cultural conditioning as a factor in film perception. The convention to show someone running very fast to shoot with a long lens and in *slow motion*. If you showed a long lens, slow motion shot of someone running to a person who had never seen film or video before, they might not understand at all that the person is running fast. More likely they would perceive the person as almost frozen in time through some sort of magic.

Manipulating Perspective

There are many other tricks that can be used to alter the audience's perception of space. In *The Lady from Shanghai* (Figures 4.7 and 4.8), Welles uses a subtle and very clever trick to add subtext to the scene. In the film, Welles plays an ordinary seaman who is seduced into an affair and a murder plot by Rita Hayworth. There are double and triple crosses, and the Welles character is in way over his head. This scene is a meeting between him and the beautiful woman who is at the bottom of all the schemes and machinations. She asks him to meet her in an out-of-the-way public place: the aquarium. On the face of it, this seems like a perfect place for them to meet without attracting attention. In fact, she has a darker purpose.

The staging also seems perfectly straightforward. They meet and then talk while they stroll in front of the glass windows of the aquarium. Welles uses subtle tricks to make this happy, innocent

Figure 4.9. (top) This wide shot comes at the end of a chase scene in *Nine and 1/2 Weeks*; out on the town, the characters have been chased by a gang of violent thugs.

Figure 4.10. (bottom) At the moment they realize they have lost their attacker, a severe lens change *punches in* to the scene. It is a high-energy cut that gets us closer so that we are experiencing the scene along with the characters rather than as an abstract, at-a-distance chase scene. We are drawn into their excitement and identify with their exuberance. The sudden loss of depth-of-field isolates them in the landscape and gives our attention nowhere else to go. The *punch-in* changes the visual texture to match the mood.

lens language

Figure 4.11. (top) A visually powerful *punch-in* from *Gladiator*, as the main characters rise into the arena from the underground space in a wide shot.

Figure 4.12. (bottom) The switch to a very long lens (the *punch-in*) punctuates the moment and intensifies the drama as well as simply being dramatic and visually striking.

place mysterious and foreboding. First, the motivated light from the aquarium backlights them dramatically in a classic film noir fashion. As the Welles character begins to realize the danger of the situation he is in, they move to a spot where they are completely in silhouette. When he goes in for coverage, Welles doesn't chicken out. The motivated lighting is also a water effect so the ripples play across their faces. These devices subtly suggest that the character is out of his depth, underwater, which is exactly the point of the scene.

The third trick is even more clever. In the wide shots, we see the fish in the aquarium: ordinary fish and turtles of one or two feet in length. In the close-ups, however, Welles had film of the fish back-projected at a greatly enlarged size. As a result, the fish are now gigantic. Although just barely seen behind their heads, the effect is mysterious and a little frightening. In combination with the silhouette and the rippling water effects, the subtext is clear: the character is out of his depth, his head is underwater, and he may not survive. It is a masterful stroke that is completely unnoticed by most of the audience. Like all the best techniques, it is seamless and invisible.

Kurosawa uses very long lenses in a way that is stylistically distinctive. See Figure 4.14 for an example of how he uses lenses to achieve certain compositional perspectives and character relationships. Another example of lens use is the *punch-in*, shown in Figures 4.11 and 4.12.

Selective Focus

The characteristic of relative lack of depth-of-field can be used for selective focus shots. As discussed above, shallow depth-of-field can isolate the subject. The essential point is that focus is a storytelling tool. This is a drawback of 16mm film and some High Def cameras. Because they often have smaller sensors, they have far more depth-of-field than 35mm film, thus making it more difficult to use focus in this way; however many HD cameras now have sensors that are the same size as a 35mm film frame or even larger. Depth-of-field is a product of the sensor size, not whether it is film or video. See the chapter *Optics & Focus* for more on selective focus. If you want to reduce depth-of-field on a camera with a smaller sensor, some people will say "pull back and use a longer lens" or "shoot wide open." These are not always options, especially on a tight location.

Focus can also be shifted during the shot, thus leading the eye and the attention of the viewer. The term for the classic use of this is *rack focus*, in which the focus is on an object in the foreground, for example, and then, on cue, the camera assistant radically changes the focus so that it shifts dramatically to another subject either in front of or behind the original subject. Not all shots lend themselves to the technique, especially when there is not enough of a focus change to make the effect noticeable. A downside of rack focusing is that some lenses *breathe* when changing focus; this means they appear to change focal length while shifting focus.

Also with tracking shots that are very tight and close, we can watch as objects come into view, then slowly come into focus, then go soft again. Selective focus and out-of-focus can also be highly subjective visual metaphors for the influence of drugs or madness, as well. The bottom line is that focus is an important storytelling tool as well as being crucial to the overall *look* of a particular production.

Figure 4.13. (above) Japanese and Chinese traditional art do not employ linear perspective but instead they rely on above/below relationships to convey depth.

Figure 4.14. (top) Akira Kurosawa almost always used very long lenses and in this case a slightly elevated points of view to render a compressed space. In this shot from Kurosawa's *Seven Samurai*, we clearly see the influence of composition and perspective from Japanese prints and the same sense of space as in Figure 4.13.

Figure 4.15. (top) A normal lens keeps the background in focus; it can be distracting.

Figure 4.16. (bottom) A very long lens throws the background out of focus and the viewer's entire attention is drawn to the character.

Figure 4.17. (above, right) Deliberate lens flare is an essential part of the look of this scene from *Nine and 1/2 Weeks*.

Another issue in selective focus is when two or more players are in the same shot but at different distances. If you don't have enough light to set the lens to a higher f/stop (and thus you don't have much depth-of-field), it may be necessary for the focus-puller to choose one or the other to be in focus. This is up to the DP or director to decide, and they should consult before the shot — and don't forget to let the focus puller know. A few basic rules of thumb:

- Focus goes to the person speaking. It is permissible to rack focus back and forth as they speak.
- Focus goes to the person facing the camera or most prominent in the frame.
- Focus goes to the person experiencing the most dramatic or emotional moment. This may countermand the principal of focusing on the person speaking.
- If there is doubt about whom to focus on, most camera assistants put the focus on the actor who has the lower number on the call sheet.

This may sound frivolous but, it's not. Call sheets list the actors in numbered order of their characters. The lead is actor #1, and so on. If you are playing it on the fly, the safe bet is to go with the actor with the lower number on the call sheet.

If they are close enough, the AC may split the focus between them (if there is enough depth-of-field to keep both of them acceptable sharp) or by very subtly racking back and forth. Major focus racks need to be discussed in advance and rehearsed. This is true of all camera moves that are motivated by dialog or action. If the AC and the operator haven't seen what the actors are going to do, it is difficult to anticipate the move just enough to time it correctly. Rehearsal is a time saver, as it usually reduces the number of blown takes.

It is interesting to note that older books on cinematography barely mention focus at all. There is a reason for this. Until the 60's, it was the established orthodoxy that pretty much everything important in the frame should be in focus. The idea of having key elements in the frame that are deliberately out of focus really didn't fully take hold until it was popularized by fashion photographers in the 80's. It is now recognized by filmmakers as a key tool and is the reason that when evaluating and using HD cameras, a great deal of attention is paid to the size of the video sensor. There is more discussion of the other factors that affect focus and depth of field in the *Optics & Focus*, later in this book.

Figure 4.18. A high-angle shot along with a dramatic shaft of light and shadows creates a graphic composition in *Sin City*.

IMAGE CONTROL AT THE LENS

Some techniques with the lens are discussed in the chapter on *Image Control*; in this chapter we deal with altering the image quality with the lens and shutter only as they are relevant to this discussion of visual storytelling with the lens. There is a huge variety of visual effects that can be achieved with just the selection of lenses, filters, flare, and similar effects, many of which are difficult or impossible to achieve in other ways.

Filtration

Modern lenses are remarkably sharp. For the most part this is what we want. In some cases, however, we are looking for a softer image. The most frequent reason is beauty. A softer image, especially of a woman's face, will generally be prettier. A soft image may also be more romantic, dreamlike, or, in a subjective shot, may translate to a state of mind less in touch with reality. Some cinematographers tend to think only of diffusion filters but a softer image can be achieved in many different ways. More on this in the chapter *Image Control*.

Soft Lenses

Some shooters use older lenses for an image that is subtly soft in a way that is difficult to achieve with filters. Soft lenses can give a slightly greater apparent depth-of-field. This is because the fall-off from critical sharpness is somewhat masked by the softness.

Besides not being made with the latest computer-aided optical design and manufacturing, older lenses also have less sophisticated optical coatings. The coating on lenses is there primarily to prevent internal flares and reflections, which slightly degrade and soften the image. This can be seen clearly if the sun or other strong light source directly hits the lens. The internal flares and reflections are very apparent in an old lens as compared to a modern one.

Certainly the best-known recent use of this technique was the film *Saving Private Ryan,* where the filmmakers asked the Panavision camera company to remove the modern coatings off a set of lenses so that they would more closely resemble the types of lenses that were used in actual World War II combat photography.

Figure 4.19. This *god's eye shot* (a type of *high angle* shot that is either directly overhead or nearly so) from *Kill Bill* dramatically portrays the situation of the character — utterly surrounded. In filmmaking, everything must have a reason — it's not enough to do something just because "it's a cool shot."

Flare/Glare

A direct, specular beam of light that hits the lens will create a flare that creates veiling glare, which appears as a sort of milky whiteness over the whole image. This is why so much attention is paid to the matte box or lens shade and why the grips are often asked to set *lensers* — flags that keep direct light sources from hitting the lens. There are exceptions, such as in Figures 4.1 and 4.17, where deliberate flare is used as a photographic technique, generally as a device to set a certain tone or mood for the shot.

Lens Height

Variations in lens height can also be an effective tool for adding subtext to a shot. As a general rule, dialog and most ordinary people shots are done at the eye level of the actors involved. Some filmmakers attempt to avoid using many straight-on eye-level shots, as they consider them boring. Variations from eye level have filmspace implications, psychological undertones and are useful as a strictly compositional device.

Variations from eye level are not to be done casually, especially with dialog or reaction shots. Keep in mind that deviations from eye-level are asking the viewer to participate in the scene in a mode that is very different from normal, so be sure that there is a good reason for it and that it is contributing in a way that helps the scene.

High Angle

When the camera is above eye height, we seem to dominate the subject. The subject is reduced in stature and perhaps in importance. Its importance is not, however, diminished if the *high angle* reveals it to be a massive, extensive structure, for example. This reminds us that high angles looking down on the subject reveal overall layout and scope in the case of landscape, streets, or buildings. This is useful if the intent is an *establishing* or *expository* shot where it is important for the audience to know something about the layout.

As with subjective and objective camera views on the lateral plane, we can see camera angles that diverge from eye level as increasingly objective, more third person in terms of our literary analogy. This applies especially to higher angles. A very high angle is called a *god's eye shot* (Figure 4.19), suggesting its omniscient, removed point-of-view: distant, separate from the scene, a world view, philosophical and contemplative. We see all parts of the scene, all interacting forces equally without particularly identifying with any of them.

Low Angle

A low-angle shot can make a character seem ominous and foreboding, as in *Dr. Strangelove* (Figure 4.20). When a character is approaching something as seen from a low angle, little is revealed beyond what the character might see himself: we share the character's surprise or sense of mystery. If the shots of the character are low angle, we share his apprehension.

If these are then combined with high-angle shots that reveal what the character does not know, for example, we are aware of whatever surprise or ambush or revelation awaits him: this is the true nature of suspense. As Hitchcock brilliantly observed, there can be no real suspense unless the audience knows what is going to happen. His famous example is the bomb under the table. If two characters sit at a table and suddenly a bomb goes off, we have a moment of surprise that is quickly over, a cheap shock at best. If the audience knows that the bomb is under the table and is aware that the timer is clicking steadily towards exploding, then there is true suspense that engages and involves the audience in a way that simple shock never can. If the audience is on the edge of their seats knowing that the time on the clock is growing shorter, then the fact that the two characters seated at the table are nattering on amiably about the weather is both maddening and engaging.

Although any time we get away from human eye level we are decreasing our subjective identification with the characters, low angles can become more subjective in other ways. Clearly a very low angle can be a dog's eye view, especially if it is cut in right after a shot of the dog and then the very low angle moves somewhat erratically and in the manner of a dog. This type of doggie POV is practically required for werewolf movies, of course. With low angles, the subject tends to dominate us. If the subject is a character, that actor will seem more powerful and dominant. Any time the actor being viewed is meant to be menacing or frightening to the character we are associating the POV with, a low angle is often appropriate.

Figure 4.20. Kubrick is a master of choosing the right angle and lens to tell the story powerfully. In this shot, the lens height and angle make a clear statement about the state of mind of the character (*Dr. Strangelove: or How I Learned to Stop Worrying and Love the Bomb*).

lens language

Figures 4.21 (above, left) **and 4.22** (above, right). Director Orson Welles uses shifting *dutch tilt* from dutch left to dutch right to make the crazy house sequence in *Lady from Shanghai* an almost psychedelic feeling.

Dutch Tilt

In most shooting we strive for the camera to be perfectly level. It is the job of the camera assistant and the dolly grip to recheck every time the camera is moved and ensure that it is still "on the bubble." This refers to the bulls-eye or transverse bubble levels that are standard on all camera mounts, heads and dollies.

This is crucial because human perception is much more sensitive to off-level verticals than to off-level horizontals. If the camera is even a little off, walls, doorways, telephone poles, any vertical feature will be immediately seen as out of plumb. There are instances, however, where we want the visual tension of this off-level condition to work for us to create anxiety, paranoia, subjugation, or mystery. The term for this is "dutch tilt" or "dutch angle."

This is used extremely well in the mystery/suspense film *The Third Man*, where a great many shots are done with the camera off-level. Orson Welles also uses it very effectively in *The Lady from Shanghai*. In this example, he is trapped in the carnival crazy house at the end of the film. He is also still under the influence of the pills he took as part of his escape from the courthouse. In this shot, the camera is tilted radically right as he enters in the distance. Then, as he crosses frame and goes through a door to a second room, the camera, instead of tracking, tilts to the opposite angle and ends with a hard left tilt (Figures 4.21 and 4.22).

This of course is entirely in keeping with the surrealistic atmosphere of the crazy house and of his deranged, drugged state of mind, but it has another advantage as well. Tracking shots that move past walls are not at all unusual. In this type of shot we track along with the character who walks through a door into the next room. The camera passes through the wall and what we see is usually a black vertical line that represents the edge of the wall that we are magically transversing.

visual storytelling

Figure 5.2. The transition from black-and-white to color in the film *Memento* is a visual metaphor for transitioning from the past (black-and-white) to the present (color). (top) The character picks up a developing Polaroid. (middle) His POV as the Polaroid develops and starts to show color. (bottom) Back on him, the scene has transitioned to color.

Figure 5.1. (previous page) Caravaggio's *The Calling of St. Matthew*. The lighting carries a great deal of the storytelling power of the image.

VISUAL METAPHOR

One of our most important tools as filmmakers is *visual metaphor*, which is the ability of images to convey a meaning in addition to their straightforward reality. Think of it as "reading between the lines" visually. In some films, things are simply what they are. In others, however, many images carry an implied meaning that can be a powerful storytelling tool. A couple of examples: in *Memento*, the extended flashback (which moves forward in time) is shown in black-and-white and the present (which moves backward in time) is told in color. Essentially, it is two parts of the same story with one part moving forwards and the other part told backward. At the point in time where they intersect, the black-and-white slowly changes to color. Director Christopher Nolan accomplishes this in a subtle and elegant way by showing a Polaroid develop (Figure 5.2).

Telling Stories with Pictures

In other chapters we talk about the technical and practical aspects of lighting. In this chapter we look at lighting and other aspects of the visual image as key elements of storytelling.

Let's divert our attention from film for a moment and look at a painting. Studying classical art is useful in that the painter must tell the whole story in a single frame (not to mention without dialog or subtitles). Thus, the painter must employ every aspect of visual language to tell the story of the painting as well as layer it with subtext, symbolism, and emotional content. As with the films of Kubrick, Welles, and Kurosawa, it is also useful to study the visual design because nothing in the frame is accidental. Every element, every color, every shadow is there for a purpose, and its part in the visual and storytelling scheme has been carefully thought out.

First, let's look at this beautiful painting that opens this chapter, *The Calling of St. Matthew* by Caravaggio (Figure 5.1, previous page). Light has a great power to form space. In this case, the single source forms a pool of space that envelops the students. Outside it is another space, sharply delineated. Within this pool of light is knowledge and outside is darkness — ignorance. As Newton said, "What we know is a drop; what we don't know is an ocean."

Clearly the light represents knowledge, the illuminating power of the great mystery of the universe, but it is not just a symbol — it is also a crucial part of the design. It carries a major portion of the storytelling as well.

H.W. Janson discusses the painting in his book *The History of Art*: "Most decisive is the strong beam of light above Christ that illuminates his face and hand in the gloomy interior, thus carrying his call across to Matthew. Without this light, so natural yet so charged with symbolic meaning, the picture would lose its magic, its power to make us aware of the divine presence." The lighting is chiaroscuro at its best; not only does it create strong contrasts and clearly delineate the characters in sharp relief but the figures almost jump out at us. The strong directionality of the light guides the eye and unifies the composition. What is unimportant falls into shadow and thus does not distract the eye.

"In Baroque painting, light is an aggressive liberating force. A small amount of it is enough to reveal the spiritual opportunities that lie hidden." (Edmund Burke Feldman in *Varieties of Visual Experience*). Here the strong beam of sunlight is the hand of God itself, reaching into the dusky tavern to pluck Matthew out of the darkness. The light coming from outside is clearly the presence of divine truth; it penetrates the dusty darkness of ignorance in the tavern, so the shadows are equally important — ignorance, lethargy, and wasted lives. As we discussed in *Visual Language,* they also form *negative spaces* that are important compositionally.

It is a powerful painting that carries depths of meaning and content far beyond its mere visual beauty — the kind of thing we strive for every day on the set. All that is missing is a producer in the background saying, "It's awfully dark; couldn't we add some fill light?"

LIGHTING AS STORYTELLING

In visual storytelling, few elements are as effective and as powerful as light and color (which is discussed more fully in later chapters). They have the ability to reach viewers at a purely emotion gut level. This gives them the added advantage of being able to affect the audience on one level, while their conscious brain is interpreting the story at an entirely different plane of consciousness.

Film Noir

Certainly, one of the highlights of lighting as storytelling is the era of *film noir*: American films of the forties and fifties, primarily in the mystery, suspense, and detective genres, nearly all of them in black-and-white. The noir genre is best known for its low-key lighting style: side light, chiaroscuro, shadowy (Figure 5.6). This was, of course, only one of the various elements of visual style: they also used angle, composition, lighting, montage, depth, and movement in expressive new ways. Many factors came together to influence this style: technical innovations such as more sensitive, finer-grained black-and-white negative film stock; lenses better suited to darker shooting conditions; smaller, more mobile camera dollies, cameras light enough to hand-hold, and portable power supplies, all perfected during World War II, alleviated many of the logistical problems previously connected with location filming.

These enabled filmmakers to get out to the dark, mean streets of the city with its shadowy alleys fraught with unknown dangers, blinking neon lights reflected on rain-soaked pavement, and all of the mystery and menace of the city after dark. Beyond just the gritty reality and groundedness that come with actual locations, the challenges and various difficulties of lighting in and around real structures tend to force cinematographers to experiment and be bolder with their lighting; there is less of a tendency to just do it the same old way it's always been done back in the studio.

But all of this is more than just visual style: it is inherently a part of the storytelling, an integral narrative device. "A side-lit close-up may reveal a face, half in shadow, half in light, at the precise moment of indecision." (Silver and Ward). Beyond narrative, it becomes part of character as well. Noir was the birth of the protagonist who is not so clearly defined as purely good or evil. As with Walter Neff in *Double Indemnity* or Johnny Clay in *The Killing* and so many others, they are characters full of contradiction and alienation. In their very being they may be pulled between good and evil, light and dark, illumination and shadow. This reflects the confusion and sense of lost ideals that returned with the veterans and survivors of the war. It also reflects the "zeitgeist" of the times: the growing undercurrent that not all things can be known, "...the impossibility of a single, stable point of view, and thus the limits to all seeing and knowing." (J.P. Tellotte, *Voices in the Dark*) — that what is unseen in the shadows may be as significant as what is seen in the light.

Figure 5.3. (top) The *Black Maria*, developed by Edison and Dickson, the first method of controlling lighting for filmmaking.

Figure 5.4. (bottom) D.W. Griffith and his cameraman Billy Bitzer examine a piece of negative in front of some Cooper-Hewitt tubes, one of the earliest artificial lighting sources. For a more extensive discussion of the history of film lighting see *Motion Picture and Video Lighting*, by the same author, also published by Focal Press.

Figure 5.5. Although not strictly a noir film, *Citizen Kane* is of the same era and employs the same techniques of visual storytelling with lighting that is expressive, visually striking, and makes specific story points.

Here the reporter has come to the vault where Kane's memoirs are kept. As the guard brings forward the sacred book that we hope will contain the ultimate secrets, the single beam of light represents knowledge reaching into the darkened space in much the same way that it does in the Caravaggio (Figure 5.1).

Being a backlight with no fill, it leaves the characters in complete silhouette, perhaps representing their ignorance of the knowledge.

LIGHT AS VISUAL METAPHOR

Let's turn now to a more recent example, a film that uses light as a metaphor and as storytelling perhaps better than any other of the modern era: Barry Levinson's *The Natural*. Masterfully photographed by Caleb Deschanel, the film is so visually unified and well thought out that it would be possible to comment on the metaphoric or narrative use of lighting in almost every scene; here we will examine only the high points.

In the opening shot we see the title character alone, dejected and older, sitting at a railroad station. He is half in light and half in shadow, a metaphor for his uncertain future and his dark, unclear past. The train arrives and blacks out the screen. He gets on. End of title sequence. It is mysterious, suggestive, and supremely simple (Figure 5.7). *The Natural* is the tale of a talented young baseball player Roy Hobbes (Robert Redford) who is diverted from his career by a chance encounter with a dark and mysterious young lady, but makes a comeback years later as he simultaneously finds love with his long-lost childhood sweetheart. It is a story of good versus evil in the classic sense, and Levinson and Deschanel use a wide variety of cinematic and narrative devices to tell it. More than anything, they use light as a visual metaphor — a key part of the visual storytelling.

As the story begins, Roy is a young farm boy full of energy, talent, promise, and infatuation for his sweetheart Iris (Glenn Close), who always wears white. This section is shot in bright afternoon sunlight: the vibrant energy of nature with just a hint of a soft filter. It is backlit with the sun, and everything is warm and golden.

His father dies of a heart attack in the shade of a tree, and that night there is a ferocious storm: inky blue punctuated with stabs of violent lightning. A bolt splits the tree, and Roy uses the heart of the

Figure 5.6. The black-and-white *film noir* period is one of the highest achievements of film lighting as a story element. This frame is from *Mildred Pierce*.

tree to make his own bat, which he inscribes with a lightning bolt: a symbol of the power of nature — light in its most intense, primitive, and pure form. He gets a call from the majors and asks Iris out for a last meeting. They are silhouetted on a ridge against a glowing blue sky that represents night and the temptations of eros (Figure 5.9). If you look closely, it is completely unnatural (it's day-for-night with a blue filter) but beautiful and perfectly portrays their mental state. In the barn, as they make love they are engulfed in stripes of moonlight alternating with darkness. It is a radiant moment, but there are hints of danger (we will learn much later in the film that she is made pregnant by this encounter). As he boards a train to travel to his major league tryout, things darken a bit. The only light source is the relatively small windows of the train, and while they admit plenty of light, it is low angle and somewhat shadowy and malevolent.

Light and Shadow / Good and Evil

It is here that he first sees the woman who is to bring evil and temptation into his life — the *Lady in Black* (Figure. 5.10), who we first see in silhouette and from the back. Usually portrayed backlit or in shadow, as befits her evil nature, she invites him to her hotel room, shoots him, and then jumps to her death, ending his baseball hopes.

Figure 5.7. The opening shot from *The Natural* — a faceless character lost somewhere in the light and the dark, suspended in time: the past is uncertain and the future is unclear. This purgatory of being caught between them establishes the mood and tone of uncertainty and conflict between two worlds that is carried through the rest of the film.

visual storytelling

Figure 5.8. (above) After years of foundering in the narrow darkness of obscurity, Roy emerges into the light of the one thing that gives him power — the bright sunny open space of a baseball field.

Figure 5.9. (top) Early in the film, Roy and his sweetheart Iris are young and innocent, but their purity is disrupted when they meet in the blue moonlight and make love. We will only find out at nearly the end of the film that this loss of innocence leads to a son, which Roy does not know about until he is redeemed and recovers this purity that is represented by the golden sunlight of a wheat field where he plays catch with his newly discovered son.

Figure 5.10. (bottom) The *Lady in Black* — the temptation that leads to Roy's downfall. She is always lit dimly and is somewhat shadowy — an ephemeral figure; in this shot under-lit for a mysterious look. DP Caleb Deschanel gave this scene a special treatment by bi-packing a slightly out-of-focus black-and-white negative with the color negative.

Sixteen years later, we see him arrive at the stadium of the New York Knights. He is in total darkness as he walks up the ramp, then emerges into sunlight as he enters the ballpark: he is home, where he belongs (Figure 5.8). Given his first chance to play, the sequence opens with a shot of what will become an important symbol: the lighting towers of the field. They are dark and silhouetted against black storm clouds. It is twilight, halfway between day and night. As he literally "knocks the cover off the ball," there is a bolt of lightning and it begins to rain. Lightning, the most powerful form of light, is a recurring symbol throughout the film — light as pure energy, bringing the power of nature. Coming back into the dugout, we are introduced to a second visual theme: the flashbulbs of news photographers (Figures 5.13, 5.14, and 5.15).

As one of his teammates adopts the lightning bolt as a shoulder insignia, the team takes off — a symbol of the power of light and energy that Roy has brought to the squad. They are on a hot streak. Now we meet the Judge, half owner of the team. Slimy and evil, his office is completely dark, lit only by the dim light that seeps through the closed venetian blinds (Figure 5.11). His face is obscured in shadow. After the Judge tries to get him to lose so he can buy the team, Roy rebuffs him, and on his way out he defiantly flips the room lights on. Then the bookie emerges from the shadows.

Their attempt at bribery having failed, they contrive to set him up with Memo (Kim Basinger, who always wears black) at a fancy restaurant, where the only illumination is the table lamps that cast an ominous underlight on the characters, although fill is added for Roy (purity) and Memo (raw beauty). She takes him to the beach and in a reprise of the love scene between Roy and Iris they are bathed in blue moonlight. But this is a slightly different moonlight than we saw with his boyhood girl: colder and harsher; sensuous, but not romantic (Figure 5.12).

Fading Flashbulbs

Next comes a montage sequence of flashbulbs popping, symbolizing fame, celebrity, glamour, and the seduction of the fast life that will distract him from baseball. To emphasize the idea that fame and success have a corrupting influence on his focus on the game and his nightlife and partying with Memo, many of the flashbulbs go

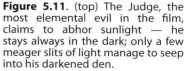

off right in his face, thus affecting his vision — a perfect metaphor for the blinding influence of celebrity. Roy descends into a slump, bringing the team down with him. In his decline, the flashbulbs still go off, but in marvelous subtlety we see them in slow motion at the end of their burn cycle as they fade out. Iris comes to a game to watch, unbeknownst to Roy. As the team is losing and Roy is striking out, Iris stands up (Figure 5.18). Her translucent white hat is backlit by a single shaft of sunlight, making her appear angelic. Roy hits a home run that breaks the stadium clock — stopping time. Photographers' flashbulbs go off, and as Roy peers into the crowd looking for Iris, he is blinded by them and can't see her (Figure 5.16). Later, they meet and go for a walk.

As he tells her the story of his dark past, they are in complete silhouette, in darkness even though it is midday. As he ends his confession they emerge into full daylight. Later, the silver bullet that has been in his stomach since the Lady in Black shot him sends him to the hospital.

Figure 5.13. (below, left) Throughout the film, flashbulbs represent the glare of fame, fortune, and celebrity. For Roy, as the new hero of the team, the newspaper photographers and flashbulbs are everywhere.

Figure 5.14. (below, top) They quickly become the flashbulbs of the paparazzi as he paints the town red with his glamorous girlfriend Memo.

Figure 5.15. (below, bottom) As the nonstop nightlife hurts Roy's performance on the field, a *slowmo* shot of a flashbulb fading to black represents Roy's loss of power — the dimming of his light.

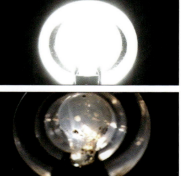

Figure 5.16. (above) His long-lost love Iris comes to a game. Roy seems to sense her presence, but as he turns to look for her, he is blinded by the glare of the photographer's flashes.

Figure 5.17. (right, top) As Roy's success on the field promises to rescue the team and spoil the Judge's plans, he watches from his shadowy lair.

Figure 5.18. (right) As Roy is faltering on the field, near defeat, Iris stands up, and a single beam of light illuminates her so that she is visible in the crowd. It gives Roy the power to hit a home run and win the game. The angelic glow makes her hat a halo to supplement the white dress and the standing pose. To reinforce the lighting effect, she is surrounded by men, all in dark clothes and hats.

Figure 5.19. (below) As a reporter comes close to uncovering Roy's dark secret, he sneaks onto the field to photograph him at batting practice. To stop him, Roy hits a ball with perfect aim that breaks the reporter's camera; the flashbulb fires as it falls to the ground: the glare of disclosure, of secrets being brought to light, is prevented by Roy's sheer talent with the bat.

Figure 5.20. (right) As Roy lays ill in the hospital before the playoffs, the Judge comes to offer him a bribe. Rather than rendering the Judge in shadow as might be the obvious choice, Deschanel arranges for the warm glow of the otherwise benevolent hospital lamps to glare on the Judge's glasses — thus the light itself manages to obscure his eyes and partly disguise his evil. This is appropriate as he appears here not as the intimidating force of evil but as a silky-voiced cajoler.

Against doctor's orders, he tries to practice in secret, but the reporter attempts to take a picture of him. Roy hits a ball that smashes his camera, which falls to the ground, and the flashbulb fires as it breaks: he is striking back at the glare of publicity that has nearly destroyed him (Figure 5.19).

The final climactic game is at night, and the stadium tower lights burn brightly. The Judge and the bookie watch the game from his skybox, which we see from below as just a pale yellow glow on the partially closed blinds: an image of evil and corruption hovering over the game (Figure 5.17). Roy is struggling as his injury plagues him, and it all comes down to one final pitch that will win or lose the pennant. Having it all rest on the final pitch is, of course, a given in any baseball movie, but the cinematography and the metaphor of lighting and lightning together with the mystical glow of the dying sparks, strongly reminiscent of triumphal fireworks, gives this scene a magical quality that makes it one of the most memorable final scenes in American cinema and visually one of the most moving.

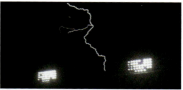

Figure 5.21. (above) The moment before the do-or-die climactic pitch is thrown, lightning (which has always brought the power of good to Roy) strikes the light towers of the baseball field.

Figure 5.22. (left, top) As Roy connects powerfully with the ball, he is framed so that the lights of the field (representing the ennobling power of baseball) are in the shot with him.

Figure 5.23. (left, bottom) Roy's home run strikes the lights of the field; one shatters, short-circuiting them all, and they explode in a shower of fireworks.

Visual Poetry

It all comes down to a 3-2 count and the last pitch — the ultimate moment. The pitch is thrown in slow motion; Roy swings and slams a home run right into the stadium lights (Figure 5.22), which shatter and short-circuit, sending a shower of sparks onto the field (Figures 5.23 and 5.24). This is a masterful touch, as drama, as storytelling, and as a truly motivated lighting effect. In one of the truly great images of contemporary cinema, as he rounds the bases in slow-motion triumph, Roy and his celebrating teammates are enveloped in these glowing fireworks, as if miniature stars of glory are raining on them. A soft, golden glow of light personified engulfs Roy and the entire team as the film ends. It is the light of pure good; Roy and the power of his raw talent as symbolized by the bat carved from the tree struck by lightning have transformed them and invigorated them with all that is good about baseball and all that it symbolizes about American democracy.

The firefly-like glow comes from the exploding lights of the field (the illuminating spirit of baseball), shattered by Roy's home run (his talent) that have just been struck by a bolt of lightning — the same lightning that has brought Roy the power of his unsullied talent when it struck the tree under which his father died and from which he took the wood to carve his almost magical bat. These are symbols and they work, but there is a more subtle visual metaphor at work and it is what makes the shot so hauntingly evocative. What is magical about this shot is that the light is everywhere: it is an omnipresent bathing glow, it is all around them, it almost seems to emanate from within them as they bask in the beauty of a pure and simple moment of triumph in baseball and the triumph of right over the insidious attempts of the Judge to infect and degrade baseball with his greed. With this elegantly simple but visceral and expressive visual image system, Levinson and Deschanel make the most of and add extra

Figure 5.24. As Roy rounds the bases, the sparks from the exploding bulbs surround him and his jubilant teammates in a soft gentle wash of light. They are enveloped in an omnipresent glow of the power of good triumphant over evil — one of the most haunting images in modern cinema. The light is all around them, part of them, within them.

layers of meaning to a great story, a great script, and a superlative cast. In this particular film, light is used as a metaphor in a very clear and sustained way. In most films, lighting is a part of storytelling in more limited and less overtly metaphorical ways, but it can always be a factor in underlying story points, character, and particularly the perception of time and space. Filmmakers who take a dismissive attitude toward lighting are depriving themselves of one of the most important, subtle, and powerful tools of visual storytelling.

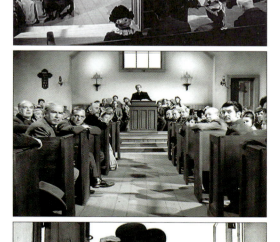

cinematic continuity

SHOOTING FOR EDITING

Filming is ultimately shooting for editorial. The primary purpose of shooting is not merely to get some "great shots" — in the end it must serve the purpose of the film by giving the editor and the director what they need to actually piece together completed scenes and sequences that add up to a finished product that makes sense, has emotional impact, and accomplishes its purpose.

Thinking about Continuity

Movies get made one scene at a time, and scenes get made one shot at a time. No matter how large and complex a production is, you are always still doing it one shot at a time. As you do each shot you have to keep the overall purpose in mind: that this shot must fit in with all the other shots that will make up the final scene.

Continuity is a big issue in filmmaking. It's something we have to be aware of at all times. Continuity mistakes can easily render several hours of shooting worthless or can create huge problems in editing. So what is continuity?

Basically, continuity means a logical consistency of the story, dialog, and picture so that it presents the appearance of reality. Here's a simple example: in a wide shot, he is *not* wearing a hat. Then we immediately cut to a close-up and he is wearing a hat. It appears to the viewer as if a magic hat suddenly appeared on his head. This would be a serious continuity error — the audience would surely notice it. When the audience is aware of continuity errors, it makes them aware they are watching a movie, it breaks the illusion.

Types of continuity

There are several categories of continuity:

- Content
- Movement
- Position
- Time

Continuity Of Content

Continuity of content applies to anything visible in the scene: wardrobe, hairstyle, props, the actors, cars in the background, the time set on the clock. As discussed in the chapter *Set Operations*, it is the script supervisor in conjunction with the various department heads who must ensure that all of these items match from shot to shot.

These kinds of problems extend from the very obvious — she was wearing a red hat in the master, but now it is a green hat in the close-up — to the very subtle — he was smoking a cigar that was almost finished when he entered and now he has a cigar that is just started. While the script supervisor, on-set wardrobe, and prop master are the first line of defense in these matters, it is still up to the director and camera person to always be watchful for problems.

As with almost anything in film there is a certain amount of cheating that is possible; the audience can be very accepting of minor glitches. Absolutely perfect continuity is never possible and there is a large gray area.

Continuity of Movement

Anything that is moving in a shot must have a movement in the next shot that is a seamless continuation of what was begun. Whether it be opening a door, picking up a book, or parking a car, the movement must have no gaps from one shot to the next. This is where it is so critical to be aware of how the shots might be cut together.

Figure 6.1. (previous page) A continuity sequence from *High Noon*. The geography is very clear and well established. It is possible to be a bit looser about some of the rules of continuity, and in fact the editor does so a few times in this scene.

As discussed in *Shooting Methods*, to play it safe in shooting any type of movement and be sure that the editor is not constricted in choices, it is important to overlap all movement. Even if the script calls for the scene to cut away before she fully opens the door, for example, it is best to go ahead and let the camera roll for a few seconds until the action is complete. Never start a shot exactly at the beginning of a movement — back up a bit and roll into it, then let it run out at the end.

One prime example of this is the *rock in*. Say you shot a master of a character walking up to the bank teller. He is there and is talking to the teller in the master. You then set up for a close-up of him. You may know that the edit will pick up with the character already in place, but the safe way to do it is to have the character do the final step or two of walking up as shot in the close-up OTS position.

There are times, however, when focus or position is critical. It is difficult to guarantee that the actor will hit the mark with the precision necessary to get the shot in focus. In this case a "rock in" is the way to go. The technique is simple: instead of actually taking a full step back, the actor keeps one foot firmly planted and steps back with the other: then when action is called, he can hit his mark again with great precision. The most important aspect of continuity of movement is *screen direction*, which is discussed in more detail later.

Figure 6.2. Occasionally continuity of time can be reinforced by cutting to the clock, but this cannot be the primary means of keeping the audience aware of *when* they are.

Continuity of Position

Continuity of position is most often problematic with props. Props that are used in the scene are going to be moved in almost every take. Everyone must watch that they start and end in the same place, or it can be an editor's nightmare. This is often the dividing line between a thoroughly professional performer and a beginner: it is up to the actor to use the props and place them exactly the same in every take. If, for some reason, there is a mismatch in placement of a prop between the master and a element of coverage, it is up to the director to either reshoot one or the other or to do some sort of repair coverage that will allow the editor to solve the problem.

This can be done in a variety of ways. One simple example: if the actor put the glass down on the left side of the table in the master, but it is one the right side in the medium, one solution is to do a shot where the actor slides it across the table. This solves the problem, but there is one drawback: the editor has to use that shot. This may end up creating more problems than it solves.

Continuity of Time

This does not refer to the problem of resetting the clock so that it always reads the same time (that is prop continuity and comes under continuity of content), rather it has to do with the flow of time within a scene. For example, if Dave North is walking away from Sam South in the wide shot, then you cut to a close-up of Sam South; by the time you cut back to Dave North, his action must be logical time wise. That is, if the close-up of Sam South was for two seconds, when cutting back to the wide shot, Dave North can't have walked fifty yards away, (there wasn't enough time for that).

Within the scene, certain conventions help maintain pacing and flow, particularly in cases where a character moves within a scene. The action or background at the beginning of the move may be important, as they may be important at the end of the scene (otherwise why are they being shot?) The middle part of the move, however, is often not important information. If the character has to cross a wide room or walk up a flight of stairs, it may be helpful to skip

cinematic continuity

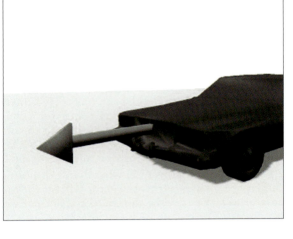

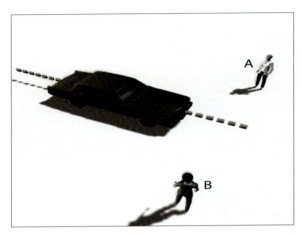

Figure 6.3. (above) The position of the viewer (or camera) establishes *the line*, sometimes called *the 180° line* or the *action axis*. The woman at top (A) will see the car moving to her left (**Figure 6.4**, above, right)

Figure 6.5. (right) The woman at the bottom (B) will see the car moving to her right.

Figure 6.6. (below) If both of the women are viewing the car from the same side of its movement of direction, then they will both see it moving in the same direction.

Figure 6.7, (below, right) This is the basic principle of screen direction. If we cross over to the other side of the line of action, it will reverse the screen direction.

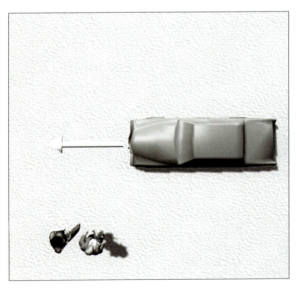

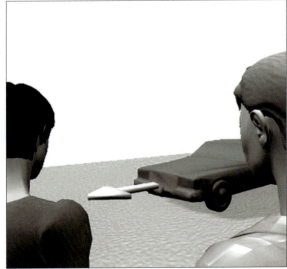

Figure 6.8. Screen direction plays a major role in David Lean's directing of *Lawrence of Arabia*. To emphasize the inevitability of Lawrence's fate, all movement in the film is from left to right.

over some of that move. To just skip it would be, of course, a jump cut and an error in continuity, but there are several work-arounds. The simplest is to let the character exit frame, then enter frame in the next shot. This is a simple form of an *elliptical cut* (when the cut between two shots spans a substantial amount of time), and a good deal of movement time can be left out without disturbing continuity. This is a culturally conditioned film convention that audiences worldwide have come to accept. To preserve movement continuity and screen direction, if the actor exits the left side of frame, she must enter the next frame on the right side (Figure 6.26).

In *The Technique of Film and Video Editing*, Ken Dancyger points out another device used by Kurosawa in *Seven Samurai,* by Kubrick in *Paths of Glory,* and, of course, in many other films: a tight close-up of the character that tracks or pans as the character moves. As long as the direction, action, and speed match that of the wide shot, the movement of the character can be longer or shorter than the real time move would take. If the character changes direction in the shot, this must be preserved when cutting back to a wider shot.

THE PRIME DIRECTIVE

Most of these techniques and rules are based on one principle: to not create confusion in the mind of the audience and thus distract them from the story or annoy and frustrate them. Let's take a fundamental example (Figures 6.3 through 6.7). Two women are standing on opposite sides of the street. Woman *A* sees the car going left. Woman *B* sees the car going right. If we move them to the *same* side of the street, they will both see the car going in the same direction in relation to their own sense of orientation (left/right): their *perception* of the car will be the same. The movement of the car establishes direction, but there is another aspect: where the women are viewing the movement from is also important; this is defined by *the line,* sometimes called the *180° line*. These two establish the spatial orientation of the scene and are the basis of *screen direction*.

SCREEN DIRECTION

Anybody standing on the same side of a scene will see things from the same orientation, as in Figures 6.3 through 6.7, as long as they are on the same side of *the line*. Let's take this simple two shot (Figure 6.10). From our first camera position, the woman Lucy is on the left and the man Ralph is on the right. Then, in **C**, the camera position

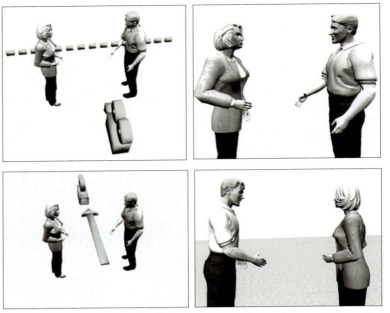

Figure 6.9. (above) Where the camera can go without creating this jump in directional relationships is defined by a 180° semicircle on one or the other side of the line. The camera can go anywhere in that 180° arc and screen direction is maintained. The camera can go closer or farther away, higher or lower as long as it stays on the same side of the line.

Figure 6.10. (top, left) When starting a scene, which side of the line the camera is on establishes screen direction.

Figure 6.11. (top, right) With the camera on one side of them, the woman will be on the left and the man will be on the right.

Figure 6.12. (bottom, left) If the camera is shifted to the other side of the line, their positions are reversed.

Figure 6.13. (bottom, right) The man is now on the left and the woman is on the right — the screen direction is reversed. These two shots could not be cut together without creating a jarring effect.

is shifted to the other side of the line. In **D**, the audience will see, for no reason they can understand, that Ralph is on the left side facing right and Lucy is on the right side facing left. It will confuse the audience: they won't be able to readily understand and assimilate the information. While their brains try to sort it out, their attention will be drawn away from the story. Not only will they be distracted from what the characters are saying, but if it happens often enough, it will annoy and frustrate them. What is it that delineates where we can put the camera to maintain continuity and where we can't?

The Action Axis

There is an imaginary axis between these two characters. In our first example of the car, the movement direction of the car establishes what we call the *line*. In all of these diagrams, it is represented by the large dashed line. The line is referred to by several terms; some people call it the *action axis* or the *action line*. If we stay on one side of it for all our shots — everything cuts together perfectly (Figure 6.10). If we cross over to the other side — the characters will jump to opposite sides of the screen. Safe locations for the camera are symbolized by the 180° half circle (Figure 6.9). This semicircle is a symbol only; in practice the camera can go nearer or farther, higher and lower, in relation to the subjects; the lens focal length can change, and so on — what is important is that by keeping the camera on the same side of the line, the screen direction does not change.

These Are the Rules — but Why?

The basic rules of *not crossing the line* are well known to all working filmmakers, but many do not stop to consider the fundamental theory and perceptual issues that underlie this principle. It is important to understand it at a deeper level if you are to be able to solve the trickier issues that do not conveniently fall into one of the basic categories of this system. More importantly, it is only when we understand the whole theoretical system that we can truly understand when it is permissible to break the rules.

First, we have to consider directionality. What do we mean by that? What is something that's not directional? Not much, really. A featureless cylinder or a globe painted all the same color are non-

Figure 6.14. The line established by clear and easily understood geography. The action line is practically visible itself in this shot from *High Noon*. Interestingly, the filmmakers actually purposely violate the line a few times in this scene, but since the geography is so strong, these violations do not create a continuity problem.

directional, but just about everything else is. A woman looking at a building is directional. More importantly, her *look* is directional. Movement is also directional. Say we took that featureless globe and rolled down the sidewalk. Its line of movement is the line. If we see it from one side of the line, its going to our left, and if we see it from the other side of the line, it is going right. The imaginary line exists between any two objects that have some sort of relationship — even between a book and a telephone sitting on a table.

What Establishes the Line?

The line is established by the first view of the scene the audience sees; once the physical relationship of the scene has been established, it must remain consistent in order to avoid confusing the audience. Is the line always there? No, the line only exists once it has been created by something in the scene. As we saw in the example of the two women and the car, your first camera setup in the series of shots establishes the line, but it works in conjunction with specific visual elements of the scene itself. Several things can establish the line for a particular scene. They are:

- A look
- Movement
- A specific action
- Exiting frame
- Physical geography

The Purpose of Screen Direction

Screen direction serves two important purposes: it gives the audience clues about the story and it helps keep the audience from getting confused about where someone is or what they are doing. Avoiding confusion is the fundamental reason for all film continuity.

Figure 6.15. (left) In this sequence from *High Noon*, leaving town is clearly established as going left.

Figure 6.16. (right) When the marshall decides he must stand and fight, we clearly see him turn the carriage around and head back the other way. When the carriage is moving to the right, we know that they are going back toward town.

Figure 6.17. Early films, such as the *Great Train Robbery*, which treated cinema as a "filmed play," maintained a static frame and constant, unchanging left/right relationships as viewed by the audience. Since the camera never moves, it never changes the directional relationships of the actors or the set.

Figure 6.18. (below, top) An example of a true reverse from *Seven Samurai*. The camera jumps cleanly and completely to the other side of the line (**Figure 6.19**, bottom).

Directional Conventions

The classic example of this is in low-budget cowboy movies of the fifties. In these films it was always well established that one direction on screen was *towards* town and the opposite direction was *away* from town (Figures 6.15 and 6.16). Once we knew that we could tell if the good guys or the bad guys were heading toward town or away, any deviation from this would have been very confusing.

Another convention applies to trains, planes, and automobiles. If someone is leaving the east and going to the west, the plane or vehicle should be traveling left in the frame and vice versa. This is derived from the fact that nearly all maps have north at the top, so west is left and east is right.

Deliberately Breaking the Rules

One of the aims of editing is to *not* confuse the audience. If a character is walking towards the left of the screen in one shot and without explanation in the next shot he is walking toward the right, the audience will (even if only subconsciously) wonder why he changed. Their attention will be momentarily drawn away from the story as they try to sort it out.

This is the basic principle of all continuity in film shooting and editing. For example, she was just wearing a red dress outside the restaurant, but once she stepped through the door she is wearing a blue dress. Is this a different day? A dream sequence? What happened? Of course, a filmmaker can use this as a storytelling device. Perhaps most famously is the breakfast sequence in *Citizen Kane*. In three seamlessly cut together shots we see Charles Foster Kane and his wife at the same dining table in the same room. We only know that time is progressing because they are wearing different clothes and makeup in each shot. Through this simple device the deterioration of their marriage is told with great efficiency. Most famously, in the payoff shot she is reading a newspaper put out by a rival publisher: we know the marriage is doomed. Similar devices can indicate we've gone into a fantasy sequence or flashback. They can be quite subtle (a small change in makeup or hair) or dramatic: the little match girl on the street is suddenly in a gorgeous ball gown.

Exceptions to the Rule

There are several important exceptions to the 180° rule and *the line*.

- If we see things change position *in the shot*, then we understand that things have changed position. If a car is moving right in the shot, and then we see it turn around so that it's going left, then there's no problem (Figure 6.16).
- When the camera position moves *during* the shot.
- If you cut away to something completely different, when you cut back, you can change the line.
- In the case of something that is moving, you can cut to a neutral axis shot, then go back to either side of the line.

A neutral shot is one where the movement is either directly towards or away from the camera (Figures 6.20). In cases where the camera moves during the shot, in essence, the line itself has moved. Some people tend to think of the line as very rigid and static, that once the line is established it can never move the whole rest of the time you are shooting the scene, but actually it is fluid and can change throughout the scene, as we will see later.

There is another exception, although it must be applied with caution. Remember, the whole point of the rule is to not confuse the audience. That is its only reason for being; it is not a carved in stone dictum that exists independently. That means that if we can cross the line without confusing the audience, then we're still OK.

Example — a courtroom. It's layout is very clear and visually strong. At the front of the room is the bench, a large identifiable object with the judge sitting at it. On one side is the jury, and facing the judge are the counsel tables. It is familiar and understandable. In a situation like this you have a great deal of leeway in crossing the line without creating confusion. Another example would be rock climbers ascending a cliff. You can jump to the other side and no one is going to misunderstand what happened.

Reverse

Another case of crossing the line is when you deliberately go to the other side for a reason. Say two people are seated on a sofa and we do extensive coverage of them from in front of the sofa, the most logical place to shoot from (Figure 6.22). Clearly the line has been well established. But now there is another important action. A new character has to enter through the door and have a conversation with the two people on the sofa. It always better to show a character entering the room rather than just having them enter frame, when we don't know where they came from.

Second, we wouldn't really know where the door is and that he is entering the same room. Since they have not seen the door before, for all the audience knows, we have gone to a completely new scene and this man is entering another room somewhere. What we would really like to do is put the camera in the back of the room behind the sofa, so we see them in the foreground and see him entering, but that would be crossing the line, so we can't do it, right?

Yes, you can do it. It's called a *reverse*, but you can't just do it willy-nilly. You can't do it on a close-up; that would be just crossing the line. The important thing is that we still see the two people in the foreground, but we see the new character and the door in the background. There is motivation for being on the other side; there is an understandable reason.

Another factor in a successful reverse is how big a difference it is. Just crossing the line slightly would probably not work. It is when you definitively and unquestionably are on the other side of the line that a reverse is understandable. The audience does have to do some mental reorientation, but given the proper clues they can do so easily and it is not distracting to the viewers. Another way to cross the line is to see the camera move to the other side of the line, as in a dolly move. Then there is no confusion.

TURNAROUND

You would never do the over-the-shoulder on one actor, then move the camera to do the OTS on the other actor, then go back to the first for the close-up, and so on. This would be very inefficient and time consuming. So naturally you do all the coverage on one side, then move the camera and reset the lighting. The term for this is that you *shoot out* one side before you move to the other side, which is called the *turnaround*. The group of OTS's and close-ups that match the ones done on the first actor are called the *answering shots*. Every shot you do in the first setup should have an answering shot. After window and door matching, the turnaround is the other major area where cheating is employed, such as in cases where some physical obstacle precludes a good camera position for the turnaround, or perhaps the sun is at a bad angle, or maybe it's a complex lighting setup and there simply isn't time to relight for the answering shot.

Figure 6.20. Cutting to a neutral angle such as a car coming directly toward you can help transition from one side of the line to the other.

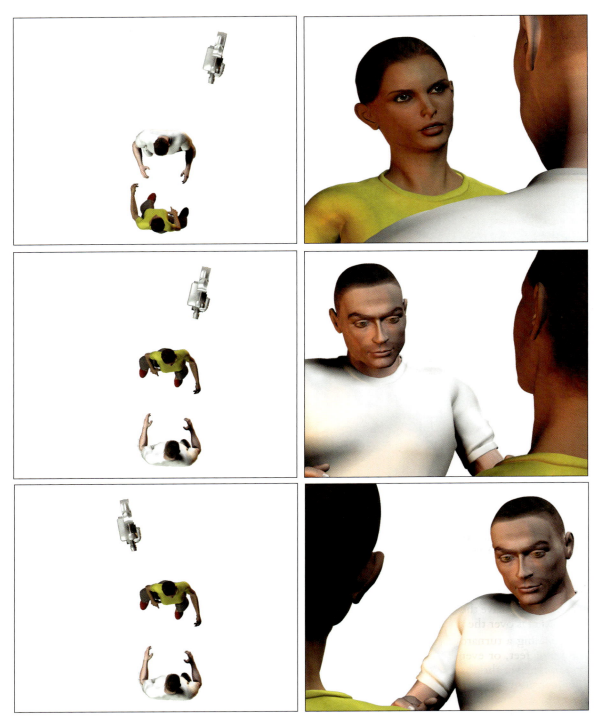

Figure 6.21. Sometimes it is necessary to cheat a turnaround. If for some reason there is no time to set up and light a real turnaround, or if the new background is somehow unuseable, then it is possible to cheat the shot by merely spinning the actors around (middle two frames).

However, if you only spin them, the camera ends up being over the "wrong" shoulder. Based on the shot in the top right frame, the answering shot should be over her *right* ear. In the middle frames, we see it is over her *left* ear. In the bottom two frames we see it done correctly: the actors are reversed in their postions, but the camera is shifted to camera left so that it is now over the correct shoulder for the cheated shot.

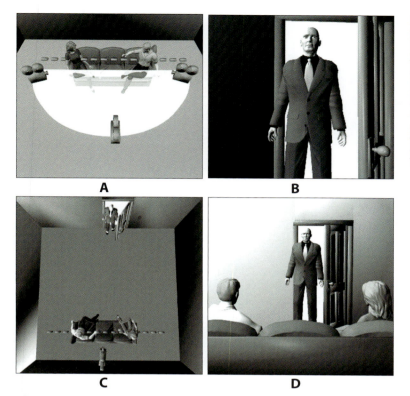

A   B

C   D

Figure 6.22. In this scene of a couple sitting on a couch (**A**), the action line is clearly established. We can do any shots we want as long as we stay on the correct side of the line. A new character enters (**B**), and we would like to include him in a shot that shows all three. Doing so puts the camera definitely on the wrong side of the line, as in **C**.

Even though it is technically an error, the shot works fine because it is done boldly and the sofa helps the viewers orient themselves (**D**).

Cheating the Turnaround

In any of these cases, it is possible to leave the camera and lights where they are and just move the actors. This is a last-ditch measure and is only used in cases where the background for one part of the coverage is not usable or there is an emergency in terms of the schedule — if for example, if the sun is going down. The theory is that once we are in tight shots on the coverage, we really don't see much of the background.

It is not correct, however, to just have them switch places. In our sample scene, we are over the shoulder of Jennifer, looking at Dave. In the OTS of Dave, we are seeing over Jennifer's right shoulder. If we did a real turnaround, we would be over Dave's left shoulder (Figure 6.21). In this illustration we see two cases: in #1 we rotate the camera 180°. This is a real turnaround. In case #2 we just spin the actors and leave the camera where it is. You can see the problem: the camera is over the wrong shoulder.

In cheating a turnaround, you have to either move the camera a couple of feet, or even better, just slide the foreground actor over so you are over the correct shoulder. (Fortunately, moving the foreground actor seldom involves any substantial relighting.) The key to a successful cheat is that the background either be neutral or similar for both actors as established in any previous wide shots. In some cases, moving props can help establish the cheat.

PLANNING COVERAGE

Which brings us to another key point that is easily overlooked: whenever you are setting up a master, take a moment to think about the coverage. Make sure that there is some way to position the camera for proper answering shots. Particularly if one character's coverage is more dramatic or more crucial to the story than the other, it is very

Figures 6.23 (left) **and 6.24** (right). Maintaining the same direction while going through a door is usually desirable, but not always necessary.

There is a continuity error in this scene. Can you spot it? See the text for the answer.

easy to get yourself backed into a corner or up against an obstruction that makes it difficult or impossible to position the camera for a proper answering shot.

An answering shot should be the same focal length, focus distance, and angle as the shot it is paired with. In a pinch, if you can't get quite far back enough (or close enough), you can cheat a bit with a different focal length to end up with the same image size, which is by far the most important issue. As with all issues of continuity, anything that the audience won't notice is OK.

Cuttability

So that's the 180° rule and we can shoot *anywhere* in the 180° circle, right? Well, not quite. First let's define what makes shots *cuttable*. When we put a sequence together, it is important that when one shot follows another, it does so smoothly, not jarringly.

An example: our two people are on the sofa. We are doing a shot from the side that includes both of them and the arms of the sofa. Then we move in just a bit and get a similar shot of the two of them but without the sofa arms. How would it look if we cut these two together? Suddenly the image size changes just slightly, as if maybe the film broke and some frames are missing — sometimes called a *jump cut*. For two shots to be cuttable, there needs to be a more substantial change. If instead of moving in just slightly, for example, we moved in a lot so that the shot is just a close-up shot of one of the characters. Then the two shots would be cuttable.

The 20% and 30 Degree Rules

How do we know how much we have to change to make two similar shots cuttable? It's called the 20% rule. In general, a shot must change by *at least* 20% to be cuttable (Figure 6.25). That can be a 20% change in angle, in lens size, or camera position. It's a very rough guideline, of course. Many people find that 20% just isn't enough of a change for a smooth cut. At best, it is an absolute minimum — it is wise to make more of a change to ensure a good edit.

Another rough guideline is the 30° rule. This is just a variation of the 20% rule (Figure 6.25). Let's go back to our 180° circle. Without changing the lens, or moving closer or farther away, and as long as we move 30° to the left or right along that circle, we're OK (sort of). With lens changes, it is more subjective. Depending on other factors in the shot, moving up or down one prime lens size — say from a 50mm to a 35mm, may or may not be enough. Frequently, it is necessary to change two lens sizes: say, from a 50mm to a 25mm. In the end it comes down to a judgment call.

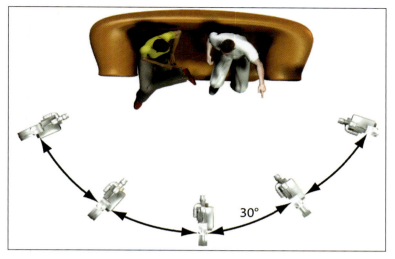

Figure 6.25. The *20% rule* and the *30° rule* are pretty much the same thing. What is important is not some exact figure, but the crucial element is that the two shots appear *different enough* to the audience so that they cut together smoothly. You should consider these guidelines an absolute minimum. Often they are not enough of a change. It is best to combine the 30° move with another change, such as a different focal length to ensure cuttability.

OTHER ISSUES IN CONTINUITY

Other general principles apply when the subjects are in motion or for groups larger than a two shot.

Moving Shots

Two types of shots predominate in moving shots: the driving shot, and walk and talk. The same rules apply to both. At first glance we would think that the direction of the car or the walk is the major axis, but in fact it is only a secondary axis. The major axis for screen direction is between the two people, not the direction of their walk or the movement of the car.

Going Through a Door

There are two schools of thought on door entrances and exits. Some will say that if a character goes through a door going to the right (in an exterior shot), they have to emerge on the other side, also going right (in the interior shot). Others maintain that once someone goes through a door it is a *new deal,* and anything goes. Again, it is a subjective call. If there is a very clear connection between the two, and the directionality and continuity of movement is very strong, then it is a good idea to maintain directional continuity between the two. If there is a great deal of difference between the interior and exterior and there is a greater change in angle, camera position, or lens size between the two, it is possible to go to the other side when the character comes through other side of the door (Figures 6.23 and 6.24). However, there is a small continuity problem in this scene when Bogie enters the off. Can you spot the mistake? Take a very close look before you read the next paragraph.

He is using a different hand opening the door: right hand in the hallway shot and left hand on the shot inside the office. Similarly, when a character takes a turn around a building, if the camera cuts when the character disappears around the corner, when we pick him up on the other side, the screen direction should be maintained.

Entering and Exiting Frame

As we noted before, exiting frame establishes screen direction, since it shows the character taking a definite direction of travel. Once a character exits either frame left or right, they should enter the next from the *opposite* side (Figures 6.26). You can think of it as an *imaginary pan.* As the character exits frame, you mentally pan with her:

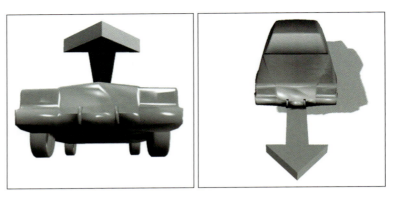

Figure 6.26. (above) When a character exits the frame, this establishes a direction that must be observed when the character reenters. Think of it as if you were panning the camera.

Figures 6.27 and 6.28. (above, right and far right) To be truly neutral, the object or character must be angled to exit the top or bottom of the frame.

this positions you correctly for the next shot of entering frame. Of course, there will be times when you do an actual pan as characters pass the camera, but there are just as many occasions when you will want to cut, either because the pan is awkward, would reveal parts of the location you don't want to see, or even when the two shots are in very different locations even though you want the audience to perceive the two parts of the walk to be in the same place. This is called location stitching (for an example see Figures 6.52 through 6.54). As with all continuity sequences, if something else comes in between the exit and the entrance, anything goes.

Neutral Axis to Exit Frame

If the character or a moving vehicle exits the frame on a completely *neutral axis*, then you are free to go anywhere you want on the next cut. For something to exit on a truly neutral axis, however, it has to exit either above or below the frame (Figures 6.27 and 6.28). A neutral axis resets screen direction; once you go to a neutral axis shot of any type, you are free to come back to the scene with a new screen direction established for the scene. This can be used as an editorial device and also as a way to save the scene in editing, just as you would with a *cutaway*.

Three Shots

Screen direction is basically the same in *three shots* (or when there are more characters in the scene), but one thing to watch out for is overlapping the person in the center. If you break it up as a pair of two shots, the person in the center will appear in both shots and there will be unavoidable problems. The center character will "pop" as you cut from shot to shot (Figures 6.29 through 6.31).

Keep the Nose Out

For the same reason it is important to avoid getting a part of the foreground person in the shot when doing a clean single over the shoulder of the second character. When two characters are fairly close to each other in the master, it is often difficult to completely frame the second person out, especially if they move around a lot. Often their nose, or a hand, or some small piece of them will creep into the single. This is not only compositionally annoying but will cause continuity problems. It will often be necessary to shift the off-screen character back a bit so they don't creep in. You don't want to do it so much that you "miss" his presence in the coverage. If there is a large shift, be sure to set a new eyeline for the on-screen character so that their head doesn't shift too much from the master. It may be necessary for the actor to look at a mark rather than at the other actor, which is something to avoid, as it does make it difficult for the performer.

Prop Continuity in Coverage

The principle of overlapping applies to foreground props as well as three shots. If, for example, there is a candlestick on the table between two characters, you need to pay attention to its continuity as well as that of the actors: this is where having a good *continuity supervisor* really pays off. Although all types of continuity are ultimately the responsibility of the director, keeping an eye on such things is the primary job of the script supervisor (another name for the continuity person, although on sets they are often referred to as *scripty*). However, the DP and even more so the camera operator (if the cinematographer is not also functioning as the operator) has to keep an eye on such things. Since the operator is constantly scanning all parts of the scene, it is often the operator who picks up on small mistakes in continuity, screen direction, and eyelines. If it is left in its position from the master, it will seem to jump back and forth as you cut from medium shot on one actor to medium on the other. Your choices are to cheat it out of the mediums altogether (the safest) or cheating it back and forth for each medium, which is a bit riskier.

Mistakes in prop continuity are easy to make, especially on small productions where you may not have a full prop crew on the set or when you don't have an experienced continuity supervisor. It is important to stay vigilant for even the smallest details, as bad continuity is something that will mark your project as "amateurish." On the other hand there is such a thing as "too much continuity." Sometimes, fledgling script supervisors can become so obsessed with tiny details that won't really be apparent to the audience that they can start to get in the way of the production. It is important to find a balance; only being on the set and then watching the finished production with an audience provides that experience.

Eye Sweeps

When an off-screen character walks behind the camera, the on-screen character may follow with her eyes. Many inexperienced directors are reluctant to do this, as they think it won't work. It's perfectly OK as long as the eye sweep is slightly above or below the lens. As always, it is important that the actor not look directly into the lens, even for just a moment. The most important thing about eye sweeps is that they match the direction and speed of the crossing character. This means that the on-screen actor will move their head in the opposite direction of the movement of the crossing, since we are essentially crossing the line in a reverse. If you are shooting the eye sweep first, it may be desirable to shoot a few different speeds because when the crossing is shot later, the speed may not match.

Figure 6.29. (left) A three shot with a character in the middle.

Figures 6.30 and 6.31. (middle and right) If coverage is not clean singles, then you need to be sure that hand and head continuity match for the character that appears on both sides of the coverage. In this example we see that he is gesturing with different hands. This will drive your editor crazy. The safe way to shoot a scene like this is to shoot each actor as clean singles. Even if you shoot it as shown here, shooting clean singles in addition will provide safety coverage if you need it.

| A | B | C |

| D | E | F |

Figure 6.32. This master from *Ronin* (**A**) establishes the main group and their places around the table. The next cut (**B**) reveals the woman at the head of the table (separate from the group) in a way that shows her relationship to them; it orients us to the overall arrangement. This is a *reverse*. This cut to a three shot maintains the screen direction established in the master (**A**). This is a good example of how seeing a piece of the table helps to keep us grounded in the scene. If it wasn't there, we would definitely miss it. (**B**) This over-the-shoulder of the girl is on the opposite side of the line from (**D**); it is outside the group. However, since the previous sequence of shots has clearly established all the relationships, there is no problem. (**E**) This single on the man in the suit also benefits from seeing a piece of the table. If it was necessary to move the table to get the shot, the set dressers will often have something smaller that can stand in for it. (**F**) This shot is from the POV of the man in the suit, but we don't see any of him in the foreground. In this case we are said to be "inside" him — not inside his body, but inside his field of vision.

Group Shots

Scenes with more than three characters generally require a good deal of coverage. If there is a dominant direction to the arrangement of the group, that will most likely dictate a screen direction line based on where you shoot the master from. In practice it may be possible to shoot from almost anywhere as long as you get the proper answering shots and coverage. However, it may be better to pick a line and stick to it. This will reduce confusion in the audience's perceptions. If there is a dominant character standing apart from the group, this will often establish the line. These frames from a group scene in *Ronin* illustrates some of these principles (Figure 6.32). Notice in particular the slight difference between **B** and **F**. Both are shots down the middle of the axis; **B**, however, is an over-the-shoulder past the man in the suit, while **F** does not include him, and is more of his POV.

Chase Scenes

Chase scenes can be problematic for screen direction. As a general rule of thumb you want to maintain an overall direction within the scene, but there is considerable room for variation. When the chase itself changes direction, your screen direction may change as well. For car chases especially, some directors prefer to mix it up more to slightly disorient the audience and emphasize the kinetic nature of the chase; the same applies to fight scenes or other types of action.

Cutaway Eyeline Continuity

Since cutaways are not part of the main scene but are physically related to it, directional continuity must be maintained between the location of the scene and the cutaway element. This is especially important for cutaways that involve a look from the additional character, which they often do (Figures 6.33 and 6.34). Since you are moving away from the main scene and it is usually for a quick pickup shot, often you will be up against limitations of the set or other problems that will make it necessary for you to cheat the additional character a bit. In this case, it is important to be careful about the eyelines. Because the audience is acutely aware of where an actor's eyes are directed, wrong eyelines are something they will always be aware of. Careful attention must be paid to eyelines: it is very easy to get them wrong.

Look Establishes New Line

In a related issue, let's focus on the couple at the table. In our scene of a couple in a restaurant, the conversation between the couple has its own line. When she turns to look at the gangster, that establishes a new line that must be respected in all shots that involve the couple at the table and the gangster (Figures 6.35 through 6.37). It does not replace the line established by the couple's conversation, which must still be used for any coverage at their table.

Eyelines in Over-the-Shoulder Coverage

When shooting over-the-shoulder coverage, the camera height will generally be at eye level for the characters. If the two performers are of unequal height, some modification is usually necessary. In this case, the camera height will approximately match that of the character over whose shoulder you are shooting.

Eyelines for a Seated Character

The same principle applies when one or more of the characters is seated or on the floor, but with an important exception. Since shooting over the shoulder of the standing character might be an extreme angle, it also works to keep the camera at the eye-level of the seated performer, which makes it sort of a *past the hips shot*, (not an official term, by the way, but maybe it should be).

In situations like this, for the clean singles, when there is a difference in height or level of the characters in coverage, the eyelines may also need some adjustment. This does not apply to over-the-shoulders, as we can see the off-screen performer's head and thus we know the actual eye-level. In this case the eyeline of the seated characters should be slightly above the lens, and the eyeline of the standing character should be slightly below the lens. Be careful not to overdo this. As with all eyelines and cheats, the final judgment should be made while looking through the lens. How it looks and how it will work in editing always trumps a rote rule: the goal is workable editing, not merely formal technique.

Figure 6.33. (left) This master establishes the background group and that the man with the mustache is looking to the left of the camera.

Figure 6.34. (right) In the cutaway to the background group, the directional relationships are maintained and most importantly the man with the mustache is still looking to camera left. There can be no question but that he is looking toward the foreground group.

Figure 6.35 (left) Two people at a table establishes a strong action line.

Figure 6.36. (middle) If one of them looks off-screen to something else, this establishes a new line beween the two, as in **Figure 6.37** (right).

Figure 6.38. (top) The opening frame of a very long, slow, deliberate zoom out from *Barry Lyndon*.

Figure 6.39. (bottom) The last frame from that same zoom. Kubrick uses this type of *slow disclosure* thematically throughout the film, always ending in a perfectly balanced formal composition, often based on a painting of the period. The slow zoom out works on many levels, both visually and storywise.

OTS and Inserts

Inserts generally are not critical in terms of screen direction except in a general way. One instance where they are important is reading inserts. This type of insert is quite common as the master scene, or even an over-the-shoulder is usually not tight enough to allow the audience to actually read what the character is looking at. In these cases, it is important to conform to the eyeline and screen direction of the character reading the material, even if they are not holding it.

Moving Action

Once you thoroughly understand the underlying principles and the cognitive reasons for the these rules, it is easier to see when there are exceptions and flexibility. It is important to remember that "the line" is not some physical thing that has an independent existence on the set. The line is only in relation to where you have first established the scene by the camera placement of the first shot that appears on screen. Also, the line moves, as we saw in the example of the couple and the gangster in the restaurant (Figures 6.35 through 6.37).

Most importantly, in a scene with moving action, such as a fight scene, the line will be shifting constantly. In highly frenetic fight scenes photographed with lots of angles and cuts to be edited in a rapid fire sequence, the director and editor might want to ignore the line altogether to add a sense of action and disorientation to the scene. In general, however, it is good to observe screen direction rules — especially if the two people fighting are not physically distinct in look or wardrobe. Otherwise the audience might end up rooting for the wrong guy.

INTRODUCTIONS

When you are bringing the viewer into a scene, you can think of it much the same as bringing a stranger into a party. Some of the concepts have been mentioned before, but now let's consider them in the context of narrative continuity. There are four basic introductions that need to be made: place, time, geography, and the main characters.

Many aspects of introductions and transitions are functions of the script, but they must be actualized by the director and the cinematographer on the set. Some are improvised at the time of shooting because they may be based on some prop or aspect of the set or location that has not been apparent before, such as a perfect full moon just above the scene.

The Place

We need to let the audience know where they are. Establishing shots and variations are discussed in the chapter *Shooting Methods*. There is an important exception to this called slow disclosure. In this technique, instead of opening with a wide shot, the scene begins with a tight shot of a character or another scene element. Only as the scene progresses does the camera pull back to reveal where we are and what is going on. This is a variation of the basic reveal where the camera starts on something that either moves or the camera moves past it to show some other scene element.

Not only a master formalist but also a great visualist (he started his career as a still photographer for *Look* magazine), Stanley Kubrick uses slow disclosure masterfully in *Barry Lyndon* (Figures 6.38 and 6.39). Throughout the film, one of the key formal devices is the very long, very slow zoom back. He starts with a telling detail of the scene and then very deliberately pulls back to reveal more and more. As with so many other aspects of the film (its perfectly composed fixed frames based on paintings of the period, the emphasis on formal geometry, and the slow pacing of action and editing) this slow pull back underlines the rigid formalism of society and culture at that time as well as the inevitability of Lyndon's decline. These long pullbacks also serve as editorial punctuation between sequences and contribute to the overall pace of the film. For these shots, Angenieux created a special lens for Kubrick: the Cine-Pro T/9 24-480mm. Famously, he also had an ultra-fast Zeiss F/0.7 still photo lens converted for motion picture use on this film to use with the candle-lit scenes.

The Time

Beyond establishing *where* we are, the viewer must know *when* we are. Internally within the scene, this is either a function of a transition shot or other types of temporal clues. In these two frames from *Ronin* (Figures 6.40 and 6.41) the director needed to find a way to establish that fifteen or twenty minutes had passed.

This can be much more difficult than conveying that days have passed or that it was summer and now it's winter — that can be accomplished by a simple exterior shot of the green trees which dissolves to a shot of the same tree barren of leaves and a layer of new-fallen snow on the ground. Here he has done something very subtle. In the first shot we see the bellboys starting to put decorations on a tree in the hotel lobby. In the second shot, as the camera pans to follow the character's exit, we see that the decorations have been completed. For the audience, this is completely subconscious, but it conveys the passage of time in a subliminal way.

Figure 6.40. (top) Devices to convey a short passage of time are often more difficult than demonstrating a long passage of time between cuts. In *Ronin*, the director uses the fact that the Christmas tree is being decorated in one shot. The bellhops enter with a box of decorations for the tree.

Figure 6.41. (bottom) In the next shot, the tree is fully decorated. It is very subtle but, the audience will subconsciously register that some short amount of time has passed between the two shots.

Figures 6.42 (top), **6.43** (middle), **and 6.44** (bottom). A simple and purely visual establishing sequence opens *The Maltese Falcon*. It starts on the Golden Gate bridge, so we know we're in San Francisco; pulls back to reveal the window and sign, so we know we're in an office, and then down to the shadow on the floor that introduces the name of detective agency and the name of the main character. It is an elegant visual introduction.

The Geography

This was discussed previously, but it deserves mention here as there are several aspects to establishing the geography that relate to actual shooting on the set. Establishing the place usually just serves the purpose of showing us where the scene will take place. This is just called the establishing shot. Establishing the geography is a bit different than just letting the viewer know where the action takes place. Where an establishing shot is generally an exterior view of the building, establishing the geography relates to the scene itself, particularly, but not exclusively, the interiors. It is not enough that the audience knows the general location of the scene, but it is also important that they have a general comprehension of the layout of the place — the overall geography. This prevents confusion as characters move around or as the camera cuts to other viewpoints within the scene.

The Characters

Introducing the characters is of course mostly a function of the script and the actors, but a general principle is to introduce key characters in some way that visually underlines some aspect of their importance, their nature, and their story function. Also, making this introduction visually interesting helps the audience remember the character: a form of visual punctuation.

For the entire first half of *High Noon*, we have been waiting for the arrival of the bad guy on the noon train. He has been discussed, feared, even run away from. When we finally meet him (Figures 6.45 through 6.47), Zinnemann handles his introduction cleverly. As he first gets off the train, we do not see his face. Then for an entire sequence of shots, we see him being greeted, strapping on his guns, and still we do not see his face. Finally, his former lover is getting onto the train; she is leaving town only because he has come back. She turns to look at him, and it is only then that we first see his face. It is a dramatic and distinctive way to introduce him.

OTHER EDITORIAL ISSUES IN SHOOTING

In the course of shooting the scene, it is important to not be so focused on the essential action and storytelling that there is no thought of the small shots that will help the editor put the scene together in a way that is seamless, logical, and also suits the tone, pacing, and mood of the sequence. These include cutaways, inserts, and character shots that contribute to the overall ambiance.

Jump Cuts

Disruptions of continuity can result in a jump cut. Although clearly an error in methodology, jump cuts can be used as editorial technique. Truffaut and others of the nouvelle vague in France in the early sixties were among the first to employ jump cuts effectively. According to Ken Dancyger, in his discussion of *The 400 Blows*: "How did the stylistic equivalent of the personal story translate into editing choices? The moving camera was used to avoid editing. In addition, the jump cut was used to challenge continuity editing and all that it implied. The jump cut itself is nothing more than the joining of two noncontinuous shots. Whether the two shots recognized a change in direction, focus on an unexpected action, or simply don't show the action in one shot that prepares the viewer for the content of the next shot, the result of the jump cut is to focus on discontinuity. Not only does the jump cut remind viewers that they are watching a film, it is also jarring. The jump cut asks viewers to tolerate the admission that we are watching a film or to temporarily suspend belief in the film." (Ken Dancyger, *The Technique of Film and Video*

Figures 6.45. (top) A dramatic and suspenseful introduction of the main bad guy in *High Noon*. His arrival has been talked about and dreaded for the entire movie up until this point, but when he arrives on the noon train, the director delays showing his face until the most dramatic story moment. As he gets off the train, we see him only from the back.

Figure 6.46. (middle) As his former girlfriend is boarding the train to escape the coming violence, she turns to see him and their eyes meet.

Figure 6.47. (bottom) Our first view of him is both a dramatic *reveal* and her subjective *POV*: it makes for a powerful moment. Notice how their eyelines match; if they did not, it would not seem like they were looking at each other. In order to match, they need to be *opposite*: she is looking toward the left of the frame and he is looking toward the right side of frame.

Editing). Jump cuts as a stylistic device stem from Jean Luc Goddard's first feature, *Breathless*. Film lore is that he just shot the scenes in such a way that they could not be edited conventionally (such as running the camera for long periods as the characters drive around Paris) and simply had to come up with a stylish way of covering up his error. True or not, it made jump cuts a stylistic device, which just goes to show, if you play it right, even your mistakes can become legendary.

Figure 6.48. (right) We see the Sheriff turn his head and look, which *sets up* the subjective POV (*High Noon*).

Figure 6.49. (left) His subjective POV of the clock. From an editorial point of view three things are important: the POV is properly set up, the screen direction is consistent between the two shots, and his eyeline is correct. He is looking up and to the left and the clock is on the wall and facing right.

THE SIX TYPES OF CUTS

Some aspects of editing are beyond the scope of what we deal with in day-to-day production on the set, but directors and cinematographers must know most of the major concepts of editorial cutting in order to avoid mistakes and to provide the editor with the material she needs to not only cut the film together seamlessly, but also to control pacing and flow, delineate overall structure, and give the scenes and the whole piece unity and cohesion. There are six basic types of cuts, some of which have been discussed. They are:

- The content cut
- The action cut
- The POV cut
- The match cut
- The conceptual cut
- The zero cut

The Content Cut

The content cut applies to whenever we cut to a new shot within a scene only to add new information or carry the story forward. In its simplest form, content cutting is used in the coverage of a conversation. We cut from the master, to the over-the-shoulder, to the close-up. Nothing changes in these shots except the content. We were seeing both of them, and now we see one of them, and so on.

The content cut is just a part of the overall forward progression of the narrative. As with all cuts, it must obey the basic rules of the line and the 20% rule in order to be cuttable.

The Action Cut

The action cut, sometimes called a continuity cut or a movement cut, is employed whenever action is started in one shot and finished in the next. For example, in the first shot we see him opening the door, and in the next shot we see him emerging from the other side of the door. Or she reaches across the table, then cut to her hand picking up the cup of coffee. Shooting for the action cut must be done properly if it is to work in editing.

First of all, you should always overlap the action. In this example, it would be a mistake to have her reach for the cup of coffee, then call "cut" as soon as her arm extends, then proceed to a close-up of her arm coming in to pick up the shot. There is a grave danger that there will be a piece missing, which will result in a jump cut. In this case, if her arm extends only to the edge of the table in the first shot, but when we see it in the next shot it is all the way to the middle of the table, that missing part will be very noticeable.

As discussed in *Shooting Methods*, shooting the overlap also gives the editor the choice of exactly when to time the cut. If the editor has some freedom to time the cut, small problems in movement can be smoothed over. In this small example, the overlapping action is fairly small. In the case of entering and exiting doors, getting in and out of vehicles, and so on, fairly substantial overlaps should be shot. This is especially true if there is important action or dialog going on during the move. In that case, the editor needs the ability to adjust for performance and narrative flow as well as simple continuity.

In shooting close shots that continue the action in a larger shot, it is also important to match the speed of the action. In the case of picking up coffee, the actor may have been in the middle of a big speech as she reached for the coffee and thus did it slowly and deliberately. If a good deal of time has passed between shooting the wide shot and picking up an insert of the hand picking up the coffee, it is possible that she will not be doing the dialog, and all she is doing is sticking her hand in the frame to grab the cup. In this case, it is very easy for her to forget the pacing of the original shot and think of this as something new. The urge is to just stick her hand in and grab it.

Cutting on Action

While shooting for an action cut it is important to always be aware of the possibilities of the cut point. It is always best to cut "on the action." If someone is seated at a desk and rises to go to the door, you want to shoot while he is rising from the chair. If the phone rings, you want to cut to the next shot while he is reaching for the phone, and so on. Cutting on action makes for a smoother cut and a more invisible one. The audience is a bit distracted by the action and less likely to notice the cut. Take the example of answering the phone: in the medium shot, the phone rings, he picks it up and starts talking. Then we cut to a close-up of him talking. In this case, it is critical that his head be in exactly the same position and that he is holding the phone in exactly the same way. If any of these fails, it will be bad continuity and will be distracting. Cutting as he reaches for the phone helps avoids these problems.

The POV Cut

The POV cut is sometimes called "the look" and we briefly discussed it in *Shooting Methods*. It is one of the most fundamental building blocks of continuity and is especially valuable in cheating shots and establishing physical relationships. A POV cut occurs anytime a look off-screen in the first shot motivates a view of something in the next shot (Figure 6.50). The simplest case:

- Shot 1: A character looks off-screen and up.
- Shot 2: A view of a clock tower.

There will be no question in the mind of the viewer that we are seeing the tower as he would see it — that is, from his point-of-view. In order to do this, the POV shot must satisfy certain conditions.

- Direction of look. If it is to a shot of the clock tower, clearly, he has to look up. Further, he must look up at approximately the right angle. If his gaze only rises about 10°, for example, and the clock tower is ten stories high, it won't work. Similarly, if we have seen in a wide shot that the clock tower is on his right side, then his look must go to the right as well.
- Angle of the POV. The shot of the clock tower must bear some logical relationship to where the viewer is. If we have seen that he is standing on the plaza right under the tower, then we cannot cut in a shot of it as seen from a hundred yards away over the trees.

Figure 6.50. A subjective POV or *the look*. *(top)* We see him turn his head. Second from the top: his eyeline is set, so we know where he is looking. Third from the top: his subjective POV of the airplane. Its position matches his eyeline. In the bottom frame is a *connecting shot* that shows us both and clearly establishes his relationship to the airplane. A connecting shot is not absolutely necessary but it is helpful.

The POV cut is a classic means of cheating locations. For example, our story is based on him seeing a murder in the building opposite him, but unfortunately, the building opposite our location is unavailable for use. In this case, the POV cut from him looking out the window to a POV of his view through the window of the building across the street will sell the concept that he can see the murder.

As discussed in the chapter on *Shooting Methods*, it is easy to over rely on the POV cut (and on the use of separation in dialog scenes) to the extent that it makes the scenes artificial and empty. It is always best to get a connecting shot that ties it all together if at all possible. Like with cutaways and inserts, shooting a connecting shot is a good safety. Even if the script doesn't call for one, it is one of those things that the editor may thank you for later. Safety first — one the most amateurish mistakes a director can make is to wrap a scene without getting all the coverage that the editor will need to cut it smoothly.

Executing a Subjective POV

In order to make the POV cut work, it is essential to execute the shots properly. A subjective POV consists of several pieces. First, you must establish the person looking, or the audience will not know whose POV it is.

Secondly, it is usually necessary to see that person "look" — often this is done by showing them turn their head or in some other way appear obviously appear to be looking at something. This part of the setup is essential in letting the audience know that the next shot will be the character's POV.

Third is the actual POV itself, their view of the thing they are looking at. Generally this needs to be a somewhat normal lens because an extremely long lens or very wide lens would not represent normal human vision and wouldn't look like someone's point of view. To finish it off, many editors also use the shot of the character returning their head to the position they were in before the POV, but this is not absolutely essential.

The Match Cut

The *match cut* is often used as a transitional device between scenes. An example from a western: the telegrapher sends the message that the governor has not granted a pardon; the hanging will go on as scheduled. From the telegrapher, we go to a shot of the telegraph pole (probably with an audio cut of the clicking of the telegraph). Then from the shot of the telegraph pole we cut to a shot of the gallows: a vertical pole approximately the same size, shape, and in the same position as the telegraph pole. One image exactly replaces the other on screen.

One of the most effective uses of a match cut is in *Apocalypse Now*, where Coppola cuts from the spinning blades of the ceiling fan in the Saigon hotel room to the spinning blades of a helicopter deep in the combat zone. Great care must be taken in shooting both sides of a match cut. It is not enough that the objects be similar in shape: the screen size (as determined by focal length) and the position in the frame must also match. One method is to have a video of the previously shot scene and play it back on the director's monitor. For precision work, a monitor with an A/B switch allows the image to be quickly switched back and forth from the freeze frame of the video to the live picture from the monitor. As an additional guide, a grease pencil or china marker can be used to outline the object on the monitor.

Figure 6.51 (top). In *2001: A Space Odyssey*, Kubrick uses an edit that is both a *conceptual cut* and a *match cut*. In the first frame (top) the ape has discovered the bone as a weapon and tool and throws it into the air. In the next frame (middle) we see the bone traveling through the air. Then there is a match cut (bottom) to a spaceship. Kubrick has not only communicated that the original tool (a bone) has led to a world where space travel is possible, but he has also moved the story forward from the past to the future in an elegant way; no need for a clumsy title card that says "10,000 Years Later" or some other device — the conceptual cut says it all.

The Conceptual Cut

A *conceptual cut* is one that depends on the content of the *ideas* of two different shots more than on the *visual content*. A famous example of a conceptual cut and also a match cut is at the beginning of Kubrick's *2001: A Space Odyssey*: the cut that spans tens of thousands of years is used to transition from prehistoric times to the era of space travel (Figure 6.51). This is a match cut because the direction, movement, shape, and screen size of the bone almost exactly matches that of the spacecraft. It is also a conceptual cut, however, in that Kubrick is using the bone as a metaphor for human's very first use of a tool. The spacecraft then is the ultimate result of the first use of tools—a tool that can carry humans into space. These types of cuts are usually spelled out in the script as they require a good deal of preparation. What is relevant for the cinematographer and the director working on the set is that these shots must be previsualized, planned, and executed with an eye toward their final purpose.

There are other types of conceptual cuts that are not match cuts, meaning that the visual contents of the two shots are not at all related. For example, in a war film, the general might say, "We'll bomb 'em back to the stone age," and slam his fist down on the table. This cuts

Figures 6.52 (left), **6.53** (middle), **and 6.54**. This scene from *Ronin* appears to be one continuous pan, but in fact when a passing pedestrian wipes the frame, there is a cut that enables the filmmaker to use two entirely different locations as the beginning and end of the same shot. This is called *location stiching* or *location splicing*.

immediately to a shot of an explosion. The cut is carried over by the action, by the idea, and by the sound edit (fist slamming and explosion). Audio often plays a role in conceptual cuts. One of the most elegant examples is from *Citizen Kane*. Mr. Thatcher stands next to a Christmas tree hovering over a fifteen year-old Charles Kane and says "Merry Christmas..." and the next shot is years later. The audio continues with "...and a Happy New Year." The soundtrack completes the continuity even though the subject of the second shot is a different location and years later. It is an elegant jump over years. This is also an *elliptical cut* — meaning an edit that skips over a period of time. Good editing is as much about what you leave out as it is about what you leave in or the how you arrange it.

The Zero Cut

The *zero cut* is a type of match cut that rarely gets mentioned in discussions of shooting and editing. A variation of this technique is used by John Frankenheimer in *Ronin* (Figures 6.52 through 6.54). In this case, the camera tracks with a man as he walks down a street. An extra wipes the frame (blocking it entirely for a frame or two) and the character walks on. There is nothing especially remarkable about the shot. The trick is that it is actually two shots that were done thousands of miles and weeks apart. The first part of the shot was done on location in Europe, and the second part of the shot is on a studio lot in Los Angeles. This gives the director the opportunity to use the strong points of two locations combined into one continuous shot. This is actually a form of *location stitching* (also called *location splicing*) where footage shot in two or more locations is edited to make it look like the whole scene was filmed in one place.

This technique is the same one Hitchcock used in his "one shot" film *Rope*. It is what made it possible for him to shoot the entire film so it appears to be one long continuous take, even though a roll of film in the camera lasts only 11 minutes. Although *Rope* gives the impression of one long take, it is a myth that there are no cuts at all; in fact, there are a few, most of them at the reel changes.

lighting basics

THE FUNDAMENTALS OF LIGHTING

I'm sure you've heard this, "If you light it right..." or "With good lighting, the scene will..." What does that mean? What is "good" lighting?

Lighting has nearly infinite permutations and variations. There is certainly no one "right" way to light a scene. As a result, there is no chance that we can just make a simple list of "proper" lighting techniques. What we can do, however, is try to identify what it is we want lighting to do for us. What jobs does it perform for us? What do we expect of "good" lighting? Starting this way, we have a better chance of evaluating when lighting is working or us and when it is falling short. Naturally, these are generalizations. There are always exceptions, as there are in all aspects of filmmaking — staging, use of the lens, exposure, continuity, editorial, and so on.

What are the Goals of Good Lighting?

So what is it we want lighting to do for us? There are many jobs, and they include creating an image that has:

- A full range of tones and gradations of tone
- Color control and balance
- Shape and dimension in the individual subjects
- Separation: subjects stand out against the background
- Depth and dimension in the frame
- Texture
- Mood and tone: emotional content
- Exposure

Full Range of Tones

In most cases, we want an image to have a full range of tones from black to white (tonal range is always discussed in terms of grayscale, without regard to color). There are exceptions to this, of course, but in general, an image that has a broad range of tones, with subtle gradations all along the way, is going to be more pleasing to the eye, more realistic, and have more impact.

In video and High Def, a proper test chart is essential in preparing the camera to achieve this — to make sure that your camera setup will allow you to capture a full range of tones in your image. This means that your black will be truly black and your white truly white and also that there is a smooth transition throughout the grayscale range with every nuance of gray tone represented.

Naturally, this may not be the final image structure you are aiming for. It's not meant to be — it's a reference that you can reliably return to time after time and a standard from which to judge the contrast and range of your camera setup and thus your scene lighting. From there you have a known starting point for beginning to create the image structure that is right for the scene you are shooting.

Color Control and Color Balance

There are two sides of use of color in lighting and use of the camera. Color balance refers to adjusting the video camera to the lighting conditions (or in film selecting the right film stock or using the correct filter), while color control refers to altering the lighting through the use of different lighting units or putting gels on the lights. First, (unless you are going for a specific effect), the lighting itself must be color balanced. The two most common standards are daylight balance (5500K) and tungsten balance (3200K), but other balances are possible either using a gray card or a test chart or by white balancing

Figure 7.1. (previous page) Dramatic shafts of light through rain and smoke make this frame from *Nine and 1/2 Weeks* a powerful and striking visual.

to a neutral card. This would likely be the most desirable route with lighting you can't control, such as in an office with fluorescent lighting you can't change. Up until the eighties, it was conventional to precisely color balance all lighting sources in a scene. Now with constantly improving video cameras, better film stocks, and most of all, changing visual tastes, it is common to mix slightly, even radically, different color sources in a scene (see the chapter *Color* for examples). In making these decisions you will need to pay close attention to exposure, color balance, filtration, correct processing (for film), and proper camera setup (in the case of video cameras). Color control is also important in the mood and tone of a scene (Figure 7.3).

Shape

Flat front lighting (Figure 7.11) does not reveal the shape and form of the subject. It tends to flatten everything out, to make the subject almost a cartoon cutout: two-dimensional. Lighting from the side or back tends to reveal the shape of an object — its external structure and geometric form.

This is important not only for the overall depth of the shot, but it also can reveal character, emotional values, and other clues that may have story importance. Naturally, it also makes the image more real, more palpable, more recognizable; this is important not only for each subject in the frame, but to the overall picture as well.

Separation

By separation, we mean making the main subjects "stand out" from the background. A frequently used method for doing this is a backlight. Another way to do it is to make the area behind the main subjects significantly darker or brighter than the subject. In our quest to make an image as three-dimensional as possible, we usually try to create a foreground, midground, and background in a shot; separation is an important part of this.

Figure 7.2. (top) Color plays a major role in imagemaking: issues of color balance in relation to camera white balance are crucial to achieving the image you want. If the camera and monitor are not properly calibrated, your task is going to be much more difficult.

Figure 7.3. (above) Out of the ordinary color is frequently appropriate for sci-fi, horror, or fantasy sequences.

Figure 7.4. Two devices are used to add visual texture to this light: a 4x4 *cuculoris* (also called a *cookie*) and a heavy smoke effect.

Depth

As images, what are film and HD? They are flat rectangles — it is a two-dimensional medium (3D is another matter). As lighting people, cinematographers, and directors, a big part of our job is trying to make this flat art appear as three-dimensional as possible — to give it depth and shape and perspective, to bring it alive as a real world as much as possible. Lighting plays a huge roll in this. Use of the lens, blocking, camera movement, set design, color, and other techniques play a role as well, but lighting is our key player in this endeavor.

This is a big part of why "flat" lighting is so frequently the enemy. Flat lighting is light that comes from very near the camera, like the flash mounted on a consumer still camera: it is on axis with the lens. As a result it just flatly illuminates the entire subject evenly. It erases the natural three-dimensional quality of the subject.

Texture

As with shape, light from the axis of the lens (flat lighting) tends to obscure surface texture of materials. The reason is simple: we know texture of the subject from the shadows. Light that comes from near the camera creates no shadows. The more that light comes from the side, the more it creates shadows, which is what reveals texture. Texture can also be present in the lighting itself (Figure 7.4).

Mood and Tone

Let's recall our discussion of the word "cinematic." Used in conversation, it is often used to describe something that is "movie-like." For example, someone might say a particular novel is cinematic if it has fast-moving action, lots of description, and very little exposition. That is not how we will use the term here. In this context, we will use the term cinematic to describe all the tools, techniques, and methods we use to add layers of meaning, emotion, tone, and mood to the content.

As every good camera and lighting person knows, we can take any particular scene and make it look scary or beautiful or ominous or whatever the story calls for, in conjunction with use of lens and camera, of course. Many tools affect the mood and tone of a scene: color, framing, use of lens, frame rate, handheld or mounted camera — indeed everything we can do with camera and lighting can be used to affect the audience's perception of the scene.

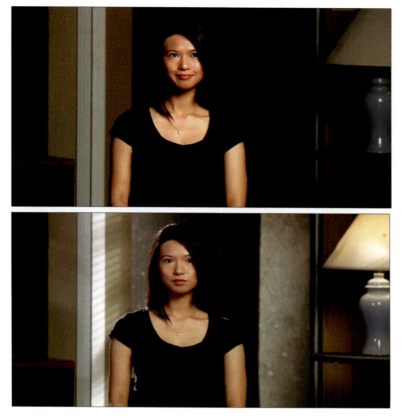

Figure 7.5. (top) Lighting can create depth and three-dimensionality in a scene. Here, the actress is lit only with a soft key; the scene is flat, two-dimensional and doesn't seem real. In **Figure 7.6** (bottom) the addition of a backlight, a practical lamp, and lighting through the window and in the hallway makes the scene more three-dimensional and realistic.

Exposure and Lighting

Lighting does many jobs for us, but none of them matter if you don't get the exposure right: incorrect exposure can ruin whatever else you have done.

In terms of lighting, just getting enough light into a scene to get an exposure is usually not difficult. What is critical is correct exposure. Certainly, it is a job for lighting, (in addition to the iris, frame rate, gain, and shutter angle) but don't forget to think of it as an important image making and storytelling tool. Most of the time we want nominally "correct" exposure (see the chapter *Exposure*).

It is important to remember in this context that exposure is about more than just "it's too light" or "it's too dark." Exposure for mood and tone is obvious, but there are other considerations as well. For example, proper exposure and camera settings are critical to color saturation and achieving a full range of grayscale tones.

There are really two ways in which you have to think about exposure. One is the overall exposure of the scene; this is controlled by the iris, the shutter speed, gain and neutral density filters. All of this controls exposure for the entire frame. Except for some types of neutral density filters (called *grads*), there is no chance to be selective about a certain part of the frame.

Another aspect of exposure is balance within the frame. As is discussed in the chapter on exposure, film and video can only accommodate a certain brightness range. Keeping the brightness range within the limits of your particular film or video camera is mostly the job of lighting. Again, it's not merely a technical job of conforming your lighting to the available latitude: the lighting balance can also affect the mood, tone, style, and overall look of the scene.

Figure 7.7. Strong, simple primary colors can be a powerful element in any image.

SOME LIGHTING TERMINOLOGY

Key light: The dominant light on people or objects. The "main" light on a scene.

Fill light: Light that fills in the shadows not lit by the key light. Lighting is sometimes described in terms of the *key/fill ratio*.

Backlight: Light that hits a person or objects from behind and above. A rim/edge light might be added to separate a dark side of a face or object from the background or make up for a lack of fill on that side. Frequently, back light can be overexposed and still record well on tape or film. Also sometimes called a *hair light* or *shoulder light*.

Kicker: A kicker is a light from behind that grazes along an actor's cheek on the fill side (the side opposite the key light). Often a kicker defines the face well enough that a fill is not even necessary. It should not be confused with a backlight, which generally covers both sides equally.

Sidelight: A light comes from the side, relative to the actor. Usually dramatic and creates great chiaroscuro (if there is little or no fill light), but may be a bit too harsh for close-ups, where some adjustment or slight fill might be needed.

Topper: Light directly from above. The word can also refer to a flag that cuts off the upper part of a light (see chapter *Tools of Lighting*).

Hard light: Light from the sun or small lighting source such as a Fresnel that creates sharp, well-defined shadows. Even a large 10K is still only a small source in relation to the subject being lit.

Figure 7.8. Lighting is your primary tool in establishing mood and tone, which add layers of meaning to the content. This shot is lit with a *Mighty Mole* bouncing off the concrete floor.

Soft light: Light from a large source that creates soft, ill-defined shadows or (if soft enough), no shadows at all. Skylight on an overcast day is from many directions and is very soft.

Ambient light: There are two uses of this term. One means the light that just happens to be in a location. The second use of the term is soft, overhead light that is just sort of "there."

Practicals: Actual working prop lights — table lamps, floor lamps, sconces, and so on. It is essential that all practical lamps have a dimmer on them for fine-tuning control; small dimmers for this purpose are called *hand squeezers*.

Upstage: Part of the scene on the other side of the actors, opposite the side the camera is on. **Downstage** is the side the camera is on. Comes from theater when stages were raked (tilted) and upstage was the part farthest away from the audience.

High key: Lighting that is bright and fairly shadowless with lots of fill light; often used for fashion and beauty commercials.

Low key: Lighting that is dark and shadowy with little or no fill light. Can also be described as having a high key/fill ratio.

Bounce light: Light that is reflected off something — a wall, the ceiling, a white or neutral surface, a silk, or just about anything else.

Available light: Whatever light already exists at the location. May be natural light (sun, sky, overcast day) or artificial (streetlights, overhead fluorescents, etc).

Motivated lighting: Where light in the scene appears to have a source such as a window, a lamp, a fireplace, and so on. In some cases the light will come from a source visible in the scene; in some cases, it will only *appear* to come from a source that is visible in the scene.

Figure 7.9. (top) Hard light creates sharp, well-defined shadows.

Figure 7.10. (bottom) Soft light creates soft shadows that fall off gradually.

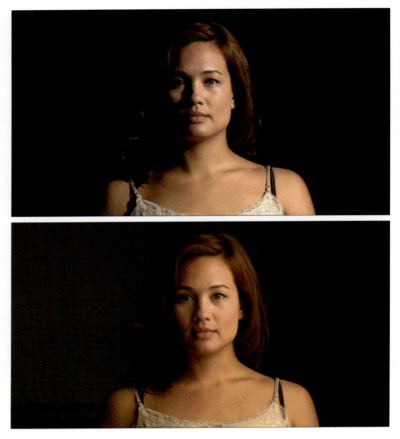

ASPECTS OF LIGHT

What are the variables when we work with light? Given its nearly infinite possibilities, the number of factors are surprisingly few:

- Quality (hard vs soft)
- Direction
- Altitude
- Color
- Intensity
- Texture

Although understanding light is a study that lasts a lifetime and there are nearly infinite ways to light a scene, when we boil it down to the basics, there are really only a few variables that we deal with in lighting. These are the aspects of light that we work with as we work on a scene.

Hard Light and Soft Light

What makes hard light hard? What makes soft light soft? How do we distinguish between them? There are many ways to light any scene; the variations are endless. The styles and techniques of lighting are nearly infinite. Oddly, there are really only two types of light (in terms of what we are calling *quality of light*) when you really boil it down to the basics: *hard light* and *soft light*. There are all sorts of subtle gradations, and variations between completely hard and fully soft, but in the end there are just these two types that exist at opposite ends of a continuum.

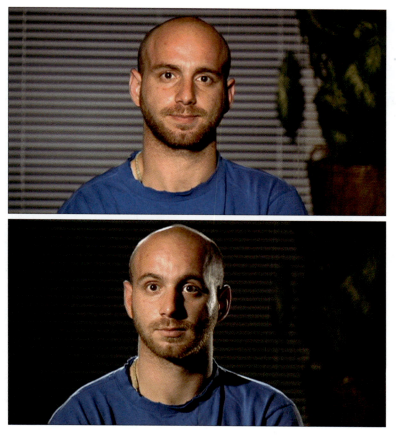

Figure 7.11. (top) Flat front lighting creates no depth, no sense of three-dimensionality. It looks fake and "lit" — something we try to avoid.

Figure 7.12. (bottom) Light from the sides or back (anything other than flat front lighting) creates depth, dimension, a more realistic feel.

Hard Light

Hard light is also called *specular* light. It is light that casts a clear, sharp shadow. It does this because the light rays are traveling parallel, like a laser. What creates a beam of light with the rays pretty much parallel? A very small light source. The smaller the source, the harder the light will be. This is an absolutely crucial point: how hard or soft a light appears is a function of the size of the source.

Outside on a clear, sunny day, take a look at your shadow: it will be sharp and clean. Even though the sun is a large star, it is so far away that it appears as a small object in the sky — which makes it a fairly hard light.

Soft Light

Soft light is the opposite; it is light that casts only a fuzzy, indistinct shadow; sometimes no shadow at all. What makes light soft? A very large source. Go outside on a cloudy day and you will have little or no shadow at all. This is because instead of a small, hard source (just the sun), the entire sky is now the light source — it's enormous. See Figures 7.9 and 7.10 for examples of hard and soft light.

How do we make soft light on the set? There are two ways. One is we *bounce* a light off a large white object. Typically we use things like *foamcore* (a lightweight artist board often used for temporary signs or mounting photographs). The bigger the *bounce* is, the softer the light will be. You can use almost anything light-colored as a bounce: a white wall, an umbrella, a piece of white styrofoam building insulation (also called *bead board*). For larger applications, there are several materials that come in sizes from 4'x4' up to as large as 20'x40' and

Figure 7.13. (top) *Upstage* is on the other side of the actors, away from the camera. Light from the upstage side (the side away from camera) gives pleasant shadows and is flattering to the face.

Figure 7.14. (bottom) *Downstage* is on the same side of the actors as the camera. Lighting from the *downstage* side is unpleasant for the face, puts the shadows in the wrong place, and more flat front lighting.

sometimes even larger. On the film *Memoirs of a Geisha*, for example, very large *silks* were used to cover virtually the entire set, which was several acres in size.

Another way is to direct the light through *diffusion*. In the past, photographers used things like thick white tracing paper or white shower curtains as diffusion. Nowadays, there are many types of diffusion available in wide rolls and sheets. It is amazing for its ability to withstand the intense heat of being put right in front of a powerful light. Diffusion may be attached directly to the *barn doors* of a light or held in a frame in front of the light, or attached to a window, etc.

Figure 7.15. A powerful *backlight* and a *bounce* off the book create a look that perfectly reinforces the character of Col. Kurtz and his mental state of isolation and insanity in this scene from *Apocalypse Now*.

Many types of diffusion material are available in varying grades — from very *light,* almost translucent up to very *heavy* diffusion. A popular light diffusion is *opal*; it is so thin you can almost see through it. This doesn't make the light very soft, but sometimes we want a very subtle effect. Heavier diffusion is much thicker, and it makes the light much softer. About the heaviest, softest diffusion we normally use on the set is a cotton cloth called *muslin*.

Direction

The direction from which the key light comes at the actors is one of the most critical aspects of lighting. The most commonly used terminology is *front, 3/4 front, side, 3/4 back,* and *backlight*. The direction of the light is a major determinant not only of the shadows, but it is also an important factor in the mood and emotional tone of a shot. If most of the light comes from the side or back, the scene will tend to be "darker," more mysterious, more dramatic.

This is especially important if you are trying to make a scene appear underlit, such as a moody scene where you want the audience to perceive the scene as very dark. It is rarely a good idea to try to accomplish this effect by radically underexposing: a scene lit mostly from the back will appear dark without underexposing.

Avoid Flat Front Lighting

Flat front lighting occurs when the key light is very close to the camera. The result is an image with few if any shadows and very little depth or dimension. The result is an image that is very flat and without shape. Also, the subject is rarely separated from the background or other objects in the frame. This reminds us that one of the key jobs of lighting is to direct the eye and "pick out" key elements of the frame, usually the actors.

There are exceptions, of course, but as a general rule, flat front lighting is shapeless, dull, and boring. See Figure 7.11: the lighting is hardly better than the average driver's license photo. In Figure 7.12, the light has moved to the side and a *backlight* plus *kicker* is added. As a general principle, the more your key light comes from the sides or back, the more it is going to give the subject depth and dimension and serves as a positive element in the composition.

Figure 7.16. (top) This rig by Tony Nako for *X-Men* uses dozens of Kino-Flo units to create a soft overhead ambient light to suggest an overcast winter day.

Figure 7.17. (above) Overhead ambient light created with handmade soft boxes. In this case the soft ambient is supplemented with hard light keys and other units for emphasis and shape.

Light from the Upstage Side

Particularly when lighting a dialog scene, it is almost always a good idea to light the actors from the *upstage side*. Upstage means the side away from the camera. If a key light is on the same side of the actors as the camera, it is *downstage*. It is not always possible, but whenever possible it is best to light from the upstage side. See Figures 7.13 and 7.14 for examples.

Backlight and Kicker

Two lights that by definition come from the back are *backlights* and *kickers*. Backlight is sometimes referred to as a *hair light* or *shoulder light* (Figure 7.12). It outlines the subject, separates them from the background, and gives the subject more shape and depth.

A *kicker* is a light that comes from 3/4 back and brushes along the cheek of the subject. It is an extremely useful light. Once you start looking for them, you will see kickers everywhere, even on simple interview shots. As cinematographers take advantage of the higher speed of new film stocks and HD cameras and their ability to "see" into the shadows, there is a tendency to use less and less fill light on subjects. The kicker can be useful to define the shadow side of the face even if there is no fill light at all. Men tend to benefit from a hard kicker, while a soft kicker frequently works better for women.

Intensity

How bright or intense a light is clearly affects exposure, but remember that no matter how bright or dark the overall light of a scene is (within limits), we can adjust it by exposing correctly with the iris, shutter, or neutral density filters. What is important here is the *relative intensity* of different lights within a scene, the relative *balance* of the various lights. These are really two completely different ways to think about the intensity and exposure of lighting in a scene: the

Figure 7.18. *Blown out* windows and strong contrast in the film *Domino*. All effects of this type depend on some smoke to make the light rays visible.

overall lighting level and then the *comparative difference* between lights in a scene — which is usually referred to as the *contrast ratio* between the *key* and *fill*.

Take a look at Figure 7.18 — the windows are completely *blown out*, meaning they are extremely overexposed. Most of the time, we try to control the windows so they are not overexposed and thus without detail and visually distracting in the frame. Occasionally the scene calls for a more extreme look and the DP will choose to blow out the windows. In this scene from *Domino,* the windows are not only blown out, but it is hard light and the slight haze in the room creates defined shafts.

Texture

Texture occurs in several ways. One is the inherent texture of the subject itself, but the one that concerns us here is texture of the light itself. This is done by putting things in front of the light to break it up and add some variation of light and shadow. Things you put in front of the light are called *gobos*, and a particular type of gobo is the *cuculoris* or *cookie*, which comes in two types.

Hard cookies are plywood with irregular cutouts (Figure 7.4). *Soft cookies* are wire mesh with a subtle pattern of translucent plastic.

Other tricks include putting a shadow-casting object in front of the light; traditionally these include things such as vertical *Charlie bars* — vertical wooden bars used to create shadows. This effect can also be accomplished with strips of tape on an empty frame. Another method is to put lace in a frame and place it in front of the light.

Color

Color is such a large and important issue that we devote an entire chapter to the subject. There are several aspects to the subject of color as we use it in filmmaking:

- The image-making side of color: how we use it to make better images.
- The storytelling aspect of color; that is the emotional cultural context of color. One of the best references on this topic is *If It's Purple, Someone's Gonna' Die*, by Patti Bellatoni, a fascinating and practical look at using color in filmmaking.
- Color is important at the camera (choice of film stock or proper video camera setup) and in terms of controlling color at the light source, which involves both using color-balancing gels and the choice of the proper lighting instruments, which come in both daylight balance and tungsten balance.

Figure 7.19. (top) This scene from *Kill Bill* is primarily lit from the practical source in the table.

Figure 7.20. (above) A practical table lamp used as a key in this scene from *The Big Combo*. Practical lamps figure prominently in the *film noir* genre.

BASIC LIGHTING TECHNIQUES

Lighting is a vast and complex subject; we don't have space here to go into great depth but, we can review some basic concepts. For a more comprehensive discussion of lighting, grip, and electrical distribution, see *Motion Picture and Video Lighting* by the same author, also a Focal Press book.

There are, of course, dozens of very different ways to light a scene. The incredible variety of lighting styles and techniques is what makes it a lifelong learning experience. First, some basic principals:

- Avoid flat front lighting. Lights that come more from the sides and back are usually the way to accomplish this. Any time a light is right beside or behind the camera, that is a warning sign of possible flat, featureless lighting.
- Use techniques such as backlight, kickers, and background/set lights to separate the actors from the backgrounds, accentuate the actor's features, and create a three-dimensional image.
- Be aware of the shadows and use them to create chiaroscuro, depth, shape the scene, and mood. Don't be afraid of shadows; some cinematographers say that "...the lights you don't turn on are as important as the ones you do turn on."
- Use lighting and exposure to have a full range of tones in the scene — this must take into account both the reflectances of the scene and the intensity of the lighting you put on them.
- Whenever possible, light people from the upstage side.
- When appropriate, add texture to your lights with gobos, cookies, and other methods.

Back Cross Keys

One of the most useful and commonly used techniques is *back cross keys*. It's simple, straightforward, and fast but also very effective. Take a look at the next ten dialog scenes you see in feature films, commercials, or television: there's a good chance that most or even all of them will be lit with this technique. (Figures 7.21 and 7.22)

The idea is simplicity itself. For a two-person dialog scene (which constitutes a large majority of scenes in most films), one upstage light serves as one actor's key light and also the second actor's backlight. A second light does the opposite: it is the second actor's key light and the first actor's backlight. That's all there is to it, but you may want to add some fill, backlights, or whatever else the scene calls for.

Figure 7.21 and 7.22. Two sides of scene lit with *back cross keys*: one light on each side is one actor's key and the other actor's backlight. Both lights are from the upstage side. In this case, the woman's key is coming through a window and some lace to add texture. His key is hard without any softening or texture. See the DVD or website for more on this lighting technique.

Ambient Plus Accents

Especially on larger sets, it is often difficult or impractical to light every corner of the set with many different hard or soft light units. It is often better to establish an *ambient base* — which means to simply fill the set with a soft, featureless overhead light. This gives you a basic exposure for the entire set, but it is usually somewhat bland and low in contrast. For some scenes, this might be the desired effect, such as this scene in a frozen landscape (Figures 7.16). In most cases, however, you will want to add some accents to feature actors or emphasize certain elements of the set (Figure 7.17). Establishing an ambient base can be accomplished in a number of ways:

- Overhead lights often in conjunction with an *overhead silk*
- *Chicken coops, space lights,* or *softboxes*
- Bouncing a light off the ceiling
- Leaving the overhead fluorescents on
- Large skylights or glass roof

Lighting with Practicals

This is a method that may be used by itself or in conjunction with other methods. A *practical* is something that works — whether it be a table lamp or a refrigerator. Here, we are only talking about lights, whether they be table lamps, sconces, floor lamps, or whatever.

Practical lamps play a part in almost any scene they are in, particularly if it is a night scene. The film noir genre in particular constantly used practical lamps as a major element in the frame as a lighting source.

One of the few absolute rules in lighting is that every practical must be on a dimmer of some sort. In most cases this will be a hand squeezer, a small hand-held dimmer that is usually made from an ordinary wall dimmer. The reason for this is obvious — with most kinds of lights, we can control the intensity with scrims, grip nets, neutral density gels, and flooding/spotting.

With practical lamps we don't have these methods of control, so a dimmer is the quickest and most precise way to control the brightness. One possible way to control a practical lamp is to precisely cut neutral density gel and fit it into the lampshade. This works, but it is time-consuming and crude. Given that these lamps appear in the frame, it is essential to be able to control them much more precisely than that, so hand squeezers are essential.

We want them to appear bright, or the lamp won't look like it's on. This means they are right on the edge — too bright and they will burn out, which means they are not only overexposed and without detail but they may also be a distraction in the composition.

Figure 7.23. Natural window light is extremely soft as long as there are no direct rays of the sun. It is not merely the light from the sky (a huge wrapping source), it is also the light bouncing off the ground, nearby buildings, and so on.

Lighting through the Window

In the old studio days, sets were commonly lit *from the grid* (overhead pipes). This is still done, but these days, locations are used as frequently as sets built in studios. On locations, it may be possible to rig a temporary grid of some sort through the use of various grip equipment such as *wall spreaders* or other means.

Also, locations are lit *from the floor*, meaning that lights are placed on stands. This works, but it has disadvantages, among them that the working area can be cluttered with stands, grip stands, and cable. For this reason, many DPs prefer to light from the outside — through window, doors, skylights, etc. This also has a naturalistic look almost by default; most rooms with windows naturally get a great deal of their light from the windows. Some cinematographers and gaffers go so far as to say always light from outside, although clearly there will be situations where this is not possible. This method also means that the set will be less crowded, so moving from setup to setup is quicker and easier and also gives the director much greater freedom in selecting their frame.

Available Natural Light

The term *available light* is used in two ways on film sets. One of them means whatever light is there in a location; usually an exterior location but it can refer to rooms that have windows, skylights, or ordinary room lighting as well. In general, the term "available light" means working with the existing lighting on the location. There is a third, less serious use of the term. Some might say that a particular DP is an "available light" cinematographer, as in "he uses every light available on the truck."

Available Light Windows

Window light can be some of the most beautiful light of all, if you use it right (Figure 7.23). Windows can be disastrous — for example, if you place an actor against a window and the camera is placed so that the actor is in front with the view out the window behind them. In normal daylight conditions, this will produce a very high-contrast situation, and you have to choose between having the outside view properly exposed and the actor in complete silhouette or exposing for the actor and having the window view overexposed and blown out. (See "The Window Problem" on the DVD or website).

There are work arounds, of course. One is to use a big light on the actor to bring up their exposure. This generally requires a very large unit and it can be difficult to make it look natural; also, the light has to be daylight balance. The other alternative is to bring down the exposure of the window. The easiest way to do this is to *gel* the window with *ND* (*neutral density* gel), which can reduce the light coming through the window by one, two, three, or even four stops (the ND designations for this are ND .3, .6, .9, and 1.2).

If you want to use tungsten balance lights inside the room, you can also add *85 gel*, which converts daylight (5600K) to tungsten balance (3200K). Or you can use gel that combines them: 85N3, 85N6, etc. But there is another alternative: change the shot. This not only makes lighting easier, but it will generally produce a better-looking shot. If the director is flexible about the staging, you'll get a better image by placing the camera so that the actor is beside the window and the background of the shot is no longer the view out the window, but rather something inside the room. This not only solves the exposure imbalance, but it also gives the actor soft window light from the side. This can be some of the most beautiful lighting there is.

What makes window light so beautifully soft? We have to distinguish between *window light, sky light,* and *sunlight.* Many people think of window light being "sunlight." Direct sun is hard and contrasty. *Sky light* is the light coming from the sky itself, which is a huge radiating source and thus very soft. Also coming through a window might be sun bounced off neighboring buildings, the ground, clouds, etc.

Figure 7.24. This dark, moody scene is lit primarily from the window with four *MaxiBrutes* through a 12x12 *Hilight* diffusion, supplemented by the library lamps on the table. A very slight smoke effect is added for atmosphere.

Figure 7.25. (top) For this re-creation of a noir look, his key is just a bounce off the paper in the typewriter.

Figure 7.26. (bottom) The overall setup is very simple: a *Tweenie* bounces off the typing paper, a *Betweenie* gives him a backlight/kicker, and another Betweenie adds a slight glow to the map. The practical lamps have very little influence on the scene; they are mostly just props.

MOTIVATED LIGHT

Light in a scene may come from many sources, including lights that are actually in the frame such as practicals, windows, skylights, signs, and so on. In some cases, these sources are visible but do not provide enough output for proper exposure. In this case, the sources may only serve to *motivate* additional lighting that is off-screen. Some cinematographers and directors prefer that most or all lighting in a scene be motivated in this way — that the viewer somehow understands where the light is coming from. In these frames from *Honeydripper* (Figures 7.29 and 7.30), the light is *motivated* by the lamps, but the actual illumination comes from sources not shown in the frame.

Carrying a Lamp

Often we want the lamp to appear to be lighting the subject, but for some reason, it just won't do it. If we turn the lamp's brightness up enough to light the actor, then the shade will be completely blown out; or it might be that the actor just isn't close enough to be properly lit by the lamps. In this case, we use a technique called *carrying* the lamp. To do this we set a small lamp in a place where it will hit

Figure 7.27. (top) Her only source is the practical lamp itself. A very small source adds a *catchlight* in the eyes.

Figure 7.28. (bottom) The lamp works for her even when she leans back, but only in a fairly narrow range of distance from the practical.

lighting basics

Figure 7.29. (top) In the establishing shot from *Honeydripper* the oil lamps are clearly shown to be the motivation for the direction, color, and softness of the light, which is then used to great effect in this two-shot.

Figure 7.30. (bottom) Once the sources have been established in the wide shot, the lighting of the mediums and close-ups makes sense and seems appropriate. This is an example of both *motivated lighting* and *carrying* a lamp.

the actor from the same direction as the light from the lamp. It also needs to be the same quality of hard or soft and the same color; table lamps tend to be on the warm side, often about 2800K or warmer.

Figures 7.25 and 7.26 show a modern take on a film noir look that employs a different method of carrying a lamp. Here the lighting is actually very simple: it's a Betweenie (300 watt Fresnel) that is bouncing off the piece of paper in the typewriter. Another *Betweenie* gives the actor a backlight, and a third one puts a small splash on the map behind him.

The typing paper bounce gives him a moody look appropriate for the scene and doesn't create problematic shadows like a hidden light from below would. If we try to light the actor with the practical

Figure 7.31. (top) If the practical is set high enough to give proper exposure to the subject, the lamp itself is completely blown out.

Figure 7.32. (middle) When the practical lamp is set to a level that gives it the proper exposure, then the subject is underexposed.

Figure 7.33. (bottom) A separate source is added to "carry" the lamp. It comes from the same direction as the lamp and gives the illusion that the practical lamp is lighting the actor. The source in this case is a MolePar in a snoot box with a dimmer.

lamp as in Figure 7.31, the lamp is totally blown out. If we dim it down enough to see the lamp (Figure 7.32), then the actor gets lost.

The solution was to have a light just out of frame on the left and below the table level. With this rig on a dimmer, it was possible to achieve the correct balance between the practical light and the actor's key. The key to this technique is to make sure the light you are using to carry the practical is hitting the actor from the same angle as would the light from the practical lamp. It needs to be the same color and quality (in terms of hard versus soft) as well.

DAY EXTERIORS

Working with daylight can be a lot trickier than people think. Some producer and directors believe that working with available daylight will always be faster and easier. Sometimes, but not always. If it's an overcast day (soft light), then nothing could be simpler.

If you are dealing with direct sun, however, controlling it can require constant attention and adjustment. When dealing with actors in direct sun, you have several choices: *diffusion* of the harsh sun, *filling* and *balancing* the shadows, finding a better location or angle for the shots, or moving the shot into *open shade*. See video examples on the DVD and website.

Fill

You can use *bounceboards* or lights to fill in the shadows and reduce the contrast. Grip *reflector boards* (Figure 7.34) have a *hard side* and a *soft side* and yokes with brakes so they can be set and will stay as positioned. The sun moves quickly, however, and it is almost always necessary to *shake them up* before each take. For this reason, a grip has to be stationed beside each board to re-aim it for each take. It is also important to *table* them if there is a break in filming. This means adjust the reflector to a horizontal position so it doesn't catch the wind and blow over. Be sure to secure them heavily with *sandbags*. Between scenes, they should be laid on the ground on their sides so as not to damage the surfaces.

Even the soft side of a reflector board can be a bit harsh; one good strategy is to aim the hard side through medium diffusion (like 216) or the soft side through light diffusion (such as Opal), which just smooths it out a bit.

Silks and Diffusion

Another choice is to make the sunlight softer and less contrasty. For tight shots, a 4x4 frame with diffusion can soften the light and can be held by a grip stand, with plenty of sandbags, of course. For larger shots, frames with silk or diffusion are made in many sizes: 6'x6', 8'x8', 12'x12', 20'x20' and even 20'x40'. These larger sizes require solid rigging and should only be done if you have an adequate grip crew who know what they are doing: a 12'x12' silk has enough area to drive a sailboat at 10 knots, meaning it can really do some damage if it gets away from you in a wind.

Open Shade and Garage Door Light

The simplest and often most beautiful solution to working with harsh direct sun is simply to get out of the sun entirely. If the director is flexible about the scene, it is usually not only faster but also better lighting to move the scene to a shady spot; best of all is *open shade*, which is the shady side of a building, trees, and so on, but open to the sky. Here the subject is lit by the soft light of the radiating sky dome, reflection off the rest of the terrain and so on. The only

danger here is your background: since the exposure will be a couple of stops down, it is critical that you not frame the shot so that the hot background behind the actor will be in direct sun and thus severely overexposed. (Figures 7.36 and 7.37).

A variation on this is *garage door light* (Figure 7.38). This is open shade with the darker interior as a background. It can be both beautiful and dramatic. It doesn't have to be an actual garage door, of course; the key is that it is open shade with a darker background such as you would have with an actor positioned right in a large open entrance such as a garage door. Also, a good deal of the light on the actor is being bounced off the surrounding landscape or buildings and also the ground level surface in front of them, which gives them a nice underlit fill. All of these methods are simply ways of dealing with the fact that sunlight is often too harsh and contrasty.

Sun as Backlight

If all other options are unavailable, an alternative is to turn the shot so that the actor has their back to the sun. This does two things: first of all the actor is lit by the bounce off the surroundings. In most cases this is not quite enough, but the addition of a simple bounce board (foamcore, beadboard, or a folding silk reflector) helps. This involves working with the director to adjust the shot. Remember that shots rarely exist on their own; they are usually part of an entire scene. This means that thinking it through and planning for the sun angles must be done before starting to shoot the scene. Once you have shot the master for a scene, it is often not possible to cheat the actors around to take advantage of the sun's position, although for some close-ups it may be possible. It is also important to think ahead about the sun's movement, especially if the scene is going to take a long time to shoot or there is a lunch break during filming.

Figure 7.34. This grip is standing by to *shake up* the *reflector board*. This means he re-aims it for every shot. The sun moves surprisingly fast and it is usually necessary to re-aim the reflector for nearly every take. This reflector board also has a layer of CTO gel on it to warm up the backlight.

Figure 7.35. The grips are *Hollywooding* a light silk to move with the actors for the dolly shot. Hollywooding is a term for handholding a silk, light, or flag.

LIGHTING FOR HIGH DEF VIDEO

High Def is much closer to film than non-High Def video but there are still differences. It tends to *see into the shadows* more than film, and it sees detail much more than film. This means that shadows you would expect to go black or nearly black in film are still visible in HD. This can have the effect of ruining the illusion; the same is true of HD's tendency to see more fine detail. The makeup and wardrobe departments must be especially on their toes. Tiny imperfections of sets and props can suddenly become obtrusive where on film they were more than acceptable. This is a big part of the "video look," which, while far less apparent on High Def, can still be a problem if not dealt with properly. This problem is more complex than just detail resolution: it can be partially dealt with by using diffusion filters but by no means entirely. Dealing with it in this way may mean using diffusion filters where you don't want to.

The idea that HD requires less lighting is a bit of a myth. However, it is true that because HD cameras can shoot at higher ISOs without unacceptable noise, then lighting for HD cameras often calls for less intensity of lighting. This means that you can use a 5K where a 10K might have been necessary for film lighting. How many lights you use is based on shaping the light, accenting certain elements, and so on. Between film and video, the number of lights seldom changes, but their size often does. This is because high-definition video *sees* into the shadows a great deal more and thus give the impression of being *faster* than film. This is much the same as happened with the introduction of high-speed lenses and high-speed film in the 80's and 90's. Overenthusiastic supporters claimed that fewer people would be needed on the crew and fewer lights. None of this is true in the

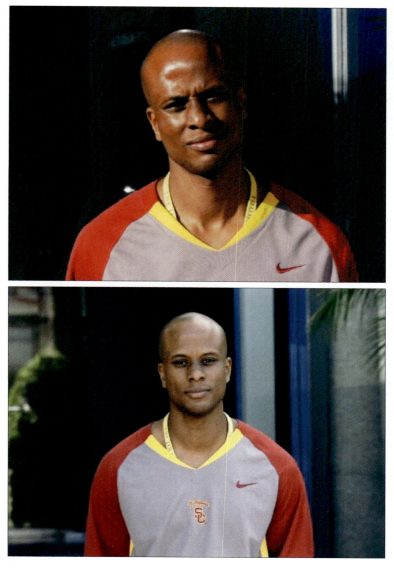

Figure 7.36. (top) Direct sunlight is harsh, contrasty, and unflattering. If you do have to shoot in direct sun, try not to do so during the middle part of the day. Sunlight is softer and at a lower, more flattering angle early in the day or late in the afternoon.

Figure 7.37. (bottom) Here we just have the actor back up a few feet so he is under the awning of the building. This is *open shade*; it is softer and less contrasty.

larger sense, of course — not if you really care about the quality of your lighting. At best, you need a smaller generator and lighter gauge distribution cable and slightly smaller lights.

Think of it this way — say you light a scene beautifully with four lights: a 12K creating a beautiful shaft of light through the window, a 10K raking down the hallway, a 2K bounce for a key on the scene, and a baby-junior for a backlight. Let's now assume that the speed of your video camera *doubles* (a very big jump in speed). Does this mean that you all of a sudden need fewer lights?

Not unless you want to do less lighting — that is, give up something important. You still need four lights to accomplish what you did before. The only difference is that instead of a 12K you need a 6K, instead of a 10K you can use a 5K, and so on. Doubling the speed is a giant leap technologically, but in terms of exposure and lighting it is only one stop. Can you get an exposure using fewer lights? Of course you can. But as a cinematographer or director, if you are willing to say that *just* getting an exposure is your only goal

Figure 7.38. An example of *garage door light*. The subject is just inside the door, which puts her in open shade. The sun is still hitting the ground, buildings and the rest of the background behind the camera, which results in a soft bounce on the actress.

in lighting, then you don't need to be reading books like this one. It is true that there are more and more cases where you can shoot purely with *available* light — that is, where you can get visually interesting, even beautiful scenes only with the light that already exists at a location. However, this is not a high def or even a video phenomenon, the same is true with film stock, which has improved vastly in the last few years. For example, look at the movie *Lost in Translation*, in which nearly all of the night exteriors of Tokyo were shot purely with available light.

lighting sources

Figure 8.2. (above) A *12K HMI Fresnel*.

Figure 8.1. (previous page) An *Airstar* balloon light used for a large night exterior.

THE TOOLS OF LIGHTING

Cinematographers do not need to know all the details of how each piece of lighting equipment works, but it is essential that they know the capabilities and possibilities of each unit, as well as its limitations. A great deal of time can be wasted by using a light or piece of grip equipment that is inappropriate for the job. One of the DPs most important functions is ordering the right lighting equipment for the job and using it appropriately. Motion picture lights fall into seven general categories: *HMIs*, tungsten *Fresnels*, tungsten *open face lights*, *fluorescents*, *xenons*, *practicals*, *LED* lights, and *sunguns*.

DAYLIGHT SOURCES

Lighting units can generally be divided into those that output *daylight balance* or *tungsten balance* light. Several types of light are daylight balance: HMIs and *color correct fluorescents* and LED units among them.

Color Rendering Index

Lights are classified according to *Color Rendering Index* (CRI), which is a measure of the ability of a light source to reproduce the colors of various objects faithfully in comparison with a natural light source. This means that a light with a low CRI will not render colors accurately. A CRI of 90 or above (on a scale of 0 to 100) is considered necessary for film and video work (and also still photography). The CRI is especially important when judging fluorescent and other gas discharge sources. For most HMIs and color-correct fluorescents, LEDs, and other units designed for film work, the color rendering index is greater than 90.

HMI Units

HMIs generate three to four times the light of tungsten halogen, but consume up to 75% less energy for the same output. When a tungsten bulb is color-corrected to match daylight, the advantage increases to seven times because a great deal of the spectrum is absorbed by the blue gel (color temperature blue or CTB). See the chapter *Color*). Because HMIs (Figure 8.2) are more efficient in converting power to light, they generate less heat than a tungsten lamp with the same output.

HMI stands for the basic components: H is from the Latin symbol for mercury (Hg), which is used primarily to create the lamp voltage. M is for medium-arc. I stands for iodine and bromine, which are halogen compounds. The halogen serves much the same function as in a tungsten halogen lamp in prolonging the useful life of the bulb and ensures that the rare earth metals remain concentrated in the hot zone of the arc.

HMI lamps have two electrodes made from tungsten, which project into a discharge chamber. Unlike tungsten bulbs, which have a continuous filament of tungsten wire, HMIs create an electrical arc that jumps from one electrode to another and generate light and heat in the process. *Color temperature (see the chapter Color)* as it is measured for tungsten bulbs or sunlight does not technically apply to HMIs (or to other types of discharge lighting such as fluorescents) because they produce a quasi-continuous spectrum. In actual practice, though, the same measurements and color temperature meters are used for all types of video and motion picture lighting sources.

Our eyes are unreliable in judging color because our brain adjusts and compensates; it will tell us that a wide variety of colors are "white." A *color meter* or *vectorscope* is a far more dependable ways of judging color; however, they do not measure CRI.

Figure 8.3. A combination of *Kino Flo* and tungsten units on a *blue-screen* efx set. (Photo courtesy of Kino Flo.)

Ballasts

All HMIs require a ballast, which acts as a current limiter. The reason for this is simple: an arc is basically a dead short; if the current were allowed to flow freely, the circuit would overload and either blow the fuse or burn up. Early ballasts for HMIs were extremely heavy and bulky (200 pounds or more) because they contained current limiters that consisted of heavy copper wire wound in a coil like a transformer. Fortunately, few of these remain in use.

The invention of the smaller and lighter electronic ballast was a major improvement. Electronic ballasts also allow the unit to operate on a *square-wave* (unlike the *sine wave* of normal alternating current electricity).

The most significant new development in HMIs is the new *flicker-free* ballasts, which use square-wave technology to provide flicker-less shooting at any frame rate. With some units there is a penalty paid for flicker-free shooting at frame rates other than sync sound speed: it results in a significantly higher noise level. If the ballasts can be placed outside or shooting is MOS, this is not a problem. It is not usually an issue as high-speed shooting rarely involves recording audio. For a more detailed discussion of flicker and how to avoid it, see the chapter *Technical Issues*.

Header cables are the power connection from the ballast to the light head itself. Many larger HMIs can only take two header cables; a third header will usually result in a voltage loss too great to get the lamp to fire up. *Square-wave* refers to the shape of the sine wave of the alternating current after it has been reshaped by the electronics of the ballast. Flicker is discussed in more detail in the chapter on

Figure 8.4. (above) The ballast acts as a transformer to provide operating voltage and also starting voltage, which can be as high as 20,000 volts. It is also a current limiter.

Figure 8.5. (right) An 18K HMI with a *Chimera softbox* in use on a day exterior location.

Technical Issues, but suffice it to say here that the normal sine wave of AC current leaves too many "gaps" in the light output that become visible if the camera shutter is not synchronized to its rhythm. By squaring the wave, these gaps are minimized and there is less chance of flicker. This is especially important if you are shooting at anything other than normal speed; high-speed photography in particular will create problems. It is important to note that flicker can be a problem in video also, just as with film cameras.

Voltages as high as 12,000 *VAC* (volts AC) or more are needed to start the arc, which is provided by a separate ignitor circuit in the ballast. This creates the power needed for the electric current to jump across the gap between the two electrodes. The typical operating voltage is around 200V. When a lamp is already hot, much higher voltages are needed in order to ionize the pressurized gap between the electrodes. This can be from 20 kV to more than 65 kV (kilo-Volt). For this reason, some HMIs can not be restruck while they are hot — which means you may have to wait for the light to cool before you can start it again. This can be a major hindrance when the whole film crew is waiting on it. *Hot restrike,* which generates a higher voltage to overcome this resistance, is a feature on most newer HMIs. HMI bulbs can change color temperature as they age. It is important to check the color temperature of HMI bulbs periodically with a color meter to see if they need correcting gels to keep them consistent with other lighting units in use on the project.

18K and 12K HMI

The 18K and the 12K HMIs are the most powerful fresnel lights currently available. Like all HMIs they are extremely efficient in light output per watt of input power. They produce a sharp, clean light, which is the result of having a very small source (the gas arc) which is focused through a very large lens (Figure 8.2).

These large lights are invaluable where very large areas are being covered or there is a need for high light levels for high-speed shooting. They are also a natural for sunlight effects such as sunbeams through a window or any other situation where a strong well-defined beam is needed. They are also among the few sources (along with HMI PARs) that will balance daylight and fill in the shadows sufficiently to permit shooting in the bare sun without silks or reflec-

Figure 8.6. Larry Mole Parker of Mole-Richardson does a side-by-side test of a *carbon arc* light and a *12K HMI PAR.*

tors. The fact that they burn approximately "daylight blue" (5500 degrees kelvin) is a tremendous advantage in these situations: no light is lost to filters. Often when a 12K or 18K is used to fill in sunlight, it is the only unit operating on a generator. If it was drawing on one leg only, the load would be impossible to balance and might very well damage the generator. In this case a *ghost load* on the other legs is necessary.

Most 12 and 18Ks are 220 volt lights, but some are 110 volt units which can make load balancing difficult. Lights that run on 220 volts require *three-phase* power. Most power available on a movie set, or in most buildings, is 110 volts in the United States. In Europe, Great Britain, and most of the rest of the world, 220 volt power is the standard. For more on electricity and power supplies for lighting, see *Motion Picture and Video Lighting*, also from Focal Press.

As with any large light, coordinate with the *gennie* (generator) operator before firing it up or shutting it down. The power surge when they start up can be a significant strain on the power supply. Don't start up all the large lights at the same time. Be sure to clarify with the rental house what type of power connectors are used on the lights when you are placing your lighting and grip order for the job.

6K & 8K

6K and 8K HMIs can handle many of the same jobs as the bigger lights, particularly where the area covered is smaller. Although they generally have a smaller lens, they still produce a sharp, clean beam with good spread. In many applications they perform admirably as the main light: serving as key, window light, sun balance, and so on. Some 6Ks and 8Ks accept 110 volt input and, some require a 220 volt power supply. They may require a variety of connectors or a set of *Siamese splitters,* (called Y-cords in Great Britain).

When ordering any large lamp, it is crucial to ask these questions and be sure the rental house will provide the appropriate distribution equipment or adapters — remember, if you don't order it, it won't be there. You must be very thorough when placing an order. Failure to do so may result in the light not being functional. Some makes of HMIs provide for head balancing. This is accomplished by sliding the yoke support backwards or forwards on the head. This is a useful feature when adding or subtracting barn doors, frames, or other items that alter the balance of light.

Figure 8.7. *Lite Panel LED* lights mounted in a car and also as a fill light on the camera. This type of camera mounted fill light is called an *Obie*, named for actress Merle Oberon, for whom it was invented. Due to their light weight, compact size and, ability to run off batteries, LED units are very popular as camera mounted lights. (Photo courtesy of Litepanels.)

4K and 2.5K

The smaller HMIs, the 4K and 2.5K, are general purpose lights, doing much of the work that used to be assigned to 5K and 10K tungsten lights. Slightly smaller than the bigger HMIs, they can be easily flown and rigged and will fit in some fairly tight spots.

1.2K and Smaller Units

The smallest lamps, the 1.2K, 575, 400, and 200 watt HMIs, are versatile units. Lightweight and fairly compact, they can be used in a variety of situations. The electronics ballasts for the small units have become portable enough to be hidden in places where larger units might be visible. They can also be *wall-plugged*, which means no generator or other supplemental power supply is needed on location.

HMI PAR Units

Some of the most powerful, intense lights available are HMI PARs; they have the high output of HMIs and the tightly focused beam of the PAR reflector. The largest units are 12K and 18K, but HMI PARS are made in smaller sizes as well, down to 125 watts. *Arri Lighting* (part of the *Arriflex* group) makes a popular unit called the *Pocket PAR* in these smaller sizes.

One particularly versatile unit is the 1.2K HMI PAR, made by several manufacturers. What makes it special is that it is small enough (in wattage) to be plugged into a 20 amp household circuit, but being PARs they have a healthy output, which in conjunction with their daylight balance means they have a wide variety of uses in daylight situations: fill when bounced or through diffusion or for a small shaft of light through a window.

Rules for Using HMI Units

- Check the stand and ballast with a VOM meter for leakage by measuring the voltage between the stand and any ground. There will usually be a few volts, but anything above 10 or 15 volts indicates a potential problem.
- Keep the ballast dry. On wet ground, use apple boxes, rubber mats or other insulation material.
- Avoid getting dirt or finger marks on the lamps: oil from the skin will degrade the glass and create a potential failure point. Many lamps come provided with a special cleaning cloth.
- Ensure that there is good contact between the lamp base and

the holder. Contamination will increase resistance and impair proper cooling.

- The filling tip (nipple) should always be above the discharge, or there is a risk of a cold spot developing inside the discharge chamber.
- Running at above rated voltage may result in failure.
- Very long cable runs may reduce the voltage to a point that affects the output and may result in the lamp not firing.
- Excessive cooling or direct airflow on the lamp may cool the lamp below its operating temperature, which can result in a light with a high color temperature and inferior CRI.

Potential Problems

HMIs (or any light with a ballast) may sometimes fail to function properly. Be sure to have a few extra header cables on hand: they are the most common cause of malfunctions. The safety switch on the lens can also cause trouble. Never try to bypass it, however; it serves an important function. HMIs should never be operated without the glass lens, which filters out harmful ultraviolet radiation that can damage someone's eyes. When they do fail to fire:

- Check that the breakers are on. Some HMIs have more than one breaker.
- *After* killing the power, open the lens and check the micro-switch that contacts the lens housing. Make sure it is operating properly and making contact. Wiggle it, but don't be violent — the light won't operate without it.
- If that fails, try another header cable. If you are running more than one header to a light, disconnect and try each one individually. Look for broken pins, dirt in the receptacle, etc.
- Check the power. HMIs won't fire if the voltage is low. Generally they need at least 108 volts to fire. Some have a voltage switch (110, 120, 220); be sure it's in the right position.
- Try the head with a different ballast and vice-versa.
- Let the light cool. Many lights won't do a hot restrike.

XENONS

Xenons are similar to HMIs since they are a gas discharge arc with a ballast. They feature a polished parabolic reflector that gives them amazing throw and almost laser-like beam collimation. At full spot they can project a tight beam several blocks with a relatively small amount of spread. Xenons are very efficient with the highest lumens per watt output of any light. Xenons currently come in five sizes: a 1K, 2K, 4K, 7K and 10K. There is also a 75 watt sun-gun unit. The 1K and 2K units come in 110 and 220 volt models, some of which can be wall-plugged. This produces a high-output light that can be plugged into a wall outlet or a small portable generator. Larger xenons are extremely powerful, and must be used cautiously: they can quickly crack a window. Just one example of their power: with ASA 320 film stock and the light set at full spot, a 4K delivers f/64 at 40 feet from the light, considerably more than you would get with a 4K HMI or equivalent tungsten lamp.

The current supplied by the ballast to the bulb is pulsed DC; as a result, flicker is not a problem for xenons, and they can be used for high-speed filming up to 10,000 fps. Xenons do, however, have some disadvantages: all xenons are expensive to rent and have a cooling fan that makes them very difficult to use in sound filming. Also,

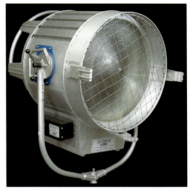

Figure 8.8. A 20K Fresnel tungsten. (Photo courtesy of Cinemills.)

Figure 8.9. A Mole-Richardson *Baby Baby* 1K. This is a 1,000 watt tungsten Fresnel. It is a "baby" for two reasons: a 1K Fresnel is called a baby, but this is also the baby version of that as it is smaller than a studio 1K.

Figure 8.10. A scrim set for a Betweenie. Most lights come with a scrim set to control intensity. A *double* (red rim) reduces the output by one stop, and a *single* (green rim) reduces it by one-half stop. Also included are a *half-double* and a *half-single*. This is called a *Hollywood scrim set* because it includes two doubles.

because of the bulb placement and reflector design, there is always a hole in the middle of the round beam, which can be minimized but never entirely eliminated.

Due to the parabolic reflectors, flagging and cutting are difficult close to the light: flags cast bizarre symmetrical shadows. Also, the extremely high and concentrated output means that they burn through gel very quickly. Many people try to compensate by placing the gel as far as possible from the light. This is a mistake — the safest place to gel is actually right on the face of the light.

Seventy-five watt xenon sunguns were developed for the Navy. They are excellent for flashlight effects. They come in both AC and DC configurations. Most have motorized flood/spot controls that can be operated during the shot. As with larger xenons, there is a hole or a hot spot in the center of the beam (depending on the focus) that cannot be eliminated. Xenon bulbs do not shift in temperature as they age or as voltage shifts.

LED Lights

A new and very popular source is LED lights (Figure 8.7), which are small and extremely energy efficient, which also means that they produce much less heat than tungsten lights (where the electricity produces 90% heat and only 10% light). LEDs have been incorporated into all types of units, although few of them have the long reach of a PAR or a fresnel. For lighting fairly close to the scene, however, they have many advantages. Their compact size means they can be hidden in many places on the set and also makes them easier to handle and rig on location. There are also many LED lights that run on batteries — these can be very useful for handheld work, camera mounting and other conditions where AC power may not be available or it is just not practical to run and AC power cord. Certainly a hand-held camera operator is not going to want to be dragging a power cable around all the time.

TUNGSTEN LIGHTS

Tungsten lamps are just bigger versions of ordinary household bulbs; they all have a filament of tungsten wire just as invented by Thomas Edison. There are two types of tungsten fresnels: *studio* and *baby*. The *studio* light is the full-size unit, and the *baby* is a smaller housing and lens, making it more compact for location use (Figure 8.9). As a rule, the baby version is the studio housing of the next smaller size (the body of a baby 5K is similar to the body of a studio 2K). In most countries outside the United States, the electrical supply is 220 volts; different bulbs are used that are suited to the appropriate voltage.

Fresnels

Fresnel units are lights with lenses. Most film lights employ the stepped Fresnel type lens, with a few exceptions that use a simpler *plano-convex* lens such as a *Dedo* or an *ellipsoidal* (*Leko*). A Fresnel lens is a stepped ring design that reduces the thickness of the lens to save on cost and also prevent heat buildup in the glass, which can cause cracking.

Twenty

The biggest tungsten light now in use is the 20K. It is a large unit with tremendous output. Many jobs that were formerly done by the 10K are now done with this light. Most 20K units use bulbs that run at 220 volts (which may require special electrical distribution), and several models come with a built-in dimmer (Figure 8.8).

Figure 8.11. (top) The Mole-Richardson open face 2K or *Mighty Mole*.

Figure 8.12. (middle) A 1K *MolePar*.

Figure 8.13. (bottom) A *Big Eye* 10K, so called because it has a lens that is larger than a standard studio 10K.

Tenners

The 10K tungsten Fresnel comes in three basic versions:

- The baby 10K provides high-intensity output with a fairly compact, easily transportable unit with a 14-inch Fresnel lens.
- The basic 10K, known as a "tenner" or studio 10K, has a 20-inch Fresnel.
- The largest light of this group is the *Big Eye* tenner, which has a 24-inch lens. The Big Eye is a very special light with quality all its own. The DTY (10K) bulb provides a fairly small source, while the extremely large fresnel is a large radiator. The result is a sharp, hard light with real bite but with a wraparound quality that gives it almost a soft light quality on subjects close to the light. This is a characteristic of all very big lights that gives them a unique quality.

It is important to never use a 20K, 10K, or a 5K pointing straight up (this applies to large HMIs and xenons as well). The lens blocks proper ventilation and the unit will overheat. Also, the filament will not be properly supported and will sag and possibly touch the glass.

Senior/5K

Although it is available in both versions, the *baby 5K* is far more popular than the larger unit. It can work as a general purpose big light and a fill used against a 10K. The 5K is also called a *senior*.

Junior/2K

The *2K Fresnel* is also known as a *deuce* or a *junior*. It has enough power to bring a single subject or actor up to a reasonable exposure, even with diffusion in front of the lens. Juniors are also useful as backlights, rims, and kickers. *Baby juniors* (called *BJs*) are the more compact and an extraordinarily versatile unit.

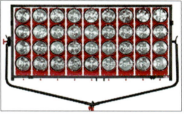

Figure 8.14. (above) The *Dino*, or in this illustration, Mole-Richardson's *Moleeno*, consists of 36 1K PAR bulbs. (Photo courtesy of Mole-Richardson.)

Figure 8.15. (top) *Skypans* rigged for a large set by lighting director Tony Nako and gaffer Michael Gallart. Skypans are very simple lights — just a socket for the bulb and a pan reflector. They can use 5K, 10K or 20K bulbs. Also on the trusses are 5K Fresnels and space lights. (Photo by Michael Gallart).

Figure 8.16. (left) The *Ruby Seven*, a PAR based unit that offers additional controllability. (Photo courtesy of Luminaria.)

Figure 8.17. (above) Two *Mole FAY* lights *boxed in* with some 4x8 floppies for control.

Baby/1K

Thousand watt units are known as *1Ks* (one K) or *babies*. The 1K is used as a key light, a splash on the wall, a small back light, a hard fill, and for dozens of other uses. The baby can use either a 750 watt bulb (EGR) or a 1,000 watt bulb (EGT). Most are now used with the 1K quartz bulb, but are still called 750s. The *Baby 1K*, also called a *Baby Baby*, is the small size version. Because of its smaller lens and box, it has a wider spread than the studio baby.

Tweenie /650

The *Tweenie* is "between" the 1K and the Inky. With the new high-speed films, the Tweenie is often just the right light for the small jobs a baby used to do, even as a key light. It is very useful for a number of small jobs, easily hidden, and can function as a quick accent or an eyesight.

Betweenie, InBetweenie, Inky and Pepper

These are similar to Tweenies but smaller. The *Betweenie* is a 300 watt unit and the *InBetweenie* uses a 200 watt bulb and is often used instead of an *Inky* (also 200 watts). At 100, 200, or 300 watts (depending on the bulb and size of the housing), the *Pepper* is a smaller unit, but up close it can deliver a surprising amount of light. The Inky at 200 watts is great for a tiny spritz of light on the set, as an eye light, a small fill, or for an emergency last-minute light to just raise the exposure a bit on a small area.

Open Face

Some 2K, 1K, and 650 units are available as *open face* lights — that is, they have no lenses, but they do have some spot/flood focusing. Their light is raw and can be uneven, but they do have a tremendous output for their size. They are good for bounce or shooting through diffusion (Figure 8.11). They are a good source when all you need is raw power and the control that a Fresnel affords isn't necessary.

PARS

PAR stands for *parabolic aluminized reflector*. A parabola is an ideal shape to collect all of the light rays and projects them out in the same direction. It is the shape of reflector that is going to give the narrowest, most concentrated beam. In conjunction with this, all PAR units have a lens, which functions primarily to concentrate or spread the beam. Tungsten parts generally come with a fixed lens that is part of the unit: they are pretty much the same as a car headlight. HMI PARs always come with a set of interchangeable lenses: these

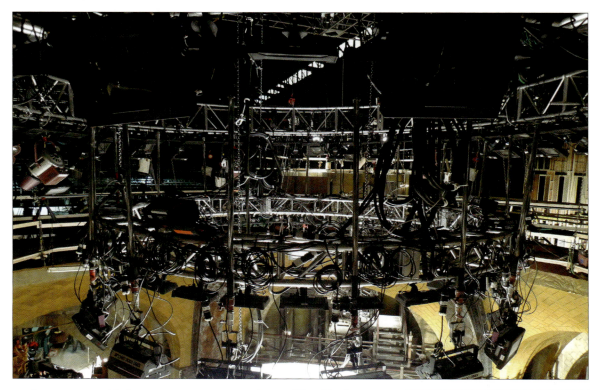

go from a very wide beam to a very narrow beam. The disadvantage of PARs is that the beam generally covers only a very small area and is not a very complimentary light for actors because it tends to be uneven and raw; nor is it easily controllable, but it is useful for many purposes that call for just raw light power.

PARs come in two basic varieties: film versions come in a solid rotatable housing such as Mole-Richardson's *MolePar* (Figure 8.12), which feature barn doors and scrim holders, and in a flimsier theatrical version called a PAR can. Theatrical lights are not generally as sturdily built because they are generally hung in a theater and then left alone. They don't get the rough treatment and adverse conditions that film and video lights do. PARs (especially the very concentrated NSP bulbs) can quickly burn through even the toughest gels, melt bead board, and set muslin diffusion on fire.

PARs with a *dichroic* coating have an output that is very close to daylight (blue) balance. Small PAR 48s and 36s are also available at lower voltages, as well as 110 volt. Nearly all types of bulbs are also available in 220 volts. As single units, they may be used in units such as the PARcan or MolePAR. PARcans are used extensively in concert lighting; they are lightweight and inexpensive. The MolePAR is more rugged and better suited to work on a film set.

PAR Groups

PARs are also made in groups, one of the best known being the *Maxi Brute*, a powerful unit with tremendous punch and throw. They are used in large night exteriors and in large-scale interior applications: aircraft hangars, arenas, and so on. They can also be used directly or through gel, muslin, and so on, when very high light levels are needed to get through heavy diffusion. All PARs generate very intense and concentrated heat; use caution when setting them up — they can crack windows and char wood and other materials.

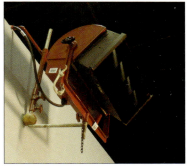

Figure 8.18. (above) A Mole-Richardson *2K Zip Softlight*. *Zip* means it is more compact than a regular softlight. It is mounted on a *set hanger* (also called *wall hanger*). 2K Zips are very popular for just this sort of use: they fit into small spaces and when put up near the ceiling of a set or location, they don't hang down so far that they interfere with the shot.

Figure 8.19. (top) A complex rig supporting a variety of lights. The middle ring holds 108 lights from LED units to strobes to Mole 5K tungsten Fresnels. Also hanging from this rig are space lights including one very large space light — see Figure 8.24. (Photo by Michael Gallart.)

Figure 8.20. A Mole-Richardson *6K HMI PAR* unit.

MaxiBrutes and *Dinos* are similar in design but different in size. Maxi's come in configurations of 6, 9, or 12 x PAR 64 lamps, the most common being the 9 lamp head. A *Dino* or *Moleeno* is 36 x PAR 64 lamps. Other variations of this design exist as well (Figure 8.14).

Fay lights are clusters of 650 watt PAR 36s and come in configurations up to 9 or 12 lamps. *Wendy lights,* developed by cinematographer David Watkin, come in large panels with the same PAR 36 lamps (usually DWE). Vittorio Storaro has also developed a series of lights that use 28 volt *ACL* bulbs (*Aircraft Landing Lights*).

All the bulbs on most multi-PARs are individually switchable, which makes for very simple intensity control. All PAR group lights allow for spot, medium, and flood bulbs to be interchanged for different coverages. The FAY bulbs are dichroic daylight bulbs; tungsten bulbs (FCX) can also be used. They can be used as daylight fill in place of HMIs. They are not exactly daylight balance but are very close to and can be corrected with gels if necessary.

Most people refer to any PAR 36 dichroic bulb as a FAY, but in fact there are several types. FAY is the ANSI code for a 650 watt PAR36 dichroic daylight bulb with ferrule contacts. If the bulb has screw terminals, it is an FBE/FGK. With diffusion these units can be used as a large-source soft light (Figure 8.17).

The Ruby

Multi-PAR units are an outstanding source of raw *firepower*. They provide a lot of output per watt that can be concentrated into a small area or flooded with some degree of precision. Multi-PAR units also tend to be less expensive to rent than large Fresnel lights.

Although with some units you can swivel the outside banks of lights inward or outward, it is not possible to truly *spot* them. The *Ruby Seven* solves this with a mechanism that tilts the outer ring in or out, moving on the axis of the center bulb (Figure 8.16).

HMI PARs

HMI PARs are available from 18K and 12K down to 1.2K, 575s, 200s, and even smaller. The larger units are extremely powerful. The smaller ones can be moved easily, where moving a scaffold and heavy light is a major operation. HMI PARs are different from tungsten units in that they have changeable lenses that can be added to make a narrow spot, a medium flood, wide flood, and an extra-wide flood. Every HMI PAR will come with its own set of lenses. As with tungsten PARs, the beam is oval and the separate lenses can be rotated to orient the pattern.

SOFT LIGHTS

Studio soft lights consist of one or more 1,000 watt or 1,500 watt bulbs directed into a *clamshell* white painted reflector that bounces light in a random pattern, making a light which is apparently as large as the front opening. They vary from the 1K studio soft (the Baby soft, also known as a 750 soft) up to the powerful *8K Studio Soft*, which has eight individually switchable bulbs.

All soft lights have certain basic problems: they are extremely inefficient in light output; they are bulky and hard to transport; and like all soft sources, they are difficult to control. While the large reflector does make the light "soft," the random bounce pattern makes the light still somewhat raw and unpleasant.

As a result of this rawness, some people put some diffusion over the soft light for any close-up work. Big *studio softs* through a large frame of 216 is a quick way to create a large soft source in the studio. Often

Figure 8.21. (top) *Barger Baglights* with Chimera softboxes in use on a hair product commercial. The reason there are so many lights is that they are dimmed up and down for different shots or when the model moves. Also, since this is a hair commercial, light coming from any directions makes for more reflections and sheen on the hair so it looks its best. This is a key advantage of tungsten lights: they can be controlled from a dimmer board. In comparison to a 5K with a Chimera, the Bargers have wider, more even throw and take up less real estate on the set.

Figure 8.22. (bottom) A reverse angle of the scene; DP Tom Denove is taking an incident reading at the model's position and using his other hand to shield the backlights from influencing the reading: this is correct procedure for taking an incident reading, which is the reading that determines what f/stop the lens will be set at. In most cases you don't want the backlight to influence that reading.

used with the studio is the *egg-crate*, which minimizes side spill and does make the beam a bit more controllable. Soft lights see most of their use in television studios where they provide a soft source without additional rigging. However, tungsten softlights in television news studios have been almost entirely replaced by Kino Flo units for one simple reason: to save on air conditioning costs. The color-correct fluorescent lights generate substantially less heat, which can be a real problem for studios, where they might be in use 24 hours a day. Since they are more or less permanently flown, their bulkiness is not a problem.

Small compact versions of the 2K and 1K soft lights are called zip lights (Figure 8.18). They have the same width but half the height of a soft light of similar wattage. Because of their compactness, zips are great for slipping into tight spaces.

Barger Baglights

Barger makes a type of softlight that is compact and efficient; it consists of several 1K tubular bulbs in a housing. It is always used with a *Chimera*, which is a self-contained softbox that fits on the front of the light. This has many advantages. Normally to make a light soft, it is necessary to put a diffusion frame in front of it; then to control the spill, several flags are needed. This means there might be as many

Figure 8.23. An extra-large *space light* (suspended from the same circular truss shown in Figure 8.20) in a lighting rig designed and executed by gaffer Michael Gallart and lighting director Tony Nako. (Photo courtesy of Michael Gallart.)

Figure 8.24. A *China ball* suspended from a C-stand. These are a cheap and extremely lightweight source of softlight and are easily rigged.

Figure 8.25. The *Softsun 100K* by Lightning Strikes, currently the most powerful light available.

as six stands. This becomes a real problem when you need to move the light quickly. A softbox such as a Chimera makes the entire unit fit on one stand. They are often used with a soft *eggcrate* on the front, which helps control the spill. Figures 8.21 and 8.22 show Barger Baglights in use on a commercial with DP Tom Denove. The reason there are so many lights on the shot is that the model is constantly in motion. Every light is on a dimmer, and they were constantly being dimmed up and down for different shots. The Fresnels were controlled by a dimmer board, but the Barger Baglights were controlled by turning switches on and off, which is a real advantage of the Barger. Each bulb inside has its own switch on the back of the unit, making intensity control quick and easy.

COLOR-CORRECT FLUORESCENTS

Color-correct fluorescent tubes have gained enormous popularity in recent years. Pioneered by the Kino Flo company, they are extremely lightweight, compact, and portable sources. Achieving a truly soft light can be difficult and time consuming. Whether it's done by bouncing off a large white surface or by punching big lights through heavy diffusion. Either way takes up a lot of room and calls for a lot of flagging to control it.

Kino Flos had their origin in 1987. While working on the film *Barfly*, DP Robby Mueller was shooting in a cramped interior that didn't leave much room for a conventional bounce or diffusion soft source. His gaffer Frieder Hochheim came up with an answer: they constructed high-frequency fluorescent lights. By using remote ballasts, the fixtures were maneuverable enough to be taped to walls, and mounted behind the bar. Kino Flos were born (Figure 8.27).

Unlike conventional fluorescent ballasts, which can be quite noisy, especially as they age, their ballasts were dead quiet and their light was flicker-free due to the higher than normal frequency. There are now several companies that make these types of lights, including Mole-Richardson. The ballasts are high-frequency, that eliminates the potential problem of flicker which is always present with fluorescent type sources. Second, the bulbs are truly color-correct. Colored bulbs are also available for various effects, as well as for greenscreen, bluescreen or redscreen. Kino makes a variety of extremely large rigs that can either frontlight or backlight an effects screen.

An added bonus of color-correct, high-frequency fluorescents is that they generate considerably less heat than either tungsten or HMI, which is a great advantage in small locations. For example, they are extremely popular in television newsrooms, which often have lights on 24 hours a day.

OTHER TYPES OF UNITS

Besides Fresnels, open face, LED, and fluorescent sources, there are a number of other kinds of lights that are commonly used for film and video lighting.

Softsun

Lightning Strikes makes the *Softsun* series of lights in a variety of sizes from 3.3K to an amazing 100K (Figure 8.25). SoftSuns require no warmup time. They achieve maximum power and proper color temperature the moment they are turned on. SoftSuns are also the only daylight color temperature light source that can be dimmed with minimal shift in color temperature.

Cycs, Strips, Nooks and Broads

When just plain output is needed, broad lights are strictly no-frills, utilitarian lights. They are just a box with a double-ended bulb. As simple as it is, the broad light has an important place in film history. In classical Hollywood hardlighting, the fill near the camera was generally a broad light with a diffuser. The distinctive feature of the broad light is its rectangular beam pattern, which makes blending them on a flat wall or cyc much easier: imagine how difficult if would to be smoothly combine the round, spotty beams of Mighties or Fresnel lights.

The smallest version of the broad is the *nook*, which, as its name implies, is designed for fitting into nooks and crannies. The nook light is a compact, raw-light unit, usually fitted with an FCM or FHM 1000 watt bulb. The nook is just a bulb holder with a reflector. Although barn doors are usually available, nooks aren't generally called on for much subtlety, but they are an efficient and versatile source for box light rigs, large silk overhead lights, and for large arrays to punch through frames.

A number of units are specifically designed for illuminating cycs and large backdrops. For the most part they are open face 1K and 1.5K units in small boxes; these are call cycs, cyc strips, or *Far Cycs* (which create a more even distribution up and down the background).

Chinese Lanterns and Spacelights

Chinese lanterns (*China balls*) are the ordinary paper globe lamps available at houseware stores (Figure 8.24). A socket is suspended inside that holds either a medium-base bulb (household, ECA, ECT, BBA, BCA, etc.) or a 1K or 2K bipost. Just about any rig is possible if the lantern is large enough to keep the paper a safe distance from the hot

Figure 8.26. Balloon lights require minimal rigging. The museum would have not permitted installation of a heavy-duty lighting grid above the Egyptian temple. In this setup, the balloons have black skirts, which contain and control the spill. (Photo courtesy of Sourcemaker.)

Figure 8.27. Color-correct fluo-rescents by Kino Flo. Their light weight makes rigging them easier and quicker. Notice how the large window at left rear has been *blacked out* with a large *solid* of black duvetyne. A pipe has been rigged to the ceiling to support some of the lights. Note also the *snoot boxes* on the two tungsten *zip lights*. (Photo courtesy of Kino Flo.)

bulb. Control is accomplished by painting the paper or taping gel or diffusion to it. Similar in principle are *spacelights* (Figure 8.23), which are basically big silk bags with 1, 2, 6, or 12 1K *nook lights* inside. For establishing an even overall base level on a set, they can be quite useful. When cabling, you will want to separate them into different circuits to give you some degree of control over the level. China balls are inexpensive and very easy to rig.

Self-Contained Crane Rigs

There are a number of units that consist of several large HMIs rigged on a crane (Figures 8.28 and 8.29). Most also carry their own genera-tor. Musco was the first of these, but now there are several to choose from. These units can provide workable illumination up to a half mile away and are used for moonlight effects and broad illumination of large areas. The main Musco unit comes with its own 1,000 amp generator, which is typical of this type of unit. The 6K heads are individually aimable by a handheld remote control.

Ellipsoidal Reflector Spots

The ellipsoidal reflector spot (ERS) is a theatrical light, but it is used as a small effects light because of its precise beam control by the blades. Called lekos in the theater, on a film set you will frequently hear them referred to as *Source Fours*. (*Source Fours* is manufactured by *Electronic Theater Controls* (ETC).)

Because the blades and gobo holder are located at the focal point of the lens, the beam can be focused sharply and patterned gobos can be inserted to give sharply detailed shadow effects. These lights come in a size defined by their beam angle. The longer the focal length, the narrower the beam. They also make a unit that has a zoom. Some ERS spots have a *gobo* slot that will hold a metal disk that will project a pattern. These patterns come in a vast array of designs.

Figure 8.28. (above) A Mini Musco in use at the Universal Studios *backlot*.

Figure 8.29. (right) A self-contained crane rig on Wall Street. (Photo by Michael Gallart.)

Balloon Lights

Balloon lights provide a powerful and flexible new tool for night exteriors (Figures 8.1 and 8.26). They can be either HMI or tungsten sources. They generate a soft, general fill light for large areas. Perhaps their greatest advantage is that they are much easier to hide than a crane or scaffolding. They are also faster to set up and to move. The disadvantage is that they can be very time consuming and expensive to gel. Wind is a factor when flying balloon lights. The smaller the balloon, the lower the acceptable wind speeds. A good reference is to observe flags: if they're flapping straight out, it's too windy. This introduces an element of uncertainty into their use. Larger balloon lights usually come with an operator.

Handheld Units

Portable handheld, battery-operated units are generally called sunguns. There are two basic types: tungsten and HMI. Tungsten sunguns are either 12 volt or 30 volt and powered from battery belts. Some are designed as sunguns, but some are 120 volt lights converted by changing the bulb and power cable. Typically, a tungsten sungun will run for about fifteen minutes. Sunguns with HMI bulbs are daylight balance and more efficient in output than tungsten units.

DAY EXTERIORS

Day exteriors can be approached in three ways: filling with large daylight balance units such as a *Brute Arc* or HMI, bouncing the existing light with reflectors, or covering the scene with a large silk to control the contrast. Sometimes it is some combination of several of these techniques (Figure 8.30.)

Controlling Light with Grip Equipment

Once you have a light working, you have to control it. As soon as you get beyond what can be done with the barn doors, it becomes the province of the grip department. Grip equipment is wide and varied, but in relation to lighting control it falls into three basic categories: reduction, shadow casting, and diffusion.

Reducing the amount of light without altering the quality is done with *nets*, which are frames covered with a netting material; the purpose is the same as a metal scrim on a light: it reduces intensity without changing the color or hard/soft quality of the light. Just as

Figures 8.30. A day exterior with *negative fill* (the black *12x12 solid* that creates a shadow side) and *shiny board* reflectors that are aimed through 4x4 frames with diffusion. The fill is an *8x8 frame* with *Ultrabounce*, a reflective material. This setup reverses the direction of the light source (the sun). The shiny boards are necessary in order to raise the level of the actors so that they are not significantly darker than the background, which would otherwise be seriously overexposed.

with metal scrims, a *single* (color coded green) reduces the light by one-half stop and a *double* (color coded red) reduces the light by a full stop. The same frames used for nets can be covered with white silk-like material that is a medium heavy diffusion. When they are covered with black *duvetyne,* they are *flags* or *cutters*, which can control spill, cast shadows, or block off flares from the lens. The same silk-like material or solid black duvetyne (a fire-resistant cloth) also comes in larger sizes for butterflies and overheads. These come in various sizes, denoted in feet: 4x4, 6x6, 8x8, 12x12, and 20x20. (Figure 8.30).

FOR MORE INFORMATION ON LIGHTING

Lighting is a vast subject; here we have room only to cover the basics. For more on lighting techniques, photometric data, grip equipment and methods, electrical distribution, bulbs, and scene lighting examples, see *Motion Picture and Video Lighting* by the same author, also published by Focal Press.

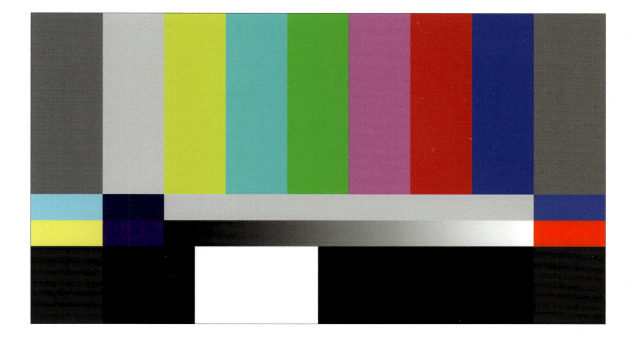

HD cinematography

HIGH DEF AND STANDARD DEF

Standard Def video (*SD*) is video as it has been since the invention of television. In the United States, this meant *NTSC* video (*National Television Standards Committee*) and in Europe, Asia, and many other areas, *PAL* (*Phase Alternating Line*). *Secam* is another format used in France and the former USSR. NTSC consists of 525 scan lines from top to bottom in each frame and approximately 30 frames per second. PAL is 625 lines per frame and 50 frames per second. Officially, NTSC is now being replaced as a broadcast standard in the United States, Mexico, and Canada by *ATSC* (*Advanced Television Standards Committee*).

Standard Def video will soon be part of history as it is gradually giving way to *High-definition* (*HD* or *High Def*) video that varies from 720 lines from top to bottom up to 1080 lines measured vertically as *lines*. These are display standards for television monitors. For shooting, some cameras now offer even higher resolutions (sometimes called *Super High Def*) and even though they have to be *down-converted* for viewing on a home TV or in a theater, they still result in better images. High Def video comes in many formats, including HDCAM, HDCAM-SR, DVCPRO HD, D5, XDCAM HD, HDV, AVCHD, and also 2K and 4K and others, which will be discussed in more detail later in this chapter.

ANALOG AND DIGITAL VIDEO

Digital cinematography is a form of video, but not all video is digital; before *digital video* there was *analog video*. Although it didn't make much of an impact at the time, there was even *analog High Def* video as far back as the late 70s. High Def did not really take off as a recording medium for professional production until it became *digital High Def*. Most of what we will discuss about video applies equally to Standard Def and High Def and other formats. SD video can be analog or digital. *Digital Video* is used in *DV, DVCam,* and *MiniDV*. *DigiBeta* is a very high-quality SD digital video format.

Analog

Although analog video is on its way out, a little history will help us understand how video works in the digital age. For most of the last 50 years since its invention, video was in analog form. Before computers were invented, even before things like transistors and integrated circuits, video was done with vacuum tubes, which understand *voltage* — variations in electrical potential. Except for the very beginning when it was mechanical, all early television/video was based on this principle.

Voltage from the video *sensor* (chip or tube) goes up and down in response to variations in brightness in the picture. If we look at a representation of the changes in voltage of a video signal, it looks like this: we measure it as going from zero (no voltage at all) representing pure black, up to .7 (700 millivolts — pure white). *Analog* means "something that represents something else." An example: the hands of a clock are not "time" — they are an *analog representation* of time. In analog video, we represent a picture as variations in voltage. It works, but there is a problem: every time you make a copy of an analog video, it gets worse. Just like when you make a photocopy, it is never as good as the original. There's another problem — computers can't work with analog, which means all those great things we can do with computers won't work on analog video.

Figure 9.1. High-definition *color bars,* used for camera and monitor testing and calibration.

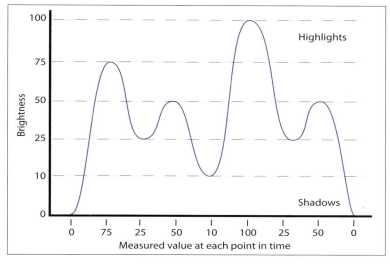

Figure 9.2. An analog signal is a variation in voltage over time.

Digital Video

A digital video signal is composed of a series of values that represent a stream of information that can be reproduced as an image. The conversion to digital video has wide-ranging implications, not only for image acquisition but for editing, image manipulation, storage, theater projection, and broadcast transmission as well.

What is digital? It means converting an image into a form that a computer can read: zeros and ones. As the image is projected by the lens onto the image plane, it is still fundamentally an analog image. If it's not one's and zeros, the computer simply can't understand it.

Figure 9.2 shows a typical video signal in analog form. Along the bottom axis, we *measure* the signal at regular intervals; every time we measure it, we get a specific value from 0 to 100. For the example in Figure 9.2, the values would be:

    0
    75
    25
    50
    10
    100 and so on.

It's easy to convert this to a binary form the computer can understand, which would be:

    0 = 0
    75 = 1001011
    25 = 11001
    50 = 110010
    10 = 1010
    100 = 1100100

For digital video, some form of an *analog-to-digital converter (ADC)* is part of the camera and outputs the digital signal. In its simplest form, an ADC reads the variations in voltage of a continuous analog signal and translates that into binary output. It does this by sampling the analog signal at regular time intervals, which is the *sampling rate*. The sampling rate or *sampling frequency* defines the number of samples per second taken from a continuous signal. It is normally measured in *hertz (Hz)*, which is *frequency* or *cycles-per-second*.

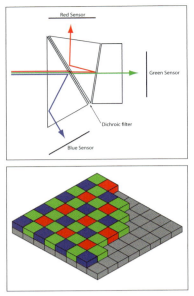

Figure 9.3. (top) The prism block of a 3-chip camera.

Figure 9.4. (above) A Bayer filter sensor, which is used in single-chip video design. Note that there are twice as many green pixels as their are blue or red pixels.

TYPES OF VIDEO SENSORS

Digital video requires something that serves the same function as film, which is, after all, just a medium that records and reproduces the patterns of light and dark that are focused on it by the lens. In digital video, electronic sensors perform this function.

Two types of video sensors are widely used: *CCD* (*Charge-Coupled Device*) and CMOS (*Complementary Metal Oxide Semiconductor*). Each type has its advantages and disadvantages. A CCD consists of a photo-voltaic region containing capacitors which convert light energy to an electrical charge. As with the silver based grains in motion picture film emulsion, a minimum number of photons are necessary to cause a change. Tiny lenses focus the light onto each of the millions of capacitors on the light sensing layer. CCDs are most often referred to my how many pixel elements (the capacitors) they have — measured in megapixels, or millions of pixels. This has become a shorthand for the quality of an image sensor, but there are other factors that determine image quality as well. CMOS sensors have the advantage of high noise immunity and relatively low power consumption.

Three-Chip vs Bayer Filter Sensors

There are two methods used to record the images: *three-chip* and *Bayer filters*. Increasingly, high-end pro digital HD cameras often use a single sensor (similar to digital still-photo cameras), with dimensions about the same size as a 35mm film frame or even larger. An image can be projected onto a single large sensor exactly the same way it can be projected onto a film frame, so cameras with this design can be made with *PL* (Arriflex type mount), *PV* (Panavision type mount), and similar systems of attaching lenses. This means that a large range of extremely high-quality motion picture lenses can now be used on these HD cameras.

In a single-chip design, clearly there has to be a way to record the three channels of color (red, green, blue). One way to do this is with a *Bayer filter*, which is an array, or mosaic, of color filters that sits on top of the video sensor. The pattern is G, R, G, B, which means that half of the filters are green, which is the dominant color in human perception. Using this method requires a process of *deBayering* and *demosaicing* before it begins to look like a useable image.

Since depth-of-field is largely dependent on the size of the frame at the image plane, the larger sensors also let these cameras achieve the same shallow depth of field as 35mm motion picture film cameras, which is important because many cinematographers consider selective focus an essential visual tool.

Three-Chip Design

Three-chip cameras typically use three 1/3-inch, 1/2-inch or 2/3-inch sensors in conjunction with a prism block that separates the incoming image into its primary colors, with a separate sensor capturing each color. Three-chip designs have advantages in terms of color reproduction, but they have optical design problems that make it difficult to use traditional prime lenses (although some specially designed prime lenses have been built for these cameras) and are incapable of achieving 35mm depth-of-field unless used with optical adaptors that permit the use of lenses designed for 35mm; however, these adapters result in a loss of image sharpness and a substantial loss of light.

DIGITAL VIDEO

Digital video exists in many forms: DigiBeta, DV, DVCam, DVCPro, HDV and MiniDV and the many varieties of High Def. These differ in methods of compression, recording formats, tape speed, and tape cassette size, but all are similar in that they take an analog signal from their video sensors and convert it to digital.

As with all things digital, the equipment available changes almost on a daily basis; as you decide what to use for your project, side-by-side comparisons will be most helpful. Naturally the producer will be most concerned about the cost/benefit ratio of the various formats and different HD cameras, which can vary widely in their rental prices. These are the producer's concerns, but it is your job as the cinematographer or director to make sure that the cost concerns are balanced with both the visual quality the system can produce and what its other capabilities are. Since HD technology is changing so rapidly, unless you are shooting with a camera you know well, a comparison test of the cameras you are considering is a good idea. Most camera rental facilities will be glad to arrange some testing time for you.

A downside of having such rapid progress in the quality and engineering of video camera formats is that cameras and other gear tend to become obsolete relatively soon. Some cinematographers own 16mm or 35mm cameras that are decades old but still take as good a picture as the day they were made: better even, as the film stocks constantly improve.

Many cameras offer interchangeable lenses, and the quality of video lenses is improving; many cameras also have mounts that will accommodate film-style lenses. The size and quality of the video sensor is also important, not only for image quality but for focus — the *smaller* the sensor the *greater* the depth-of-field (see the chapter *Optics*). At first glance this might seem like a good thing, but remember that depth-of-field is an important storytelling tool; too much depth-of-field restricts the possibility of using this important tool.

Standard Def

Standard Definition video can be recorded on several types of cameras: BetaCam, DigiBeta, DV, VHS, and so on (there are many). Some of these are analog and some are digital. There is no question but that the days of analog and standard def video are coming to an end: digital HD simply offers far too many advantages. DV (digital video) cameras, and DigiBeta (a high-end digital pro format) are SD video recorded digitally. Standard Def is 525 lines (in the NTSC system) or 625 lines (in the European-based PAL system), although not all lines are actually displayed on a typical monitor; some are outside the viewable area.

High Def

So what is High Def? Basically, HD is anything that is more than 525 lines/625 lines (NTSC or PAL). There is 720 HD, which is 720 lines in each frame. This can be 720P (progressive) or 720I (interlaced). In interlaced video, the lines of video are scanned on the monitor in an alternating fashion: first all of the odd lines and then all of the even lines. In progressive video, the video lines are written from top to bottom for each frame. Many HD cameras shoot 1080 lines, which can also be progressive or interlace. Most HD cameras can also shoot at 24FPS or 25FPS (Europe and elsewhere) for a more film-like look or 30FPS which has long been the video standard.

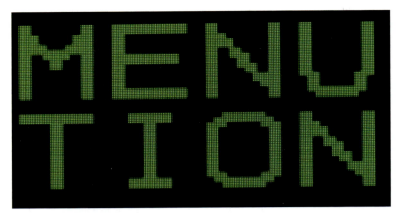

Figure 9.5. Pixels on a screen. They are enlarged here to see detail. The term *pixel* is derived from *picture element*. All digital imaging is based on pixels.

SHOOTING FORMATS

Digital formats are defined either by how many horizontal and vertical lines (or lines of pixels) they are composed of (such as 1080x1920 or 720x1280 — usually classified as 1080 or 720) or by their resolution as expressed in how many horizontal lines of pixels there are (such as 2K or 4K).

What's in a "K"?

2K and 4K capture are rapidly becoming the standard for HD acquisition in professional work. A 2K image is one that measures 2048 (2K or 2x1024) pixels across horizontally. A 4K image measures 4096 pixels across or 4x1024. By comparison, HDCam (a Sony format) is most frequently shot at 1080. 2K is slightly more resolution than 1080 and 4K is four times the resolution. The vertical measure of pixels may vary somewhat as not all frames or camera sensors share the same aspect ratio. "K" refers to kilo (one thousand) and 1024 is derived from binary code, the same as a kilobyte. A "K" is increments of 1024 pixels measured horizontally.

2K, 4K and Higher Resolution Formats

These types of video that offer higher resolution than the 1080 standard are referred to as *2K, 4K, 5K, 8K* and so on. Some people call these higher-resolution formats *Super High Def.* It is important to remember that this is a different way of describing a video format. 720 and 1080 refers to the number of video lines measured vertically. (This is described in more detail later in this chapter after we talk about formats.) For more detail on formats and aspect ratio, see the chapter *Professional Formats*. The term *format* can refer to either the type of camera (HD, DV, film, etc.) or the shape of the frame, which is *aspect ratio*; many HD video cameras can shoot in several different aspect ratios.

DIGITAL COMPRESSION

Digital cinema cameras are capable of generating extremely large amounts of data up to hundreds of megabytes per second. To help manage this huge data flow, nearly all cameras and the recording hardware designed to be used with them utilize some form of *compression*. *Prosumer* cameras typically use high compression to make the video files more compact for recording and storage. While this allows footage to be comfortably handled even on smaller, less powerful computers, the convenience comes at the expense of image quality. The software is also constantly improving in its ability to high resolutions.

Lossy and Lossless Compression

A *lossless* compression system is one that is capable of reducing the size of digital data in a way that allows the original data to be completely restored, byte for byte. This is done by removing redundant information. For example, if an area of the image is all pure white, where normally the digital code would be a long list of zeros, the compression might write a code that means "there is a row of 5000 zeros," which will use only a few bits of data instead of thousands. Much higher compression ratios (lower data rates) can be achieved with *lossy* compression. With lossy compression, information is discarded to create a simpler signal. These methods take into account the limits of human perception: they try to lose only information that won't be missed by the eye — at least that's the theory. Lossy compression may be invisible to the eye but can have a negative effect on post-production and later generations of duplication.

Chroma Subsampling

Many cameras use *chroma subsampling* as a basic form of compression. In this technology, the *luminance* (black-and-white brightness) is sampled at a different rate than the *chrominance* (color). It is based on the idea that a real RGB signal (such as you might get from gathering independent signals from the red, green, and blue sensors in a three-chip camera), contains redundant information: in essence, each of the channels contains a duplicate black-and-white image. An RGB signal has potentially the richest color depth and highest resolution, but requires enormous bandwidth and processing power.

With chroma subsampling, there might be twice as many samples of the luminance as for the chrominance. This would be expressed as 4:2:2, where the first digit is the luminance channel and the next two digits are the chroma channels — they are sampled at half the rate of the luminance channel. Video that is 4:4:4, has the same chroma sampling for color channels as for luminance. There are other variations — for example, Sony's HDCam cameras sample at 3:1:1. You may occasionally see a fourth digit, such as 4:4:4:4; in this case the fourth number is the alpha channel, which contains transparency information.

Because the human visual system is much more sensitive to luminance than to color, lower-resolution color information can be overlaid with higher-resolution luma (brightness) information, to create an image that looks very similar to one in which both color and luma information are sampled at full resolution.

MPEG and JPEG

Other types of compression are *MPEG* and *JPEG*. MPEG stands for *Motion Picture Experts Group*, and JPEG is an acronym for *Joint Photographic Experts Group*. Various forms of MPEG are used for both video and audio. Both MPEG and JPEG are types of *codecs*: which means *compressor—decompressor*.

Some compression systems compress footage one frame at a time, interpreting the video as a series of still frames; this is called *intraframe* compression. *Interframe* compression systems can further compress data by eliminating redundancy between frames. This leads to higher compression ratios, but can sometimes put a bigger processing load on the editing system. As with HD cameras, codecs and editing software and hardware are constantly improving. It is usually possible to *transcode* older formats into whatever codec you want, but there is almost always some loss of quality in the process.

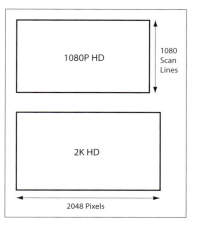

Figure 9.6. Different methods for defining the resolution of an HD format. Resolutions such as 720 or 1080 refers to the number if scan lines measured *vertically*. 2K and 4K refer to the number of pixels measured *horizontally*. In this case a 2K frame is 2048 pixels across.

RAW

With most HD cameras and recording systems, the scene information is compressed and is processed by the camera electronics according to choices made by the cinematographer, and these choices are *baked in* — they cannot be changed later. Cameras that record in the *RAW* format do minimal processing to the image: they record the raw data that came out of the video sensors. RAW images are also produced by many digital still cameras and are considered superior because they are not compressed, which can reduce quality. The kinds of choices the cinematographer can make are described later in this chapter.

Digital Negative

Think of RAW as a *digital negative*. What does this change? The basic idea of RAW is to simply record all of the data that comes off the sensors, essentially unchanged. *Metadata* is recorded at the same time; this is a file "about" the image, such as any camera settings, and so on.

RAW image files can in essence fill the same role as film negatives in traditional film-based photography: that is, the negative is not directly usable as an image, but has all of the information needed to create a final, viewable image. The process of converting a RAW image file into a viewable format is sometimes called *developing* the image, in that it is analogous with the motion picture film process that converts exposed negative film into a projectable print.

Like a traditional negative, a RAW digital image may have a wider *dynamic range* (latitude) or wider color *gamut* than the eventual final image format can show. Gamut defines the limits of color reproduction in a particular colorspace. The selection of the final choice of image rendering is part of the process of white balancing and color grading, which is exactly the same as making two very different *looks* by printing differently from the same negative. RAW images have high image quality, finer control of parameters, and 12 or 14 *bits* of information recorded for each pixel.

With a motion picture negative, you can always go back to the original. If you shot the negative right to begin with, you can do anything you want with it, now or in the future. If five years from now, you decide you want to make the look of the film entirely different, you can. You can do the same with RAW; it is archival and non-destructive, and you can manipulate the image later.

There are many types of RAW files — different camera companies use variations on the idea. RAW files must be interpreted and processed before they can be edited or viewed. The software used to do this depends on which camera they were shot with. Also, RAW files shot with a Bayer-filter camera must be *demosaiced* (the mosaic pattern imposed on the image by the Bayer filter must be interpreted), but this is a standard part of the processing that converts the RAW images to more universal JPEG or TIFF files.

Bitrate

Video compression systems are often characterized by their *bitrates*. *Bitrate* describes how much data (computer bits) is required to represent one second of media. One cannot directly use bitrate as a measure of quality, because different compression algorithms perform differently. More advanced compression algorithms at a lower bitrate may deliver the same quality as a less advanced algorithm at a higher bitrate. Bitrate is especially important when you get to output for DVDs or Internet delivery, which may have limits on how much bitrate they can handle.

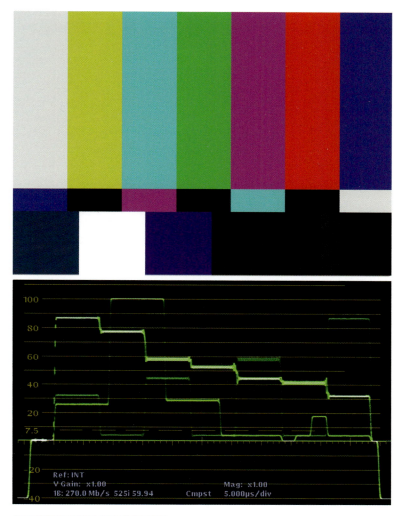

Figure 9.7. (top) SMPTE 75% color bars as they are seen on a video monitor. The primary and secondary colors are arranged in order of brightness. On the far left top is a 75% gray patch. In the bottom row, second patch from the right is a 100% white patch. (bottom) The color bars as seen on a *waveform monitor,* which measures the voltage of the video signal. Also on the lower row at the right on the color bars is the PLUGE, which can be clearly seen on the waveform signal.

MONITORING ON THE SET

When shooting digitally, recorded scenes can be played back instantly, either by rolling back the tape or, in a file-based system (video recorded on hard drives or flash memory), selecting individual takes — in a file-based system, every take is an individual data file and can be accessed randomly.

This means a cinematographer can have a much better understanding how the final image will look. This assumes that there is a good-quality monitor on the set, that its viewing conditions are good (all excess light screened off), and ideally, the cinematographer has access to a waveform monitor/vectorscope (discussed in the next section). In some cases, a separate *DIT* (*Digital Imaging Technician*) monitors the signal with the waveform/vectorscope and a high quality monitor. The DIT works with the cinematographer to control the image.

With a properly calibrated high-definition display, on the set monitoring, in conjunction with data displays such as histograms, waveforms, RGB parades, and various types of focus assist, can give the cinematographer a far more accurate picture of what is being captured. However, all of this equipment may not be possible in shooting situations. It is critical that a working cinematographer be able to work without monitors and other displays.

Figure 9.8. SMPTE 75% color bars as displayed on the *vectorscope*. As a check on system alignment, each primary and secondary color is placed in boxes. If they are not in their boxes, then something is wrong.

The vectorscope is really just the color wheel (see Figure 12.1 in the chapter *Color*) represented electronically: around the circle is hue and how far away from the center is chroma saturation. If the camera is photographing a black-and-white scene (zero saturation), then the vectorscope will display only a dot in the center.

THE WAVEFORM MONITOR AND VECTORSCOPE

To see the various elements of the video signal, two special test oscilloscopes are used: the *waveform monitor* and the *vectorscope* (Figures 9.7 and 9.8). Usually combined into one unit, these tools are invaluable; it is essential to understand what they are telling you. On a video shoot, the waveform monitor is your light meter and the vectorscope is your color meter. Color monitors, even sophisticated ones, can be unreliable, but information for the waveform and vectorscope can almost always be trusted.

Waveform Monitors

The waveform monitor displays the luminance video signal information. It allows you to analyze the information from an entire frame or from just one line of video. The waveform monitor displays the signal on a scale seen in Figure 9.7. The scale is from zero to one hundred or in milivots. It can be measured in *IRE* units (*International Radio Engineers*) or as percentage, which is generally used in HD video. The waveform is merely measuring the voltage of each part of the video picture: voltage represents the brightness of the image.

Zero represents pure black, and one hundred represents pure white. It is possible for the video signal to go below zero or above one hundred, but the final image will still only show pure black at zero and one hundred will still be pure white.

The Vectorscope

Used in conjunction with the waveform monitor, the vectorscope measures the *chrominance* (color) of the video signal (Figure 9.8). The scale of the vectorscope is a circle overlaid with the color *amplitude* and *phase* relationship of the three primary colors (red, green, and blue). The vectorscope displays color information only; there is no information about exposure — although you can see the effects of over or under exposure in how they affect color saturation.

The vectorscope screen for calibration shows a display of a SMPTE color bars test signal with all of the dots in their boxes and the color burst correctly placed on the horizontal axis. Chroma phase error translates as "the color is off," as shown in Figure 9.9. Notice how color is conceptualized as a circle and we rotate the circle around its center to adjust the hue (phase). How far it is from the center indicated chroma saturation. At zero saturation (black-and-white) the display is just a dot in the center.

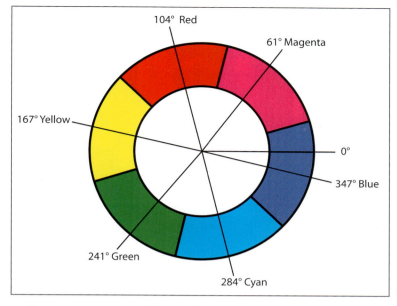

104° Red
61° Magenta
167° Yellow
0°
347° Blue
241° Green
284° Cyan

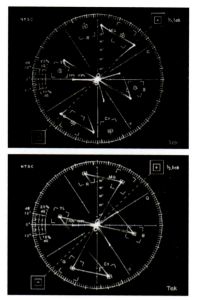

Figure 9.9. (top) *Hue* (*phase*) error; notice how the color is shifted clockwise — the dots indicating the key hues are not in their proper boxes. (Photo courtesy of Tektronix.)

Figure 9.10. (middle) Vectorscope showing correct *phase*. The dots are in their boxes and also are not too far from or too near the center, indicating correct levels of *chroma*. (Photo courtesy of Tektronix.)

Figure 9.11. (above, left)The position of primary and secondary colors on the vectorscope. As you can see, it is the color wheel. Video phase (hue) is represented as measured in degrees around the circle, starting at the three o'clock position.

All vectorscope graticules are designed to work with a color bars signal. Remember, the color bars signal consists of brightness information (luminance) and color information (chrominance or chroma). Each bar of the color bars signal creates a dot on the vectorscope's display (it's a dot because they are pure colors). The position of these dots relative to the boxes, or targets, on the graticule and the phase are the major indicators of the color signal.

Proper white balance of a video camera is indicated by dot centered on the vectorscope display when the target or signal being displayed is a white or neutral gray object. If the camera white balance is off, the spot will be shifted off-center.

VIDEO LATITUDE

Video, whether standard def or high def, has historically had a problem with latitude (dynamic range). The sensors in most high-end digital video cameras have had considerably less exposure latitude than modern motion picture film stocks. They tend to "blow out" highlights, losing detail in brightest parts of the image (Figure 9.13). If highlight detail is lost, it is impossible to recapture in post-production. Cinematographers can learn how to adjust for this type of response using techniques similar to those used when shooting on *reversal* (transparency/positive) film, which has a limited latitude especially in the highlights. For this reason, highlights are frequently a problem in HD, because digital sensors inevitably *clip* them very sharply (Figure 9.13), whereas film produces a softer roll-off effect in the brighter areas of the image. Camera companies have made great strides in giving video more latitude, and they continue to improve.

Many cameras incorporate a *knee function* in their controls, and it is essential that you understand what it does and how to use it. The *knee* region (called the *shoulder* in film, as discussed in the chapter *Exposure*) represents the *highlight* areas. The knee function allows you to control how these brighter areas are handled in image processing. It is imperative that you learn how to operate the knee function on any video camera you use. Use of the knee control on HD cameras is discussed later in this chapter. One advantage of digital imaging is that these cameras tend to have excellent low-light response and

Figure 9.12 (left) Normal exposure on an HD camera. Below it is the same frame on a waveform monitor. Notice the proper skin tones, the correct color saturation in the chart, and how all segments are shown on the gray scale. These images are from a latitude test on an HD camera.

Figure 9.13. (right) At just two stops overexposed, the skin tone is blown out, the color saturation is severely reduced and there is no *separation* visible in the lighter tones on the gray scale. *Clipping of the highlights* appears on the waveform monitor as a flatline at the top of the signal. This is at only plus two stops of exposure and already it has exceeded the *latitude (dynamic range)* of the HD camera.

can really *see* into the shadows. This also tends to bring out shadow detail, which can give the impression that they are far more sensitive to light (i.e., they have a higher ISO) than they really do. This can sometimes lead a cinematographer to be daring and shoot scenes in extraordinarily low lighting levels. Sometimes it works and sometimes it doesn't; the results can sometimes be unacceptably noisy, especially if *gain* is used. Gain boosts image brightness by adding voltage to the signal, which also adds *video noise*. Beware, this noise may not always be visible on a preview monitor, or you may see it but deem it acceptable, only to be disappointed when you see it on a larger monitor.

Clipping

An important aspect of video latitude is *clipping*, which is what happens when the brightness of an object in the scene exceeds the maximum brightness level the camera is capable of. *Clipped highlights* show as a flat line on the waveform monitor (Figures 9.13 and 9.33). In general, clipping is to be avoided at all costs; once the signal flatlines at the top, there is no information at all; it is just dead flat white, no detail, no separation. Nothing can be done to fix it; the complete lack of information makes saving it impossible; it can never be anything other than dead flat white or featureless gray. This is one of the major differences between how film and video respond to highlights. Film has the ability to gently "roll off" the overexposed highlights. One of the most important uses of the waveform monitor on the set is to watch for instances of clipping due to overexposure.

Video Noise and Grain

Motion picture film has a characteristic grain structure (although modern, low-speed film stocks are remarkably low in grain). Some filmmakers add artificial grain to their HD projects, to match intercut film footage or to make it look old or just to create a "look." Digitally recorded footage does not have a characteristic grain structure but it can have video noise (especially if the gain is turned up) which looks different. If you want your scene to have the look of film grain, it is better to add it in post rather than trying to convince yourself that video noise looks like film grain.

Color Bars and Test Charts

There are several types of reference color bars. In High Def especially, there are many different types. On the waveform monitor NTSC SMPTE color bars appear as in Figure 9.7. There are many types of color bars, some different ones are shown at the beginning of this chapter in Figure 9.1. Color bars are used for monitor adjustment and for camera testing and adjustment. For monitor adjustment, they are electronically generated by the camera and are recorded at the beginning of every tape; for camera adjustment they are a physical test chart that is photographed by the camera. These test charts need to be very precise, and the best of them can cost a thousand dollars or more. These test charts are used for testing for adjusting the camera in the field. Proper setup of the test chart is critical. It should be evenly illuminated with no glare. The standard method is to use two lights at 45°.

THE DIGITAL INTERMEDIATE (DI)

Digital Intermediates are a way of combining the best of both worlds. Although it is a part of shooting on motion picture film, it is discussed here because it involves all of the image controls that are covered in this chapter: the DI is way of utilizing the digital techniques and computer magic that are an inherent part of digital High Def. When using a DI, you shoot on film, then do your post-production and image manipulation in the digital world, with all the amazing options we have in that realm, and then you produce a film print that can be shown almost anywhere in the world. Although it is rapidly changing, the world has long been standardized on projecting 35mm film. Theaters with 35mm projectors are found in every nation. A movie printed on film in London can be projected in Kyoto or Karachi without any adaptation or special equipment.

For films that do employ the DI process, there is a crucial choice: whether to do image manipulation *in the camera* or *in post*. However, for overall color cast and altering the contrast of scene, it probably makes sense to do these in post as doing them on the set can be costly and time consuming.

The first film to use DI was *O Brother, Where Art Thou* shot by Roger Deakins (see Figure 1.14). He knew he wanted a particular look for the film: a desaturated sepia-toned look. The film was shot in Alabama in the summer, meaning that the vegetation was bright green. Deakins experimented with a variety of methods to get the look he wanted — none of which produced the results he wanted. He found that a digital intermediate allowed him to create exactly the look he was going for.

THE VIDEO SIGNAL

Even if you shoot mostly on film, it is essential to know the basics of video. Today, nearly all editing and most postproduction are done in video, even for projects shot on film, and we can envision a time in the near future when virtually 100% of it will be.

No matter how well designed and goofproof a piece of video equipment is, it is still not a matter of *point and shoot*. Even if certain systems are automated, this automation may have unwanted consequences down the line. To understand video, it is necessary to have an overview of the history of the basic video signal. Black-and-white television broadcasts began in 1936 in Britain and in 1939 in the United States television had a 4:3 aspect ratio. This matched the standard film projection frame of the time.

Interlace Video

In standard-def TV, this electron beam scans 525 lines (in the North American system). Standard-def video is usually *interlaced* (Figure 9.14). The odd-numbered lines are a *field* and the even-numbered lines are a field. This means that every frame of interlace video consists of two fields. Interlace video is not nearly as common as it once was, as most modern equipment is *progressive*.

Progressive Video

Most of the time you will be shooting *progressive*. In progressive video, the beam starts at the top and scans down line by line (1,2, 3, 4, and so on). Progressive has higher vertical resolution than interlace, but the main reason we use it is that it looks more *film-like*. Dramatic narrative productions (films with a story and actors) are usually shot *24P*, meaning that it is progressive video at 24 frames per second; 24 frames per second being the frame rate of film cameras.

NTSC and ATSC

NTSC is the standard-def television system used in the United States and some other countries almost since the beginning of television. It stands for National Television Standards Committee. It is now being replaced by High Def digital television.

In NTSC, each frame is made up of 481 horizontal lines that are visible, plus another 44 lines that are *blanked*. These lines are blanked because they occur while the scanner beam is traveling back up to the starting point at the top left of the screen. This makes a total of 525 lines for each video frame.

ATSC (Advanced Television Standards Committee) is the standard for digital High Def television wide screen 16:9 images up to 1920×1080 pixels in size — six times the display resolution of NTSC However, aspect ratios other than 16x9 are also supported.

Figure 9.14. Interlaced video consists of two sets of alternating scan lines. Each set of scan lines is called a video "field."

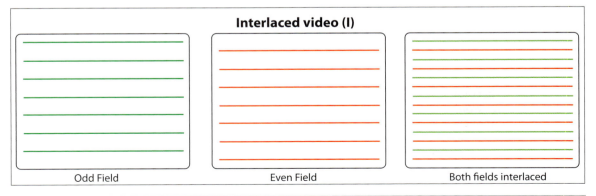

Interlaced video (I)

Odd Field · Even Field · Both fields interlaced

Figure 9.15. Component outputs on the camera: Y, Pr, Pb.

Colorspace

Cameras can render the colors of a scene differently. One of the primary factors is the *colorspace* being used. Colorspace is a video standard that defines how the colors will be handled — different colorspaces render the colors of a scene slightly differently. Some cameras are capable of using any one of a number of different colorspace configurations; these can be selected in the camera menus. There is no agreed upon standard, but *Rec 709* (a colorspace defined by SMPTE) is frequently used in HD.

Measuring Color Space on the Vectorscope

There are many different colorspace systems and notations used to derive and define color video, as we discussed earlier in this chapter. Figures 9.22 and 9.23 show the same test chart in two different colorspaces. You can see how a different colorspace changes color rendition of the image.

Color Difference Signals: B-Y and R-Y

Processing all information as R, G, B is inefficient because each separate channel contains both color information and grayscale (luminance) information, which is redundant. As we recall from the chapter on color, black-and-white (grayscale) actually conveys the great majority of information about an image. Engineers realized that there was no need to repeat the black-and-white information for every channel. For this reason, most video systems distill the chroma information into color difference signals. Luminance is notated as Y, since B already stands for blue.

There are many systems in use, but basically, color difference is derived by taking the blue component and subtracting the luminance (grayscale) information: B-Y (blue minus luminance) and for the red channel, luminance is subtracted from red: R-Y. This is called *component* video. This is abbreviated in various ways; on the camera in Figure 9.15, it is Y, P_B, P_R.

Encoded Color

One characteristic of human vision is we can't see fine detail nearly as well for changes in color as we can for changes in luminance. In other words, the picture won't suffer very much if we reduce the *bandwidth* of the color components, provided we can maintain essentially full bandwidth of the luminance signal (bandwidth is the rate of information flow). Even a full bandwidth luminance signal doesn't have very much energy in the upper end of its spectrum; the higher-frequency signals are quite a bit lower amplitude almost all the time.

HD cinematography

Figure 9.16. *HD SDI* outputs, as well as composite, timecode, and other connections on a Miranda *downconverter*.

SDI

SDI stands for *Serial Digital Interface* and is becoming the standard for HD camera output (*HD SDI*). There is also standard-def SDI (*SD SDI*). Where component video employs three cables, SDI runs on a single *BNC* cable.

Component video is analog, but SDI is digital. It also contains digitally encoded audio, timecode, and ancillary data such as embedded audio, closed captions, and other sorts of metadata. Some systems employ *dual link* SDI, which doubles the data flow.

SETTING UP A COLOR MONITOR

The most important thing you can learn about video is how to properly set up a color monitor. Even with other equipment such as a waveform monitor and vectorscope on hand, the monitor is still a crucial part of previewing and judging the picture. As we'll see in the chapter *Color*, there is no exact correlation between the mathematical representation of color and the human perception of it.

Color bars are an artificial electronic pattern produced by a signal generator, which may be in a video camera (most professional video cameras have a *bars* setting) or a separate piece of equipment on the set or as a standard piece of equipment in any video post-production facility, be it telecine, editing, or duplication. Color bars are recorded at the head of every videotape to provide a consistent reference in postproduction. They are also used for matching the output of two cameras in a multicamera shoot and to set up a video monitor. On top on the left is a gray bar: it is 80 IRE units.

Monitor Setup Procedure

To set up a monitor, start with the following steps:

- Allow the monitor to warm up.
- Shield the monitor from extraneous light. (Viewing conditions are always important with monitors).
- Turn on color bars on the camera.
- Set the contrast to its midpoint.
- Turn the chroma (color saturation) all the way down until the color bars are shades of black-and-white. Now you are ready to adjust the brightness with the PLUGE.

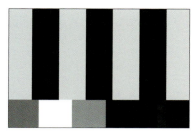

Figure 9.17. Blue-only color bars shown in black-and-white for clarity. Notice that the bands are of equal intensity, and in the upper portion the large and small bars are equally gray or black. This indicates correct phase and saturation.

Figure 9.18. Incorrect luminance; notice how all three of the PLUGE bars in the lower right are visible.

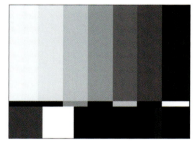

Figure 9.19. Correct monitor setup, shown here in black-and-white.

Figure 9.20. (above, left) SMPTE 75% color bars. See also Figure 9.1 on the opening page of this chapter. It is typical of the kind of color bars that will be generated by many high-end HD cameras. 75% refers to color saturation; this is considered to be more reliable to measure than 100% saturation, but 100% color bars do exist and you need to be sure what type you are working with.

The PLUGE

Notice the three narrow bars labeled 3.5, 7.5, and 11.5 on the bottom right (Figure 9.17). These are the *PLUGE*, which stands for *Picture Lineup Generating Equipment*. The PLUGE was developed at the BBC in London. It was generated at a central location in their facility and sent by wire to each studio. This way all of the equipment could be calibrated conveniently and consistently. This was the PLUGE alone, not combined with the color bars.

The middle black bar is set at 7.5 IRE, (or in the digital realm, 16, 16, 16). The first bar on the left, *superblack*, is set at about 2.5 IRE below black, and the third bar, dark gray, is set at 3.5 IRE above black. None of these really work to adjust a monitor to properly display 0 IRE black, so the following procedure is standard. Learning to calibrate a monitor is an essential skill.

- Adjust the brightness control until the middle (7.5 units) PLUGE bar is not quite visible. The lightest bar on the right (11.5 units) should be barely visible. If it's not visible, turn the brightness up until it becomes visible.

- Since 7.5 units is as dark as video gets, you should not see any difference between the left bar (3.5 units) and the middle bar (7.5 units). There should be no dividing line between these two bars. The only division you should see is between 11.5 and 7.5. This same technique is used in setting the black-and-white viewfinder on a video camera.

- The next step is to set the contrast control for a proper white level. To do so, turn the contrast all the way up. The white (100 unit) bar will bloom and flare. Now turn the contrast down until this white bar just begins to respond.

Adjusting Color

It is possible to *eyeball* the yellow and magenta. This is the down and dirty method and should only be used if other methods are not practical. The yellow should be a lemon yellow without orange or green. And the magenta should not be red or purple. This quickie method is not recommended except in emergencies; it is much better to do it the professional way. If you do eyeball a monitor, don't put too much faith in it for color reference or brightness. Monitors vary widely in color reproduction, especially in less than ideal viewing conditions on location.

Blue-Only Adjustment

Professional monitors have a blue-only switch. This turns off the red and green, leaving only the blue (Figure 9.17). If your monitor does not have a blue-only switch, you can use a piece of blue gel (full CTB) or a Kodak Wratten #47. View the monitor through the gel. If you see any of the red, green, or yellow colors, double the blue gel over to increase the blue effect.

By using the blue-only switch or a piece of blue gel, you have removed the red and green elements of the picture. Only the blue remains. If the hue is correct, you should see alternating bars of equal intensity.

- With the blue switch on (or your blue gel in front of your eye) turn the chroma or color until the gray bar at the far left and the blue bar at the far right are of equal brightness. You can also match either the gray or blue bars with their sub-bars.
- Adjust the hue control until the cyan and magenta bars are also of equal brightness. You can also match either of them with their sub-bars. Now the four bars — gray, blue, cyan, and magenta, should be of equal intensity. The yellow, green and red should be completely black. See Figures 9.17 through 9.19 for monitor views of this procedure.

Once you have set up your monitor, leave it alone until you move to another location or viewing conditions change. Unless you have a waveform and vectorscope, it's the only instrument you have to see how accurate your video is.

CAMERA WHITE BALANCE

Just as we use film stocks of different color balance and camera filtration to adjust film shooting to different color conditions (daylight or tungsten), in video, the white balance function compensates for variations in the color range of the source lighting. White balance is accomplished by aiming the camera at a color neutral surface and selecting the white balance function on the camera. The internal electronics compensate for variations in color. Naturally, it is essential that the light illuminating the white card be the same as is in the scene, just as the light on a gray reference card in film must be the same as is on the scene. This means just the lighting, not any use of color gels for effect. If you are lighting the scene with tungsten lights and plan to use green gels on the lights, you will use a pure tungsten light for the color balance. If you color balance with the green gels on the lights, the camera will remove the green.

Some people use a piece of white paper as a neutral reference, but this is not reliable. "White" paper can vary widely in color. More reliable is a standardized photo gray card or a white card made specially for this process. Using a white wall or a piece of paper to white balance should be for emergencies only — it is approximate at best.

If you are using filters on the camera to alter the color, this must be removed for white balance or their effect will be erased by the white balance. The white balance can also be used to *fool* the camera. For example, if you want the overall color balance to be warm in tone, you can put a cooling filter (blue) over the lens while doing color balance. The circuitry will compensate and when you remove the filter over the lens, the image will then be warm. Special tools are made for this purpose; the most commonly available are called *warm cards*. These are cards that are slightly blue in varying degrees and thus cause the camera to correct the picture to slightly warm. An example of incorrect color balance is shown in Figure 9.43.

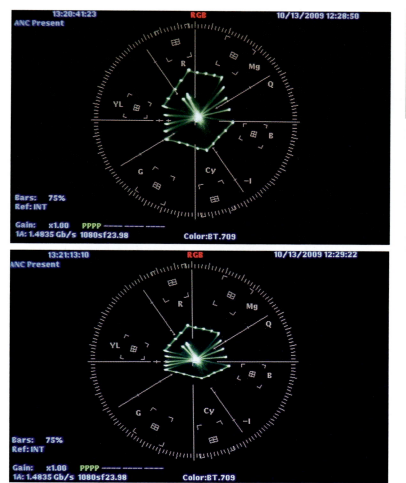

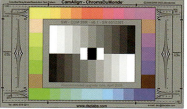

13:20:41:23 RGB 10/13/2009 12:28:50
ANC Present

Bars: 75%
Ref: INT
Gain: x1.00 PPPP ---- ---- ----
1A: 1.4835 Gb/s 1080sf23.98 Color:BT.709

Figure 9.21. (above) The Chroma du Monde test chart from DSC labs: an 11 stop gray scale surrounded by color patches of the primary and secondary colors.

Figure 9.22. (left, top) The Chroma du Monde on the vectorscope in Rec 709 color space.

Figure 9.23. (left, bottom) The same chart rendered in a different color space — in this case, NTSC.

Analog/Digital Conversion

Conversion of the video signal from analog to digital occurs in three parts; signal preparation, sampling, and quantization (digitizing). There are two types of component signals; Red, Green, and Blue (RGB), and Y, R-Y, B-Y, but it is the latter that is by far the most widely used in digital video. R-Y and B-Y, the color difference signals, carry the color information, while Y represents the luminance. Cameras, telecine, and so on, generally produce RGB signals at the sensors, but it is almost always converted to another format before output because an RGB signal is far too much information for recording.

DIGITAL VIDEO ENCODING

Digital video is fundamentally different from NTSC and PAL video in the way it is encoded and processed. Various types of processing equipment manage the digital video in different ways. These are classified by the way in which they encode the information.

4:2:2

This is a set of frequencies in the ratio 4:2:2, used to digitize the luminance and color difference components (Y, R-Y, B-Y) of a video signal. For every four luminance digital samples, there are two digital samples of each color difference channel. The human eye is not as sensitive to color as to luminance detail, enabling this form of compression. RGB video is usually represented with an equal number of bits for each of the three color component channels, but RGB is not normally transmitted and bandwidth is not as big a factor when dealing with a connection between the computer and display device.

The four represents 13.5 MHz, the sampling frequency of the Y channel, and the twos each 6.75 MHz for both the R-Y, B-Y channels. D-1, D-5, Digital Betacam, and most digital disk recorders use 4:2:2 digitizing.

4:1:1

This is a set of frequencies in the ratio 4:1:1, that is used to digitize the luminance and color difference components (Y, R-Y, B-Y) of a video signal. The 4 represents 13.5 MHz, the sampling frequency of the Y (luminance) channel, and the 1s each represent 3.75 MHz for the R-Y and B-Y chrominance channels.

4:2:0

This is a set of frequencies in the ratio 4:2:0, that is used to digitize the luminance and color difference components (Y, R-Y, B-Y) of a video signal. 4:2:0 is used in PAL DV and DVCam, DVDs and a few other formats. The 4 represents 13.5 MHz, the sampling frequency of the Y channel, while both the R-Y and B-Y are sampled at 6.75 MHz. In 4:2:0, 3/4 of the chrominance values have been deleted.

YUV

YUV is another way of indicating chroma subsampling. Y is still luminance; U and V are the chrominance channels. YUV = four Y samples, four U samples, and four V samples per unit of time.

IS IT BROADCAST QUALITY?

Broadcast quality is a term that frequently gets misused. It does not mean, as many people think, a "good-quality" picture or merely a certain level of resolution. Broadcast quality is actually a complex set of technical standards for the timing, synchronization, and levels of the video signal. It is something that can only be measured with sophisticated test equipment. It is largely the province of video engineers, but it is important to understand the concept, particulary as it is used to refer to cameras.

DO IT IN THE CAMERA OR IN POST?

One question that comes up frequently in digital shooting is, "should we fix the look in the camera or shoot it 'straight' and fix it in post?" Some people take a traditional purist approach and insist on doing everything in the camera. In HD, this is referred to as being "baked in," meaning that alterations to the video signal (such as color balance, gamma, knee compression, and so on) are recorded and may be difficult to change later on. That is a fine approach, but it ignores the incredible tools that are available for image manipulation in post production. Sometimes cinematographers feel that the only way that can retain control of the image is to do everything in camera, but increasingly, it is important to be involved in the post process as well.

When shooting in the RAW format, however, nothing is actually baked in and all final decisions are always still possible in postproduction. What can be altered is the *LUT* (Look Up Table)used for viewing; this LUT can also be used to serve as a guide in postproduction. See the chapter *Image Control* for more on LUTs.

The Decision Matrix

Here's an organized way to think about the problem:

- Do you have the proper tools to do a "look" on the set? A high-quality monitor is absolutely essential, and a waveform monitor and vectorscope are necessary if you are doing anything extreme, particularly with gamma or exposure.
- Are you and the director solidly in agreement on the look you are going for and you're sure it's the approach you want to take? Especially important for any extreme look that you may later want to back off from.
- Are you, the DP, going to have access to the postproduction process and are you sure your views will be listened to?

In some cases it is better to do it on the set so there are no surprises later. This ensures that your lighting and exposure (and maybe the director's choice of shots) will fit in with the look you are creating. Otherwise, if you are seeing a "plain vanilla" image on the monitor, you are taking a risk that some things may not be lit or exposed properly for the look you plan to do later.

The 50% Rule

Some DPs use the *50% Rule* and take any look half the way there on the set, the rest of the way in post. This is especially important if you are doing something in the camera that may cause problems later on. One example is very high color saturation. This may exceed the gamut limits and may also introduce excessive noise into the image.

By going to 50% of the look, you keep your options open should you want take it back to a less radical image in post or if the more extreme look causes problems (such as noise) with the video signal.

A Different Approach

There is a third way that combines the best of both worlds: metadata. In cameras that shoot in the RAW format, alterations to the video signal are recorded in the metadata that accompanies each video file. This means that you have them if you want them, but are not bound by them: they are there for viewing and post-production but not *baked in*, which means you have great freedom to alter the look of the image later on, even years later — or you can keep it the way you decided on set.

10 Things to Remember When Shooting HD

Here are some tips specific to lighting for HD and shooting with High Definition cameras:

- Never overexpose high def.
- Control highlights: HD has trouble with them.
- Avoid using gain whenever possible.
- Nail exposure when you can, but if not, err on the side of underexposure, not overexposure.
- 23.98 fps is the most frequent choice for narrative storytelling. 29.97 fps is usually preferred for sports.
- A potential problem is too much depth-of-field. This is not a problem with full frame HD cameras as they are roughly the same DOF as 35mm film cameras.
- Another problem is seeing too much detail in things like makeup, sets, and wardrobe.
- Shoot at 23.98 or 29.97, not 24 or 30. This is important for audio sync. There are times when you will need to shoot actual 24 or 30 fps; consult with your editor.

TIMECODE AND EDGECODE

In editing, it is important to be able to identify each clip and individual frames. The *Society of Motion Picture and Television Engineers (SMPTE)* formalized *timecode* as a method of giving each frame a unique address. This code is an eight-digit number, based on the 24-hour clock and the video frame rate. Timecode measures time in *Hours:Minutes:Seconds:Frames*. Since most tapes are one hour or less, the first segment (Hours) is often used to designate the *roll number* of the tape. This is important in postproduction as it prevents duplication of timecodes when using more than one tape, which is important, since all but the shortest of productions involve multiple tapes — keeping track of your footage is an important job.

The values range from 00:00:00:00, to the largest number supported by this format; 23:59:59:29, or, no more than 23 hours, no minutes or seconds greater than 59, and no frames above the highest allowed by the rate being used (29 in this case for 30 frames/sec). This format represents actual clock time — the duration of scene or program material, and makes time calculations easy and direct.

There are two ways to do timecode in the course of shooting. In the first method, each tape is cued up to the beginning and the timecode is set to start at all zeros, except for the hours, which designates tape number. In the second method, the timecode is left to run free, based on clock time. This gives each tape unique numbers, unless you shoot more than 24 hours, but this is generally not a problem.

Video Frame Rate

The frame is the smallest unit of measure within SMPTE timecode. Some timecode readers display a small blip or other symbol at the end to indicate odd or even field (on interlaced video, where there are two fields per frame), but there is no number designation for it.

The frame rate is the number of times per second pictures are displayed to provide motion. There are four standard frame rates (frames/sec) that apply to SMPTE: 24, 25, 30, and 30 *Drop-Frame*.

- 24 fps Frame rate based on U.S. standard motion picture film
- 25 fps Frame rate based on European motion picture film and video, also known as SMPTE EBU (PAL/SECAM color and b&w)
- 30 fps Frame (also called *30 frame Non-drop*)
- 30 fps Drop-Frame

Remember that 24 fps can either mean actual 24 frames or it can mean the variant 23.98; the same applies to 30 fps, which is discussed following. The frames figure advances one count for every frame of film or video, allowing the user to time events down to 1/24th, 1/25th, or 1/30th of a second. Unless you have an application that specifically calls out one of the above frame rates, it doesn't matter which timecode is used as long it is consistent. Most SMPTE applications outside of broadcast video use the 30 frame non-drop rate because it matches real clock time.

Drop-Frame and Non-Drop-Frame

29.97 video can be written in either drop-frame or non-drop-frame format. The difference between the two is that with drop-frame format the frame address is periodically adjusted (once every minute) so that it exactly matches real time (at the 10-minute mark), while with non-drop-frame format the frame address is never adjusted and gets progressively further away from real time. See the following section for an explanation of drop-frame numbering.

Figure 9.24. (top) The timecode panel on a Sony F900.

Figure 9.25. (bottom) Most cameras offer the choice of *free run* timecode (*F-Run*), where timecode runs continuously even when the camera is not running, or *record run* (*R-Run*) where the timecode advances only when the camera is recording. On this camera, in between the two is the *Set* function, which is used to set the timecode. For identification of tapes, the hour (first two digits of the timecode) is set to correspond to the number of the tape.

29.97 Video

Before the introduction of color, video ran at a true 30 frames per second (fps). When the color portion of the signal was added, video engineers were forced to slow the rate down to 29.97 fps.

The reason for this is to prevent interference with the *color subcarrier*, which is the part of the video signal that carries color information. This slight slowdown of video playback leads to disagreement in the measurement of video versus real time; one second is not evenly divisible by 29.97. A frame rate of 29.97 fps is 99.9% as fast as 30 fps. It is 0.1% (or one-thousandth) slower: 29.97 fps / 30 fps = .999 (or 99.9%). This means that a frame rate of 30 fps is 0.1% (or one-thousandth) faster than 29.97: 30 fps / 29.97 fps = 1.001 (or 100.1%).

If it were running at precisely 30 fps, one hour of video would contain exactly 108,000 frames. 30 frames x 3600 seconds = 108,000 frames total. However, since video does not actually run at 30 fps, playing back 108,000 frames of video will take longer than one hour to play because: (108,000 frames) / (29.97 frames/sec) = 3,603.6 seconds = 1 hour and 3.6 seconds. In timecode this is written as 01:00:03:18. All of this means that after an hour, the playback is 108 frames too long. Once again, we see the relationship of 108 frames out of 108,000, or 1/1000th. Sixty seconds of 30 fps video contains 1800 frames. One-thousandth of that is 1.8. Therefore, by the end

Figure 9.26. A timecode slate (smart slate) in use on a film set. As shown here, it can be set up to display the date for a couple of frames after slating.

of one minute you are off by 1.8 frames. You cannot adjust by 1.8 frames per minute, because you cannot adjust by a fraction of a frame, but you can adjust by 18 full frames per 10 minutes. Two frames in 2000 accumulates 18 frames in 18,000, and there are 18,000 frames in 10 minutes.

How Drop Frame Solves the Problem

Because 10 minutes is not evenly divisible by 18 frames, we use drop-frame timecode and drop two frame numbers every minute; by the ninth minute, you have dropped all 18 frame numbers. No frames need to be dropped the tenth minute because actual frames and timecode frames are once again in agreement.

Thus the formula for the correcting scheme is: drop frame numbers 00:00 and 00:01 at the start of every minute except the tenth. (This also translates to dropping two frame numbers every 66 2/3 seconds.) This sequence repeats after exactly ten minutes. This is a consequence of the ratios of the numbers: Two frames in 2000 accumulates 18 frames in 18,000, and there are 18,000 frames in 10 minutes (30 frames, times 60 seconds, times 10 minutes. Also, 10 minutes of NTSC video contains an exact number of frames (17,982 frames), so every tenth minute ends on an exact frame boundary. This is how drop-frame timecode manages to get exactly one hour of video to read as exactly one hour of timecode.

To Drop or Not to Drop?

It is not necessary to use drop-frame timecode in all instances. Drop-frame is most important in applications where exact time is critical, such as broadcast television. For short pieces that are not going to be broadcast, standard timecode is acceptable; the slight mismatch will be of no consequence. In 25 Hz video (all countries that don't use NTSC), such as in 625/50 video systems, and in 24 Hz film, there is an exact number of frames in each second. As a result, drop-frame is not necessary. There is no drop-frame in 24P High Def video which helps to simplify things.

TIMECODE SLATING

When slating with timecode on tape-based cameras, always pre-roll audio and timecode for at least five seconds. This is critical for syncing up the dailies in telecine. Tape-based timecode-driven equipment (which includes the telecine and audio syncing decks, as well as playback and edit decks) takes at least five seconds to come up to speed and lock. Not having good pre-roll can definitely cause problems. Pre-roll is handled by the sound recordist. Where in the old days, the AD would call "roll sound" and the mixer would only call "speed" when the old tape decks finally lumbered up to the correct speed, the mixer now waits the appropriate time for pre-roll to lay down before calling "speed." This is not necessary with cameras that record to a hard drive or flash memory (file-based cameras).

In telecine there is an *offset* that occurs. Sometimes the smart slate numbers and the sound don't line up. This must be dealt with at some point down the line. There is a valuable additional feature with the Denecke timecode slate. As the clap stick is help open, the timecode rolls freely so that it can be checked. On some slates when the clapper is brought down, the timecode freezes momentarily, which makes it easier for the editor to read it without searching for the exact frame that matches the clap; after that, the date appears momentarily.

TAPELESS PRODUCTION

One advantage (in some cases a disadvantage) of digital cinematography is that there are many options for the actual recording, transport, postproduction and archiving. All the options can be a bit confusing sometimes and almost always require some research and testing. It is important to test your workflow at the beginning of the project. The results of your tests may affect what camera you choose, how you archive the data, and so on.

It is now clear that the future is tapeless cameras, which record directly to digital media such as hard drives, Panasonic's *P2 cards*, even directly to laptop computer. Tapeless cameras shoot as *file-based*, which means that each individual shot is a separate computer file that can be randomly accessed. These files are like any computer file: they can be quickly copied, transferred, or backed up.

Metadata

Metadata means "data about data." Digital files from tapeless cameras can have identifying information attached to them, which makes them more useful and vastly easier to keep track of, sort, and classify. They contain metadata that can be searched just as one would search for a specific file on a computer. Metadata can contain a myriad of information: timecode, date and time, length of shot, which camera and lens was used, and in some cases (with GPS) even where the shot was taken. As discussed elsewhere, metadata is an important part of shooting and working with RAW video files.

With film and tape cameras, it is often the custom to *bump* a slate: shoot the slate as a separate shot. Don't do this with a tapeless camera, because you will just end up with a disconnected shot that may have no relation to the scene it is slating.

Some of the characteristics of tapeless/file-based workflow are:
- Content is entirely in discrete, identifiable files.
- Can be transferred in faster than real time.
- Has all the advantages of metadata.
- Requires substantial efforts in content and asset management.
- Is almost entirely computer based, thus does not rely on expensive dedicated tape decks, and so on.

Tapeless Workflows

Tapeless, file-based workflow is substantially different from working off recorded tape. The advantages are numerous, but there are some pitfalls you need to steer clear of, one being loss of data. There are many ways to approach tapeless workflow, and each editor generally fine tunes the method to suit their equipment, work style, and type of job.

With tape, it is rare to lose the footage or have it be unplayable (although it can happen); in a tapeless workflow, every individual shot is a separate computer file recorded at high speed onto a hard drive or flash memory. It is easy for data to become corrupted or be lost in a hard drive failure, or to simply have the unit lost, damaged or, destroyed. It is also easy to misplace or erase video files. Hard drives are highly unreliable as a form of video storage; always be sure to back up to at least two hard drives — three is better.

To guard against these catastrophic losses, many productions employ a *data wrangler*, whose only job is to download the footage from the camera, put it in the right location, and above all — back it up! The data wrangler replaces and does mostly the same job as a *loader* on a film shoot.

Some important things to remember when handling video and audio data files on the set:

- Plan for how much media you will need. Remember that unless you have a separate download capability (such as a card reader), you will need to use the camera to download files. This means the camera will be out of commission. It may take longer than you might think to download full cards.
- Make sure you have the correct cables. Some cameras use USB, some are Firewire, HDMI, eSata, and other interfaces.
- Always have spare cables!
- Plan for double or triple backup. The downloaded files are your entire investment in money, time, and creative effort. Things can go wrong; don't assume that they are safe and/or all playable. Files get corrupted all the time. Hard drives crash frequently!
- Periodically test the files to make sure they are playable and properly labeled.
- Three separate hard drives is the best plan for security.
- Do not try to separate the files or folders. Many tapeless cameras record the "essence" (actual video files) separately from the metadata and pointer files. Don't try to only drag the video files to a separate hard drive.
- There are only two kinds of hard drives in the world: those that have failed and those that are going to fail.
- Metadata is the additional identifying information that accompanies video files. Timecode is the most obvious example, but there are many others such as date and time of recording, take length, and file size. Investigate metadata, it can be very helpful in post.
- Be sure to plan your file transcoding (conversion to another file type) before you shoot. Most camera files need to be converted in some way before they are editable. Some files are "native" to particular editing systems; some are not.
- Decide what file type you want to work with, there are many: DPX, TIFF, RAW, ProRes HQ, H.264, .r3d, MPEG, DNX, and so on.
- Don't just test the files, also test your editing software, the hardware you will be using, and the hard drives you will be using. Test the entire workflow of your project, all the way through to delivery.
- Be sure to check on your requirements for *deliverables* — the video and audio standards required by the person or organization you will be sending the finished product to.

DIGITAL FILE TYPES

Container Files: Quicktime and MXF

Quicktime is a *wrapper* or *framework* format. It functions as a *container* for many different types of video and audio in a variety of codecs. These video types are referred to as essence files. *MXF* is also a container format; it is an acronym for *Material Exchange Format*. It is a wrapper file format designed for interchange of material between systems and across platforms. It records the actual video, audio, or data as "essence" accompanied by metadata. Wrapper files come in many forms, so just saying that "it's a Quicktime file" doesn't tell you the whole story.

Cineon and DPX Files

Originally created for scanned images, the pixel data in Cineon files (.cin) correlates directly to the image as it would appear on projection print film. It was originally designed to function as part of a postproduction workflow.

DPX (Digital Picture Exchange) is a file type used for digital intermediate (DI) and was originally derived from the Cineon format. Like Cineon files it is designed to closely reproduce the density of each channel from the scanned original negative. DPX was designed to transport images on a file-per-frame basis. It includes many built-in information fields, organized into functionally separated headers. This structure allows a wide variety of different image types to be carried while providing support for rapid, efficient reading and processing of a received file.

COMPRESSION AND CODECS

As previously discussed, the term *codec* stands for *compressor-decompressor* or *coder-decoder*. As with HD cameras, editing systems and other hardware, they are always in flux as new technologies, hardware and software improve their performance. It is generally possible to convert any particular codec into another one (transcoding) but there is almost always some loss of quality in the process.

Intra-frame versus Interframe Compression

The term *intra-frame* coding refers to the fact that the various lossless and lossy compression techniques are performed only within the current frame, and not relative to any other frame in the video sequence. In other words, no temporal processing is performed outside of the current picture or frame.

Inter-frame compression works with blocks of frames, known as a GOP or *Group of Pictures*. It works by comparing the similarities and differences between the images within the GOP. Within the group there are I, B, and P frames. I frames are basically the reference and don't need additional information to be decoded. P frames are *predicted* based on information from other frames. B frames are *bi-directionally* predicted from other frames.

Wavelet Compression

Wavelet compression can be either lossy or lossless. It is a mathematically based compression that is well suited to reducing large video files to a very compact size. It is used in *JPEG 2000* and *Redcode* among other implementations.

Bit Depth

Digital video defines each pixels brightness and color as a *computer word* comprised of *bits* (zeros and ones). In the simplest example, a pure black-and-white image (with no gray at all) would only need a zero (black) or a one (white) to represent every pixel in the image.

In a color image, every pixel is formed through a combination of the three primary colors: red, green, and blue. Each primary color is often referred to as a *color channel*. The *bit depth* for each primary color is termed the *bits per channel*.

The greater the number of bits per channel, the more subtle the range of colors. For example, a system that records 8 bits per channel can use a total of eight 0's and 1's for each pixel. This allows for 2^8 or 256 different combinations — 256 different intensity values for each primary color. When all three primary colors are combined at each pixel, this allows for as many as $2^{8\times3}$ or 16,777,216 different colors.

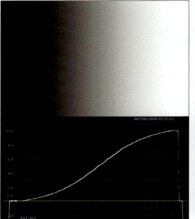
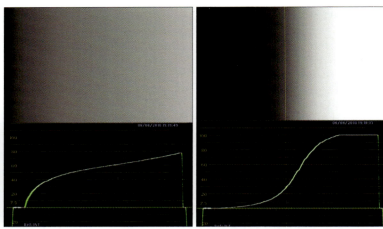

Figure 9.27. (left) A gradient gray-scale with normal gamma (contrast).

Figure 9.28. (center) The same gray scale with low gamma (low contrast). Nothing reaches true white and the shape of the curve changes drastically.

Figure 9.29. (right) Increased gamma (high contrast). This results in a much steeper curve. Notice how the white areas clip and the dark areas are crushed down to zero.

In 8-bit video, these values range from 0 to 255. In 10-bit video, these values range from 0 to 1023. In both cases, 0 represents the absence of something, either white or a color, while either 255 or 1023 represents the maximum amount of a color.

An 8-bit grayscale is essentially sufficient to smoothly represent all the shades of gray our eye can perceive but 8-bit color shows banding — clear divisions between different shades of color.

To avoid *banding*, color needs to be stored in 10-bit files. This provides smaller differences between color values, which prevents banding, but results in much larger files; however, keep in mind that 10-bit video has four times as much color information as 8-bit. Some systems employ 12-bit, 14-bit, and even 16-bit imaging.

MPEG

An acronym for *Motion Picture Experts Group*, which developed the standard, *MPEG* is by far the most widely used codec in various types of video. There are several variations of the MPEG standard currently in use.

- *MPEG-1* was used primarily for compact discs. It is not high enough quality for DVD.
- *MPEG-2* was chosen as the compression method for digital TV and DVD video.
- *MPEG-4 AVC* is a more efficient method of coding video. H.264 is also known as MPEG-4 Part 10. It is also widely used for DSLRs (digital single lens reflex cameras) — still photo cameras, many of which have the capability to record good 1080P HD video. Because it delivers good quality video at very low bit rates, it is also widely used as the codec for video on the Internet.

AVC-Intra/MPEG-4/H.264

AVC-Intra was developed by Panasonic and is compliant with *MPEG-4/H.264* standards. It is now used in some cameras made by other companies. It is 10-bit intra-frame compression. It is an *intra-frame* codec, meaning that the compression happens within each frame as opposed to interframe compression schemes where the compression of each frame may depend on other frames with the GOP (group of pictures).

MPEG-4 is also the compression scheme chosen for Blu-Ray high definition video discs. For recording camera video, H.264 is used in some cameras because of its ability to compress large amounts of

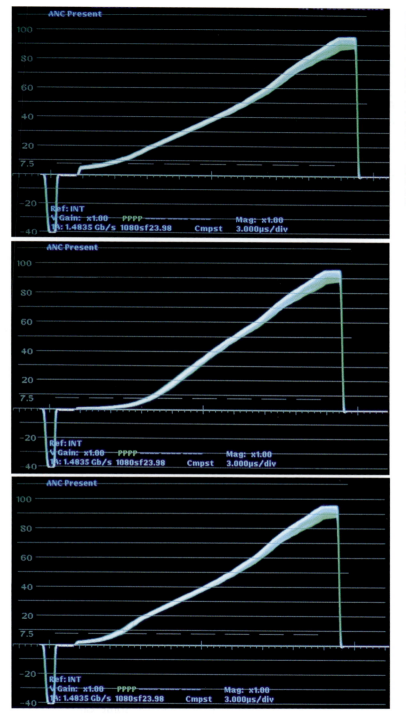

Figure 9.30. (top) A gradient gray-scale on the waveform monitor and black gamma (left-hand part of the curve representing the shadow areas) at normal.

Figure 9.31. (center) Black gamma at minus 99 at 35%. This means that the dark areas that are at 35% bright-ness and below are made darker. On the camera in this illustration, black gamma is selectable from 0 to minus 99 and at 50% (everything from middle gray down), 35%, 25%, and 15%.

Figure 9.32. (bottom) Black gamma at minus 50 at 15%; only the very darkest areas of the frame are affected.

data reasonably well; however there is definitely a price to be paid in picture quality, as is true of all heavy compression schemes. Another problem is that it can be difficult for editing systems to deal with H.264. For this reason, the footage is usually transcoded to another codec before being ingested into the non-linear editing application. Plug-ins for various editing applications are usually available from the camera manufacturers, as is free-standing conversion software for most codecs.

Figure 9.33. (top) In this frame the knee (brightest part of the grayscale at far right on the curve) is clipped: the curve flatlines at 108%.

Figure 9.34. (bottom) The same grayscale, and same exposure, but *knee* control is dialed down. This keeps the brightest parts of the shot from clipping with changing the rest of the picture.

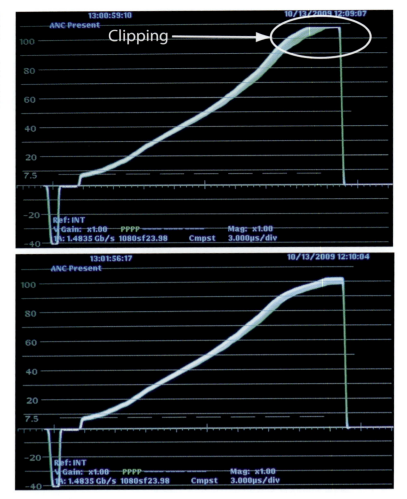

Other Codecs

TIFF is *Tagged Image File Format*. It can be a container for either lossy or lossless image data. Some post processes deal with the video files as a series of *TIFF* images that can be very large but also very high quality. *JPEG (Joint Photography Experts Group)* is another file type usually associated with still cameras and computer graphics but also used in video. JPEG is a lossy format but can reputedly achieve compression ratios of as high as 10:1 without noticeable loss of visual quality but if overused can result in very poor picture quality. *Motion JPEG* renders the video as a series of lossy JPEG images.

Each frame is compressed separately (intra-frame) and is thus not as efficient as inter-frame codecs, however, it imposes less of a load on the processing power of the computer. With inter-frame codecs, the computer needs to constantly refer to other frames as it displays each individual frames. *JPEG2000* is a more complex and computationally intense codec that is wavelet based. *OpenEXR* is a *high dynamic range* (HDR) file format. High dynamic range means that it can handle images with greater latitude/brightness ration/dynamic range (see the chapter on *Exposure* for a discussion of latitude and dynamic range). It supports 16 bits per channel and has an extraordinary dynamic range of 30 stops. It can be used as either a lossy or lossless codec.

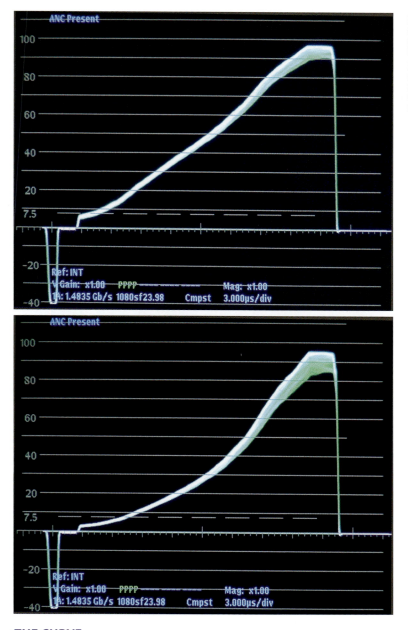

Figure 9.35. (top) Shot on the camera, this curve shows the gamma at normal, which is .45 on this camera.

Figure 9.36. (bottom) With the camera set at a high gamma, the picture becomes very contrasty, which we can see represented as a much steeper curve.

THE CURVE

The video signal is largely the same as film's response to light and the curve as seen on a waveform monitor is the same as the Hurter and Driffield or *D log E* curve that is discussed in the chapter *Exposure*. Different terminology is used for video: in film densitometry, the highlights are called the *shoulder,* and the dark areas are called the *toe*. In video the brightest areas are called the *knee,* and the darkest areas of the frame are simply called the *shadow areas*. In the illustrations in this chapter, a gray gradient from black on the left to pure white on the right was shot with an HD camera and the waveform monitor was photographed. This gives a more readable representation of how the various controls of knee, gamma and black gamma change the image. These controls apply to all types of video except RAW, which records the image without any alterations; however, it is criti-

Figure 9.37. (top) The external switches on a typical HD camera. The second switch is H, M, L, which means high, medium, or low gain. In the operations menus, you can select what values each one represents. Many operators choose minus 3dB, 0dB and plus 3dB gain for the high, medium and low values.

The third switch (*Output*) can select colors bars as the output (bottom position) or set the camera for normal operation (middle position) or top position for *automatic knee control* (*DCC or Dynamic Contrast Control*).

The last switch can select preset, which means that the camera cannot be white balanced; instead, the color balance is controlled only by the built-in color filters (see Figures 9.38).

All the way on the left is a switch that actuates auto black balance (sets the black level to zero IRE) and auto white balance, which adjusts the color balance when the camera is aimed at a neutral white or neutral gray target.

Figure 9.38. (middle) On the left are two wheels that control neutral density (the numbers) and color filters (letters). Sony provides a chart that shows what each setting of the wheels does. Other cameras use different schemes for these controls.

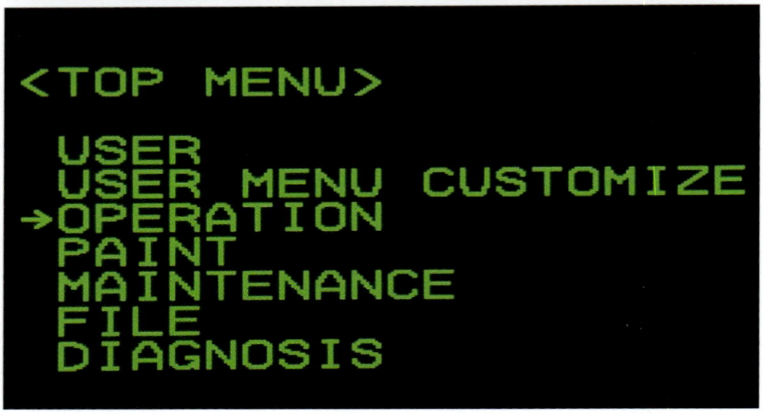

Figure 9.39. (bottom) A typical *top menu* on an HD camera, it provides access to the various *submenus*. The two most frequently used are *Operation* and *Paint*. The Operation menu only controls how you use the camera (setting values of the gain switch, for example). The Paint menu is where you control the look of the picture.

Other cameras will have different menu structures and terminology, but the basic controls of the look are the same.

cal for a cinematographer to understand how these controls affect the image even if they are shooting with a RAW camera.

The curves for film and video are important sources of information and it is important to understand what they mean and what they can tell you about each film stock or video camera setup. In addition to viewing the curves to show what different controls have done to the image, most color correction software also includes curves that you can alter directly — Photoshop has curves as well. By altering them directly, we mean that you can push or pull on various parts of the curve to alter the slope in different parts of the image. Recall that changing the slope affects the gamma (contrast) for that region of the curve. These curves can be used to alter the overall luma (brightness) or color balance of individual regions of the image.

CONTROLLING THE HD IMAGE

Certain basic controls are available on nearly all HD cameras and in post; these are the primary tools used to create a "look." In some HD cameras these can be controlled in the camera and are *baked in* to the recorded image. They become a permanent alteration to the video signal and can be difficult or impossible to alter later. In any case, cinematographers will always want to have some control over their images, whether on the set or in postproduction.

In cameras that shoot RAW, changing these parameters on the camera doesn't actually alter the image, they only alter how the image appears on the monitor. As will be discussed in the chapter *Image Control*, LUTs are used to control the monitor display.

The available image controls on most cameras include:

- Gain or ISO
- Gamma
- Knee
- Black Gamma and Black Stretch
- Color saturation
- Matrix (color fine tuning)
- Color balance (day, tungsten, etc)

With these basic controls it is possible to "create your own filmstock" and change an image in an amazing variety of ways.

Figure 9.40. (top) A test shot with the RED camera at ISO 200.

Figure 9.41. (bottom) A test shot at ISO 2000. Although the results are surprisingly good, there is noticeable noise.

Figure 9.42. (top) Correct color balance is achieved by either balancing to a white card or gray card.

Figure 9.43. (bottom) Incorrect color balance happens when you either don't white balance or use the wrong filter (some HD cameras have built-in filters for tungsten or daylight balance; some do it electronically. In this case, the tungsten balance filter on the camera was used in daylight, resulting in a blue cast on the entire image.

Gain/ISO

On some HD cameras, the control of *sensitivity to light* is called *gain*. Gain is measure in *decibels* (*dB*). Increasing the gain is electronic amplification. The trade-off is electronic noise. On some HD cameras, sensitivity is rated in ISO. Figure 9.40 shows frames from an HD camera rated at ISO 200 and Figure 9.41 is ISO 2000. The results are quite good, but there is always a price to pay for increased ISO or gain — more noise. Many cinematographers set cameras at minus 3dB to reduce noise, but others disagree with this practice.

Gamma

Gamma is contrast or, more precisely, the slope of the curve (specifically the middle part of the curve). Overall contrast is one of the most basic components of a visual image, and many DPs make this the first adjustment they make. A typical normal gamma is .45; raising this number makes the image more contrasty and lowering it makes the image less contrasty (Figures 9.33 and 9.34).

Black Gamma/Black Stretch

Black gamma is the contrast of the shadow regions. It is an extremely useful tool in shaping the image. On most cameras, you can choose how much of the shadow region you want to affect, either only the very darkest shadows or all the way up to from middle gray down to pure black. *Black stretch* is reducing the contrast of the shadows, thus reducing the overall contrast of the image and allowing the camera to see into the shadows a bit more (Figures 9.30 through 9.32).

Knee

The *knee* is brightest parts of the scene — the highlights. Even with slight overexposure of the highlights, video will usually *clip*. Film has a much better ability to *roll off* the highlights more gradually. For this reason control of the knee is critical. Knee controls are generally in two parts: *point* and *slope*. *Point* is a measure of where on the curve this parameter starts to take effect. *Slope* is the relative gamma of the knee regions. See Figures 9.33 and 9.34 for a more visual example of the knee. Many cameras also have *automatic knee control*.

Color Saturation

Chroma (color) *saturation* is simply how much color you have — how much saturation there is. Zero saturation is a black-and-white image. Oversaturation means that the image is recorded with more chroma than was present in the actual scene.

Matrix

No, you don't have to decide between the red pill or the blue pill. The *matrix* allows fine-tuning control of color. The matrix includes *color space*; there are several HD color spaces defined by *SMPTE* (*Society of Motion Picture and Television Engineers*). See the chapter on *Color* for an explaination of color space. See Figures 9.22 and 9.23 for examples.

Color Balance

Some people think of *color balance* (often called *white balance*) as simply adjusting the camera to *daylight* or *tungsten balance*. In fact, altering the color balance is one of the easiest and most accessible image controls. In Figures 9.42 and 9.43, the image manipulation is as simple as it can get: this camera has built-in color balance filters for daylight and tungsten; here the camera is set on the "wrong" color filter. Using warm cards and gels to adjust the color balance was discussed earlier in this chapter.

exposure

EXPOSURE: THE EASY WAY

Frankly, exposure can get pretty technical, so it's important to grasp the basic concepts first before we plunge into the world of H&D curves, the Zone System, and the mathematics of densitometry. Let's take a look at exposure the easy way.

This introduction is a bit simplified, but it will provide a working understanding of exposure that is useful without being too technical. First of all, there is one notion that has to be put away right now. Some people think of exposure as nothing more than "it's too dark" or "it's too light." There are many more crucial aspects to exposure that are important to understand.

What Do We Want Exposure to Do for Us?

What is it we want from exposure? More precisely, what is "good" exposure and what is "bad" exposure. Let's take a typical scene, an average one. It will have something in the frame that is very dark, almost completely black. It will also have something that is almost completely white, maybe a white lace tablecloth with sun falling on it. In between, it will have the whole range of dark to light values — the middle grays, some very dark grays, some very light grays and, some right in the middle — halfway between black and white.

When we shoot this scene, we want it to be reproduced on film or video exactly as it appeared in real life — with the black areas being reproduced as black in the finished product, the white areas reproduced as white, and the middle grays reproduced as middle grays.

Now of course, there will be times when you want to deliberately under or overexpose for artistic purposes, and that is fine. In this discussion we are only talking about theoretically ideal exposure, but that is what we are trying to do in the vast majority of cases anyway. So how do we do that? How do we get the film or video to exactly reproduce the scene in front of it? Let's look at the factors involved.

The Bucket

Let's talk about the recording medium itself. In film shooting it is the raw film stock; in video it is the sensor chip, which takes the light that falls on it and converts it to electronic signals. For our purposes here, they are both the same: exposure principles apply equally to both film and video, with only a few differences. They both do the same job: recording and storing an image that is formed by patterns of light and shadow that are focused on them by the lens. For convenience here, we'll refer to it as film but, it's the same either way.

Think of film as a bucket that needs to be filled with water. It can hold exactly a certain amount of water, no more, no less. If you don't put in enough water, it's not filled up (underexposure). Too much and water it slops over the sides and creates a mess (overexposure). What we want to do is give that bucket the exact right amount of water, not too much, not too little — that is ideal exposure. So how do we control how much light reaches the film?

Controlling Exposure

We have several ways of regulating how much light reaches the film. The first is the iris or aperture, which is nothing more than a light control valve inside the lens. Obviously, when the iris is closed down to a smaller opening (Figure 10.2), it lets less light through than when it is opened up to a larger opening (Figure 10.3). How open or closed the iris is set for is measured in f/stops (we'll talk about that in more detail later). Remember, the film or sensor wants only so much light, no more no less. If our scene in reality is in the bright sun, we can

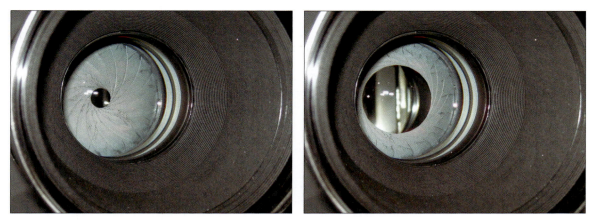

close down the iris to a small opening to let less of that light through. If our scene is dark, we can open up the iris to a wider opening to let in all the light we can get — but sometimes this will not be enough.

There are other things that control how much light reaches the image plane (the surface of the film or video sensor). One of these is shutter speed, which is a measure of how long the light reaches the film during each frame. Most of the time when we are shooting at 24 frames-per-second (FPS), then our shutter speed is 1/48th of a second. In each frame, the light is falling on the film or sensor for 1/48th of a second. If we have way too much light for the iris to help us with, then if we expose each frame for a much shorter time, then there will be less exposure in every frame — problem solved.

Change the Bucket

There is another, more basic way to change the exposure: use a different bucket. Every type of film has a certain sensitivity to light; the same is true of every video sensor. This means that some are more sensitive to light and some are less sensitive. It is rated in *ASA* or *ISO*, which generally ranges from about ISO 50 (low sensitivity) to ISO 500 (high sensitivity).

A film with a low sensitivity needs lots of light to make a good image. Typically films that are ISO 50 or thereabouts are only good for outdoor shooting, where the sun provides tons of light. High ISO films (such as ISO 500) will give you a good image even with very little light, as do HD cameras with higher ISOs.

A high-speed film is like using a smaller bucket — you don't need as much to fill it up. A low-speed film is like a larger bucket — it takes more to fill it up, but on the other hand we have more water. In the case of film and video images this means that we have more picture information, which in the end results in a better image.

The Four Elements of Exposure

So we have four elements to contend with in exposure:
- The amount of light falling on the scene.
- Aperture — a light valve that lets in more or less light.
- Shutter speed. The longer the shutter is open, the more light reaches the film or sensor.
- ASA or ISO (sensitivity). Using a higher ISO film is an easy fix, but it involves a penalty: faster films tend to be grainier and have less resolution than low-speed films. This applies to digital cameras as well — using a higher ISO will result in more image *noise*.

Figure 10.4. (top, left) An overexposed image. Notice how the highlights are burned out — they have no detail.

Figure 10.5. (below, left): The same image "fixed" — it's better, but the highlights are still burned out. There is no process that can bring back burned-out highlights; that information is lost forever.

Figure 10.6. (top, right) An underexposed image.

Figure 10.7. (below, right) The underexposed image "fixed," almost back to normal but very grainy and flat.

We'll Fix It in Post

One thing you will hear sometimes, especially on a set is "don't worry, we'll fix it in post." There is nothing wrong with making an image *better* in postproduction: there are many incredible tools you can use to improve the look of your footage. What you don't want to do is take the attitude that you can be sloppy and careless on the set because "everything can be fixed in post." It's simply not true. When it comes to exposure, fixing it in post generally means scrambling to come up with an image that is merely acceptable.

Improving or fine-tuning an image in post is a part of the process. It always has been, but now with all the great digital tools we have available (including things we can do in post-production on film projects), we have even wider latitude to adjust the image. However, this is not to be confused with "fixing" a mistake, which almost never results in a better image.

Whether we shoot film or video, we always make some adjustments in the post-production process, slight changes in color and exposure. Mostly this is done to ensure consistency within a scene and consistency across the whole project. The key to this is that they are slight adjustments. If you start trying to repair problems caused by mistakes made during shooting, there are almost always negative consequences. Here are some examples: Figure 10.4 is a badly *overexposed* image and Figure 10.6 is a badly *underexposed* image.

Once you "fix" the overexposed frame, some parts of it (the middle tones and shadows) are OK, but what is still not good are the highlights — they are still blown out, they have no detail, no tone, no color. Fixing the underexposed frame is different: the highlights are OK, but in the shadows there is a huge amount of video noise. This one was fixed digitally; on film the result would be similar, except in film it is increased film grain. In the "fixed" underexposed frame, it's flat and dull and low in contrast and the color is flat.

The Bottom Line

Here's the key point: exposure is about much more than just it's "too dark" or "too light," Exposure affects many things: it's also about whether or not a image will be noisy or grainy, it's about the overall contrast of the image, and it's about whether or not we will see detail and subtleties in the shadows and in the highlights. It's also about color saturation and contrast — the colors in the scene will only be full and rich and reproduced accurately when the exposure is correct. *Overexposure* and *underexposure* will severely *desaturate* the color of the scene; this is particularly important in *greenscreen* and *bluescreen* (see the chapter *Technical Issues*). In these situations, we want the background to be as green (or blue) as possible, in order to get a good *matte*. This is the main reason we have to be so careful about exposure when shooting greenscreen or bluescreen. As explained in *Technical Issues*, checking exposure of the background is critical when shooting any form of *chroma key*, the generic name for greenscreen and bluescreen composite matte shooting.

The bottom line is this: you will get the best image possible only when your exposure is correct. This is true of still photos on film, motion picture film, digital photography, *Standard Def (SD)* video, (including *DV*) and all forms of *High Def (HD)*.

How Film and Video Are Different

There is one crucial way in which film and High Def video are different. With HD, it is absolutely critical that you not overexpose the image. This is not as critical with film. Film stock is fairly tolerant of overexposure and doesn't do as well with underexposure; HD on the other hand is very good with underexposure, but remember, you will always get a better picture with exposure that is right on the money: this is the crucial thing to remember about exposure.

We should note however, that what we said about film applies only to negative film (which is what we almost always shoot on commercials, music videos, feature films, and short films). There is another type of film called *reversal film* (also known as *transparency* or *positive film*). This is just like slides or transparencies in still film: the same film that ran through the camera comes back from the lab with correct colors, not reversed like negative film. Reversal film reacts the same way as HD video: overexposing it is disastrous, but it's pretty good with underexposure.

Two Types of Exposure

There are really two ways to think about exposure: overall exposure and balance within the frame. So far we've been talking about overall exposure of the entire frame; this is what you can control with the iris and shutter speed (and some other tools and methods we'll talk about later, such as *neutral density filters*).

You also have to think about balance of exposure within the frame. If you have a scene that has something very bright in the frame and also something that is very dark in the frame, you may be able to expose the whole frame properly for one or the other of them, but not both. This is not something you can fix with the iris, aperture, changing ASA/ISO, or anything else with the camera or lens. This is a problem that can only be fixed with lighting and grip equipment; in other words, you have to change the scene.

In the next section, we'll move on to a more technical and in-depth discussion of exposure and densitometry (the science of measuring exposure): it's exposure the hard way. I won't kid you, it gets a little complicated, but bear with it, this is important material to know.

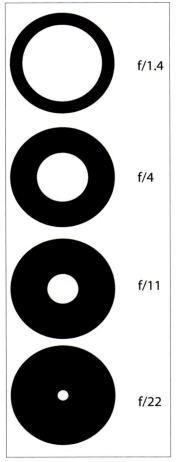

Figure 10.8. The aperture or iris at various f/stops.

LIGHT AS ENERGY

Human eyes are sensitive to a small portion of that spectrum that includes the visible colors from the longest visible wavelengths of light (red) to the shortest wavelengths (blue).

Intensity of light is measured in foot-candles (in the United States) or in lux (in metric countries). A foot-candle (fc) equals about 10.08 lux (or, for a rough conversion, multiply foot-candles by 10 to get lux). A foot-candle is the light from a standard candle at a distance of one foot. One lux is the illumination produced by one standard candle at a distance of 1 meter. When a film is exposed for 1 second to a standard candle 1 meter distance, it receives 1 lux of exposure. What's a standard candle? It's like the standard horse in horsepower, it just is. To provide some points of reference:

- Sunlight on an average day ranges from 3,175 to 10,000 fc (32,000 to 100,000 lux)
- Typical TV studios are lit at about 100 fc (1,000 lux)
- A bright office has about 40 fc or 400 lux of illumination
- Moonlight is about 1 lux (roughly a tenth of a foot-candle)

The f/stop is covered in more detail in the chapter on *Optics*, but for our discussion here it is important to know how it fits into the exposure system. F/stop and lighting calculations apply equally to both film and all forms of video, as does most of the information in this chapter.

F/STOPS

Most lenses have a means of controlling the amount of light they pass through to the film or video sensor; this is called the *aperture* or *iris*. The f/stop is the mathematical relationship of overall size of the lens to the size of the aperture.

Stop is a short term for f/stop. A stop is a unit of light measurement. An increase in the amount of light by one stop means there is twice as much light. A decrease of one stop means there is half as much light. The f/stop is the ratio of the focal length of a lens to the diameter of the entrance pupil, as shown in Figure 10.8. This works out to each f/stop being greater than the previous by the square root of 2.

F/stop is derived from the simple formula:

$$f = F/D$$

f/stop = focal length/diameter of lens opening

If the brightest point in the scene has 128 times more luminance than the darkest point (seven stops), then we say it has a seven stop *scene brightness ratio*.

EXPOSURE, ISO, AND LIGHTING RELATIONSHIPS

The units we deal with in exposure are:

- F/stops
- ASA, ISO, or EI (different names for the same thing)
- Foot-candles or lux
- Output of sources as affected by distance
- Reflectance of objects

It turns out that all of these can be arranged in analogous ways. They all follow the same basic mathematical pattern. Remember that f/stop numbers are fractions: the relationship of the aperture diameter to the focal length of the lens. For example, f/8 really means 1/8; the diameter is 1/8 the focal length. F/11 is 1/11, which is obviously a smaller fraction than 1/8. Each time we open the aperture one whole f/stop, we double the quantity of light reaching the film; each time we close it one stop, we halve the light reaching the film.

The relative f/stop scale (Table 10.1) is tiered to show that the same relationships that apply to whole f/numbers, such as f/8 and f/11, apply to intervals between them. So the difference between f/9 and f/13 is one whole stop, and so on. Modern digital meters measure in 1/10ths of a stop. This is helpful for calculations and comparisons, but for most practical purposes, this level of accuracy is not necessary. One-third of a stop is the practical limit of precision, given the vagaries of optics, lab chemistry, sensor sensitivity, and telecine transfer. This is not to say that accurate exposure is not important, only that the degree of precision in the overall process has limits.

Inverse Square Law and Cosine Law

As light emanates from a source, it does not drop off in intensity at a linear rate. For example, if the lamp is 11 feet from the subject, moving it to 8 feet will increase the subject illumination by 1 stop, just as opening the lens diaphragm from f/11 to f/8 would do. The inverse square law applies to point sources, strictly speaking, but spotlights follow it fairly well at the distances usually utilized.

Light decreases with the *square of the distance* from the source. In everyday terms, it you get 1/4 the amount of light every time you double the distance from the source. We rarely estimate light levels by mathematical calculation, but it is important to understand the basic principle involved.

Figure 10.9 illustrates the inverse square law graphically. A similar principle is the cosine law (Figure 10.10). As a surface is turned away from the source, less of the surface is "visible" to the source and therefore there is less exposure. Mathematically, the decrease in exposure is equal to the cosine of the angle of the surface, so this is called the cosine law.

ISO/ASA

Since one-third stop is the minimum exposure difference detectable by the unaided eye (for most *negative* stocks), film sensitivity is rated in no finer increments than this. This scale is tiered to make the relationships between intervals more easily seen. Just as ISO 200 is 1 stop faster than ISO 100, ISO 320 is 1 stop faster than ISO 160. (Table 10.2).

Although this is obvious, memorizing this scale makes it easier to see the differences between odd intervals, such as ISO 80 to ISO 32 (1 1/3 stops.) The scale may be expanded in either direction by adding or subtracting digits (the intervals below 6 are 5, 4, 3, 2.5, 2, 1.6, just as the intervals below 64 are 50, 40, 32, 25, 20, and 16.

Foot-candles: The ISO scale can also be applied to foot-candles. Doubling the foot-candles doubles the exposure. The third-stop

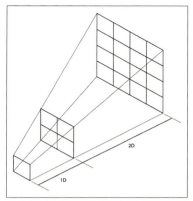

Figure 10.9. (top) The inverse square law. This is important not only to understanding expsoure measurement, but to lighting as well. Every time you double the distance, you get 1/4 the amount of light.

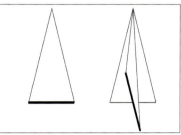

Figure 10.10. (bottom) The cosine law: how the angle of the subject affects its exposure level.

Table 10.1. (top) Light levels and exposure. "X" represents a given amount of light; each step to the left doubles the amount of light at the subject.

Table 10.2. (bottom) ISO or ASA in one-third stop increments. The same series can be interpreted as percentage of reflection, footcandles or shutter speeds — which serves to remind us that all these measures of exposure are interrelated.

Light	2048x	1024x	512x	256x	128x	64x	32x	16x	8x	4x	2x	X
F/Stops	1	1.4	2	2.8	4	5.6	8	11	16	22	32	45
1/3 Stops	1.1 / 1.3	1.6 / 1.8	2.2 / 2.5	3.2 / 3.6	4.5 / 5	6 / 7	9 / 10	13 / 14	18 / 20	25 / 29	36 / 40	

6		12		25		50		100		200		400		800	
	8		16		32		64		125		250		500		1000	
	10		20		40		80		160		320		640		1250

F/STOPS		- 1/3	- 2/3	-1	-1 1/3	-1 2/3	-2	-2 2/3	-3	-3 1/3	-3 2/3	-4	-4 1/3
REFLECTANCE	100%			50%			25%			12%			6%
		80%			40%			20%			10%		
			64%			32%			16%			8%	

Table 10.3. The relative relationship between f/stops and reflectance.

intervals give the intermediate fc values. For example, the difference between 32 fc and 160 fc is 2 1/3 stops.

Percentage of Reflection: The ISO scale from 100 on down relates to percentage of reflection. For example, ISO 100 can represent 100%, pure white. Other reflectances, such as 64% and 20%, can then be seen to be 2/3 stop and 2-1/3 stops darker than pure white (Table 10.3).

Shutter Speeds: Referring to the ISO scale (Table 10.2), it can be seen that, for example, 1/320 sec. is 1-2/3 stops faster than 1/100 sec. This can be helpful when unusual combinations of shutter angle and frame rate produce odd effective shutter speeds.

LIGHT AND FILM

It is the energy in each photon of light that causes a chemical change to the photographic detectors that are coated on the film. The process whereby electromagnetic energy causes chemical changes to matter is known as photochemistry.

All film is coated onto a base: a transparent plastic material (celluloid) that is 4 to 7 thousandths of an inch (0.025 mm) thick. Onto the base, an *emulsion* is adhered where the photochemistry happens. There may be 20 or more individual layers coated here that are collectively less than one-thousandth of an inch in thickness. Some of the layers coated on the transparent film do not form images. They are there to filter light, or to control the chemical reactions in the processing steps. The imaging layers contain sub-micron-sized grains of silver halide crystals that act as the photon detectors.

These crystals are the heart of photographic film. These crystals undergo a photochemical reaction when they are exposed to various forms of electromagnetic radiation — light. In addition to visible light, the silver halide grains can be sensitized to infrared radiation. A halide is a chemical compound of a halogen (any of a group of five chemically related nonmetallic elements including fluorine, chlorine, bromine, iodine, and astatine) with a more electropositive element or group, in this case silver. Silver halide grains are manufactured by combining silver nitrate and halide salts (chloride, bromide, and iodide) in complex ways that result in a range of crystal sizes, shapes, and compositions.

The unmodified grains are only sensitive to the blue part of the spectrum, and thus are not very useful in camera film. Spectral sensitizers are added to the surface of the grains to make them more sensitive to blue, green, and red light (remember, we're talking about black-and-white film here). These molecules must attach to the grain surface and transfer the energy from a red, green, or blue photon to the silver halide crystal as a photo electron. Other chemicals are added internally to the grain during its growth process, or on the surface of the grain. These chemicals affect the light sensitivity of the grain, also known as its *speed* — that is, how sensitive to light it is.

The speed of an emulsion is quantified by standards set by the *ISO (International Standards Organization)* or *ASA (American Standards Association)* rating. ISO is the technically the correct designation, but by tradition, many people still refer to it as ASA. The higher the ISO, the lower the light level the film is capable of responding to. For color film, manufacturers list the sensitivity of film as *EI* or *Exposure Index*. Higher ISO means the film is *faster*; the trade-off is that the increased light sensitivity comes from the use of larger silver halide grains. These larger grains can result in a blotchy or *grainy* appearance to the picture. Photographic film manufacturers are constantly making improvements that result in faster films with less grain. For Kodak, a major advance was the introduction of *T-grains* in the 80's. These tabular grains are roughly triangular, which allowed them to be packed closer together, thus reducing apparent grain. Fuji has a similar technology called nano-structured grain. A grainy look is sometimes added to the image to make it look like old film.

Figure 10.11. A typical black-and-white negative.

The Latent Image

When the shutter is open, light affects the chemistry of the emulsion and a latent image is formed. When a photon of light is absorbed by the chemical sensitizer sitting on the surface of a silver halide grain, it forms the latent image. A silver halide grain contains billions of silver halide molecules, and it only takes 2 to 4 atoms of uncombined silver to form the latent image site. In color film, this process happens separately for exposure to the red, green, and blue layers of the emulsion. The reason for this is simple: there is no way to sensitize a grain to color; you can only sensitize it to a specific band of the spectrum. The image that is formed is called *latent* because it remains invisible until chemically developed.

Any photon that reaches the film, but does not form a latent image, is lost information. Most color films generally take 20 to 60 photons per grain to produce a developable latent image. This is called the *inertia point* for the film. Below the inertia point, no image is recorded at all because there is no chemical change in the emulsion. Video receptors are electronic and of course quite different in operation, but the basic theory is quite similar. With some small differences, exposure theory and practice are the same for film and video.

Chemical Processing

In order for the latent image to become visible, it must be made visible and stabilized to make a *negative* or a *positive* (Figure 10.11). In black-and-white film, the silver halide grains have to be sensitized to all wavelengths of visible light, so the silver halide grains are coated in just one or two layers. As a result, the development process is easier to understand.

- The film is placed in developing chemistry that is actually a reducing agent. Those grains that have latent image sites will develop more rapidly. If the film is left in the developing chemistry for the proper amount of time, only grains with latent image information will become pure silver. The unexposed grains remain as silver halide crystals.

- The development process must be *stopped* at the right moment. This is done by rinsing the film with water, or by using a *stop bath* that stops the development process.

- After development, some of the altered halide and all of the unaltered silver halide remains in the emulsion. It must be removed or the negative will darken and deteriorate over time. The removal of this undeveloped material is accomplished with fixing agents, usually sodium thiosulfate (hypo) or ammonium thiosulfate. The process is called *fixing*.

- The film is washed with water to remove all the processing chemicals. Then it is dried.

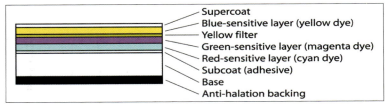

Supercoat
Blue-sensitive layer (yellow dye)
Yellow filter
Green-sensitive layer (magenta dye)
Red-sensitive layer (cyan dye)
Subcoat (adhesive)
Base
Anti-halation backing

Figure 10.12. (left) Color negative with its distinctive orange mask.

Figure 10.13. (right) The layers of color negative film.

When all the steps are finished, the film has a negative image of the original scene. It is a negative in the sense that it is darkest (has the highest density of opaque silver atoms) in the area that received the most light exposure. In places that received no light, the negative is clear, or at least as clear as the film base can be.

Other types of chemistry can result in a *positive* image, This is called positive film or reversal film. In still photography, the images are often referred to as *transparencies* or *slides*. Reversal film has finer grain and sharper resolution, but it is also extremely sensitive to exposure error. Also, since the film is already positive, there is no printing of the negative, which is where small corrections in exposure and color balance can be corrected when a print is made for projection. Making prints from a negative also has a safety factor: the original negative only has to be sent through a printing machine a few times, which decreases the chance of dirt and damage.

Color Negative

Color negative is three layers of black-and-white film, one on top of the other (Figures 10.12 and 10.13). The difference is that each layer is treated with a different spectral sensitizer so that it is receptive to a different band of the spectrum. These translate to roughly red, blue and green. Some color negative films have four color layers.

- With color film, the development step uses reducing chemicals, and the exposed silver halide grains develop to pure silver. Oxidized developer is produced in this reaction, and the oxidized developer reacts with chemicals called couplers in each of the image-forming layers. This reaction causes the couplers to form a color, and this color varies depending on how the silver halide grains were spectrally sensitized. A different color forming coupler is used in the red, green, and blue, sensitive layers. The latent image in the different layers forms a different colored dye when the film is developed.
- The development process is stopped with a stop bath.
- The unexposed silver halide grains are removed using a fixing solution.
- The silver is removed by bleaching chemicals.
- The negative image is then washed to remove as much of the chemicals and reaction products as possible.

The overall orange hue on color negative film is the result of masking dyes that help to correct imperfections in the color reproduction process; this is easily removed in making color prints or in *film-to-tape transfer.*

Film's Response to Light

There are two steps in the making of a negative:

- Exposure. The useful property of silver halide is that its state is altered when subjected to light, in direct proportion to the amount of light energy absorbed. This change is not visible, it's still a *latent image.*

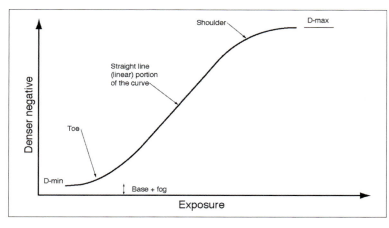

Figure 10.14. The Hurter and Driffield D Log E curve for negative density.

- Development. Silver halide that has been altered by contact with light can be reduced to pure silver if placed in developing fluids. The activity of the developer and time of development will determine how much of the sensitized halide will be converted. The chemistry for color film is different from the solutions used for black-and-white films, but the basic concepts are the same.

DENSITOMETRY

To understand film we must look at its response curve. This classical approach to densitometry (the scientific analysis of exposure) was devised by Hurter and Driffield in 1890 and so is called the *H&D curve* or sometimes the *D log E curve*. This is sometimes shortened to *Log E* curve (Figure 10.14). It plots the amount of exposure (E) in logarithmic units along the horizontal axis and the amount of density change in the negative "D" along the vertical axis.

In theory, it makes sense that we would want the film to change in density in exact proportion to change in the amount of light reflected by different parts of the scene. After all, we are trying to make an image that accurately portrays the real scene, right?

Let's look at a theoretical *linear* film (Figure 10.15). For every additional unit of exposure, the density of the negative changes exactly one unit. That is, there is an exact correspondence between the amount of light in the scene and the change in the density of the negative. Sounds perfect, doesn't it? The slope of the line for this film would be 45 degrees exactly.

The slope of this line is a measure of the *contrastiness* of the film. In a film where large changes in exposure only change the negative density a little (low contrast reproduction), the slope is very shallow. Where a film is very contrasty, the slope is very high; in other words, small changes in the amount of light cause the film density to change drastically. The extreme is something called *litho* film, which is used in the printing industry. Everything in litho film is either black or white — there are no shades of gray. In other words, if the light is above a certain level, the image is completely white. If it is below a certain level, it is completely black. This is as contrasty as a film can get. The slope for litho film (which is strictly black-and-white with no grays) would be a vertical line.

No film acts in the perfectly linear manner of this first example (i.e., the changes in the film exactly correspond to the change in the amount of light). In this diagram, we see a film that only changes 1/2 unit of density for each additional unit of light. This is a *low-*

Figure 10.15. A theoretical ideal film — one that exactly reproduces the exposure changes of the subject in a one-to-ratio with negative density.

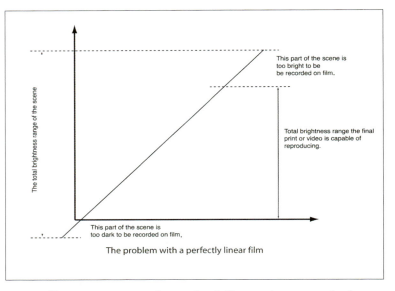

The total brightness range of the scene

This part of the scene is too bright to be be recorded on film.

Total brightness range the final print or video is capable of reproducing.

This part of the scene is too dark to be recorded on film.

The problem with a perfectly linear film

contrast film. Figure 10.16 shows the difference between a high-contrast emulsion and a low-contrast one. In the high-contrast example, for each additional unit of exposure, it changes 2 units of negative density. Looking at the brightness range of the exposure against the brightness range of the negative density, we see that it will show more contrast in the negative than actually exists in the scene. The slope of this line is called the gamma of the film: it is a measure of its contrastiness.

Contrast refers to the separation of lightness and darkness (called *tones*) in a film or video image and is broadly represented by the *slope* of the characteristic curve. Adjectives such as *flat* or *soft* and *contrasty* or *hard* are often used to describe contrast. In general, the steeper the slope of the curve, the higher the contrast. The term *gamma* refers to a numerical way to describe the contrast of the photographic image: gamma is the slope of the middle, straight part of the curve.

Gamma is measured in several different ways as defined by scientific organizations or manufacturers. They are all basically a way of calculating the slope of the straight-line portion of the curve by more or less ignoring the shoulder and the toe portions of the curve. Gamma does not describe contrast characteristics of the toe or the shoulder, only the straight line portion. But there is another wrinkle. In the lowest range of exposure, as well as in the highest range, the emulsion's response changes. In the lowest range, the film does not respond at all as it "sees" the first few units of light. There is no change in photochemistry at all until it reaches the inertia point where the amount of light first begins to create a photochemical change in film or an electrical change on a video tube. After reaching the inertial point, then it begins to respond sluggishly: negative density changes only slightly for each additional unit of light. This region is the *toe* of the curve. In this area, the changes in light value are compressed.

At the upper end of the film's sensitivity range is the *shoulder* in film terminology, and the *knee* in video. Here also, the reproduction is compressed. The emulsion is becoming overloaded; its response to each additional unit of light is less and less. The end result is that film does not record changes in light value in the scene in a linear and proportional way. Both the shadows and the highlights are some-

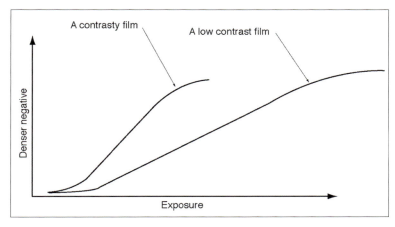

A contrasty film

A low contrast film

Denser negative

Exposure

what crushed together. This is, in fact, what gives film the "film look" that video has never been able to achieve (High Def comes a lot closer than previous systems but still has trouble with the high-lights). It is a way of compressing very contrasty scenes so that they "fit" onto the film negative.

The Log E Axis

Let's think about the log E axis (horizontal) for a moment. It is not just an abstract scale of exposure units. Remember that it represents the various luminances of the scene. All scenes are different, and thus all scenes have different luminance ratios. What we are really plotting on the horizontal axis is the range of luminances in the scene, from the darkest to the lightest.

In 1890, the German physiologist E. H. Weber discovered that changes in any physical sensation (sound, brightness, heat) become less noticeable as the stimulus increases. The change in level of stimulus that will produce a noticeable difference is proportional to the overall level: if three units of light create a perception of brightness that is just noticeably brighter than two units, then the smallest perceptible increase from 20 units of light will require 30 units. To produce a scale of steps that appear to be uniform, it is necessary to multiply each step by a constant factor. In fact, the perception of brightness is logarithmic.

What Is a Log?

First a bit of mathematics. (Just a little, so don't worry). An under-standing of logarithms is useful both in film and in video, where log files are an important concept. Logarithms are a simple way of expressing large changes in any numbering system. If, for example, we wanted to make a chart of something that increases by multiplying by 10: 1, 10, 100, 1000, 10,000, 100,000, we very quickly reach numbers so large as to be unwieldy. It would be extremely difficult to make a graph that could handle both ends of the range.

In log base 10, the most common system, the log of a number represents the number of times 1 must be multiplied by 10 to produce the number. 1 must be multiplied by 10 once to make 10, so the log of 10 is 1. To arrive at 100, you multiply 1 by 10 twice, so the log of 100 is 2. The log of a number is the exponent of 10: $10^2 = 100$, the log of 100 is 2. 10^4 is 10,000, so the log of 10,000 is 4. This means that we can chart very large changes in quantity with a fairly small range of numbers. Logs are used throughout lighting, photography, and video.

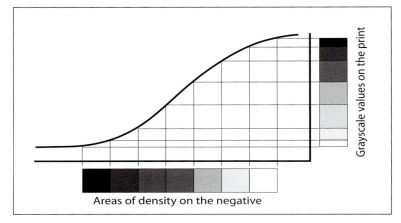

Figure 10.17. Grayscale compression in the toe and shoulder of a film negative and a film print.

Grayscale values on the print

Areas of density on the negative

BRIGHTNESS PERCEPTION

Our perception of brightness is logarithmic, and we shall see that this has far-ranging consequences in all aspects of lighting for film and video. If we chart the human perception of brightness in steps that appear smooth to the eye, we can follow its logarithmic nature. It is apparent that each step up in a seemingly even scale of gray tones is, in terms of its measured reflectance, spaced logarithmically. As we shall see later, this phenomenon is in fact fundamental to the entire process of lighting and image reproduction.

Remember that these are not fixed values (the darkest point on the log E axis is not a certain number of *candles-per-sq-foot,* for example), because we open or close the aperture of the camera to adjust how much light reaches the film and we use faster or slower film and so on. What really counts is the *ratio* between the darkest and lightest, and that is what we are plotting on the log E axis. This is called the brightness range of the film, sometimes abbreviated as *BR*. Each unit on the log E axis represents one stop more light.

CONTRAST

The word *contrast* has different meanings, depending on whether you are talking about the contrast of the subject we are photographing or the negative that we will use to make the print. In general, contrast refers to the relative difference between dark and light areas of the subject or negative.

Negative contrast refers to the relative difference between the more transparent areas of the negative and those that are more opaque. The negative is described in terms of density. These densities can be measured with an instrument called a densitometer, which measures how much light passes through the negative and how much is held back. The contrast of photographic subjects can vary a great deal from one picture to another. On clear, sunny days the contrast of an exterior scene can be great, while on cloudy days it can be relatively low in contrast. The contrast of a given scene depends on how light or dark the objects in the picture are when compared to one another and how much light is falling on them. Let's get back to our theoretically "ideal" film. This film would change the density of the negative exactly one unit for each one unit of change in the brightness of the subject.

Figure 10.17 shows the problem with this. No reproduction medium now known is capable of reproducing anything near the brightness range exhibited in most real-world situations. Nearly all film emulsions are non-linear. This linearity fails for two reasons.

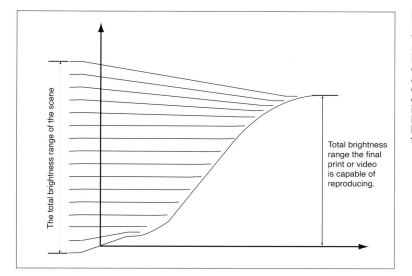

Figure 10.18. Compression of the real-world brightness values so that they fit onto the film. This is what makes it possible to make usable images even from scenes with high-contrast ranges. The same principle applies to video, whether analog or digital. A great deal of the progress of video as a more acceptable imaging medium has been improvements in its ability to compress the image brightness in a way that gets closer to what film can usefully manage.

- It takes a certain amount of light energy to initiate the activation of the photosensitive elements in the emulsion (the inertia point). Thus, the density rises gradually at first in this area called the toe, finally accelerating into the straight line portion of the curve.
- With increasing exposure to light, more silver halide is converted, until it has no more sensitive material to activate. At that point, increasing the exposure does not increase the ultimate density of the developed negative. This "saturation" occurs gradually and produces what is known as a shoulder.

The toe of the film is a result of the fact that film reacts slowly to small amounts of light. It is only when greater amounts of light reach the emulsion that the change becomes linear. This is the straight-line portion of the film. The film base itself always has some density, however slight. On top of this there is always a slight amount of fog due to light scattering in the camera, the lens, the emulsion, and also chemical fog in the processing. The cumulative effect of all of these is called base plus fog. Density measurements are usually described as *x density above base plus fog*.

This toe and shoulder behavior actually results in a compression of the actual scene. If the contrast gradient of the film is correct and exposure is correct, this compression behavior will allow more of the brightness range of the scene to be represented on the final print. In effect, it is the failure of film emulsion and video receptors to accurately represent the real world that allows us to produce photographs and video that are usable. Each film emulsion reacts to light in a special way. Some react more quickly to low light than others, creating a rather abrupt initial rise in density or *short toe*. Others react more gradually to increases in light and have what is called a *long toe*.

Another important factor is the range of subject luminance that can be usefully recorded (Figure 10.16). Low-contrast films can continue to build density over a long luminance range, whereas contrasty films saturate rather quickly and tend to "block" at either end. This is how we can match the type of film used to the type of scene being photographed. Cinematographer David Watkin used a low-contrast film stock on *Out of Africa*, where he dealt with many very contrasty situations in the harsh African sun. Both Fuji and Kodak now make emulsions that are more moderate in contrast.

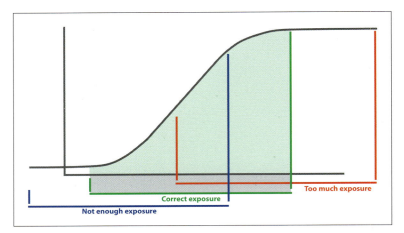

Figure 10.19. Changing exposure shifts the image up and down the curve; too much exposure pushes it off the shoulder, and too little crushes it into the toe.

Too much exposure

Correct exposure

Not enough exposure

Determining the precise film speed, coupled with precise exposure, is critical when the range of light in the scene is greater than the scale of the film. In Figure 10.19, we see three exposures of the same scene, represented by the bars at the bottom of the diagram. Not enough exposure places much of the information completely off the low end of the curve, while too much exposure places it off the high end. In either case, once you are off the curve, further changes in exposure register no change in the negative; the film doesn't "see" them. The ideal exposure places all of the information where it makes some change on the negative; in effect we don't want any part of the negative to be wasted.

If there is too much exposure, two things happen. First, even the darkest parts of the scene are in the middle range of the curve: even the darkest shadows will reproduce as middle gray tones. Graphically, overexposure appears as a shift of the subject brightness range (log E) to the right. (In effect we are making the scene values brighter by opening up the aperture.) Here we see that this overexposure places the scene values too much in the shoulder. Some information is lost in the flat part of the shoulder: lost because the differences of scene brightness value result in no change in the final density of the negative.

Further, because everything is shifted to the right, none of the scene values fall in the toe of the curve: there will be no deep black values at all in the final print, even though they existed in the original scene. Underexposure is shown as a shift of the log E values to the left. Here every subtle nuance of the high tones will be recorded because they fall in the straight line portion of the curve. But at the dark end of the scale — trouble. The dark values of the scene are mushed together in the toe. There is little differentiation of the medium gray values, the dark gray values, and the black shadows: in the final print they will all be a black hole. There will be no detail in the shadows — whether or not we can see detail is how we judge shadows and highlights; it is a phrase you will hear often in discussions of exposure — *separation and detail* in the shadows or highlights. If there is no separation of tones and no visible detail in the shadows, they are underexposed. The same applies to the highlights: lack of separation and detail means they are overexposed. Exactly what constitutes a lack of separation and detail can be a bit subjective, since some areas of a scene might be properly represented as pure black or pure white. Choosing which areas you expect to have details and separation can be a little bit of a judgment call.

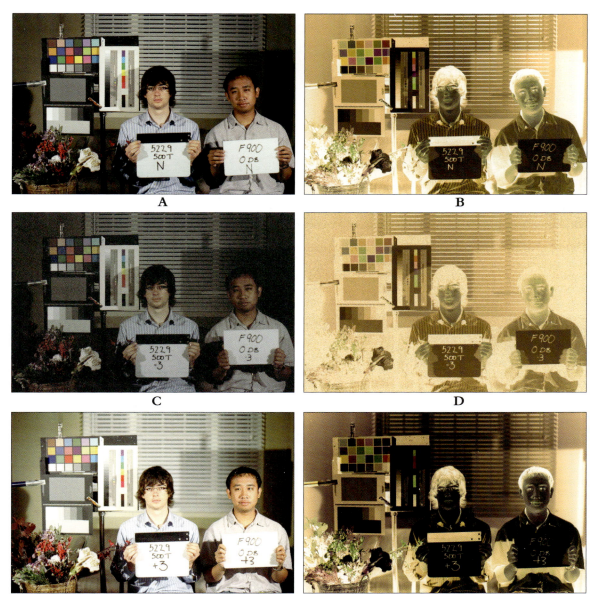

Figure 10.20. Exposure on film. (A) is normal exposure — good contrast, a full range of tones, and minimal grain. (B) is the negative of the normal exposure. Notice that it also has a full range of tones from near total black (which will print as white) to almost clear negative (which will print as black). (C) is a severely underexposed frame — three stops under. It's dark but also very grainy and doesn't have a full range of tones, hardly anything above middle grays. (D) is the negative of the badly underexposed shot; it's what we call a "thin" negative. (E) is three stops overexposed and (F) is the negative of this shot, it's what is called a "thick" negative, difficult to get a good print from.

"Correct" Exposure

"Correct" exposure, then, is essentially the aperture setting *that will best suit the scene brightness range of the scene* (the horizontal axis: log E) to the characteristic curve of the imaging medium. What is needed is to slip the scene values comfortably in between the toe and the shoulder. A typical scene with a seven stop range of light values fits nicely on the curve if we place the exposure exactly in the middle. It is important to remember, however, that correct exposure is a purely technical thing; there are occasions where you will want to deviate from ideal exposure for pictorial or technical reasons. The relation-

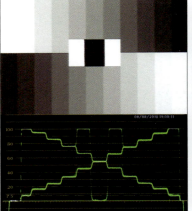
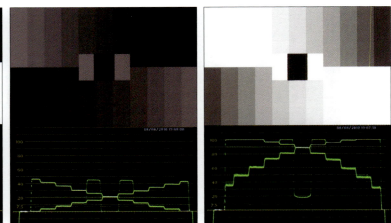

Figure 10.21. (left) An *11-step gray-scale* properly exposed. On the waveform monitor, the darkest areas are down at 0% (pure black) and the white bars are 100% (pure white). The rest of the tones are evenly distributed. The "X" is *linear,* meaning that contrast is normal. These illustrations show the image on top and the waveform monitor display for that image underneath.

Figure 10.22. (middle) A badly *underexposed* shot of the grayscale. On the waveform the tones are all crushed together at the bottom.

Figure 10.23. (right) In this very *overexposed* shot, all of the lightest steps of the grayscale are blown out pure white, with no separation. On the waveform they are clipped: flat-lined at the top. Notice that the steps are no longer linear. This clearly shows how overexposure in HD video is much more than just being "too light" — everything about the image is adversely affected.

ship of the gamma (the angle of the straight-line portion of the film) to the toe and the shoulder is what determines a film's *latitude*. It can be viewed as two characteristics: room for error and the emulsion's (or video camera's) ability to accept a certain brightness range — which is called its latitude.

Higher Brightness Range in the Scene

The problem is exacerbated if we consider a scene that has more than seven stops of brightness (seven stops is just an average; it all depends on the particular film stock or video camera). Here there is no aperture setting that will place all of the values on the useful part of the curve. If we expose for the shadows (open up the aperture), we get good rendition of the dark gray areas, but the light values are hopelessly off the scale. If we "expose for highlights" (by closing down to a smaller f/stop), we record all the variations of the light tones, but the dark values are pushed completely off the bottom edge and don't record at all; there is no information on the negative, no detail to be pulled out.

How do we deal with this situation? This is done by lighting or by modifying the existing lighting. This is one of the most essential jobs of lighting and grip work: to render the scene in a scale of brightness values that can be accommodated by the optics and emulsion of a film camera or by the optics and electronics of video.

DETERMINING EXPOSURE

In measuring and setting exposure on the lens, shutter, frame rate, with neutral density filters, or by altering the brightness levels of the scene, we have two basic tasks:

- To manipulate the brightness ratio of the scene so that it can be properly reproduced on film or video.
- To set the aperture so that the scene values fall on the appropriate part of the curve.

In practice these often turn out to be two sides of the same coin. The first task is essentially the work of lighting and lighting control, and the second task involves measuring the scene and making a judgment about the best setting for the lens.

VIDEO EXPOSURE

The same principals of exposure apply to video; the same ideas of the curve, toe and shoulder, also apply, although in video the highlights are called the *knee* and the darkest parts of the scene (called toe in film) are simply referred to as shadow areas. Exposure is even

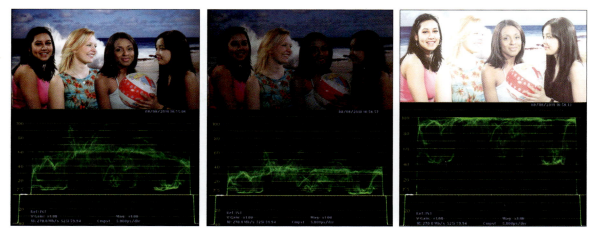

more critical in video than in film for two reasons: although they are constantly improving, video cameras tend to clip the highlights if overexposed.

Figures 10.21 illustrates an 11-step grayscale at correct exposures. Notice that in the underexposed frame (Figure 10.22) all the tones are *crushed* together. Simply making it brighter in post will not restore a full range of tones. The result will be dull and flat with lots of video noise. In the overexposed frame (Figure 10.23) the highlights are clipped. There is no information there; they will just be burned out white as in Figure 10.23.

On this page (Figures 10.24, 10.25, and 10.26) are the *Cambelles,* standardized test subjects made by DSC Labs. They illustrate the same principals: proper exposure gives you a full range of tones from black to white, and the tones are rendered as they appeared in the scene. In the underexposed frame, (Figure 10.25), all tones are crushed and not rendered properly. In the overexposed frame (Figure 10.26), the highlights are clipped and there are no true blacks. There is absolutely no way to fix this in post; once the highlights are clipped, all information is lost. Trying to make it darker in post will not bring back the highlights. They are lost and cannot be recovered; they will be burned out white no matter what you do.

THE TOOLS

The two most basic tools of the cinematographer's trade are the *incident meter* and the *spot meter*. There is a third type of meter, the *wide angle reflectance meter*, but it has extremely limited use in film.

The Incident Meter

The *incident meter* measures scene illumination only — in other words: the amount of light falling on the scene. To accomplish this purpose, most incident meters use a hemispherical white plastic *dome* that covers the actual sensing cell (Figure 10.27).

The diffusing dome accomplishes several purposes. It diffuses and hence "averages" the light that is falling on it. It also approximates the geometry of a typical three-dimensional subject. Unshielded, the dome will read all of the front lights and even some of the side-back and back light that might be falling on the subject. Left to itself, the hemisphere would provide a reasonable average of all the sources falling on the subject. In practice, many people use their hand to shield the back light off the reading and use a combination of hand shielding and turning the meter to read the backlight and usually the key, fill, side lights, and back lights separately.

Figures 10.24. (left) A properly exposed frame and its representation on the waveform monitor. Notice how there is a full range of tones from very dark to almost pure white. The two patches of surf beside the blonde model's head are very close to 100% (pure white) on the waveform.

Figure 10.25. (middle) The shot is badly underexposed: very little of the frame even reaches middle gray (50%), and the tones of the scene are crushed together at the bottom.

Figure 10.26. (right) This frame is badly overexposed: there are no real blacks or dark areas at all (the darkest tone in the scene only gets down to 40% on the waveform), but worse, all the light tones are clipped at the top. They reach 100% and then flat-line — there is no information at all, just blank white, blown out. Clipping cannot be fixed in post.

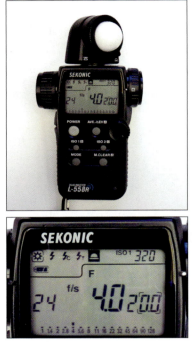

Figure 10.27. (top) A *Sekonic Dual-Master* light meter. It is a combination of both an *incident meter* and a *spot meter*. It can read both continuous light and strobes.

Figure 10.28. (bottom) A closeup of the readout for the Sekonic meter. In the upper right is the ISO (320 in this case). On the left is the frame rate — 24 frames per second (24 f/s). Middle right is the reading: f/4. The smaller numbers are 1/10 of a stop, in this case 2/10th, which you would probably round off to 1/3 of stop, for a lens setting of f/ 4 and 1/3rd.

At the bottom is a graphic indicator of the f/stop. This meter can take several readings and average them if you wish.

Figure 10.29. (below) A *reflectance* or *spot meter* by Pentax. This one has a *Zone scale* added to the barrel.

The classical practice, however, is to point the hemisphere directly at the lens and eliminate only the backlights, then take a reading exactly at the subject position. Reading key, fill, and backlight separately is in fact only a way of determining the ratios and looking for out-of-balance sources. In most instances, reading the key light is what determines the exposure — how the lens aperture will be set. Later we will look at applications that go beyond the simple classical approach and are useful in dealing with unusual situations. Most meters that are used with the diffusing dome also come with a flat diffusing plate that has a much smaller acceptance angle (about 45° to 55°). This means that the angle of the light falling on the plate has an effect on the reading, just as it does in illuminating a subject.

The flat plate makes taking readings for individual lights simpler and is also useful for measuring illumination on flat surfaces, such as in art copy work. Incident meters are generally also supplied with a lenticular glass plate that converts them to wide acceptance reflectance meters. These see little use on most sets as they have very wide acceptance angles and it is difficult to exclude extraneous sources.

For the most part, incident meters are set for the film speed and shutter speed being used (either electronically or by using slide-in plates) and then read out directly in f/numbers.

The Reflectance Meter

Reflectance meters, (most frequently called *spot meters)* read the *luminance* of the subject, which is itself an integration of two factors: the *light level falling on the scene* and the *reflectivity* of the subject. It is why they are called reflectance meters. (Figures 10.27 through 10.29).

On the face of it, this would seem to be the most logical method of reading the scene, but there is a catch. Simply put, a spot meter will tell us how much light a subject is reflecting, but this leaves one very big unanswered question: how much light do you want it to reflect? In other words, incident meters provide absolute readouts (f/stops), while spot meters provide relative readouts that require interpretation. While many spot meters were formerly calibrated in exposure value (*EV*) units, most provide direct readout in f/stops, which can be a source of confusion.

Think of it this way: you are using such a meter and photographing a very fair-skinned girl holding a box of detergent in front of a sunset. You read the girl's face: f/5.6, the box reads f/4, the sky is f/22. So where are you? Not only do we not know where to set the aperture, we don't even know if the situation is good or bad. Let's step back a moment and think about what it is that light meters are telling us. To do this we have to understand the cycle of tone reproduction and lay down a basic system of thinking about it.

THE ZONE SYSTEM

We must remember that the exposure values of a scene are not represented by one simple number: most scenes contain a wide range of light values and reflectances. In evaluating exposure we must look at a subject in terms of its light and dark values: the subject range of brightness. For simplicity we will ignore its color values for the moment and analyze the subject in terms of monochromatic values.

Let's visualize a continuous scale of gray values from completely black to completely white (Figure 10.39). Each point on the gray scale represents a certain value that is equivalent to a tonal value in the scene. In everyday language we have only vague adjectives with which to describe the tones: "very dark gray," "medium gray,"

"blinding white," and so on. We need more precise descriptions, especially if we are tying to communicate exposure concepts to other people. Fortunately, a great still photographer named Ansel Adams developed a method of dealing with exposure in a more scientific and precise manner called the *Zone System*.

Using Adam's classic terminology in describing the grayscale, we will call the most completely black section Zone 0 and each tone that is one f/stop lighter is one zone "higher." For example, a subject area that reflects three stops more light than the darkest area in the scene would be designated Zone IV. It is crucial to remember that these are all relative. Zone 0 is not some predetermined number of foot-candles — it is the darkest area in this scene.

Still photographers might be accustomed to thinking of ten zones in all, but if there is a great contrast range in the scene, there might well be zones XII, XIII, or more. (Zone system purists will no doubt object to such an extreme simplification of the method, but it is sufficient for the present discussion, since few cinematographers do their own darkroom work.) What we are measuring is subject *brightness (luminance)*, which can vary in two ways: the inherent *reflectance* of the different parts of the subject matter and the *amount of light* that falls on it. Reflectance is a property of the material itself. Black velvet reflects about 2% of the light that falls on it. A very shiny surface can reflect up to 98% of the light. This is a brightness ratio of 1:48. This is what makes a material dark or light — how reflective it is.

However, this is the reflectance ratio if the *same amount* of light falls on both objects. In reality, different amounts of light fall on different areas in the same frame (indeed, we make our living making sure they do, as we manipulate the lighting of a scene). In natural light situations the reflectance ratio can be as much as 3200:1. Picture an extreme example: a piece of black velvet in deep shadow in the same scene with a white rock in the sun.

The brightness range of a typical outdoor subject is about 1000:1. This is 15 stops and here's the rub: imaging systems cannot reproduce this range of subject brightness, just as the human eye cannot accommodate such a range.

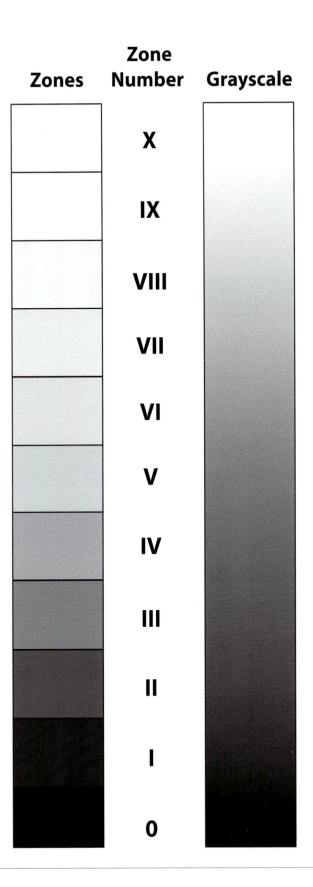

Zones	Zone Number	Grayscale
	X	
	IX	
	VIII	
	VII	
	VI	
	V	
	IV	
	III	
	II	
	I	
	0	

Figure 10.31. Zones 0 through X and a continuous grayscale. By convention, zones are represented in Roman numerals.

Zones in a Scene

Examine a typical scene with the spot meter — see Figure 10.32. If you assign the darkest value to Zone 0 you can then find areas that are 1, 2, 3, 4, 5, 6, 7, and perhaps 8 or 9 stops brighter than the darkest area: these are Zones I through X. This is an important exercise and is vital to understanding exposure control. Ignoring the effect of color contrast can be difficult sometimes. It can be helped by viewing the scene through a viewing glass, which is a neutral density filter.

Now picture each of these tonal values arranged in ascending order. What you have is a grayscale, and fortunately it is a commonly available item. Most grayscales are made to reasonable rigorous densitometric standards and are useful calibration tools. Let's take a look at what it really is (Figure 10.31).

THE GRAY SCALE

There are a great many grayscales but, they all have one thing in common: they vary from black to white. Most are divided into six to ten steps, but they certainly don't have to be: some are 20 steps or more. How white the white is and how black the black is vary somewhat depending on the printing quality and the materials involved. Some scales include a piece of black velvet, since black paper can never be truly black. For our purposes, we will consider only grayscales where each step represents one full "stop" increment over the previous, — where each step is $\sqrt{2}$ times the reflectance of the previous one (Table 10.4).

Why 18%?

Zone V is the middle zone of a ten-zone scale, and we would therefore assume it to be 50% reflectance. It isn't — it is 18% reflectance. The reason for this is that the eye perceives changes in tone logarithmically rather than arithmetically, as we saw above. If each zone were, for example, 10% more reflective than the previous, the eye would not read it as a smooth spectrum.

Discussion of the zone system is always in terms of grays, but any color can be interpreted in terms of its gray-scale value. The importance of value cannot be stressed too much. The value relationships between colors carry about 90% of the information in any picture. In a black-and-white photograph the gradients of light and shadow on surfaces contains the information about form, clearly defining all the objects. Color contributes a relatively small amount of actual picture information, but a great deal of the beauty and interest of the picture.

Zone X	100%
Zone IX	70%
Zone VIII	50%
Zone VII	35%
Zone V	18%
Zone IV	12%
Zone III	9%
Zone II	6%
Zone I	4.5%
Zone 0	3.5%

Table 10.4. Percentage of reflectance for Zones. These are reflectance values of the subject.

ZONE	DENSITY	DESCRIPTION
0	0.02	Pure black - Dmax.
I	0.11	1st perceptible value lighter than black.
II	0.21	Very, very dark gray.
III	0.34	Fully textured dark gray.
IV	0.48	Dark middle gray.
V	0.62	Middle gray - 18% reflectance.
VI	0.76	Light middle gray.
VII	0.97	Fully textured light gray.
VIII	1.18	Very light gray.
IX	1.33	First perceptible gray darker than pure white.
X	1.44	Pure white - Dmin.

Table 10.5. Zones, negative density and description.

Zone X
Zone VIII
Zone VII
Zone VI
Zone V
Zone IV
Zone III
Zone II
Zone I
Zone 0

Figure 10.32. Zones in a black-and-white print. In this example shot, there is no Zone IX. (Photo by author.)

In fact, it works out as in Table 10.4. Each step is greater than the previous by $\sqrt{2}$; a familiar number, no? The square root of 2 is also the derivation of the f/stop series. What appears middle gray (Zone V) to the eye is actually 17 1/2% reflectance, which is universally rounded off to 18%. There's more: it turns out that if you take dozens of spot readings of typical scenes, most will turn out to have an average reflectance of about 18%. Simply put: 18% is the average reflectance of the normal world. Clearly it is not the average reflectance in a coal mine or in the Sahara at mid-day, but in the most of the rest of the world, it is a reasonable working average. This gives us a solid ground on which to build. In fact, it is the standard on which incident meters are built.

As you recall, in the introduction to incident meters we noted that most incident meters, when set for film speed and shutter speed, read out directly in f/stops. How do they do this? How can they know if we are photographing diamonds on a white background or a chimney-sweep in the basement? They don't know, they just assume that we are photographing a scene of average reflectances and the diffusing dome averages the light and the meter calculates the f/stop needed to photograph the scene for good exposure based on these assumptions. (Amazingly, in most situations, this works perfectly, although there are some cases that require a bit more interpretation, such as a subject lit mostly with backlight.) More simply, if we are photographing a card that is exactly 18% reflectance (a photographic gray card) and we read the light with an incident meter, then set the aperture to the stop the meter indicates, the print will in fact come out to be Zone V.

Try this experiment. Set a photographic gray card in even, uniform light. Read it with a spot meter and note the f/stop the meter indicates. Then read the light falling on the gray card with an incident meter. The two readings should be the same. This is the central concept — the key that unlocks the world of exposure control:

- An incident reading,
- An average 18% reflectance,
- A spot meter reading of a gray card and
- Zone V

...are all the same thing but looked at from a different perspective. The result of this is that there are many different ways to read the exposure of a scene and arrive at the same result:

- You can read it with an incident meter.
- You can place a gray card in the important part of the scene and read it with a spot meter.
- You can find something in the scene that is Zone V and read it with the spot meter.

Let's think about that last one, because it really points us in a whole new direction. It depends on you making a certain judgment: you have to look at a scene in the real world of color and decide that it is about Zone V or middle gray. What about the next logical step: what if there isn't anything in the scene that is middle gray? What do we do then? Let's remember that each step on the grayscale is one stop different from its neighbor. So if Zone V equals f/4 (given a particular film and shutter speed), then Zone VI must be f/5.6 and Zone IV must be f/2.8, right?

So if there is nothing in the scene that equals Zone V, but there is something in the scene that equals Zone VI, we're still in business. If we read it and it equals f/5.6, then we know that Zone V would be f/4. We also know that Zone V (f/4 in this example) is the same as an incident or average reading and is therefore the correct f/stop to set on the lens.

I think you can see where this leads us. We don't have to confine ourselves to just reading things that equal Zone V and Zone VI. In fact, we can do it with any zone. It all depends on your judgment of what gray tone a subject brightness should be. In real life, it takes years of practice and mental discipline to accurately determine subject brightnesses in terms of grayscale values, but in the long run it is a useful skill. If you can previsualize what grayscale value you want a particular subject to be in the final print, you then have the power to "place" it where you want it in the exposure range. This turns out to be a powerful analytical and design tool.

Place and Fall

What do we mean by "placement"? We just saw its simplest form. We "placed" the skin-tone value of the hand on Zone VI. We can, if we want, place any value in the scene. Say we have a gray background in the scene that the director wants to be "light gray." We decide that by light gray, she means Zone VII (two stops above middle gray). We then read the background with a spot meter and it indicates f/4. We then count down two stops and get f/2. If we set the lens at f/2, that gray background will photograph as "light gray" or Zone VII, two steps above middle gray.

Let's try the reverse as a thought experiment. Say we had the same background under exactly the same lighting conditions, but the director decided she wanted it to be dark gray, which we take to mean Zone III. We read it with the spot meter and of course nothing has changed; the spot meter still indicates f/4, only now we want the gray background to appear much darker, so we "place" it on Zone

III, which we do by counting "up" two stops to get f/8. Common sense tells us that if we photograph the same scene at f/8 instead of f/2, it is going to come out much darker: the background will not be Zone III (dark gray) instead of Zone VII (light gray).

Nothing has changed in the actual set; we have changed the value of the final print by "placing" the value of the background differently. But what's the flaw in this ointment? There is more in the scene than just a gray background, and whatever else is there is going to be photographing lighter or darker at the same time. This brings us to the second half of the process: "fall."

If you place a certain value in a scene on a certain zone, other values in that scene are going to fall on the grayscale according to how much different they are in illumination and reflectance. For our example, let's assume we are using a Pentax Spotmeter that has a zone dial attached to it. The Pentax reads in EVs. Typical white skin tone is a Zone VI. You read an actor's face and find that it reads EV 10. Turn the dial so that 10 aligns with Zone VI. Now read the exposure indicated opposite Zone V: this is the exposure to set the lens aperture, adding adjustments for filter factors, and so on.

A Zones Example

Let's try an example. We are lighting a set with a window. We set a 10K to simulate sunlight streaming in through the window. We then read the curtains and the spot meter indicates f/11. We have decided that we want the curtains to be very "hot" but not burned out. On the film stock we are using today, we know that white "burns out" at about three stops hotter than Zone V. So we want to "place" the curtains on Zone VIII (three stops hotter than the average exposure). By placing the curtains on Zone VIII, we have determined the f/stop of the camera: it will be f/4, right?

We then take an incident reading in the room where the people will be standing. The incident reading is f/2.8. This means that people standing in that position will photograph one zone too dark. Maybe for this scene that's OK, but let's assume we want to actors to have normal exposure that will result in normal skin tone values. In other words, Zone VI "falls" at f/4 (one stop above the incident reading, which equals Zone V). Their skin tone will come out as Zone V instead of Zone VI.

To correct the situation we have to change the balance. If we just open up the lens, we are shifting the placement of the curtains and they will burn out. We must change the ratio of the illumination, not just shift the aperture of the camera. We can either tone down the 10K hitting the window with a double scrim (one stop) or we can raise the exposure of the subject area by increasing the light level there one stop. Either way are manipulating the subject values of the foreground to "fall" where we want them, based on our "placement" of the curtains on Zone VIII. We could "place" the foreground values where we want them and then see where the curtains "fall." It's the same thing. By reading the scene in different ways, you can "place" the values of the negative where you want them to fall.

Placement is important in determining subject brightness ranges and contrast ratios and in reading subjects that you can't get to for an incident reading. In order to expose by placement, you must pre-visualize which zone you want a subject value to reproduce as. For Ansel Adams, pre-visualization was what it was all about, and remember, he dealt mostly with landscapes where he had no control over lighting. Since we usually control the lighting, we can take pre-visualization one step further.

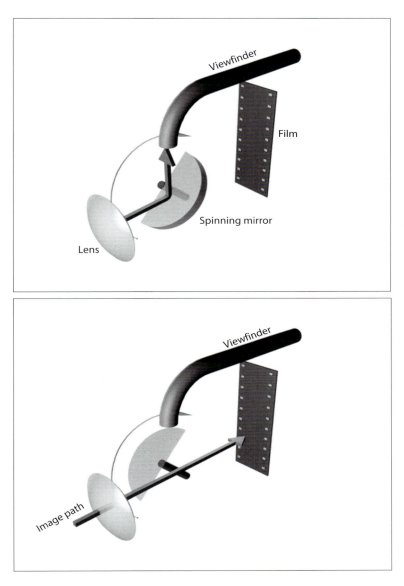

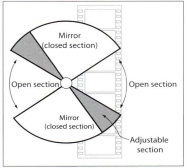

Figure 10.33. (above) Adjustable rotating shutter. Shutter angle adjustment in video or High Def cameras is done electronically.

Figure 10.34. (left) The spinning mirror shutter alternates between sending the image to the viewfinder and letting the image reach the film plane.

Reading Exposure with Ultraviolet

Ultraviolet lights present a special problem. Several companies make ultraviolet light sources. They include *Wildfire* and *Nocturn*. When combined with props or clothing painted with UV-sensitive fluorescent paints or dyes or with objects that naturally fluoresce, an incident reading is meaningless. The only valid means of assessing exposure is a reflected reading. A wide-angle reflectance meter will work if you have one, or have an adapter for your incident meter. If that is not available, a spot reading will work.

EXPOSURE AND THE CAMERA

Nearly all film cameras have rotating reflex shutters, which control exposure by alternately rotating closed and open sections past the film plane. While the closed section is in front of the film gate, the film moves, while the open section is in front of the gate, the film is exposed (Figure 10.34). The exposure time of the camera is determined by two factors: the speed at which the shutter is operating and the size of the open section. The speed is determined by the frame rate at which the camera is operating. The open section of the rotating shutter assembly is referred to as the "shutter angle" and is measured in degrees. Sensibly, most shutters are half open and half closed, which makes the shutter angle 180°. Some shutters are 165° and many are adjustable (Figure 10.33).

With the camera operating at 24 fps and a 180° shutter, the exposure time is 1/48th of a second (1/50th at European 25 fps). This is commonly rounded off to 1/50th of a second and is considered the standard motion picture exposure time.

Exposure time can then vary in two ways: by changing the frame rate (which is common) and by varying the shutter angle (which is less common). Exposure is determined by this formula:

Shutter speed for 180° shutter =
$$\frac{1}{2 \text{ x fps}}$$

Exposure in seconds =
$$\frac{\text{shutter opening (degrees)}}{360 \text{ x frames per second}}$$

Exposure Time — Shutter Speed versus Shutter Angle

To calculate exposure on shots where the camera is ramping (changing frame rate and thus shutter speed during the spot), here is a quick comparison of exposure times when expressed in 1/xx seconds versus xx degrees.

These calculations are based on 24 fps, which is the most frequently used frame rate for narrative filmmaking (30 fps is more often used for sports). To convert shutter speed to shutter angles at 24 fps:

(24 x 360) / Time shutter is open
24 x 360 = 8640 / (xx where xx is 1/ xx sec)

Thus, the equivalent shutter angle for 1/50 sec shutter speed is:

8640 / 50 = 172.8 (172.8 degrees shutter angle)

Table 10.6 shows shutter speed and the equivalent conversion in degrees:

Shutter Speed	Shutter Angle
1/32	270
1/48	180
1/50	172.8
1/60	144
1/96	90
1/120	72

Some cameras (such as the RED) have variable shutter speeds from 1/32 to 1/2000, or the equivalent shutter angles. To find a shutter speed that relates to a particular shutter angle, do the calculation in reverse. At 24 fps the equation would be:

(24 x 360) / Shutter Angle

(e.g., 8640 / xx, where xx is xx degrees).

So the shutter speed for 144 degrees:

8640 / 144 = 60

camera movement

Along with sequential editing, the ability to move the camera is the most fundamental aspect that distinguishes film and video from photography, painting, and other visual arts. As we have seen, moving the camera is much more than just going from one frame to another. The movement itself, the style, the trajectory, the pacing, and the timing in relation to the action all contribute to the mood and feel of the shot. They add a subtext and an emotional content independent of the subject.

We talked about the cinematic uses of camera moves in *Language of the Lens*; here we can cover the techniques and technology of moving the camera. The most basic use of the camera is where you put it. Camera placement is a key decision in storytelling. More than just "where it looks good," it determines what the audience sees and from what perspective they see it. As discussed in the chapter on *Shooting Methods*, what the audience does not see can be as important as what they do see.

Since Griffith freed the camera from its stationary singular point of view, moving the camera has become an ever increasing part of the visual art of filmmaking. In this section we will look at the dynamics of camera movement and also take a look at some representative ways in which this is accomplished. The dolly as a means of moving the camera dates from the early part of the 20th century. The crane came into its own in the 1920s (see Figure 11.2 for a modern version). Shots from moving vehicles were accomplished in the earliest of silents, especially with the silent comedians, who didn't hesitate to strap a camera to a car or train.. After the introduction of the crane, little changed with the means of camera movement until the invention of the Steadicam by Garrett Brown. It was first used on the films *Bound for Glory* and Kubrick's *The Shining*.

MOTIVATION AND INVISIBLE TECHNIQUE

In narrative filmmaking, a key concept of camera movement is that it must be motivated. The movement should not just be for the sake of moving the camera; doing so usually means that the director is suffering from a lack of storytelling skills. Motivation can come in two ways. First, the action itself may motivate a move. For example, if the character gets up from a chair and crosses to the window, it is perfectly logical for the camera to move with her. Not necessary, but clearly one way to do it.

Both the start and the end of a dolly move or pan should be motivated. The motivation at the end may be as simple as the fact that we have arrived at the new frame, but clearly it must be a new frame — one with new information composed in a meaningful way, not just "where the camera ended up." A big part of this is that the camera should "settle" at the end of any move. It needs to "alight" at the new frame and be there for a beat before the cut point. This is especially important if this shot might cut to a static shot.

Particularly with the start and end of camera moves that are motivated by subject movement, there needs to be a sensitivity to the timing of the subject and also a delicate touch as to speed. You seldom want the dolly to just "take off" at full speed, then grind to a sudden halt. Most of the time, you want the dolly grip to "feather" in and out of the move.

The camera movement itself may have a purpose. For example, a move may reveal new information or a new view of the scene. The camera may move to meet someone or pull back to show a wider shot. Unmotivated camera moves or zooms are distracting; they pull

Figure 11.1. (previous page) Setting up a crane.

Figure 11.2. A Chapman *Lenny Arm* rigged on a camera car for some moving shots in Greenwich Village. The grip who will operate it wears a safety harness. (Photo courtesy of Mark Weingartner.)

the audience out of the moment and make them conscious that they are watching a fiction; they do, however, have their uses, particularly in very stylized filmmaking.

There are many ways to find a motivation for a camera move, and they can be used to enhance the scene and add a layer of meaning beyond the shots themselves. They can also add a sense of energy, joy, menace, sadness, or any other emotional overlay. Camera movement is much like the pacing of music. A crane move can "soar" as the music goes upbeat, or the camera can dance with the energy of the moment, such as when Rocky reaches the top of the museum steps and the Steadicam spins around and around him. Motivating and timing camera moves are part of the goal of invisible technique. Just as with cutting and coverage in the master scene method, the goal is for the "tricks" to be unnoticed and not distract from the storytelling.

Basic Technique

There is an endless variety of ways to move the camera, and it would be impossible to catalog every one here. It is useful to look at a few basic categories of types of moves to provide a general vocabulary of camera dynamics. The most fundamental of camera moves, the pan and tilt, can be accomplished in almost any mode, including handheld. The exception is when a camera is locked off on either a non-movable mount (as it might be for an explosion or big stunt) or where it is on a movable head, but the movements are locked down and there is no operator. Many types of effect shots require the camera to be locked down so that not even the slightest movement of the camera is possible. Sandbags on the tripod or dolly, or even braces made of C-stands or lumber may also be used.

Beyond the simple pan and tilt or zoom, most moves involve an actual change of camera position in the shot. Other than handheld, these kinds of moves involve specific technologies and also the support of other team members: the grip department. Grips are the experts when it comes to mounting the camera in any way other than right on a tripod or a dolly, and they are the people who provide the rigging, the stabilization, and the actual operation when it comes to performing the actual move.

A good grip crew makes it look easy, but there is considerable knowledge and finesse involved in laying smooth dolly track on a rough surface (Figure 11.3) or rigging the camera on the front of a roller-coaster. Every detail of rigging is beyond the scope of this chapter, but we will touch on some of the major issues.

TYPES OF MOVES

Pan

Short for panoramic, the term *pan* applies to left or right horizontal movement of the camera. Pans are fairly easy to operate with a decent camera head — which sits atop the tripod or dolly, holds the camera, and permits left/right, up/down, and sometimes sideways tilting motions. There is one operational limitation that must be dealt with. If the camera is panned too quickly, there will be a strobing effect, which will be very disturbing.

As a general rule of thumb, with a shutter opening of 180° and a frame rate of 24 or 25 fps, it should take at least 3 to 5 seconds for an object to move from one side of the frame to the other. Any faster and there is a danger of strobing.

Tilt

The tilt is up or down movement without changing camera position. Technically, it is not correct to say "pan up," but as a practical matter everybody says it. The tilt, being a vertical move, is used much less frequently than the pan. For better or worse, we live most of our lives on a generally horizontal plane, and that is the way most action plays out in narrative, documentary, and informational filmmaking. As we will see later in this chapter, cranes, Steadicams and aerial mounts are to a large extent used to break out of the confined horizontal plane and make the scenes more truly three-dimensional.

Filmmaking is confined, to a large degree, by where we can put the camera. Certainly the ability of the Steadicam and similar rigs to move with action up and down stairs and slopes has opened up a new variety of moves, that help with this three-dimensional effort and keeps us "with" the characters as they move through space. Given the technology now available and the ingenuity of our grips and camera assistants, there is hardly anywhere a camera can't go.

Move In / Move Out

Move the dolly toward or away from the action. Common terminology is *push in* or *pull out*. For example, to the dolly grip: "When he sits down, you push in." This is different from a punch-in (see following). Moving into the scene or out of it are ways of combining the wide shot of a scene with a specific tighter shot. It is a way of selecting the view for the audience in a way that is more dramatic than just cutting from wide shot to closer shot. It has the effect of focusing the viewer's attention even more effectively than just doing a wide establishing and then cutting to the scene; by moving in toward the scene, the camera is saying "of all the things on this street, this is the part that is important for you to look at."

Figure 11.3. A very simple pipe dolly rig for this Imax shot in China. Pipe dolly rigs are especially useful for situations like this where a rental dolly is unavailable and it is impractical to fly one in. Many people carry the wheels and hardware with them and build the dolly and track with locally available materials. (Photo courtesy of Mark Weingartner.)

Of course, there are infinite uses of the simple move in/move out. We may pull back as the character moves out of the scene or as another character enters; the move is often just a pragmatic way of allowing more room for additional elements of the scene or to tie in something else to the immediate action we have been watching. Conversely, when someone leaves a scene, a subtle push-in can take up the slack in the framing.

Zoom

A zoom is an optical change of focal length. It moves the point of view in or out without moving the camera. Visible zooms are not popular in feature film making — certainly not since the end of the 1970s. The reason is simple: a zoom calls attention to itself and makes the audience aware they are watching a movie — something we usually want to avoid in invisible technique. When a zoom is used, it is important that the zoom be motivated. Also, it is best to hide a zoom. Hiding a zoom is an art. The zoom may be combined with a slight camera move, a dolly move, a slight pan, or with a move by the actors so that it is unnoticeable.

Difference Between a Zoom and a Dolly Shot

Say you want to go from a wide or medium to a close-up during the shot. On the face of it, there would seem to be no real difference between moving the dolly in or zooming in. In actual effect, they are quite different, for several reasons.

First, a zoom changes the perspective from a wide angle with deep focus and inclusion of the background to a long lens shot with compressed background and very little of the background. It also changes the depth-of-field, so the background or foreground might go from sharp focus to soft. These might be the effects you want, but often they are not. Second, the dolly move is dynamic in a way that a zoom cannot be. With a zoom your basic point of view stays the same because the camera does not move; with a dolly the camera moves in relation to the subject. Even if the subject stays center frame, the background moves behind the subject. This adds a sense of motion, and also the shot ends with an entirely different background than it opened with. This is not to say that a zoom is never desirable, just that it is important to understand the difference and what each type of move can do for your scene as a visual effect. Many people will also "hide" the zoom by making some other type

Figure 11.4. (top) An ordinary *track with* move. Camera move matches the direction of the subject.

Figure 11.5. (middle) Countermove.

Figure 11.6. (bottom) Dolly across the line of movement. This one has to be used with caution. If the entire shot is not used, the screen direction will be flipped without explanation. See the chapter *Cinematic Continuity* for further discussion of this issue.

of move at the same time so that the zoom is not noticeable. This is the biggest problem with a zoom: it draws attention to itself and makes the audience aware they are watching a movie.

A very dramatic effect can be produced with a combination of zoom and a dolly. In this technique you zoom out as you dolly in. This keeps the image size relatively the same, but there is a dramatic change of perspective and background. This was used very effectively in *Jaws*, when Roy Scheider as the sheriff is sitting on the beach and first hears someone call "shark." It was also used effectively in *Goodfellas* in the scene where Ray Liotta is having lunch with Robert De Niro in the diner. At the moment Liotta realizes he is being set up for killing by his old friend, the combination move effectively underscores the feeling of disorientation.

Punch-in

Different from a push in, which involves actually moving the camera, a punch-in means that the camera stays where it is, but a longer focal length prime is put on or the lens is zoomed in for a tighter shot. The most common use of a punch-in is for coverage on a dialog scene, usually when going from an over-the-shoulder to a clean single. Since moving the camera forward from an over-the-shoulder may involve repositioning the off-camera actor and other logistics, it is often easier to just go to a longer lens. There is some slight change in perspective, but for this type of close-up it is often not noticeable as long as the head size remains constant.

MOVING SHOTS

Tracking

The simplest and most clearly motivated of camera moves is to track along with a character or vehicle in the same direction (Figure 11.4). For the most part, the movement is alongside and parallel. It is certainly possible to stay ahead of and look back at the subject or to follow along behind, but these kinds of shots are not nearly as dynamic as tracking alongside, which gives greater emphasis to the moving background and the sweep of the motion.

Countermove

If the camera always moves only with the subject, matching its direction and speed, it can get a little boring. In this case, the camera is "tied to" the subject and completely dependent on it. If the camera sometimes moves independently of the subject, it can add a counterpoint and an additional element to the scene. Certainly it can be dynamic and energetic; it adds a counterpoint of movement that deepens the scene (Figure 11.5). Whenever the camera moves in the opposite direction, the background appears to move at twice the rate it would move if the camera was tracking along in the same direction as the subject. A variation is to move across the line of travel, as in Figure 11.6. A variation of the countermove is where the dolly moves in the opposite direction and the subjects cross the axis of motion as in Figure 11.10.

Reveal

A simple dolly or crane move can be used for an effective reveal. A subject fills the frame, and then with a move, something else is revealed. This type of shot is most effective where the second frame reveals new content that amplifies the meaning of the first shot or ironically comments on it.

Circle Track Moves

When ordering a dolly and track, it is quite common to also order at least a couple of pieces of circle track. Circular track generally comes in two types: 45° and 90°. These designate whether it takes four pieces or eight pieces to make a complete circle, which defines the radius of the track. A very specific use of circle track is to dolly completely or halfway around the subject; this type of move is easily abused and can be very self-conscious if not motivated by something in the scene. Some companies specify by radius.

On important note on setting up a circle track scene: as it is quite common to use circle track to move very slowly around the subject in a tight shot, focus pulling can get quite complex. The best way to simplify a circle move is to set up the shot so that the subject is positioned at dead center of the radius of the track.

Crane Moves

The most useful aspect of a crane is its ability to achieve large vertical moves within the shot. While a crane may be used only to get the camera up high, the most basic variety of crane shot is to start with a high angle view of the overall scene as an establishing shot and then move down and in to isolate a piece of the geography: most often our main characters, who then proceed with the action or dialog. This is most often used to open the scene by combining the establishing shot with the closer-in master of the specific action.

The opposite move, starting tight on the scene and then pulling back to reveal the wide shots, is an effective way to end a scene as well and is often used as the dramatic last shot of an entire film — a slow disclosure. Depending on the content of the scene and the entire film, it can have a powerful emotional content. If, for example, the tight shot is of the young man bleeding to death on the pavement, pulling back to a wide shot of the deserted street, with no help in sight can have a tragic, hopeless feel. Such shots make a very specific statement and should not be used casually. The ability of the crane to "swoop" dramatically and flowingly can be used for exhilarating and energetic effect; more than any other type of camera move, it can really "dance" with the characters or the action.

Another aspect of the crane that is important to keep in mind is that most cranes are capable of going below the level of their mounting surface. This can be used to get you down into a ditch or other place where setting a tripod or dolly would be impractical. Of course, such use can always be enhanced by building a platform for the crane. This has the effect of raising the top end of the move. Since you are now also using the below the surface capability, you can employ the full range of motion of the crane for the most dynamic shot.

Figure 11.7, 11.8 and 11.9. (left, center and right) A *going to meet them* camera move. This is a very dynamic shot as the subject distance changes. This can be used to start with a wide tracking shot and end up with a tight close-up or vice-versa.

Figure 11.10. (below) An example of a complex and dynamic move: a shot of this type tracks, pans and subject distance and direction change all at the same time.

Rolling Shot

The term *rolling shot* is used wherever the camera is mounted on a vehicle, either on the picture vehicle or a camera car that travels along with the picture vehicle. The "picture" vehicle is the one being photographed.

CAMERA MOUNTING

Handheld

Handheld is any time the operator takes the camera in hand, usually held on the shoulder, but it can be held low to the ground, placed on the knees, or any other combination. For many years, handheld was the primary means of making the camera mobile in cases where a dolly was not available or not practical (on stairs, for example). Now, with so many other ways to keep the camera mobile, handheld is most often used for artistic purposes.

Handheld has a sense of immediacy and energy that cannot be duplicated by other means. It suggests a documentary approach and thus subtly implies that "you are there," and "it's really happening."

Camera Head

The camera cannot be mounted directly on a tripod or dolly. If it was, there would be no way to pan or tilt the camera. On dollies, cranes and car mounts, there is also an intermediate step: the leveling head (Figure 11.11). This is the base the camera head sits on, which allows for leveling of the camera. In the case of a tripod, leveling is accomplished by lengthening or shortening one of the legs to get the camera level. Camera heads make smooth, stable, and repeatable moves possible. Camera heads have two main types of mounts: the flat *Mitchell plate* (Figure 11.11) and the *ball head*, which allows for leveling the head quickly. Heads fall into the following categories.

Fluid Head

These use oil and internal dampers and springs to make extremely smooth left/right and up/down moves possible (Figure 11.12). The amount of resistance is adjustable. Most camera operators want the head to have a good amount of resistance working against them.

Geared Head

These heads are operated with wheels that the operator can move very smoothly and precisely repeat moves (Figure 11.13). The geared head has a long and venerable history in studio production. The geared head is useful not only for the ability to execute smooth and repeatable moves but also because it can handle very heavy cameras.

Remote Head

Geared heads can also be fitted with motors to be operated remotely or by a computer for *motion control* (*mo-co*). Remotely controlled heads are used for a variety of purposes and have made possible the use of cranes, which extend much farther and higher than would be possible if the arm had to be designed to carry the weight of an operator and camera assistant.

Underslung Heads

These are fluid heads, but the camera is not mounted on top; it is suspended on a cradle below the pivot point. Underslung heads can rotate vertically far past where an ordinary fluid head can go and thus are good for shots that need to go straight up or down or even further. They are specialized rigs, but they have many uses.

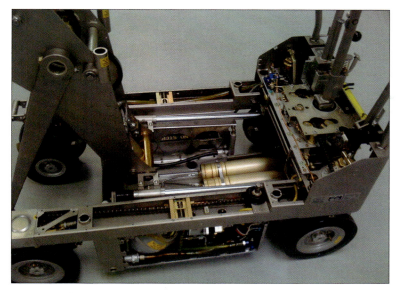

Dutch Head

Dutch angle is when the camera is tilted off horizontal. The variations are dutch left and dutch right. As with many obscure terms in film, there is much speculation as to the origin. In fact, it goes back to 17th century England, when a Dutch royal, William of Orange, was placed on the throne of Britain. There was much resentment, and anything that was considered "not quite right" was called "dutch." Hence, dutch doors, dutch dates and dutch auctions. Specially built dutch heads are also available that convert back and forth between dutch and normal operation very quickly.

The Tripod

Often called "sticks," the tripod is the oldest and most basic type of camera mount but still sees constant use on all types of film and video sets. Being smaller, lighter, and more portable than just about any other type of mount, its versatility makes up for its shortcomings. It can be quickly repositioned and can be made to fit into very tight, odd places. Its main advantage is that it can be transported just about anywhere.

High-Hat

The high-hat is strictly the mounting surface for the camera head; most have no leveling capability at all, but some do. It is used when the camera needs to go very low, almost to the surface. It is also used when the camera needs to be mounted in a remote place, such as on top of a ladder. The high-hat is usually bolted to a piece of plywood that can be screwed, bolted, or strapped in to all sorts of places.

Rocker Plate

The drawback of a high-hat is that the camera head (fluid or geared) still has to go on top of it. As a result, the lens height is still at least 18 inches or more above the surface. If this just isn't low enough, the first choice is usually to prop it on a sandbag. The pliable nature of the sandbag allows the camera to be positioned for level and tilt. Any moves, however, are pretty much handheld. If more control is desired, a rocker plate can be used. This is a simple device that allows the camera to be tilted up and down. Smooth side-to-side pans are not possible.

Figure 11.14. (top) A true nodal point head by Cartoni. (Photo courtesy of Cartoni, S.p.A.)

Figure 11.15. (middle) A compact and highly maneuverable crab dolly — the Chapman Peewee. (Photo courtesy Chapman/Leonard Studio Equipment.)

Figure 11.16. (left) The inner workings of a Fisher dolly. The tanks are for hydraulic oil and nitrogen.

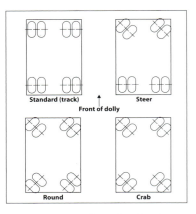

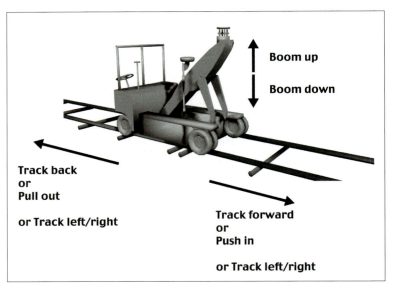

Figure 11.17. (left) Dolly wheel positions for various types of moves.

Figure 11.18. (right) Dolly and boom terminology.

Tilt Plate

Sometimes, a shot calls for a greater range of up-and-down tilt than a typical camera head can provide. In this case, a tilt plate can be mounted on top of the camera head (Figure 11.13). It is usually geared and can be tilted to the desired angle. The gearing (if there is any) is generally not smooth enough to be used in a shot.

THE CRAB DOLLY

The crab dolly is by far the most often used method of mounting and moving the camera. A crab dolly in the hands of a good dolly grip is capable of a surprising range and fluidity of movement. Figures 11.15 and 11.16 are typical dollys widely used in production today.

Dolly Terminology

Special terminology is used to describe dolly motion so that it can be communicated precisely.

Dolly In/Out

Move the dolly toward or away from the subject (Figure 11.18). When a dolly is on the floor and you want to move forward, there are two choices. "Move in" can either mean move forward on the axis of the lens or on the axis in which the crabbed wheels are aiming. These are "in on the lens" or "in on the wheels."

Dolly Left/Right

Move the dolly left or right. If the dolly is on tracks, it is left or right in relation to the axis of the track. If the dolly is on the floor, then it is left or right in relation to the subject (Figure 11.18).

Boom Up/Down

Nearly all dollies have a boom: a hydraulic arm capable of moving vertically in a smooth enough motion to be used in a shot without shakes or jarring. Some boom terms include: top floor and bottom floor.

Crab Left/Right

Most dollies have wheels that can *crab* (Figure 11.17), that is, both front and rear wheels can be turned in the same direction, allowing the dolly to move laterally at any angle. For most normal operations, the rear wheels are in crab mode and are the "smart wheels." The

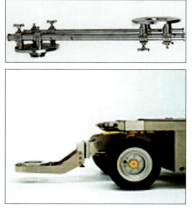

Figure 11.19. (left) A *porkchop* on a Fisher dolly. The dolly is mounted on a skateboard sled that rides on the tracks.

Figure 11.20. (top) An offset arm for a dolly, this one can also be set up for an underslung camera if needed. (Photo courtesy of J.L. Fisher, Inc.)

Figure 11.21. (bottom) A drop-down plate, sometimes called a *Z-bar*. It is used to get the camera very low but still maneuverable. (Photo courtesy of J.L. Fisher, Inc.)

front wheels are locked in and function as the *dumb* wheels. For a true crab move, all four wheels are switched to crab mode. There is another variation that can be done only with certain dollies. This is *roundy-round*, where the wheels can be set so that the dolly revolves in a full 360° circle on its own center. To do this, the front and rear wheels are crabbed in opposite directions. This can be done with Fisher dollies as well as the Panther and Elemack (Figure 11.17).

Dance Floor

Stable, shake-free dolly moves can only be accomplished on smooth floors. If there is no room for track to be laid or if the director is looking for dolly moves that can't be accommodated by straight or curved track, a *dance floor* can be built that allows the camera to move anywhere. A dance floor is built with good quality 3/4 inch plywood (usually birch) topped with a layer of smooth masonite. It is important that the joints be offset and then carefully taped. This forms an excellent surface for smooth moves. The good dolly can crab and roll anywhere, and combination moves can be quite complex. The only drawback is that you have to avoid showing the floor, unless you paint it. Smooth floors or dance floor, becomes especially critical if anything other than a wide lens is up on the camera because with a longer lens, every bump in the floor will jiggle the camera.

Extension Plate

When the camera is mounted on the dolly, it may be necessary to extend it to the left, right, or forward of where the dolly can go (Figure 11.20) — for example, if you need to place the dolly at the center of a bed. This can be done with an extension plate that mounts on the dolly, then the camera head is mounted at the end.

Low Mode

Sometimes the camera needs to be lower than the boom can go. In this case, there are two possibilities. Some dollies can have their camera mounting arm reconfigured so that it is only a few inches above the floor (Figure 11.21). If this is not available or is not enough, a Z-bar can be used to get the camera all the way to the floor. The Z-bar is basically an extension arm that extends out and then down as close to the floor as possible.

Figure 11.22. (above) The Chapman Titan II, a truck-mounted crane. The truck can run on battery power for sync-sound shots. (Photo courtesy of Chapman/Leonard Studio Equipment, Inc.)

Figure 11.23. (right) Dolly leveling with a *half apple* box, *wedges,* and *cribbing* (blocks of wood).

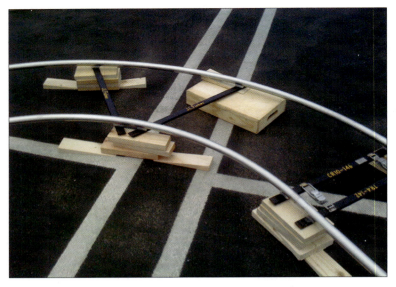

Front Porch

Some dollies have a small extension that fits on the front of the dolly — the *front porch*; this is also known as a *cowcatcher*. This can be used to hold the battery or as a place for the operator or the camera assistant to stand during a move.

Side Boards

Sideboards fit on either side of the dolly as a place for the operator or camera assistant to stand. They are removable for transportation and for when the dolly has to fit through tight spaces. These are especially important for complex moves that require the operator to shift their body position.

Risers

Six, 9, 12 or 18 inch extensions can place the camera higher than the boom travels. The longest extensions can get the camera very high but at the price of absolute stability.

Steering Bar or Push Bar

This allows the dolly grip to push/pull the dolly and also to steer the dolly in standard mode (where only the rear wheels pivot) or in crab mode, where both sets of wheels pivot.

CRANES

Cranes are capable of much greater vertical and horizontal movements than a dolly. There are two types: jib arms have no seat for the cameraperson and are usually operated by someone standing on the floor or perhaps an apple box. True cranes generally have seats for the operator, and a camera assistant. Large cranes can generally get the camera, operator and assistant up to a lens height of around 27 or more above the base. We say "above the base" because often a crane will be mounted on a platform, vehicle, or other crane for additional height. A typical crane is shown in Figure 11.22.

Both cranes and jib arms have one fundamental characteristic that may become a problem. Because they are all mounted on a pivot point, the arm always has some degree of arc as it moves up, down, or laterally. With dolly arms this degree of arc is usually negligible for all except exacting macro or very tight work that calls for critical focus or a very precise frame size.

Crane/Jib Arm

A crane is any camera support where the arm can rotate freely as well as boom up and down. For nearly all cranes, there is a pivot point, and behind this point are counterweights. This is different from a dolly, where the boom arm is fixed and operated by hydraulics. A jib arm generally means a smaller crane arm that is mounted on a dolly or sticks. Most jib arms do not have a seat for the operator and camera assistant; the camera is operated from the floor or perhaps on a small ladder or an apple box.

The counterweights extending behind the pivot point have two important consequences. First, it is important to take this backswing into account when planning or setting up a crane move. If there isn't sufficient room, at best your moves will be limited and at worst something will be broken. The second is a safety issue, and it is one that cannot be emphasized enough. Any crane can be dangerous.

When you are on a crane, the key grip or crane grip is in charge. Nobody gets on or off the crane without permission of the crane grip. The reason for this is that your weight and the camera weight are precisely counterbalanced by the weights on the back end. If you were to suddenly get off the crane without warning, the camera end would go flying up in the air and very likely cause damage or injury. With anyone getting on or off, or with any changes in equipment, the crane grip and the back-end grip communicate loudly and clearly so that every step is coordinated.

Two other safety issues when working on a crane: Wear your safety belt. Always and be extremely careful around any electrical wires. After helicopters and camera cars, cranes around high-voltage wires are the leading cause of serious injury and death in the motion picture industry. Take it seriously. The best bet is to tell your crane grip what you want and then just let him be in charge.

Crane Operation

Crane operation should always be a three-person job; anything less is absolutely not safe. (This does not apply to jib arms, which don't have seats for the operator and AC.) The key grip usually guides the move; another grip pushes and pulls the chassis, and a third grip is at the rear of the crane with weights.

This grip helps the key swing the arm and serves as a *damper* to cushion the end of the move, so that the inertia of the crane doesn't let it overshoot the mark. A good crane crew executing complex moves is a joy to watch. They make it look easy, but it calls for power, coordination, careful choreography, and nearly ballet-like precision.

The Arc

Another issue with cranes is that, because they pivot on a central point, any crane arm (or any dolly arm) moves in an arc, not along a straight vertical line. In most cases this is not a problem. It only becomes an issue with very tight shots with limited depth of focus. Very few rigs allow you to compensate for the arc. The camera support slides back and forth on rails.

Chassis Left/Right or In/Out

The chassis is a dolly or specially built platform that supports the crane. Most small and medium-size jib arms or cranes mount either on a dolly or a braced rolling platform similar to a dolly. The chassis may roll on a smooth floor or may be mounted on dolly track for more repeatable movements.

Figure 11.24. A fully tricked out car rig with camera mounted on a *hostess tray* on the driver's side for running shots.

Figure 11.25. Camera on a ladder, one of the quickest ways to get a camera up high. It is usually done with a high-hat clamped and strapped to the top rung. (Photo courtesy of Mark Weingartner.)

Crane Up/Down

These terms are the same as boom up/boom down but apply to cranes. Operationally, a crane is more difficult than a dolly. One of the main reasons is that the crane is floating freely, unlike a dolly that has specific limits and specific marks. It is relatively easy for the dolly grip to make marks on the boom arm for the high and low stop points, as well as marks on the dolly track for precise start and end points. This is not possible on a crane.

One thing that most crane grips will do is attach a rope to the camera platform and braid it with knots. These knots make it easier to grasp and pull the crane, but they also help with marking. Since the rope hangs down right under the camera, it is possible to make marks on the floor to indicate camera position, and colored tape on the rope can indicate lens height. The best crane grips can hit these marks again and again with great precision.

Non-booming Platforms

If all that is needed is height, especially for heights greater than can be accomplished with the available crane, the camera might be mounted on a construction crane such as a Condor, which is frequently used as a mounting for lights. These types of cranes can get the camera where you need it, but they usually aren't capable of booming up or down without visible shake.

Camera on a Ladder

The simplest and cheapest method of getting the camera higher than normal is to put it on a ladder, as in Figure 11.25. This is done by having the grips clamp and strap a high-hat on top of the ladder. A second ladder should stand alongside to provide a place for the focus-puller to reach the controls and perform other camera functions. Both these ladders should be well stabilized with sandbags, and a grip should always stand by for safety and assistance.

Remote on Cranes

Remote control heads have revolutionized crane shots. Since it is now possible to design cranes that do not need to support the weight of the operator and camera assistant, cranes can be longer, higher, lighter, more portable, and faster to set up.

Technocrane

All cranes move up/down and left/right. The Technocrane adds one more axis of movement. The arm can be extended or retracted smoothly during the move. It can also be revolved so that the camera spins horizontally. Other companies make similar type crane.

Cranes on Top of Cranes

Some cranes can be stacked on top of large cranes such as the Titan for additional height and mobility. Obviously, a top notch grip team is critical for this type of work, as safety is crucial. This type of rig can accomplish some highly complex compound moves. Walkie-talkies with headsets are important as coordination between the grips on both cranes is essential.

Pedestals

One type of camera mount is capable of vertical movement without arcing: the pedestal. Pedestals are the norm for television studios but are rarely, if ever used in film or video field production. Television operators are expert in their use.

CAR SHOTS

Car shots have always been a big part of film production. In the old studio days they were usually done on sets with rear projection of moving streets visible through the rear or side windows. Special partial cars called bucks had the entire front of the car removed for ease of shooting.

Rear or front projection of exterior scenes is rarely used these days, partly because the technology of shooting on live locations has been perfected as well as film or digital replacement of the background. Car shots are accomplished with car mounts. There are two basic types: hood mounts allow one or more cameras to be placed on the hood area for shooting through the windshield.

Hostess trays (named for the trays that used to be standard at drive-ins) allow the camera to be positioned on the side, usually shooting through the driver's window and the passenger's window.

Camera Positions for Car Shots

The standard positions for car shots are on the hood and either passenger or driver-side windows. Those at the side widows are accomplished with a hostess tray (Figure 11.24). The ones on the front are done with a hood mount (Figure 11.31). These two components are the standard parts of a car rig kit, but be sure to specify both if you need them. On low-budget productions where car rigs are not possible, there are some standard tricks. For shots of the driver, the operator can sit in the passenger seat. For scenes with two people in the front, the operator can sit in the back seat and do 3/4 back shots of each, two shots of both, and so on. In such cases, exterior mounted lights for the car are usually not available, so it is common to let the outside overexpose 1 to 2 stops and leave the interior slightly underexposed. It also helps greatly to pick streets with greenery or dark walls on the side of the street to hold down the overexposure of the exterior.

Vehicle to Vehicle Shooting

Camera cars are specialized trucks with very smooth suspension and numerous mounting positions for multiple cameras). Camera cars are used in two basic modes. For close-ups of the actors, the picture car is usually towed by the camera car or mounted on a low-boy trailer that is towed. The reason that it needs to be a low trailer is so

Figure 11.26. (left) A school bus lit from a camera car. On the back of the the bus are generators for units inside the bus. (Photo by Michael Gallart.)

Figure 11.27. (top) If the operator and AC are not riding on the crane it can be much longer without being excessively bulky.

Figure 11.28. (bottom) The *Cable Cam* in use for a scene on a bridge.

that the perspective relationship of the car to the road will seem natural. If the car is too high, it will look odd. Towing has two advantages. First, the position of the picture car doesn't change radically and unpredictably in relation to the cameras, which can be a problem for the camera operators and the focus pullers. Second, it is much safer because the actor doesn't have to perform and try to drive at the same time.

A simpler technology for towing shots is the wheel-mount tow. This is a small two-wheel trailer that supports only the front wheels of the car. Because the picture car is still at ground level, there are few problems with perspective. This can be an advantage if, for example, the car has to stop and someone approaches the window. This could all be done in one shot, where it would be difficult if the car is mounted on a full trailer. One safety consideration for front wheel tows: the tires are usually held onto the tow carriage with straps.

Camera positions for vehicle to vehicle usually repeat the standard positions for hood mounts. A crane may also be mounted on the camera car, which can be used for very dynamic moves such as starting with the camera shooting through the windshield, then pulling back and up to show the whole car traveling alongside.

AERIAL SHOTS

Aerial shots were also attempted very early in film history. Vibration has always been a problem with aerial shots as with the pressure of the windstream. Both make it difficult to get a good stable shot and control the camera acceptably. The Tyler mounts for helicopters isolate the camera from vibration and steady it so it can be operated smoothly.

Today, most aerial shots are accomplished with remote head mounts, with the camera mounted to the exterior of the aircraft and the operator inside using remote controls but in tight budget or impromptu situations it is still sometimes necessary for the camera operator to lean outside and balance on the pontoon — hopefully with the proper safety rig. In such cases, don't forget to secure the camera as well as any filters, matte box, or other items that might come loose in the slipstream.

Mini-Helicopters

A development in aerial shots is the use of remotely controlled mini-helicopters which are adapted with camera mounts (Figure 11.29). Generally only very lightweight film or video cameras can be flown on these helicopters.

Cable-Cam

Invented by Garrett Brown, who also conceived the *Steadicam*, the *Cable-Cam* can perform some truly amazing shots in places that a helicopter might not be usable, such as over a stadium crowd. The Cable-Cam can carry an operator or use a remote head. The unit comes with its own crew and generally requires at least a day of setup.

OTHER TYPES OF CAMERA MOUNTS

Rickshaw, Wheelchair and Garfield

Camera mounts can be put on just about anything that moves. The poor man's dolly, often used by film students, is a wheelchair. With its large-radius wheels and the operator hand-holding, it can provide some remarkably smooth dolly shots. The *Garfield* is a mount that goes on a wheelchair to allow for mounting of a Steadicam.

Figure 11.29. (top) A mini-helicopter by Flying Cam. (Photo courtesy of Flying Cam, Inc.)

Figure 11.30. (because) A low mode prism. (Photo courtesy of Century Precision Optics.)

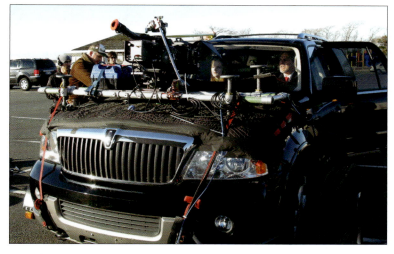

Steadicam

The Steadicam revolutionized camera movement. It can smoothly move the camera in places where a dolly would be impractical or difficult, such as stairs, rough ground, slopes, and sand. A skilled operator can pull off amazing shots that can almost be an additional character in the scene. In standard mode, the film or video camera is mounted on top of the central post and the operators video monitor and batteries ride on the sled at the bottom of the rig. The only limitation is that since the post extends down from the camera, that is the lower limit of travel for the camera. To go any lower than this, the entire rig must be switched to low-mode, which generally takes several minutes.

Low-Mode Prism

Getting the camera low to the ground can sometimes be difficult. Even if the camera is taken off the dolly or tripod, it is still mounted on the geared or fluid head. This means that the lens is still at least a foot or more off the ground. The head still has to be mounted on something; generally the lowest thing available is a high-hat.

To get even lower, a prism may be necessary. This is a prism that fits in front of the lens and optically lowers the lens so that the shot appears to be flat on the ground (Figure 11.30).

Crash Cams

For explosions, car wrecks, train crashes, and other dangerous stunts, cameras must sometimes be placed where there is great danger of them being destroyed (Figure 11.32). In this case, crash cams are used. These are usually *Eyemos* (originally a WWII combat camera) that have been fitted with crystal motors and mounts for Nikon or Canon lenses, which are a fraction of the cost of motion picture lenses.

Splash Boxes

In cases where the camera doesn't have to be actually submerged but will be very near the water or even slightly under the surface, a splash box can be used. These combine a clear optical port for the lens with a waterproof box or plastic bag that protects the camera without encasing it in a full underwater casing, which can be clumsy and time consuming to use. A splash box is something that can be used quickly for a single shot.

Figure 11.31. (left) An Arri D-21 on a hood mount for this film produced by Michael Gallart. (Photo courtesy of Michael Gallart.)

Figure 11.32. (top) A *crash cam* and armored box; in this case an Eyemo is used. (Photo courtesy of Keslow Camera.)

Figure 11.33. (middle) A multi-axis *remote control head*. (Photo courtesy of Chapman/Leonard Studio Equipment, Inc.)

Figure 11.34. (bottom) The MILO motion control rig. (Photo courtesy of Mark Roberts Motion Control.)

Underwater Housings

For actual underwater work, a fully waterproof housing is necessary. These are specially constructed rigs which have exterior controls for the on/off switch and focus. In most cases, they are specially built for particular types of cameras. Underwater housings generally have to be made for the particular type of camera being used and are seldom interchangeable. Be sure to check what depth in the water, the particular housing is built for and check the seals carefully before taking the camera under.

MOTION CONTROL

(The following is courtesy of Mark Roberts Motion Control.)

What is motion control? Some filming special effects techniques need highly accurate control of the motion of the film camera, so that the same move can be repeated many times, with each camera pass being identical to previous passes (Figure 11.34).

Where the movement of the camera is controlled by hand, it is virtually impossible to get an exact duplication of a previous pass. Traditionally, this problem has been solved by holding the camera in a fixed position (known as "locking off" the camera), and then layering the resultant takes to produce the composite image. But to look really natural, and to produce some stunning visual effects, the camera can be made to move during the pass.

Aside from the obvious benefits of multiple camera passes, this also provides a major advantage when combining live action with computer generated images (CGI). And with the latest pre-visualisation software, the director can even plan the camera move or moves beforehand, and know that the rig will be able to physically perform the move before he even gets into a studio. So, what then is motion control? It is an essential production tool in the toolbox of filming techniques, which allows that extra depth of reality in many special effects shots. (© Mark Roberts Motion Control Ltd.)

color

COLOR IN VISUAL STORYTELLING

Color is one of our most important tools and not merely because we can do beautiful things with it. Far more fundamentally is its power as a communications tool. Color affects the viewer in the same way that music or dance does: it reaches people at a gut emotional level. For this reason, it can be a powerful tool in creating visual subtext. There are three aspects of color that we must understand as cinematographers:

• Basic color theory
• Controlling color in the camera and in lighting
• Visual storytelling with color

The Nature of Light

As we recall from the chapter on exposure, light is composed of photons, which have the properties of both matter and light. Even Newton recognized that individual photons don't have "color," but they do have different properties of energy that cause them to interact in different ways with physical matter, which, when reflected is perceived by the eye/brain combination as "color."

Every beam of light has a characteristic color which can vary if the observer is moving toward or away from the light source. Visible light is a small part of the continuous spectrum of electromagnetic radiation, most of which is not directly observable, and was unknown until the 19th century. At the low-frequency (long wavelength) end of the spectrum we find radio, television, microwave, and infrared radiation.

Then we encounter a tiny slice of the spectrum, that we can see with our eyes; this extends from red to violet — the colors of the rainbow. They were originally classified as red, orange, yellow, green, blue, indigo and violet. (R–O–Y–G–B–I–V). Above violet the high-frequency colors are ultra-violet, x-rays, and gamma rays.

Indigo is no longer recognized as a color of the spectrum so the "I" is no longer used. Where formerly it could be memorized as Roy G. Biv, Roy no longer has a vowel in his last name, and it is now Roy G. Bv. It is conventional to consider visible light as a wave, as it exhibits all properties of a wave. Light can be described in terms of its *wavelength* (Figure 12.4), which is measured in *nanometers*. A nanometer is one billionth of a meter.

The Tristimulus Theory

Most people can tell you that the three primaries are red, green, and blue, but few can say why these, of all colors are the primaries. The reason lies in the physiology of our eyes.

The human retina is filled with two kinds of light receptors that are called rods and cones. The rods are primarily responsible for the perception of light and dark: value or grayscale. The cones primarily perceive color. The retina has 3 kinds of cones. The response of each type of cone as a function of the wavelength of the incident light is shown in Figure 12.5. The peaks for each curve are at 440nm (blue), 545nm (green), and 580nm (red). Note that the last two actually peak in the yellow part of the spectrum.

Figure 12.1. (previous page) Color is an important part of this still from a music video. (Photo by the author.)

Figure 12.2. The naturally occurring color spectrum and respective wavelengths in *nanometers*.

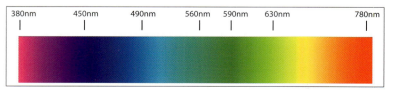

380nm 450nm 490nm 560nm 590nm 630nm 780nm

Functions of the Eye

There are many theories to explain the phenomenon of color vision. The most easily understood is the three-component theory that assumes three kinds of light-sensitive elements (cones) — each receptive to one of the primary colors of light — an extreme spectrum red, an extreme spectrum violet, and an imaginary green. There are about seven million cones in each eye. They are located primarily in the central portion of the retina called the fovea, and are highly sensitive to color. People can resolve fine details with these cones largely because each one is connected to its own nerve end. Muscles controlling the eye always rotate the eyeball until the image of the object of our interest falls on the fovea. Cone vision is known as *photopic* or daytime vision.

Other light receptors, called rods, are also present in the eye but they are not involved in color vision. Rods serve to give a general, overall picture of the field of view, and are receptive only to the quantity of light waves entering the eye. Several rods are connected to a single nerve end; thus, they cannot resolve fine detail. Rods are sensitive to low levels of illumination and enable the eye to see

Figure 12.3. Color is a crucial component of this frame from *Days of Heaven*. The primary red/orange tones function not only as pure color but also have strong associations with mood and time of day — both of which are important in the story of this film. The shooting schedule of the film was built around times of day when shots like this could be captured.

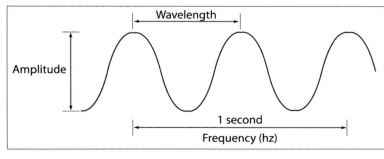

Figure 12.4. A wave is defined by *wavelength* (distance between peaks) and *amplitude* (height of the waves). Frequency is a measure of how many waves occur in a second, usually expressed as *hertz* (*hz*).

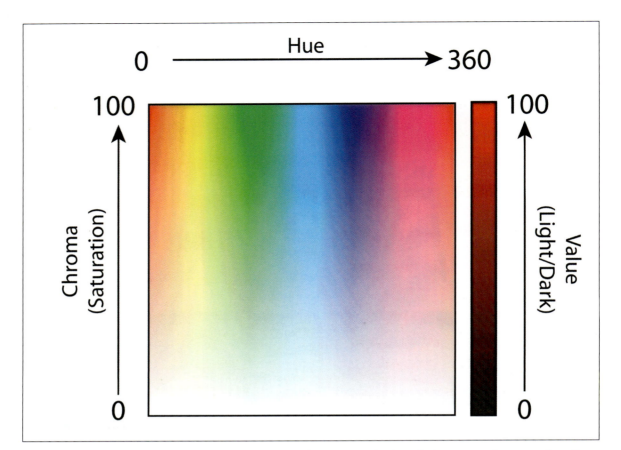

Figure 12.5. *Hue, chroma,* and *value.* Hue is measured in degrees around the color wheel (0 to 360). Hue and chroma are measured as a percentage from zero to one hundred.

at night or under extremely low lighting conditions. Therefore, objects that appear brightly colored in daylight when seen by the color-sensitive cones appear only as colorless forms by moonlight because only the rods are stimulated. This is known as *scotopic* vision.

The Purkinje Effect and Movie Moonlight

As Figure 12.6 shows, the eye is not equally sensitive to all wavelength — the eye/brain is less sensitive to blue and red. In dim light particularly, there is a definite shift in the apparent *brightness* of different colors. This was discovered by Johannes von Purkinje. While walking at dawn one day, von Purkinje observed that blue flowers appeared brighter than red, while in full daylight the red flowers were brighter than the blue. This is now called the *Purkinje effect,* which fools the brain into perceiving moonlight as slightly bluish, even though as reflected sunlight, it is the same color as daylight. This is the reason it is a convention in filmmaking to light night scenes as slightly blue, representing how we perceive moonlight, not how it actually occurs in nature.

LIGHT AND COLOR

Color is light, but the color of objects is a combination of the color of the light and the nature of the material it is falling on and being reflected by. Essentially, the color of an object is the wavelengths of light that it does not absorb. Sunlight *appears* white; it contains all colors, although not necessarily in equal proportion. Light is an *additive system* of color. Red, green and blue are the primaries. When mixed in pairs they produce magenta, cyan and yellow (a hot red, a blue/green, a bright yellow). The mixture of all colors in light creates white. The human eye has receptors (*cones*) red/green, blue/yellow, which translate light waves of differing length to the optic nerve. Because the eye is not equally sensitive to all colors, there are far-ranging implications in color theory, exposure, and even in how light meters work.

Paint is based on a *subtractive* system of color. The primaries are red, blue and yellow. The mixing of paint removes/subtracts light, All colors mixed would produce a muddy gray brown, or, theoretically, black. For our purposes we will be discussing the additive system of color, since we deal primarily with light and video color systems. An understanding of subtractive color is useful when discussing color issues with the production designer, who deals with paint.

Basic Qualities of Color

Color has four basic qualities: *hue, value, chroma and color temperature*. The first three are physical properties and are often called the dimensions of color. The last is a psychological aspect of a color.

Hue

A *hue* is a specific wavelength of light. It is that quality by which we give names to color (i.e., red, yellow, blue, etc.). The average person can distinguish around 150 distinct hues. The hue of a color is simply a definition of its wavelength: its place on the color spectrum.

Hue, chroma (saturation) and *value* (lightness/darkness) make up the three distinct attributes of color. It is convenient to arrange the hues around a *Newton color circle* (Figure 12.9). Starting from red and going clockwise, the circle proceeds from long to short wavelengths. In video, hue is generally referred to as *phase,* and we will see how the color wheel forms the basis of the *vectorscope,* which measures color in video.

Value

Value is the relative lightness or darkness of a colored surface and depends on the illuminance and on its reflectivity.

Chroma

Chroma, (also called *intensity* or *saturation* of color) is the strength of the color, or relative purity of a color — its brilliance or dullness (grayness). Any hue is most intense in its pure state; adding the color's complement (the color opposite it on the color wheel) lowers the intensity, making a color duller. A color at its lowest possible intensity is said to be neutral. For example, on video cameras that have a saturation control, turning it down to zero will produce a black-and-white picture.

Warm and Cool Colors

Another aspect of a *color* is *temperature.* The temperature is the relative warmth or coolness of a hue. This derives from the psychological reaction to color — red or red/orange the warmest and blue the coolest. Warm versus cool is a subjective description of colors.

Color Temperature

Color temperature is measured in *degrees Kelvin,* abbreviated capital K; it is more precise than describing them as *warm* or *cool.* Color temperatures over 5000K are cool colors (bluish white), while lower color temperatures (2700–3000 K) are called warm colors (yellowish white through red). A more detailed explanation of color temperature can be found later in this chapter.

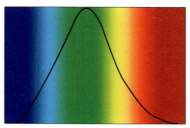

Figure 12.6. Spectral response of the human eye.

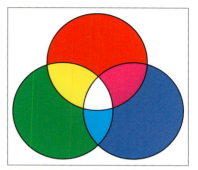

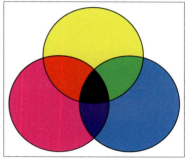

Figure 12.7. (top) *Additive color* is the system used with light, gels and filters. The primary colors in the additive system are red, green, and blue (RGB). It is called "additive" because adding the primary colors together creates white light. Also, in lighting we can create colors by adding gels to lights and mixing them.

Figure 12.8. (bottom) *Subtractive color* applies to paint and ink. The primary colors in the subtractive system are red, yellow and blue (RYB).

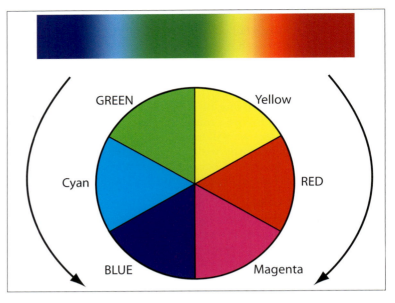

Figure 12.9. The derivation of the color wheel from the spectrum, as derived from work by Sir Isaac Newton.

THE COLOR WHEEL

For centuries artists have found it helpful to bend the linear spectrum around in a circle called the color wheel, first used by Isaac Newton (Figure 12.9). A circular spectrum better describes our perception of the continuous flow of hues, and it establishes opposites across the diameters. The color wheel is created by wrapping the visible spectrum into a circle and joining the far red end (long wavelengths) to the far violet end (short wavelengths).

Primary colors are hues from which all other colors can be mixed. In light they are red, green, and blue. Secondary colors are hues made by mixing two primaries. As a general practice, primary colors in this context are written in all caps, and secondary colors are written in caps and lower case.

> RED + BLUE = Magenta
> BLUE + GREEN = Cyan
> RED + GREEN = Yellow

COLOR MODELS

Color is surprisingly difficult to describe in graphic form. Over the centuries, dozens of color models have been devised. One of the earliest was created by the German writer Goethe. Many different color models are used to classify colors and to qualify them according to such attributes as hue, saturation, chroma, lightness, or brightness. There are a number of models that are relevant to film and video production, both for film and video. The *CIE* color system is the one most frequently used to describe the color space of film and modern video cameras.

Additive Colors

Additive colors are those relevant to light and mixing colors in light (Figure 12.7). The most common examples of this are television screens and computer monitors, which produce colored pixels by firing red, green, and blue electron guns at phosphors on the television or monitor screen. Additive color can be produced by mixing two beams of colored light, or by layering two or more colored gels or by showing the two colors in rapid succession.

Subtractive Colors

Subtractive colors are used to describe when pigments in an object absorb certain wavelengths of white light while reflecting the rest (Figure 12.8). Subtractive color has different primaries: red, blue, and yellow. Any colored object, whether natural or man-made, absorbs some wavelengths of light and reflects or transmits others; the wavelengths left in the reflected/transmitted light make up the color we see. This is the nature of print color, and cyan, magenta, and yellow, as used in four-color process printing, are considered to be the subtractive primaries. The subtractive color model in printing operates not only with CMYK, but also with printing inks.

RGB

Red, green, and blue are the primary stimuli for human color perception and are the primary additive colors, which makes sense in that our eyes work with light and react to various wavelengths by producing the sensation of color when processed by the brain. The importance of RGB as a color model is that it relates very closely to the way we perceive color with the cone receptors in our retinas. RGB is the color model used in video or any other medium that projects the color. It is also the basic color model on computer monitors and is used for web graphics. Print media, on the other hand, generally uses the secondary colors, CMYK: cyan, magenta, yellow, and black (Y).

The CIE Color System

The *CIE* color models are highly influential systems for measuring color and distinguishing between colors. The CIE color system was devised by the *C.I.E. (Commission International de l'Eclairage* — the *International Commission on Illumination*) in 1931 and has since become an international standard for measuring, designating, and matching colors. It was one of the first systems to describe color mathematically, which is what makes it precise enough to use with SD and HD video. (Figure 12.12). It comes in two varieties: CIE RGB and CIE XYZ, which is the one most used in video engineering. All possible colors can be designated on the chromaticity diagram, whether they are emitted from a light source, transmitted, or reflected off a colored surface, which changes the color of the light.

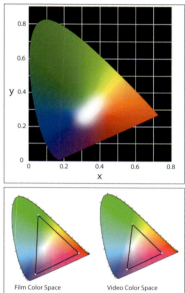

Film Color Space   Video Color Space

Figure 12.10. (middle) A diagram of the CIE color system.

Figure 12.11. (bottom) The relative color spaces of film and video. Color space describes the ability of a medium such as film, video, or a monitor to represent a range of colors.

Figure 12.12. (top) Strong primaries and color contrast make for a graphic image.

Figure 12.13. Director Zang Yimou, who started his career as a cinematographer, is known for his very bold and evocative use of color such as in his film *Ju Dou*.

One of the primary uses of the CIE diagram is to graph the differences in color space. Figure 12.12 illustrates the difference between typical film and video color space. In this diagram, film clearly has a larger color space, meaning that it can record a bigger *gamut* of colors. Gamut is a description of the range of colors a system (i.e., video, film, or a computer monitor) can represent. However, HD cameras are constantly improving in many ways; one of them is color space. Cameras vary widely in their color space, and it is something you will want to test as you are deciding what camera to use for a particular project. One very direct result of differences in color space is in video editing. Video monitors have a different *color space* than computer monitors. For this reason, many editing setups will have a video monitor for viewing in addition to the computer monitor they edit with.

Digital and Electronic Color

There are differences in the measurement system of analog and digital video. The intensity of each color is measured on a scale from 0 to 255 (in the digital system), and a color is specified by sending the monitor the RGB values. For instance, yellow is specified by telling the computer to add 255 red, 255 green, and 0 blue.

Video color (which is called *phase*) is analyzed on the *vectorscope*, which is discussed in detail in the chapter on *HD Cinematography*. Phase is a description of where the hue falls on the color wheel and is expressed as degrees. It is far more accurate to say 200° (two hundred degrees) than "sort of yellowish-green." The shortcomings of trying to describe colors in words are obvious: being able to describe color accurately is a huge advance in color control, but it is important not to develop too much of a techno-nerd attitude toward these things. A a cinematographer, you are more of an artist who deals with color on a pictorial and emotional level. For someone who is a camera technician or video engineer, however, precision is critical.

CONTROLLING COLOR

The eye will accept a wide range of light as "white," depending on external clues and adaptation. The phenomenon is both psychological (*adaptation*) and environmental. Color film, video sensors, and the color meter are all very objective about these things: they don't have a human brain to "fool" them into thinking light is white when it really isn't. These devices will tell us that there are enormous differences in the color of light in a room lit with tungsten light, one lit with ordinary fluorescents, and one flooded with noon daylight. Our perception tells us that all three are "white light," mostly because we are psychologically conditioned to think of them as white and physiologically, the eye adapts. Without a side-by-side comparison, the eye is an unreliable indicator of what is neutral light. Unfortunately, color film emulsions and video CCD's are extremely sensitive and unforgiving. An absolute color reference is essential, which may be a *vectorscope* or a *gray card* (see chapter on *HD Cinematography*).

Figure 12.14. Extreme color in this scene from *Domino*.

Color Temperature

In film and video production, the system used in describing the color of light is *color temperature*. This scale is derived from the color of a theoretical black body (a metal object having no inherent color of its own, technically known as a Planckian radiator). When heated to incandescence, the black body glows at varying colors depending on the temperature (Figure 12.15). Color temperature is a quantification of the terms "red hot," "white hot," and so on.

Named for Lord Kelvin, the 19th century British scientific pioneer, color temperature is expressed in degrees Kelvin. On the Celsius scale, the freezing point of water equals 0°. The Kelvin scale takes absolute zero as the zero point. Absolute zero is minus 273° Celsius on the Kelvin scale, thus 5500° Kelvin is actually 5227° Celsius. Degrees Kelvin is abbreviated "K" and the degree symbol is not used. Because a tungsten filament heated to incandescence is very similar to a Planckian radiator, the color temperature equivalence is very close for tungsten halogen lamps, but not for HMIs, CIDs, and fluorescents (Figure 12.15). A graphic representation of the various wavelengths is called an *SED* (*Spectral Energy Distribution*).

When a metal object (such as the tungsten filament of a light bulb) is heated to incandescence, its SED is quite similar to that of a Planckian radiator and is fairly smooth across all wavelengths, even if some are stronger than others. This is not necessarily true for all light sources. Fluorescent lights have very *spiky* outputs, which tend to be very heavy in green (Figure 12.23)

Figure 12.15. Average *color temperatures* of various sources.

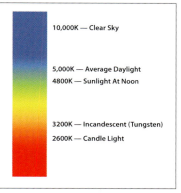

10,000K — Clear Sky

5,000K — Average Daylight
4800K — Sunlight At Noon

3200K — Incandescent (Tungsten)
2600K — Candle Light

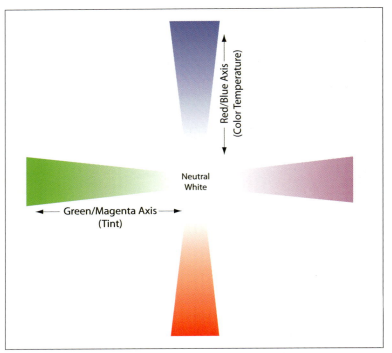

Figure 12.16. (above) The Gossen Color Pro color meter.

Figure 12.17. (right) Color is measured in two separate ways: one axis is red to blue (color temperature), which is warm/cool and magenta to green (tint).

Color temperatures can be very misleading; for many sources (especially those that exhibit discontinuous SEDs), it is only an approximation and is referred to as *correlated color temperature*. Color temperature tells us a great deal about the blue/orange component of light and very little about the magenta/green component, which can produce extremely unpleasant casts in the film, even if the meter indicates a correct reading for the color temperature.

An approximate measure of how close a source is to a pure black body radiator is the *Color Rendering Index* (*CRI*), a scale of 1 to 100 that gives some indication of the ability of a source to render color accurately. For photographic purposes, only sources with a CRI of 90 or above are generally considered acceptable.

Color Meters and the Two Axes of Color

Most light sources are not a narrow band of the spectrum; hence they are not a pure hue. Most colored light is a combination of various wavelengths; there is no one number that can describe the color accurately. Rather, it is defined on two scales: red/blue and magenta/green. As a result, most meters give two readouts (they are sometimes called three color meters, since they measure red, blue, and green), one for the warm/cool scale and one for the magenta/green scale. In the case of the a color meter, the magenta/green readout is not in absolute numbers, but directly in amount of filtration needed to correct the color to neutral on the magenta/green scale.

LB is the *light balancing* index. Its use is based on whether you are using daylight or tungsten balance film. Light balancing values are shown in Table 12.1. Light balancing works on the red/orange color scale (daylight blue to tungsten orange).

CC index is *color correction*. It describes the green/magenta aspects of the color source. It is most relevant when shooting with fluorescents, sodium vapor, mercury vapor, or other types of discharge sources that usually have a large green component. Recommended corrections are shown in Table 12.3.

Figure 12.18. In the film *Kiss Kiss Bang Bang*, the DP used cyan for night, an appropriate choice for the dark comedy/ironic tone of the film.

Mireds

Another problem with color temperature is that equal changes in color temperature are not necessarily perceived as equal changes in color. A change of 50K from 2000K to 2050K will be a noticeable difference in color. For an equivalent change in color perception at 5500K, the color temperature would need to shift 150K and about 500K at 10,000K.

For this reason, the mired system has been devised. Mired stands for micro-reciprocal degrees. Mireds are derived by dividing 1,000,000 by the Kelvin value. For example, 3200K equals 1,000,000/3200 = 312 mireds. To compute how much color correction is required, you use the mired values of the source and the final desired color. If you have source at 5500K and wish to convert it to 3200K, subtract the mired value of the desired color from that of the source. 5000K = 200 mireds. 3200K = 312 mireds and then 312 minus 200 = 112 mireds. 85/CTO orange has a mired value of +112. On the mired scale, a plus shift value means the filter is yellowish, and a minus value means the filter will give a blue shift. When combining filters, add the mired values.

Color Balance of Film and Video

The purpose of choosing the correct filmstock (daylight or tungsten) or white balancing a video camera (see the chapter *HD Cinematography*) is to make sure the film or camera renders colors accurately, as they appears in real life. Of course, sometimes you will want to alter the color for artistic purposes. No color film or camera can accurately render color under all lighting conditions. In manufacture, the film is adjusted to render color accurately under a particular condition, the two most common being average daylight, which is set for 5500K, and average tungsten illumination designed for 3200K.

Given the fact that providing tungsten light is costly and electricity intensive, while sunlight is usually far more abundant, most motion picture films are type B, balanced for tungsten. The idea is that we put a correcting filter on when we can most afford to lose light to a filter factor — in the sunlight. Kodak and Fuji have several daylight balance film stocks available.

The situation in HD and SD video is almost exactly the same, although it is done electronically. Neutral white balance on video cameras can be adjusted to any existing lighting condition, including fluorescents, mercury vapor, and other off-color sources.

Figure 12.19. Strong monochromatic color in *Kill Bill*.

COLOR BALANCE WITH GELS AND FILTERS

The term *gel* refers to color material that is place over lights, windows, or other sources in the scene. *Filter* is the term for anything placed in front of the lens to (among other things) control color. There are, however, gel-type filters that can be used in front of the lens, but these are not commonly used in film production.

There are three basic reasons to change the color of lighting in a scene, which can be done adding gels to the sources or by using daylight or tungsten units or a combination of them:

- To correct (convert) the color of the lights to match the film type or color balance of a video camera.
- To match various lighting sources.
- For effect or mood.

Gelling the lighting sources gives you more control over the scene, since not all lights have to be the same color. Using a filter on the camera makes everything uniformly the same color. The exception to this are filters called *grads*, which change color from top to bottom or left to right or diagonally depending on how they are positioned. Examples of grads in use are found in the chapter *Image Control*, where other aspects of using filters are also discussed.

The three basic filter/gels families used in film and video production are *conversion*, *light balancing* and *color compensating*. This applies to both lighting gels and camera filters. See Tables 12.1 and 12.2 for just a few of the most commonly used types. There are gels that are random, non-calibrated colors called *party gels*.

Table 12.1. *Mired values* of basic color correction/conversion gels.

TYPE	MIRED VALUE
ORANGE GELS	
Full CTO (85)	+85
1/2 CTO	+81
1/4 CTO	+42
1/8 CTO	+20
BLUE GELS	
Full CTB	-131
1/2 CTB	-68
1/4 CTB	-30
1/8 CTB	-12

Light Balancing Gels

Light Balancing gels are for warming or cooling the color temperature of the sources; which means they affect lights on the blue-orange axis (Table 12.1). They are primarily for changing a daylight source to tungsten balance or vice-versa.

Daylight sources include:

- Daylight itself (daylight is a combination of direct sun and open sky).
- HMIs, Xenons and some LED lights.
- Cool-white or daylight-type fluorescents.
- Color correct fluorescent tube that can be daylight balance.
- *Dichroic* sources such as FAYs.
- *Arcs lights* with white-flame carbons (rarely used nowadays).

Conversion Gels

Conversion gels convert daylight to tungsten or tungsten to daylight balance. They are by far the most commonly used color gels in film and video production. They are an essential part of any gel package you bring on a production.

In general, daylight sources are in the range of 5400K to 6500K, although they can range much higher. Near sunrise and sunset they are much warmer because the sun is traveling through a much thicker layer of atmosphere and more of the blue wavelengths are filtered out. The amount of dust and humidity in the air are also factors, which accounts for the different colorings of sun and sky prevalent at various times of the day, in different locales, in different weather conditions, and even at different altitudes.

CTO

Correction to match tungsten balance is achieved with either *85* (camera filter) or *CTO* (a lighting gel), both of which are orange filters. They have essentially the same effect; the reason they have different names is due to the history of their development: 85 is a *Wratten* number, which is a system developed by Kodak for filters.

CTO is the acronym for *Color Temperature Orange*. This means that it will convert 6500K to 3200K, which is excellent when correcting cooler sources such as HMIs, which are running blue or heavily skylit situations. It is also useful when going for a warmer look, because it will convert 5500K to 2940K. (5500K = mired 181, shift value of 159). Warmer equals positive. 181 + 159 = 340 mired.

An important variation of CTO is the combination of color correction and neutral density. In many cases when we are filming inside

The Basic Gel Families		
85	Conversion	Used to Convert Daylight to Tungsten
80	Conversion	Used to Convert Tungsten to Daylight
82	Light Balancing	Used to Slightly Cooling the Light
81	Light Balancing	Used to Slightly Warm the Light

Table 12.2. The basic filter families are conversion filters that convert tungsten to daylight or vice versa and light balancing filters, used to warm or cool the light source.

Figure 12.21. This shot from *Fight Club* is typical of a scene lit with ordinary fluorescent bulbs uncorrected.

a room, the windows will be the wrong color (too blue) and much too bright. The purpose of this is to avoid having to put two separate gels on a window, which might increase the possibility for gel noise and reflections, not to mention the additional cost (which can be substantial). There are two reasons lighting gels cost as much as they do: first, they are carefully calibrated in their color, and also they are incredibly resistant to heat, which is important as they are frequently just inches or a foot or two away from a blazing hot light source. They are made from polyester, high-temperature polymer, polycarbonate, or *dichroic* filters, which are thin optical coatings on glass.

CTO is used not only for color correction but also to warm up the lights. It's an old adage that everybody looks better under warm light; so warming a scene with full CTO, half CTO, or quarter CTO is a common practice. There are other warming gels as well, and every DP has preferences as to how to approach making the light on a scene warmer. Some use dimmers on tungsten lights; dimming these lights down, makes them shift toward red/orange. With video/HD it is possible to make the entire scene warmed by "fooling" the white balance" (see chapter on *HD Cinematography*).

Table 12.3. *MinusGreen* and *Plus-Green* are gels that are used to correct for the green spike in fluorescent lights. MinusGreen (which is magenta) is used to subtract the green, while PlusGreen is used to add green to your lights so that they match the green of existing fluorescents or industrial sources at the location. Values are expressed in *CC* (*color correction*) units, which is how a color meter measures *tint* — the green/magenta axis of color.

With film and video there are a wide variety of lens filters and lighting gels that can warm or cool a shot. Gel manufacturers provide a wide range of both warming and cooling gels that allow for great subtlety in lighting your shots. It is important to remember, however, that both of these methods change the color of the entire scene. Putting gels on lights or windows allows you to be selective with what lights and what parts of the scene you want to change. It's a trade-off: clearly it is faster and cheaper to use a filter or change the white balance of a camera; gelling lights or windows takes time and money, but it offers far more control of the image.

CTB

Filters for converting warm tungsten sources to nominal daylight are called *full blue*, *Tough Blue* or *CTB* (*Color Temperature Blue*). The problem with "bluing the lights" is that CTB has a transmission of 36%, while 85 has a transmission of 58%. This means that while you lose almost a stop and a half with CTB, you lose only about 2/3 of a stop with CTO. CTB is very inefficient; its most common use is to balance tungsten lights inside a room with the daylight blue window light that is coming in. The window light is liable to be far more powerful than the tungsten lights to begin with. If we then lose 2 stops by adding CTB, we are really in trouble.

Reduce Green	CC Equivilent	Use When CC Is Approx
MinusGreen	30	-12
1/2 MinusGreen	15	-5
1/4 MinusGreen	0.75	-2

Add Green	CC Equivilent	Use When CC Is Approx
PlusGreen	30	+13
1/2 PlusGreen	15	+5
1/4 PlusGreen	0.75	+3

Figure 12.22. Careful color coordination of location selection, wardrobe, and props on the John Sayles film *Honeydripper*.

The alternatives are:

- Put 85 on the windows and shoot at tungsten balance. By doing this we avoid killing the tungsten lights with a heavy blue gel, we don't have to use an 80B on the camera, and we lose 2/3 of a stop off the windows, which may help keep them more in balance.
- Put 1/2 85 on the windows and 1/2 blue on the lights.
- Put 1/2 CTB on the lights and let the windows go slightly blue. This is actually a more naturalistic color effect.
- Daylight balance lights inside: FAYs, HMIs, LEDs, or Kinos.

Light Balancing Gels

LB or light balancing gels also deal with warm versus cool color but in smaller ranges and more subtle corrections that CTO and CTB and their variations. Light balancing gels are used when only a slight correction is needed; they may also deviate from the strict blue to orange range. In the Wratten system, filters that begin with 82 are cooling filters, and those that begin with 81 are warming filters.

Color Correction Gels

CC or color correction gels deal with the magenta versus green color range, the other axis that we measure and utilize in production. These primarily come into play when dealing with sources other than tungsten or HMI lamps, especially fluorescent lights and industrial sources such as mercury vapor and sodium vapor lights.

Dealing with Fluorescent Light

One of the most common color problems we face today is shooting in locations where the dominant source is fluorescent light. The problem with fluorescents is that they are not a continuous spectrum source: in most cases they are very heavy in green.

Another problem is that even if they may appear to be approximately correct in color, their discontinuous spectra may cause them to have a low Color Rendering Index (CRI). As a result, fluorescents cannot be corrected only by changing the color with a gel on the lighting unit or filter on the camera lens. All of this also applies to sources such as orange *sodium vapor* lights (often used for street lights) and blueish *mercury vapor* (frequently used in parking lots and other industrial areas).

These are all classified as *discharge sources* because they produce light from a glowing gas excited by electrical discharge. Because of their discontinuous spectra, discharge sources can't be considered to have

Figure 12.23. Comparison of the spectrum of daylight and tungsten, both of which are fairly continuous and smooth and a typical cool white fluorescent — a discontinuous spectrum with big spikes in the green region.

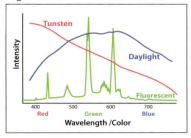

STRATEGIES FOR DEALING WITH EXISTING OFF-COLOR LIGHTS

EXISTING SOURCE	YOUR LIGHTS	STRATEGY	COMMENTS
Any fluorescents	None or fluorescents	Shoot fluorescent balance	In video, white balance the camera. In film, shoot a gray card and let the lab correct for the green.
Any fluorescent	Tungsten or any daylight sources	Replace the existing lamps with color-correct bulbs	If existing lights are accessible, replacing the bulbs with color correct lamps is not difficult.
Cool white fluorescents	HMIs or other daylight source	Gel the existing fluorescents	Adding Minusgreen or half Minusgreen will reduce the green to balance your sources.
Warm white fluorescents	Tungsten	Gel the existing fluorescents	Add Minusgreen gel to the existing lights. This will result in lights that are only an approximate color balance but with less light output. You can use tungsten lights or HMIs with CTO for tungsten balance.
Cool white fluorescents	HMI or other daylight sources	Gel the daylight sources	Add Plusgreen or half Plusgreen to your lights so they have as much green as the existing lights. In video white balance the camera. In film shoot a gray card and let the lab time out the green.
Cool white fluorescents	Tungsten	Gel the tungsten and convert to daylight balance	Add Plusgreen 50 gel to your lights which adds both blue and green correction. You can also add blue (CTB) and Plusgreen gel separately. In video white balance the camera. In film shoot a gray card and let the lab time out the green.

Table 12.4. Strategies for dealing with off-color sources.

a true color temperature in degrees Kelvin. The black body color temperature that they approximate is called the *Correlated Color Temperature (CCT)*. On location it is not always possible to replace existing lights with your own lights; this may be due to rules imposed by the management of the location or budget/schedule reasons — especially in a very large space where it might take days to correct all the existing lights. However, if you do have access to the fluorescent lights, you can simply take the existing bulbs out and replace them with color correct fluorescent tubes (Kino Flo, Optima, or other color correct bulbs). There are many options and combinations, and it can get to be a bit confusing sometimes. Table 12.4 shows a decision chart for dealing with these many different situations. On the set you may or may not have the proper gels for the lights with you. This is why a proper location scout and pre-production planning are so important, especially if dealing with industrial sources such as street lights, parking lot lights, and large factories or warehouses. A good color meter is invaluable in these situations (Figure 12.16). If you don't have one, you can hold correction gels over the lens of a digital still camera to test.

Cool White
Fluorescent

Daylight
5500K

Cool White
Fluorescent

Tungsten
3200K

Plusgreen 50

Cool White
Fluorescent

Tungsten
3200K

Fluorofilter

Cool White
Fluorescent

Daylight
5500K

Minusgreen

Warm White
Fluorescent

Tungsten
3200K

Minusgreen

1/4 CTO

Optima 32

Tungsten
3200K

Remember that correcting for undesired colors does not necessarily give these sources an adequate CRI (color rendering index), and they may never be truly color correct no matter what you do.

With video cameras, it is possible to adjust the camera to the existing lighting by proper white balancing (see chapter on *HD Cinematography*). Additional tips on shooting with fluorescents, industrial lights, or any sources that are not normal daylight or tungsten balance on location include:

- Shoot a gray card at the head of a film roll.
- Shooting with ordinary fluorescents alone and letting the lab remove the green results in a very flat color rendition. Adding some lights (such as tungsten with Plusgreen) gives a much fuller color feeling to the image.
- If you are shooting a large area such as a supermarket, factory, or office, it is often efficient to add green to your lights than to have the crew gelling existing lights.
- When you add Plusgreen or Fluorofilter to lights, they give a very strongly colored light that looks wrong to the eye.
- Video cameras don't seem to need as much green correction and tend to be more tolerant of color imbalance than film. Modern film stocks are also more tolerant of color imbalance than in the past.

Figure 12.24. (top, left) Cool White fluorescent with normal daylight. Notice how green the left side of her face is.

Figure 12.25. (top, middle) Cool White fluorescent balanced against a tungsten source with Rosco Plusgreen 50. Green is then removed by the lab.

Figure 12.26. (top, right) Cool White fluorescent with Rosco Fluorofilter, which converts them to tungsten balance.

Figure 12.27. (left) Cool White fluorescent with Minusgreen (CC 30M) balanced with a daylight source.

Figure 12.28. (middle) A Warm White fluorescent with Rosco Minusgreen and 1/4 CTO to match a tungsten source.

Figure 12.29. (right) An Optima 32 (color correct fluorescent) matched with a tungsten source.

Table 12.5. Gels can be used to correct industrial sources such as the *sodium vapor* lights used in factories and *mercury vapor* lamps that are common in parking lots and streetlights. These values are just a starting point, as industrial sources vary widely.

For best results check them with a color meter. An alternate is to hold various gels in front of the lens of reasonable quality digital still camera and check the results under good viewing conditions; including a gray card in the shot will assit in making the evaluation.

CC indicates color compensating filters, and the accompanying number and letter indicates the amount and color. For example, CC30M is thirty units of magenta, which is often the amount of compensation needed for fluorescent bulbs.

CAMERA FILTERS FOR INDUSTRIAL SOURCES

Color Balance	Existing Source	Camera Filters
Tungsten	High Pressure Sodium	80B + CC30M
	Metal Halide	85 + CC50M
	Mercury Vapor	85 + CC50B
Daylight	High Pressure Sodium	80B + CC50B
	Metal Halide	81A + CC30M
	Mercury Vapor	81A + CC50M

CORRECTING OFF-COLOR LIGHTS

HMI

HMIs sometimes run a little too blue and are voltage dependent. Unlike tungsten lights, their color temperature goes *up* as voltage *decreases*. For slight correction Y-1 or Rosco MT 54 can be used. For more correction, use 1/8 or 1/4 CTO. Many HMIs also run a little green. Have 1/8 and 1/4 Minusgreen available.

Industrial Lamps

Various types of high-efficiency lamps are found in industrial and public space situations. They fall into three general categories: *sodium vapor*, *metal halide* and *mercury vapor*. All of these lights have discontinuous spectrums and are dominant in one color. They all have very low CRIs. It is possible to shoot with them if some corrections are made. High-pressure sodium lamps are very orange and contain a great deal of green. Low-pressure sodium is a monochromatic light: they are impossible to correct.

Camera Filtration for Industrial Sources

Table 12.5 shows recommended starting points for using camera filtration to correct off-balance industrial sources. They are approximations only and should be confirmed with metering and testing. In video you may be able to correct partly with the camera's white balance function. In film, never fail to shoot a grayscale and some skin tone for a timer's guide. Only with these references will the color timer or video transfer colorist be able to quickly and accurately correct the color. For more on shooting the grayscale reference, see the chapter on *Image Control*. Pay close attention to how the grayscale is shot. An incorrectly done grayscale can do more damage than none at all; if the telecine transfer artist or film color timer adheres to it, your dailies will be very different than you expected.

Stylistic Choices in Color Control

As with everything in film and video production, stylistic choices affect the technical choices and vice-versa. This is especially true with color correction. Until a few years ago, considerable time and money were spent on correcting every single source on the set. Now there is more of a tendency to "let them go green" (or blue or yellow or whatever). This is a much more naturalistic look and has become a style all its own, influenced by films such as *The Matrix*, *Fight Club*, *Seven*, and many others.

For more detailed information on controlling color on the set and on location, see *Motion Picture and Video Lighting* by the same author.

image control

COLOR PRINTING

Negative is printed either on a continuous contact printer or on a step printer. The step printer works somewhat like a projector in that the movement is intermittent. Registration is achieved through register pins, which allows several passes to be made, as may be the case with black-and-white separation negatives.

Additive and Subtractive Printing

A printer must control the red, green, and blue components of the white-light source to achieve correct density and color balance. Two methods of control are commonly used: additive and subtractive printing. In a subtractive printer, color balance is achieved by inserting color correcting filters in the light path between the light source and the printing aperture.

Overall light density changes are made either by a variable aperture or a neutral density filter. Subtractive print involves using filter packs and neutral density filters to make corrections. As a result, it is difficult to make changes in setup. Subtractive printing is sometimes used for release prints, because there are no scene-to-scene color changes. Printing requiring any scene-to-scene color corrections is not practical on a subtractive printer. The most common printing method is additive printing. In additive printing, there are three light sources. These can then be combined in various percentages to control both the density and color balance. The red, green, and blue components are controlled with a set of dichroic mirrors.

Printer Lights

The variations in each color channel are quantified on a scale from 1 to 50. These are called printer *points* or *printer lights*. Increasing the printer light by 12 printer points adds a stop of exposure. The standard printer setup for a laboratory is usually 25-25-25 for the red, green, and blue color channel; some labs use different standards.

In theory an 18% gray card perfectly exposed and processed will print at 25-25-25. In actual practice this turns out to be only a general guideline. Some labs use 30-30-30 as their *aim density*. Beyond this, there are other minor variations due to differences in printer optics and chemistry. This can be disconcerting, but in practice it is not important. Lab numbers are self-referential — they are used within the same system at the same lab. Difference in one light causes difference in .07 to .1 density, which is 1/6 to 1/7 of an f/stop; a 3 light is 1/2 stop. Any deviations beyond this are of concern. If a lab cannot print the same negative twice without half stop deviation, then there is clearly a problem.

This standard can really only apply to answer prints and release prints, not to the *dailies,* which are the prints of a day's shooting used to review and check for problems. Dailies are also called *rushes*. Essentially printer points are a closed system within each lab. Generally, most labs are within a couple of numbers of each other. However, there are other reasons why a lab may choose to set its reference point a little higher or lower than another one. Printing machines have an overall line-up or offset known as the trim setting that is used to even out lamp, stock, filter, process, and other differences between machines so that they produce the desired result.

So prints from different labs can still look identical, even if they have different lights, because all the other factors are different as well: its only the total combination of settings that matters. If you judge your exposures by the rushes lights, you should ask the lab what the *normal* lights are for the specific stock you're shooting on.

Figure 13.1. (previous page) *CCE,* a bleach-bypass process, is a critical factor in this image from *City of Lost Children*.

One-Light Dailies

Printed dailies are increasingly rare due to the cost and the fact that the prints are generally no longer needed for editing, as it is now done digitally in almost all cases. Dailies are now usually done on video, DVD, HD, or other digital means. At most labs, you can request that your dailies be printed at a *standard light* — or a fixed light selected during camera tests. That way the DP doesn't need to juggle with lights on lab reports, but can use their eyes to judge the exposures each day.

These are called *one-light* dailies. For producers, one-light may mean a cheap deal, but for DPs it can be a useful test and feedback. If the dailies are printed at a constant setting, the DP can judge by looking at the dailies if they are too dense, too thin, or if color balance is off. The downside is that the lab does nothing to correct for mistakes or variations. This means that the producer and director see the scenes exactly as shot. They may tend to panic if they don't understand what can be done in the remaining steps of postproduction.

With video transfer of dailies there is considerable room for altering color balance and density. There is room for correction of minor color and exposure errors. In the long run, however, nothing can substitute for a properly exposed negative with the color balance shot as planned by the cinematographer.

CONTROLLING COLOR AND CONTRAST

There are many other methods of controlling the image at various stages of production. Many techniques can be used to control the amount of color saturation and contrast in a film.

- Filters such as ProMist, Fog, Double Fog, Low Cons, Ultra-Cons, and so on, cause highlights to bleed or wash into the shadows, which lowers contrast and softens color saturation. (See the section later in this chapter for more on contrast control with filters.)
- Smoke or fog (or even smog) has a similar effect to filters in that contrast and color are lowered because light is scattered more or less uniformly. Smoke has the advantage of affecting objects in the background more than in the foreground. This is more three-dimensional than a filter, which reduces the contrast uniformly for the entire scene. Artificial smoke on a closed set is somewhat controllable. A talented effects person can control whether the smoke is concentrated in the foreground or background.
- Softer lighting desaturates; harder lighting emphasizes contrast and color saturation. Specific color lighting can also be used in conjunction with postproduction to remove some color. On the film *Heart* (a remake of a black-and-white film), burgundy (magenta) gels were added to all lights. Then in printing, the magenta was pulled out of the image, thus desaturating the color by removing red and blue evenly.
- Both Kodak and Fuji offer film stocks that are higher or lower in contrast.

In the Lab

There are a number of processes that can be performed in the lab to affect the characteristics of the film negative and the print.

- *Push processing* is accomplished by leaving the film in the developing chemicals a little longer. It has the effect of increasing the apparent ISO of the film, making it more sensitive to light.

Push processing tends to increase contrast and grain. At most labs, it is easy to request a one stop, two stop, or three stop push. Be sure to write it on the camera reports.

- *Pull-processing* (pulling the film out of the developer a little early) can lower saturation a little, but is mostly used to lower contrast, especially when combined with silver-retention printing. Of course, pull-processing has the effect of lowering the effective speed of the film.
- *Double printing*. Starting with the original color negative a color *IP (Interpositve* — a positive print made from the negative) is produced. At the same time a black-and-white positive is made. These elements are then printed together. The black-and-white positive acts as a mask to control highlights and color saturation. This is a highly controllable process, since the exact density of the black-and-white positive can be varied with great subtly. This is similar to a technique used by still photographers to control prints. The final result is a desaturated dupe negative. How desaturated the image is depends on what percentage of the total exposure came from the b&w or the color IP. This technique was used in some scenes of *The Natural*, photographed by Caleb Deschanel. There was a variation in this case. Normally the black-and-white print is slightly out of focus so that hard edges are not noticeable. In *The Natural*, the color image was printed slightly out-of-focus over the sharp black-and-white image, which creates a diffusion effect.
- Bleach-bypass and other silver retention processes are discussed below.
- *Video correction*. Color and nearly all aspects of the image is easily manipulated in *telecine transfers* or using digital techniques in the computer.

Bleach-Bypass and Other Processes

Silver retention as a means of controlling the image offers several techniques for the cinematographer to alter the look of the film. All silver retention processes are based on the same phenomenon. When color film is processed, the dark areas are where the most silver is developed. The highlight areas don't have many silver halide crystals that have been affected photochemically. When color stock is developed, the silver halide crystals are replaced with color dyes. Normally, the silver itself is removed by a bleaching process. By either altering the chemistry or skipping this bleaching process (either partially or entirely), some or all of the silver is left in, which reduces contrast and color saturation.

Since most of the silver is now concentrated in the darkest areas, these parts of the image will be affected differently from the midtones and highlights. This has the effect of making the blacks denser and also desaturating the color rendition. Silver retention is usually done on the print. The effect on the print is much greater than when done on the negative. On the print, silver retention affects the blacks most; on the negative it does the reverse; it affects the whites most — it makes them very white, which results in a blown-out background.

The effect is the greatest where there is the most silver to begin with. In the print, these are the shadow areas. On the negative these are the highlights. When the process is done on the print, silver retention doesn't add as much visible grain because the effect is concentrated in the blacks. All of these techniques can be used in various combinations for a wide range of control. It is usually best to begin with selection of locations, art direction, and costuming. After that comes selection of time of day to shoot and lighting and grip control.

It is always best to use the simplest means to achieve a goal. Primary colors tend to desaturate less noticeably than pastel colors when using some sort of desaturation technique. Skintones are generally pastel; they will lose their color much faster than a primary color in the frame.

Some DPs use a contrast/desaturating technique such as *flashing* (exposing the film to small amounts of light before or during shooting), and then use a silver retention printing technique to restore the blacks in the prints. Two of the earliest films to use some of these techniques to were *McCabe and Mrs. Miller,* shot by Vilmos Zsigmond, and *Heaven's Gate,* photographed by Nestor Almendros and Haskel Wexler.

The primary technique used in *Heaven's Gate* was the simplest one of all: many of the exterior scenes were shot during morning or evening *magic hour* when the light is soft and even. This is a simple method but a very expensive one. Few productions can afford to restrict exterior filming to a few hours a day. Also, the farm location in Alberta naturally had a lot of dust in the air, which acts like smoke to soften the light. Almendros also used negative flashing and print flashing together to soften the colors and contrast.

On *Saving Private Ryan*, DP Janus Kaminski had the *anti-reflection coating* stripped off some of the lenses to make them reproduce some of the internal flares that were characteristic of lenses of the war period. These internal reflections also lower contrast. He also used a combination of on-camera flashing (the Panaflasher) and the ENR process. Combining the flashing compensates for the negative getting *heavy* from the bleach-bypass.

Darius Khondji's stunning work on *Seven* combined flashing with Deluxe's CCE printing — a silver retention process. For contrast control on the film *The Thin Red Line*, black smoke was used to create artificial clouds. Staging of scenes within the sunlit and shadow areas was also done with great care. *City of Lost Children* (Figure 13.1) employed the CCE process in addition to set design and a carefully controlled palette, all of which was facilitated by the fact that it was entirely a studio film. *Payback* used the CCE printing process, combined with shooting without the 85 filter outdoors on tungsten stock, and using a blue filter indoors. The blue-bias on the negative ensured that skintones would be consistently desaturated. The print was timed to the blue side to keep any reds from becoming more saturated.

Bleach-Bypass

Bleach-bypass is the oldest of the special processing techniques of this type. It involves simply skipping all or most of the bleach step of processing. Bleach-bypass was first used on the film *1984*, photographed by Roger Deakins. In the United States, many film labs have variations on the bleach-bypass technique. Fotokem can perform bleach-bypass on prints, original camera negative, and intermediate prints (interpositives and internegatives). CFI's process is called Silver Tint. It comes in two different levels: Standard and Enhanced. It can be used at different stages of print production.

In *Silver Tint Enhanced*, 100% of the silver is left in the print. In *Silver Tint Standard*, less silver is retained. This produces increased contrast, deeper blacks, and desaturated colors.

Skip Bleach

Skip-Bleach is FotoKem's silver retention process. skip-bleach and bleach-bypass are essentially incomplete processing in that they leave out a step that is a part of the usual processing method. The advantage of this is that it is reversible. This is because leaving the silver in has the effect of increasing the density of the negative. Density is basically silver affected by photochemical reaction: if there is more silver, there is more density. It is the same as if there was additional exposure. This is the case because you are *skipping* the bleach at the negative stage. Bleach-bypass on the negative not only makes the blacks blacker, but it also makes the whites whiter, which is to say it increases contrast. Also, overall density increases, as we discussed in the chapter *Exposure*; this is sometimes called a *thicker* negative. For this reason, most labs recommends a slight underexposure for negative intended for bleach-bypass).

This creates a look that is more radical than ENR or a bleach-bypass on the intermediates or the release print. All silver retention processes cost more than normal processing. This is true of any process in which the lab must alter its normal procedures — such as push or pull processing. In skip-bleach or similar process detailed following, there is an additional cost. Normally the silver that is taken out of the emulsion is recycled and sold. When it is left in, the lab can no longer recycle and resell it, and they need to charge the production company for that in addition to their normal fees. At most labs there is a setup fee, plus a per-foot charge.

ENR

ENR is a proprietary Technicolor process. It was invented by Ernesto Novelli Rimo (hence its name) of Technicolor Rome, and the process was first used by Vittorio Storaro on the 1981 film *Reds*. Since then, Storaro has also used it on films such as *The Last Emperor* and *Little Buddha*. It has also been used on films such as *Jade, The Game,* and *Saving Private Ryan*.

ENR is a color-positive developing technique which utilizes an additional black-and-white developing bath in order to retain some of the silver. After the film has been bleached, but prior to the silver being fixed out of the film, this extra bath allows for a controlled amount of silver to be redeveloped, adding density blacks. ENR is used on the release prints. As a result, each print roll must have the same amount of ENR applied

Not only does it make the blacks blacker, but by increasing contrast in the shadows, there is a slight increase of the shadow detail and an increase in apparent sharpness due to a small edge effect around the image. Note that this is apparent sharpness, not actual sharpness. Many people refer to ENR as a bleach-bypass process, but it is not. Bleach-bypass does have a similar effect, but chemically it is different. In the ENR process, the intensity of the effect can be varied controllably by varying the concentration of the chemistry. This makes it possible to add just a small amount of ENR that has the effect of making the blacks richer but without noticeable effect on color saturation. The ENR process that is variable in effect must be quantifiable so that the DP and lab can confer on how much is to be done. In the ENR process a densitometer is used to measure the level. In this case, it is an infrared densitometer. As a result ENR is classified in density levels, not percentages. For example, a certain print might be 50 IR. This means a .50 density, not 50%.

CCE

Deluxe, another film lab with a long history in Hollywood, uses a process called Color Contrast Enhancement or CCE. CCE raises the contrast, deepens the blacks ,and adds grain but still preserves some shadow detail. As with ENR, the amount of silver retained is read with a densitometer centered on 1000nm. According to Deluxe, a pure bleach-bypass that retains 100% of the silver might yield an IR density reading of as much as 240, which translates to four times the amount of silver that would be found in a normal print. With CCE normally processed negative (no special processes) a nominal reading at 1000nm might be around 60. With CCE, a typical reading of D-max might be around 180 to 190 IR. This translates to about 75% silver left in the print, where retention of 100% will not only increase the density of the blacks but of the mid-tones as well. By keeping the amount of silver retention in this range, there will be some desaturation of the color, an increase in grain, and denser blacks, but there will still be some detail in the blacks, unlike in 100% silver retention, where the blacks might *block up*. CCE was used on the film *Seven* (Figure 13.2) and many others.

ACE

Also a Deluxe process, *ACE* stands for *Adjustable Contrast Enhancement*. ACE is variable in effect. With ACE it is possible to enhance the blacks without significant effect on color saturation. ACE is measured in percentages.

NEC

LTC Laboratories of Paris utilizes the *NEC* process, which stands for *noir en couleur* — French for *black in color*. NEC allows for silver retention in the interpositive stage. The advantage of this is that each individual release print does not have to undergo special processing. NEC produces denser blacks but has less effect on the overall contrast and tonal rendition.

Exposure Compensation in Bleach-Bypass

When shooting film intended for a silver retention process, some change in your exposure will usually be necessary. Generally, you will want to underexpose by 1/2 to a full stop because the skip-bleach process may add as much as 1-1/2 stops. The catch is that bleach-bypass in the print stages is very expensive: for a large-scale release, it can come to hundreds of thousands of dollars. As a result, few, if any, films have bleach-bypass done for all of the prints.

Figure 13.2. The bleach-bypass look is a major element of the visual style of *Seven*.

image control

Other Image Control Techniques

Cross Processing

Cross processing was first developed by still photographers. In cross processing, the original camera film is a *reversal stock* (also called *positive film* or a *transparency*). This reversal stock is then put through processing chemistry normally used for negative film. The result is negative image on a clear based film. In other words, it does not have the distinctive *orange mask* that all color negatives have.

The effect of cross processing is increased contrast and more grain. The effect can range from subtle to radical. As a result, normal or even slightly underexposed original camera film produces the best results. Cross processing is frequently used on music videos and other projects that need a more extreme look, but it is also occasionally used on features: for example, it was used in many scenes of the film *Three Kings*.

Printing Negative as Interpositve

An alternative to cross processing is to print camera negative as an interpositive onto standard print film. Film stock normally used for interpositives is lower in contrast than normal print stock. The reason for this is that successive print stages in postproduction usually result in a buildup of contrast; to counter this, intermediate print stocks generally have a lower contrast. Both cross processing and interpositive printing result in stronger, more saturated colors, which makes them very different from bleach-bypass techniques.

Digital Intermediate

Digital intermediate is a way of having the best of both worlds. The concept is simple: you shoot on film, then do the image manipulation in the digital world with all the tools and techniques that are available there and then in the end the video files are transferred back to a negative to produce prints for projection in theaters.

Normal telecine runs at real-time speed: if the film footage was shot at 24 fps, then it is transferred to video at that same speed and you can watch it at normal speed. For a digital intermediate, however, a higher-resolution image is needed. Standard practice is to scan the film to either a 2K or 4K file; and in most cases directly to hard drives, typically a high-speed RAID.

The process provides unprecedented control over the image — far more so than traditional film color timing, which is limited to making shots lighter or darker and altering the color by controlling the relative balance of red, green, and blue.

Once the footage is digitized, all the sophisticated color correction tools that are standard in digital video become available for film. Individual sections of the image can be timed separately, contrast can be adjusted, color can change gradually within a shot, *power windows* can alter particular areas within the frame, and secondary color correction, where each color can be tweaked individually, is available. All of this happens in real-time, and with random access to all the footage; it's a nonlinear process; and with film it's done reel by reel. This degree of control is available for the entire project, allowing the creation of a look that would otherwise be impossible or require relatively unpredictable custom processing.

Scanning film to high-resolution video is slow and expensive, so it is usually necessary for filmmakers to make choices about how much data is scanned from each frame: the scan resolution, influences the economics of the entire process. Theoretically, (depending on the

Figure 13.3. A result of *cross processing* and fluorescent lighting.

film stock used), film can be considered as high as 6K. Practically, however, this is only true for first-generation camera original, and only under ideal conditions. High-res scans are made in dedicated film scanners instead of telecine machines.

DI Workflow Choices

It often makes sense to scan only the final cut negative, because it makes little sense to spend time and money scanning material that may not even end up in the picture.

On projects where the budget cannot accommodate this approach, it is possible to do just a portion of a show using the digital intermediate process, while finishing the rest with conventional techniques. Once you have done all the corrections and color balancing, the final step is a *film-out,* where the digital files are scanned back to film to create projection prints. If shooting on HD for a film-out, a test of the entire post workflow is important.

Tape-to-Tape Correction

It is important to remember that a *Digital Intermediate*, as most people use the term, is only necessary when you need a final print for theaters that still project 35mm film; it is not necessary if your project will only be projected digitally, appear on television, the Internet, or other venues that are not film projection.

However, shooting on film and then scanning to high-res digital can be employed for any type of project. In this case, it differs from the normal process of shooting on film followed by telecine in that the files that result from scanning are much higher resolution. In *tape-to-tape color correction*, once the film footage is transferred to video, and edited, the video is brought back into the same tele-

Figure 13.4. The distinctive look of *O Brother, Where Art Thou?* was achieved through the use of digital intermediate. DP Roger Deakins had tried many different film techniques but was unable to create the look he wanted through conventional methods; the digital intermediate gave him options that were not available with any other options.

cine suite where it may have been transferred to film. Here, instead of going from film-to-tape with color correction, the process goes from one tape machine to another. The telecine colorist can fine balance of color, exposure, and contrast for the entire project; the equipment they work on is capable of making adjustments to exposure, color balance, overall tone, saturation, and more. In addition to correcting each shot, an important part of this stage of the process is ensuring consistency from shot to shot and scene to scene. Using power windows, the colorist can even make changes to different parts of the frame. The telecine colorist is an important part of the image-making team; even if you know exactly what you want, it is valuable to ask for the colorist's input and opinion as well.

Digital Manipulation

The world of digital video and High Def video has opened up a whole new world of image control, whether it is in a digital intermediate or working directly on footage captured in video. With computers and the wide array of software now available, there is almost nothing you can't do with the look of your project. Editing applications provide basic image control tools and even some more advanced ones.

Other applications are designed specifically for image manipulation: *Apple Color*, *Adobe After Effects,* and *Combustion* are very sophisticated tools that are available to anyone. At the professional level, tools like *Flame* and *Inferno* and *Smoke* are visual effects and editing software; with prices up to hundreds of thousands of dollars they are not as available to those working on tighter budgets. Applications are also available for the DP or editor to do preliminary color grading and *color management* on the set or in the editing room. These can then be used a reference files for the final color correction and can either be viewed as video files by the colorist or even sent as *grading files* that the colorist can use directly or as a reference.

LOOKUP TABLES

In the case of HD footage that is shot RAW (and some other capture systems), the footage will not look at all like it will in the end, These files need processing (*demosaicing* and *debayering*) before it even begins to look like a final image (see chapter *HD Cinematography*). This makes it nearly impossible to judge contrast and color balance on the set. Some cameras output a processed image for on-set monitoring.

Figure 13.5. (top) An image from a Viper HD camera in their propriety *FilmStream* mode. (Illustration courtesy of Light Illusion.)

Figure 13.6. (bottom) The FilmStream image with an LUT applied. (Illustration courtesy of Light Illusion.)

To help visualize the final product, *LUTs* may be necessary (Figures 13.7 and 13.8). LUT stands for *Lookup Table*. Simply put, lookup tables are precalculated sets of data that are used to adjust the color of an image being displayed with the gamut and chromaticity of one video device (such as a camera) to match how that image would look using the *gamut* and chromaticity of on another device, such as a monitor. LUTs are also used when transferring video (such as a DI) to film. There are several methods for creating an LUT and different software applications to enable the DP to create their own and use them on the set.

The gamut of a particular device represents the total range of colors that can be displayed on that device. Some types of displays are capable of displaying a greater range of colors than others. Furthermore, different video and film standards employ different gamuts of color, so colors that are easily represented by one imaging medium are out of bounds for another and can't be represented. For example, film is capable of representing far more color values than the broadcast video standard.

LUTs are not absolute; in fact, DPs often build their own lookup tables to suit their own particular needs and alter them for different projects or when using different monitors. Not everyone can agree on what the "correct" lookup table for a particular video camera or digital workflow is: it's part color science and part subjective artistry. There are two basic flavors of LUT: 1D and 3D.

1D LUTs

A 1D LUT is one value of gamma or a series of measures for each color channel. 1D LUTs can be used as import and export LUTs, and as monitor (viewing) LUTs (Figure 13.7). Import and export LUTs are mainly used to convert between the logarithmic data contained in film scans and the linear data used within the application. Monitor LUTs ensure the image displayed on the monitor resembles the final output without the actual image data being modified.

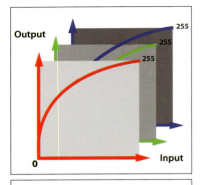

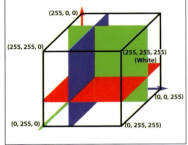

Figure 13.7. (top) A 1D LUT has separate tables for each color channel. (Illustration courtesy of Light Illusion.)

Figure 13.8. (bottom) A 3D LUT is a cube or lattice. The values of 0 to 255 in both of these are the digital color values. (Illustration courtesy of Light Illusion.)

3D LUTs

3D LUTs are a bit more complex. A 3D LUT is defined as a 3D lattice or cube where each axis is an entry point for one of the three color components (Figure 13.8). Output values are calculated by interpolating between the nearest points in the lattice. As with other types of LUTs they can be written out as a table of numbers.

The 3D cubes may be of various sizes and *bit depths*. The most common practice is to use RGB 10 bit/component log images as the input to the 3D LUT. Interpolation software routines are needed for calculating the output values from an input by looking for the nearest points defined within the 3D LUT lattice.

CAMERA FILTER TYPES

There are a few basic types of filters:

- Diffusion
- Exposure (neutral density)
- Focus (diopters and split-diopters)
- Color balance
- Color alteration
- Effects

Diffusion and Effects Filters

There are many types of diffusion filters, but they all have one common purpose: they slightly alter the image to make it *softer* or more diffuse or to reduce the contrast. They do it in a number of ways and with a variety of effects (Figures 13.9 through 13.12). Nearly all diffusion filters come in *grades*: 1, 2, 3, 4, 5 or 1/8th, 1/4, 1/2, 1, 2, and so on. Most rental house will send them out either as a set or as individual rentals. All types of filters usually come in a protective pouch and often have some soft lens tissue wrapped around them inside the pouch to make it easier to handle the glass without adding fingerprints that need to be removed later.

Diffusion filters are a very personal and subjective subject. Besides glass or resin filters, which are placed in front of the lens (or in some cases behind the lens or even in a slot the middle of it), other methods can be used. Designations for filters are not standardized, but they generally come in sets ranging from 1 to 5 or 1/8, 1/4, 1/2, 1, 2, and so on. An older type of filter that dates back to the early days of the studio system but that is still popular today are the Mitchell diffusions, which come in grades *A, B,* and *C*.

Other types of loose open material can be used, as can as grease or petroleum jelly on a piece of glass. Ordinary cellophane or plastic wrap have also been employed in emergencies. Star filters, which create a pattern of streaks around a highlight, are basically clear glass with diagonal scratches.

There are some things to beware of when using diffusion filters. They will give different degrees of diffusion depending on the focal length of the lens beings used: a longer focal length lens will appear to be more heavily diffused. Some DPs drop down to a lower degree of diffusion when changing to a longer lens. Tiffen, a major manufacturer of camera filters, has created digital filters in its *Dfx* software, which can used in postproduction to reproduce the effect of their glass filters. Be careful about judging the effect of diffusion filters on a small on-set monitor, which can be deceiving. To judge any kind of alterations to the look a large monitor is usually required.

Figure 13.9 labels: BF 1/4, BF 1/2, BF 1, BF 2

Nets

Another form of diffusion is nets or *voiles* (a mesh that is coarser than net). Many cinematographers use silk or nylon stocking material, which can have a very subtle and beautiful effect. Nets vary in their diffusion effect according to how fine their weave is. Nets can come in filter form sandwiched between two pieces of optical glass, or they might be loose pieces cut and attached to the front or rear of the lens. Camera assistants always have scissors in their kit for this and other tasks.

Attaching a net to the rear of the lens has several advantages. A net on the front of the lens can come slightly into focus with wider lenses that are stopped down. A net on the rear of this lens will not do this. Also, the diffusion effect will not change as the lens is stopped down or the focal length changes on a zoom. Attaching a net to the rear of the lens must be done with great caution as there is danger of damaging the exposed rear element of the lens or of interfering with the spinning reflex mirror. Putting a net on the rear should be done with easily removable material such as *snot tape* —

Figure 13.9. Various grades of diffusion — the Schneider Black Frost series. (Photo courtesy of Schneider Optics.)

Figure 13.10. (left) The image with no filter.

Figure 13.11. (middle) The same image with a *Black Promist 3 filter*. (Photo courtesy of Tiffen.)

Figure 13.12. (right) A *Warm Black Promist 3*. (Photo courtesy of Tiffen.)

also sometimes called *transfer tape* (a two-sided soft sticky tape that is also used for attaching lighting gels to *open frames*). For HD cameras, plastic rings that hold the net firmly are a quicker and cleaner way to apply the net to the rear element.

Contrast Filters

Various filters are used to reduce or soften the degree of contrast in a scene. These generally work by taking some of the highlights and making them "flare" into the shadows. Traditionally these were called "lo-cons." There are a number of newer, more sophisticated varieties. Two types are shown in Figures 13.13 through 13.15.

Effects Filters and Grads

There are many kinds of very special effects filters, ranging from the most obvious to the more subtle, *Sunset* filters give the scene an overall orange glow. Other filters can give the scene a color tone of almost any sort imaginable: from moonlight blue to antique sepias.

In addition to filters that affect the entire scene, almost any type of filter is also available as a *grad*. A grad is a filter that starts with a color on one side and gradually fades out to clear or another color (Figures 13.16 through 13.17). Also commonly used are *sunset grads* and blue or magenta grads to give some color to what would otherwise be a colorless or "blown-out" sky (Figures 13.18 through 13.21). Grads can be either *hard edge* or *soft edge,* denoting how gradual the transition is. The most commonly used types of grads are *neutral density filters,* which are often used to balance the exposure between a normal foreground scene and a much hotter sky above the horizon. ND grads come in grades of .3 (one stop at the darkest), .6 (two stops), .9 (three stops), and, more rarely .12 (four stops). Be sure to specify whether you want a hard or soft cut because there is a considerable difference in application. Whether you need a hard or a soft cut will also be affected by what focal length you are planning to shoot with. A longer focal length lens is better suited to a hard edge grad, while the hard edge would be visible on a wider lens. Grads can be used either horizontally or vertically. If the matte box has a *rotating stage*, they can even be diagonal. Although rare, there are matte boxes that even have a motorized rotating stages that can move the filter during the shot.

COLOR TEMPERATURE AND FILTRATION

As we discussed in *Color*, the most common system used in describing the color of light is color temperature. This scale is derived from the color of a theoretical *black body* (a metal object having no inherent color of its own, technically known as a *Planckian radiator*). When heated to incandescence, the black body glows at varying colors depending on the temperature. Color temperature is a quantification of the terms "red hot," "white hot," and so on.

There is another measure of light color that is important as well: the magenta-green content; this is an entirely different aspect of the color, and the two are completely independent of each other (see Figure 12.17 in the chapter *Color*). Since many sources in lighting tend to have a component of green, it is important to measure and correct it; otherwise the film will be heavily tinted, usually in a very disturbing and unattractive way. Sources that produce disproportionate green include fluorescents, HMIs, industrial sources such as sodium vapor and mercury vapor lamps, and many other types of bulbs with discontinuous spectrums.

How Mired Values Are Used

Another problem with color temperature is that equal changes in color "temperature" are not necessarily perceived by the eye as equal changes in color. A change of 50K from 2000K to 2050K will be a noticeable difference in color. For an equivalent change in color perception at 5500K, the color temperature would need to shift 150K and about 500K at 10,000K.

Because these changes are so unequal, the mired system has been devised. Mired stands for micro-reciprocal degrees. Mireds are derived by dividing 1,000,000 by the Kelvin value. For example, 3200K equals 1,000,000/3200 = 312 mireds. When calculating the degree of color correction needed for a particular combination, the mired system can be used. If you have a source at 5500K and wish

Figure 13.13. (left) No filter. (Photo courtesy of Tiffen.)

Figure 13.14. (middle) *Ultracon 5*, a low-contrast filter. (Photo courtesy of Tiffen.)

Figure 13.15. (right) *Softcon 5*, a different type of contrast filter. (Photo courtesy of Tiffen.)

Figure 13.16. (left) Sunset shot with no filter. (Photo courtesy of Tiffen.)

Figure 13.17. (far left) Same shot with a *Tiffen Sunset Grad*. (Photo courtesy of Tiffen.)

image control

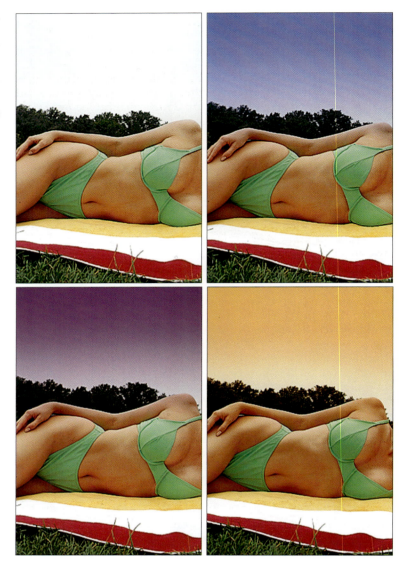

to convert it to 3200K, subtract the mired value of the desired color from that of the source. 5000K = 200 mireds. 3200K = 312 mireds. 312 minus 200 = 112 mireds. 85 orange has a mired value of + 112. In practice these calculations are done by the color meter or by using a simple get chart. On the mired scale, a plus shift value means the filter is moving toward yellowish, and a minus value means the filter will give a blue shift. When combining filters, you add the mired values to determine the final result.

What "Color Balance" Means in Film Stock

Unlike the human eye, which is assisted by the brain in compensating and adapting, no color film can accurately reproduce color under all kinds of lighting conditions. In manufacture, the film is adjusted to render color accurately under a particular condition, the two most common being average daylight (type D film), which is set for 5500K, and average tungsten illumination (type B film) designed for 3200K. There is a third, which is based on the now disused *photo bulbs*, which were 3400K (type A film), rather than 3200K, but very few films are available in this balance.

Given the fact that providing tungsten light is costly, while sunlight is usually far more abundant, most motion picture films are type B, balanced for tungsten. The idea is that we put a correcting filter on when we can most afford to lose light to a filter factor — in the sunlight. Kodak does have several excellent daylight balance films available for which no correcting filter is needed in daylight or HMI situations. They come in ISOs up to 250, which can be extremely useful on dark, cloudy days or when the sun is near the horizon. At the end of the day it gets dark surprisingly fast; this applies both to exteriors and interiors that are partially or fully lit with daylight.

There are four basic reasons to change the color of light at the source: to correct the color of the lights to match the film type (instead of using a camera filter), to match different types of lighting sources, and for effect or mood. Finally there are specialized situations like greenscreen or bluescreen.

To shoot with type B film under *daylight balance* light (in the 5500K area) an 85 orange filter is used (Figure 13.22). The 80A or 80B blue filters for shooting daylight film with warm light are rarely used, and in most cases should be combined with a UV (ultraviolet) filter because tungsten film cannot tolerate the high proportion of UV in daylight and HMIs. There is some light loss when using a correction filter, and the filter factor must be used to adjust the T/stop. For convenience, most manufacturers list an adjusted *Exposure Index* (or ISO/ASA), which allows for the filter loss; this will appear on the film can and in data sheets for that film stock.

Another form of filter that is sometimes used is a *UV* or *haze filter*. Skylight contains a great deal of ultraviolet radiation that can cause the image to go slightly blue. This is especially true at high altitudes where there is little atmosphere to filter out the UV. It is sometimes called a haze filter because it will have the effect of slightly reducing the effect of haze in the atmosphere. Two different ISOs will be listed on cans of black-and-white film. This is not related to correction filters, since none are needed. It is because black-and-white films vary in their sensitivity to colors. In most cases the ASA for tungsten light will be 1/3 stop lower. Very important: when using this adjusted EI, do not also use the filter factor. Smaller color mismatches can also be corrected with color filters, as well. If the scene lighting is 2800K, for example (too warm), then an 82C filter will correct the light reaching the film to 3200K. Types of color filters generally used in film and video production are discussed in the next section. Filter families are shown in Tables 13.1 through 13.34.

Conversion Filters

Conversion filters work with the blue and orange ranges of the spectrum and deal with fundamental color balance in relation to the color sensitivity of the emulsion. Conversion filters affect all parts of the spectrum for smooth color rendition. (*LB*) *Light Balancing* filters are warming and cooling filters; they work on the entire *SED* (*Spectral Energy Distribution*) as with the conversion filters, but they are used to make smaller shifts in the Blue-Orange axis.

Camera Lens Filters for Color Correction

Color compensating filters (*CC*) are manufactured in the primary and secondary colors. They are used to make corrections in a specific area of the spectrum or for special effects. They affect only their own narrow band of the SED. Don't make the mistake of trying to correct color balance with CC filters. Primary filters work in a limited band of the spectrum and correct only one wavelength.

Figure 13.22. (top) An *85B*.

Figure 13.23. (middle) An *80B* blue filter.

Figure 13.24. (bottom) *81A* for slight warming effect.

However, since CC filters are not confined to the Blue-Orange axis, they can be used to correct imbalances in the Magenta-Green axis, such as occur with fluorescent lamps and most types of industrial lamps. A CC-30M is often a part of the basic filter package for standard tubes. 30M is a good starting point for most uncorrected fluorescent sources (Table 13.1).

Warming and Cooling Filters

The *80 series*, which are blue conversion filters, are used to convert warm sources such as tungsten lights so that they are suitable for use with daylight film (Table 13.4).

The 81 series of warming filters (81, 81A, 81B, 81C) increase the *warmth* of the light by lowering the color temperature in 200K increments (Figure 13.24). The 81 shifts the color temp by a minimal amount: -200K. For cooling, the 82 series works in the same fashion, starting with the 82, which shifts the overall color temperature by +200K. As with most color temperature correction filters, excess magenta or green are not dealt with and must be handled separately. Table 13.2 shows the Wratten 81 and 82 filters for warming and cooling. Wratten is a system of filter classification by Eastman Kodak. *Corals* are also a popular type of filter for degrees of warming.

CONTRAST CONTROL IN BLACK-AND-WHITE

Since color filters transmit some colors and absorb others, this makes them useful in controlling contrast in black-and-white images. Most scenes contain a variety of colors. The sky may be the only blue area in a landscape shot, a field of grass may be the only largely green element in a scene, and so on. We can use this to advantage even though the shot is black-and-white.

The basic principle of contrast control filtration in black-and-white cinematography is that a filter *lightens* colors in its own area of the spectrum and *darkens* the complementary (opposite) colors. How strong an effect it has is the result of two factors: how strong the color differences of the original subject are and how strong the filter is. The scene we are shooting is the result of the colors of the objects themselves and the colors of the light that falls on them.

Color filters only increase or decrease contrast on black-and-white film when there is color difference in the scene. In a scene composed of only black, white and gray objects a color filter would only reduce exposure: it would not alter the contrast. When a filter is used to absorb certain colors, we are reducing the total amount of light reaching the film. We must compensate by allowing more overall exposure. The exposure compensation necessary for each filter is expressed as the *filter factor*.

With warm colors (red, orange, yellow), the daylight filter factors are greater than the tungsten filter factors. In the violet and blue range, the daylight factors are less than the tungsten, but for the cyan/green range of the spectrum the daylight and tungsten filter factors are nearly all equal. The same is true for magenta, which is equally red and blue. The simple rule for black-and-white filters is: expose for the darkest subject in the scene that is substantially the same color as the filter, and let the filter take care of the highlights.

Using Filters in Black-and-White Photography

These filters for black-and-white have alternate designations:

    #8 = K-2
    #15 = G-15
    #11 = X-1

Combining contrast filters for black-and-white does not have the cumulative effect that we might expect. For example, combining a #8 and #15 filter gives the same visual effect as a #15 filter alone (although the filter factor is changed by the combination of the two). Combining two filters of different groups is seldom necessary, since there is usually a single filter which will do the same job.

Polarizers

Natural light vibrates in all directions around its path of travel. A *polarizer* transmits the light that is vibrating in one direction only. *Polarizers* serve a variety of functions. Glare on a polished surface or on a glass window is, to a certain extent, polarized as it is reflected. By rotating a polarizer to eliminate that particular direction of polarization, we can reduce or eliminate the glare and surface reflection. Brewster's angle, 56° from normal, or 34° from the surface, is the zone of maximum polarization (Figures 13.25 and 13.26).

When working with glare on water and on windows it is seldom desirable to eliminate all reflections because this creates an unnatural effect. The polarizer can be used with color film to darken the sky. Maximum polarization occurs at about 90° from the sun. This works well for static shots, but care must be taken if a pan or tilt is called for because the degree of polarization may change as the camera moves in relation to the sky. If the sky is overcast, the polarizer won't help much. Polarizers reduce transmission of light, generally at least 1 2/3 to 2 stops as a filter factor, which does not change as you rotate the polarizer, however the degree of polarization may change as you pan or tilt the camera.

Beam Splitter Viewfinders and Polarizers

When using cameras with video assist and modern beam splitters, it is necessary to use special polarizing filters called *circular pola filters*. The term circular refers to technology used to make them, not their shape or the direction of the polarization. If these circular pola filters aren't used, there will be problems with either image in the finder or on the video assist. The image on the film is not affected. The reason for this is that modern beam splitters use a dielectric coating that has polarizing tendencies and since two polarizing filters can not be used together, there will be problems. The circular pola filter has a front and back and the orientation is important. The front must point towards the subject or it won't be effective.

Some camera viewfinders exhibit a magenta appearance with ordinary pola filters. On other cameras, the video goes very dark. This does not happen with circular polas.

Density Filters

Neutral density filters are used to reduce overall exposure without affecting color rendition. They can be used in extremely high-illumination situations (such as a sunlit snow scene or a beach scene) where the exposure would be too great or where reduced exposure is desired to crush depth of field. Neutral density filters combined with 85 correction filters (85N3, 85N6, and 85N9) are a standard order with any camera package for exterior work. You may want to bring a set of neutral density filters on an HD shoot as well.

Also known as *Wratten #96*, the opacity of ND filters is given in *density units* so that .3 equals one stop, .6 equals two stops, and .9 equals three stops. In gelatin filters, ND's are available in .1 increments (1/3 of a stop). If you combine ND filters, the density values are added.

		Exp. Factor
YELLOW (Absorbs Blue)	CC.025Y	-
	CC05Y	-
	CC10Y	1/3
	CC20Y	1/3
	CC30Y	1/3
	CC40Y	1/3
	CC50Y	2/3
MAGENTA (Red-blue)	CC.025M	-
	CC05M	1/3
	CC10M	1/3
	CC20M	1/3
	CC30M	2/3
	CC40M	2/3
	CC50M	2/3
CYAN (Blue-green)	CC.025 C	-
	CC05C	1/3
	CC10C	1/3
	CC20C	1/3
	CC30C	2/3
	CC40C	2/3
	CC50C	1
RED	CC.025R	-
	CC05R	1/3
	CC10R	1/3
	CC20R	1/3
	CC30R	2/3
	CC40R	2/3
	CC50R	1
GREEN (Absorbs Blue and Red)	CC.025G	-
	CC05G	1/3
	CC10G	1/3
	CC20G	1/3
	CC30G	2/3
	CC40G	2/3
	CC50G	1
BLUE (Absorbs Green and Red)	CC.025B	-
	CC05B	1/3
	CC10B	1/3
	CC20B	2/3
	CC30B	2/3
	CC40B	1
	CC50B	1 1/3

	Filter #	Exp. Factor	Mired	To Get 3200K From:
COOLING	82C + 82C	1 1/3	-89	2490K
	82C + 82B	1 1/3	-77	2570K
	82C+82A	1	-65	2650K
	82C+82	1	-55	2720K
	82C	2/3	-45	2800K
	82B	2/3	-32	2900K
	82A	1/3	-21	3000K
	82	1/3	-10	3100K
WARMING	81	1/3	+9	3300K
	81A	1/3	+18	3400K
	81B	1/3	+27	3500K
	81C	1/3	+35	3600K
	81D	2/3	+42	3700K
	81EF	2/3	+52	3850K

FILTER	CONVERSION		EXP. LOSS
80A	3200 > 5500	-131	2 stops
80B	3400 > 5500	-112	1 2/3 stops
80C	3800 > 5500	-81	1 stop
80D	4200 > 5500	-56	1/3 stop

FILTER	CONVERSION	Mired	EXP. LOSS
85A	5500 > 3400	+112	2/3 stop
85B	5500 > 3200	+131	2/3 stop
85C	5500 > 3800	+81	1/3 stop

Table 13.1. (top) *Color Correction* camera filters. (Data courtesy of Eastman Kodak.)

Table 13.2. (second from top) *Wratten* series *81* and *82* filters. (Data courtesy of Eastman Kodak.)

Table 13.3. (third from top) The *80* series.

Table 13.4. (bottom) The *85* series.

Table 13.5. Effects of filters in black-and-white photography.

WRATTEN #	COLOR	EXPOSURE FACTOR	EXPOSURE INCREASE	DEGREE	EFFECT IN DAYLIGHT
3	Light Yellow	1.5	1/2	Slight	Penetrates haze
8	Medium Yellow	2	1	Moderate	Corrects panchromatic color balance
11	Green 1	4	2	Light	Lightens green foliage
12	Yellow	2	1	Strong	Increases contrast
15	Deep Yellow	2.5	1 1/4	Heavy	Darkens sky, lightens faces
21	Light Orange	3	1 1/2	Slight	Heavy correction
23A	Deep Orange	5	2 1/4	Moderate	Penetrates heavy haze
25	Red	8	3	Heavy	Dark sky, white faces
29	Deep Red	16	4	Extreme	Strong Contrast, black sky

IR Filters

Some HD cameras are subject to IR contamination, which means that they are sensitive to infrared wavelengths to an extent that can significantly affect the look of a shot, particularly in day exteriors. IR density filters prevent this by blocking the wavelengths that cause problems. Tiffen calls their product *Hot Mirror* filters. Some cameras have built-in IR protection.

Filters and Bright Point Sources

When shooting a bright point source such as the sun, filters will almost certainly show double or triple images. This is caused by the image of the source reflecting off the front surface of the lens back onto the filter. When shooting the sun especially, it is best to go with no filters if possible, but an ND filter may be necessary.

Some sophisticated matte boxes permit the filters to be set at a slight angle, which prevents this problem. If all else fails, slightly loosen the swing-away matte box and give it a bit of an angle. Be careful, though: too much angle and you are creating an opening that will cause other types of flares and reflections. Your first AC should always be checking for light leaks of this sort, especially in situations where the sun or other strong light is hitting the camera. As an added precaution, the grips should always provide a camera umbrella or *courtesy flag* to keep light off the camera as well as the operator and focus puller.

This applies to lit bulbs in the frame, candles, or other hot spots. Candles are a particular problem, since the rest of the scene is usually very dark. Another source of trouble is car or truck headlights. When they hit the lens, they are surprisingly strong and flare out totally. You can cut a piece of Rosco scrim and place it over the headlights. Rosco scrim is an opaque material with lots of small holes. It is very effective in controlling the light, which still flares enough to disguise the scrim. If that is not available, a heavy dose of or *Streaks N' Tips* will help. Streaks N' Tips is a hair color product that is used on sets because it is easy to clean off and comes in a variety of colors.

CONTROLLING THE LOOK OF YOUR PROJECT

The look of a film or video production is a complex, interactive combination of dozens of different variables. In films where the look is very apparent, such as *Days of Heaven*, *Seven Samurai,* and *Seven* (as well as many others), there are a few prominent devices which can be readily identified; in these examples shooting primarily at magic hour, use of very long lenses or bleach-bypass processing of the release prints.

The look of the project is something that must be thought through carefully in preproduction because it may involve requesting special filters, unusual gels for the lights, arrangements with the lab or color timer, or specialized equipment such as a flicker box or lightning

Figure 13.25. (left) A scene shot through glasswith no polarizer. (Photo courtesy of Tiffen.)

Figure 13.26. (right) With a polarizer — in this case the Tiffen *UltraPo*l. (Photo courtesy of Tiffen.)

generator (for more on flicker, see the chapter *Technical Issues*). Typically the director or DP will a concept of a look for the project and then they will discuss it, look at examples, and talk about how to apply to the film. Visual examples are important for this; many DPs and directors keep books of photos and other references.

As with most issues in art, it is, of course, not nearly that simple. You can make a film at magic hour, or use long lenses or bleach-bypass, and there is a good chance that your project will look nothing like those films. These are just examples; this applies to all techniques and methods of visual production, and post-production as well. The reason is that these simple techniques are not magic bullets. Obviously, there are many variables within each technique that have to be juggled and fine-tuned to achieve the desired look. Sometimes it is a question of budget, equipment, time, crew, weather, or other factors, but this is not the point. If you educate yourself in the techniques, test, and experiment and bring all the forces to bear, you can get them right. The real issue is that these methods must be used in coordination with all the other visual elements of the production. These factors include:

- Lighting style
- Color control in lighting
- Use of lenses
- Choice of locations
- Choice of camera angles
- Set design and color scheme
- Set dressing
- Wardrobe
- Makeup
- Casting
- Choice of film or video format

The point is that you have to think globally when you consider the visual style of your production — every choice becomes part of the mix that determines the overall look, and that look is itself a key element in the overall storytelling, emotional impact, and final success of your project. Thinking globally means you also need to consult with the production designer, wardrobe designer and the editor.

Table 13.6. Filter factors and exposure compensation for neutral density filters.

FILTER	PERCENTAGE OF TRANSMISSION	FILTER FACTOR	EXPOSURE INCREASE IN STOPS
0.1	80	1-1/4	1/3
0.2	63	1 1/2	2/3
0.3	50	2	1
0.4	40	2 1/2	1 1/3
0.5	32	3	1 2/3
0.6	25	4	2
0.7	20	5	2 1/3
0.8	16	6	2 2/3
0.9	13	8	3
1.0	10	10	3 1/3
2.0	1	100	6 2/3
3.0	0.1	1000	10 1/3
4.0	0.01	10000	13
85 N3	32	3	1 2/3
85N6	16	6	2 2/3
86N9	9	11	3 2/3

image control

265

Figure 13.27. (top) Scene with no filter. (Photo courtesy of Tiffen.)

Figure 13.28. (bottom) With a neutral density filter for the sky. Although a polarizer might have achieved most of the same effect, there are two important differences: the effect of the polarizer would depend on the angle relative to the sun and it would have also have eliminated the reflections on the water, which are an important part of the image. (Photo courtesy of Tiffen.)

Figure 13.29. (above, right) For this music video shot, we used a combination of techniques. A very light net on the lens and double printing over a defocused black-and-white dupe to desaturate and soften without getting mushy. (Photo by author.)

IMAGE CONTROL WITH THE CAMERA

Frame Rate

The speed at which the film runs through the camera also has a great effect on our perception of the shot. Since film is almost always projected or transferred to video at 24 fps, running the camera at a higher speed will slow the action down and running at a lower than normal frame rate will speed the action up.

High-speed filming generally produces an image with a dreamlike effect. Low-speed filming, which speeds the action up, is most often used for a comedy effect. Low-speed filming can result in a subtle emphasis of a movement when the frame rate is from 26 to 28 fps.

Higher speeds can underscore and dramatize a particular moment. Scorsese used this very effectively in some of the fight scenes in *Raging Bull*; at times the camera was running at as much as 120 fps. It has always been possible to change the frame rate during a shot, but now many cameras can automatically compensate exposure with the aperture or shutter, thus making *ramping* during the shot far easier. Some people, however, prefer to do the entire shot high-speed and do the slower parts in post, thus giving them more control of the timing. Arriflex, Panavision, and Photo-Sonics make a number of high-speed cameras for these types of shots. In HD video, the Phantom camera can go as high as 1500 fps, and many HD cameras can go as high as 120 fps. These are discussed in the chapter *Technical Issues*.

Both high-speed and low-speed frame rates are available on some (not all) HD video cameras. If you plan to do any off-speed frames rates, be sure that the camera you will be using is capable of doing the frame rates you are planning on using.

Slow-Speed Blur

There is a special case of off-speed filming that produces a very dramatic, blurring effect that is often used in commercials and occasionally in narrative films. The effect is achieved by running the camera slower than usual, such as 12 fps, 6 fps or even 4 fps and then transferring to video *at the same rate*. The effect is blurring, but the action runs at normal speed. It looks very much like it is slowed down, but it isn't (Figure 13.30). The reason it works is that when the camera is run at a very low-speed, the shutter is open for a much longer than normal time. Shooting at 6 fps makes each frame approximately 1/12th of a second.

Figure 13.30. Slow-speed blur is a combination of shutter speed and telecine.

At 24 frames per second and 180° shutter, the film camera is exposing each frame for 1/50th of a second. The reason that it is acceptable to shoot at such a low speed is that, because of the persistence of vision, the frames perceptually overlap slightly and mask the unsharpness. The heavy blur we see when we pause on some single frames by itself reminds us that we are not taking still photos. As a still photograph this would not stand up itself, but as part of the scene, it is even more effective that a perfectly lit, well-composed detailed photograph. A particularly effective use of this technique is in *Gladiator* during the battle scene that begins the film. As the battle just after dawn, the shots are the normal frame rate of 24 fps, but as the sun goes down, shots are done at 6 fps. This gives a blurred look that effectively gives the feeling of fatigue and blurred vision that would result from an entire day of hand-to-hand fighting. In the DVD commentary, director Ridley Scott reveals that the reason this was done was that they were running out of light. By shooting at 6 fps, the shutter speed becomes 1/12th of a second, which gives a bonus of an additional two stops of exposure. In this case, the effect has a double bonus. Using slow frame rates for extra exposure can easily be used when the subject is static or has no identifiable that would reveal that the camera was running off-speed.

Shutter Angle

Another factor in the sharpness of an image is the shutter angle. Most film cameras run with a shutter of approximately 180°. This means that the film is being exposed for half the time, and for the other half, the image is being projected into the viewing system for the operator to see. Many cameras have variable shutters. The widest standard shutter is 210°, which is not appreciably different from 180°. Closing the shutter down more and more has an effect on the image. The more closed the shutter, the shorter the exposure and therefore the sharper the image.

A shutter of 90°, for example, will be a much cleaner, sharper image of any moving object. Beyond 90° there will be another effect in addition to sharpness. Since the shutter is now closed significantly longer than it is open, the subject has longer to move between exposures. This will result in a *strobe* effect with a stuttering motion effect. This effect was used extensively in *Saving Private Ryan, Three Kings,* and other films, as well as many other music videos, short films and commercials.

Figure 13.31. The distinctive look in this frame is a combination of lighting and postproduction image manipulation, primarily desaturated sepia tone. (Photo by author.)

Time Lapse

An extreme example of slow motion is *time lapse* photography. In time lapse, there is a significant amount of time between each exposure. As a result, the action will be speeded up considerably. Clouds will slide across the sky, day can turn to night in a few seconds, or a rose can bloom in less than a minute. Time lapse is usually achieved with an intervalometer. See the chapter *Technical Issues* for information on doing the calculations to determine frame rate and duration.

optics & focus

PHYSICAL BASIS OF OPTICS

Except for certain minor differences, the principles of optics and the use of lenses are the same for film and video. Nearly all principles of optics and optical design are based on a few properties of physics. The two most basic are reflection and refraction. There are a few things we need to know about the basic behavior of light in order to understand the fundamentals of optics.

Aside from lighting sources, most things in the real world do not emit visible light but reflect natural or artificial light. The reflection of light can be roughly categorized into two types of reflection: specular reflection which is defined as light reflected from a smooth surface at a definite angle, and diffuse reflection, which is produced by rough surfaces that tend to reflect light in all directions. There are far more occurrences of diffuse reflection than specular reflection in our everyday environment.

The basic rule of reflection, known to any schoolchild, is: *the angle of incidence equals the angle of reflection*. The amount of light reflected by an object is dependent upon the texture of the surface. When surface imperfections are smaller than the wavelength of the incident light (as in the case of a mirror), virtually all of the light is reflected. In everyday language — it's shiny. However, in the real world most objects have convoluted surfaces that exhibit a diffuse reflection, with the incident light being reflected in all directions.

As will be discussed in the chapter on lighting, diffusion is also a key element in controlling light that is transmitted through things: namely diffusion materials. In both cases, diffusion means the same thing: the light rays are more scattered in all directions after they are reflected or transmitted than they were before. The opposite of reflection, absorption, is of interest in two ways. First of all it is how objects have "color" (see chapter on *Color Theory*) and secondly it is how we control light on the set.

Refraction

The *refraction* of visible light is an important characteristic of lenses that allows them to focus a beam of light onto a single point. Refraction, or bending of the light, occurs as light passes from one medium to another when there is a difference in the index of refraction between the two materials.

Refractive index is defined as the relative speed at which light moves through a material with respect to its speed in a vacuum. When light passes from a less dense medium such as air to a more dense medium

Figure 14.1. (previous page) Extremely narrow depth-of-field is essential to this frame from *Seven*.

Figure 14.2. (above) A zoom mounted on an HD camera.

Figure 14.3. A *prime lens* has only one focal length, unlike a zoom, which is variable in focal length. This lens is a 25mm T/2.9 by Zeiss. A lens is defined by its focal length and its maximum wide open aperature. (Photo courtesy of Carl Zeiss AG.)

such as glass, the speed of the wave decreases. Conversely, when light passes from a more dense medium to a less dense medium, the speed of the wave increases. The angle of refracted light is dependent upon both the angle of incidence and the composition of the material into which it is entering. We can define the normal as a line perpendicular to the boundary between two substances.

The concept of refractive index is illustrated in Figure 14.4 for the case of light passing from air through both glass and water. Notice that while both beams enter the denser material through the same angle of incidence with respect to the normal (60 degrees), the refraction for glass is almost 6 degrees more than that for water due to the higher refractive index of glass. The index of refraction varies with the frequency of radiation (or wavelength) of light. This occurs with all transparent media and is called dispersion. Dispersion is a problem because it makes the image less sharp and contrasty.

F/Stop

It is one thing to have the lens form an image on the focal plane, but the amount of light that reaches it must be controlled. This is done with an aperture, which is nothing more than a variable size hole that is placed in the optical axis.

The *f/number* or *f/stop* of a lens is a measure of its ability to pass light. The f/stop is the ratio of the focal length of a lens to the diameter of the entrance pupil. However, this is a purely mathematical calculation that does not account for the varying efficiency of different lens designs.

T-stop (*true stop*) is a measurement of actual light transmission as measured on an optical bench. F/stops are used in depth-of-field and hyperfocal calculations, and T-stops are used in setting exposure.

When setting the aperture on a lens, never go backward. Most apertures have a certain amount of backlash that must be compensated for. If it is necessary to go to a larger stop (*open up*), open the lens all the way up and then reset the stop.

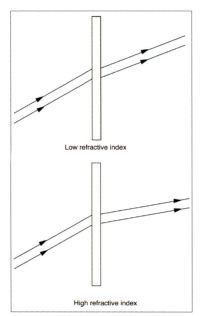

Low refractive index

High refractive index

Figure 14.4. Refraction.

FOCUS

Focus is a much misunderstood aspect of filmmaking. What is "in focus"? Theoretically, it means that the actual object is projected onto the film or video "as it appears in real life."

The human eye tends to perceive everything as in focus, but this is a result of the eye/brain interaction. The eye is basically an f/2 optic and may be considered a fairly "wide-angle" lens, so much of the world actually is in focus, certainly in brightly lit situations. But, nearly imperceptible to us, the focus is constantly shifting. This is accomplished by the muscles that control the lens of the eye. They distort its shape to shift the focus. If you look at something very close in a dimly lit situation, the background will be out of focus, but most likely you will not perceive it - because you are "looking" at the near object. By "looking" I mean that your brain is focusing your attention on the near object. This is what differentiates the eye from a camera: our mental focus is a condition of our consciousness and attention — the camera simply records everything.

As we will see later, a great number of the practices of focus — focal length, composing the frame, and even lighting — are attempts to re-create this mental aspect of focus and attention. We are using the camera to imitate how the eye and brain work together to tell a visual story in an imitation of how life is perceived by the mind.

First, the technical basics: the taking lens is the optical system that projects the image onto the film or video sensor, which is called the image plane. All imaging, whether photography, cinema, video, or even painting, is the act of taking a three-dimensional world and rendering it onto this two-dimensional plane.

When discussing focus, we often tend to think only in terms of the flat image plane, but it is more useful to remember that the lens is forming a three-dimensional image in space, not a flat picture plane. It is the flat picture plane that must be "focused" onto. It is the only part of the image that gets recorded. This will be especially relevant when we get to the circle of confusion. (Some may think we are in the circle of confusion already, but stick with it, this is important.)

The image plane is also called the *Principal Plane of Focus* — sort of the uptown business address for what we commonly call the *focal plane*. Think of it this way: we are shooting a scene that has some foreground bushes, a woman standing in the middle, and some mountains behind her. The woman is our subject. We focus the lens so that she is sharply projected onto the image plane.

In our three-dimensional model, the bushes and the mountains are projected behind the lens, but in front of her and behind her. In other words they are being projected into the camera, but in front of and behind the Principal Plane of Focus. As a result they are out of focus. By shifting the focus of the lens, or by stopping down, or using a wider angle lens, we can bring them into focus, but let's assume we are shooting wide open with a fairly long lens. By changing the focus of the lens, what we are actually doing is shifting that three-dimensional image backward and forward. If we shift it backwards, the mountains are focused on the image plane; if we shift forwards, the bushes are focused. Only objects that are projected sharply on the image plane are actually in "critical focus." But there are many objects that are only slightly in front of or behind the principal subject. If we stop down a little, thus increasing depth-of-field, they appear sharp (Figures 14.11 and 14.12). Note also that depth-of-field is different from depth-of-focus, as in Figure 14.7.

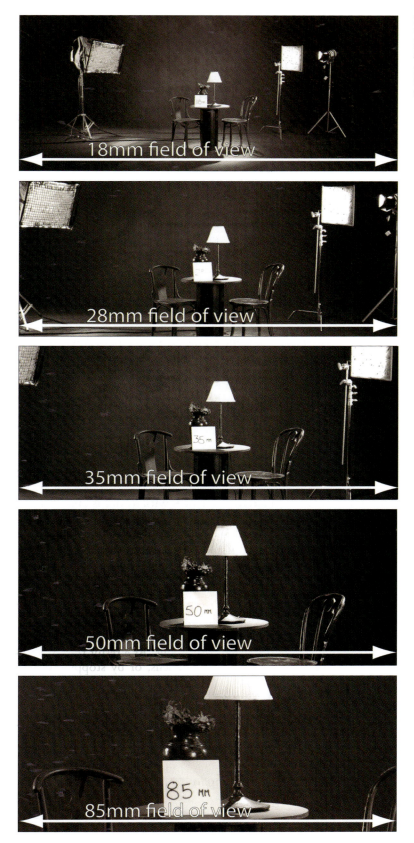

Figure 14.5. (top to bottom) Field of view of a standard set of high-speed prime lenses on a 35mm format HD camera at a 16x9 aspect ratio. The lower the number of the focal length, the wider the field-of-view of the lens. The camera remains in the same position for all these examples.

optics & focus

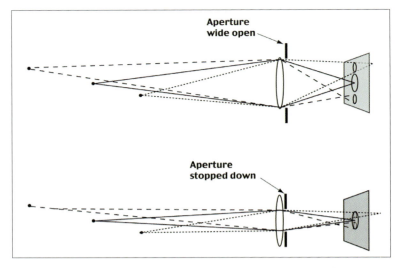

Figure 14.6. How iris opening affects the circle of confusion and thus depth-of-field.

But they are not actually sharp. This is called *apparent focus*. What is the boundary line between actual focus and apparent focus? There is none — at least not technically definable. It is a very subjective call that depends on many factors: perception, critical judgment, the resolving power of the lens, the resolving power of the film or video, the amount of diffusion, the surface qualities of the subject, lighting, and so on. Also very important is the end use of the footage. Something that appears in focus on a small television might be horribly soft on an Imax screen. There is a technical measurement of critical focus that is discussed below. It is called the circle of confusion.

Mental Focus

The viewing audience will tend to focus their attention on the part of the image that is *in focus*. This is an important psychological function that is valuable in visual imagery and storytelling with a lens.

But cinematographers are engaged not only in shaping mental perception; but they are technicians also. We need some way of quantifying focus, however arbitrary that might be. Let's think about a single ray of light — for example, an infinitely small (or at least a very tiny) point of light that is the only thing in the field of view. This sends a single ray of light toward the lens. As the ray of light leaves the object, it expands outward; no set of light rays is truly parallel, not even a laser or the light from a distant start. The lens captures these slightly expanding rays of light and reconcentrates them: this bends them back toward each other. This forms a cone behind the lens. Where these rays actually meet (and keep in mind that we are talking about the rays of a single point of light) is where the image is in focus. The lens can then be adjusted so that this single point of light is sharply focused on the image plane: that is, it appears to be just as small on the image plane as it does in life.

Now, we shift the lens so that the image of the dot of light is not exactly at the image plane. What happens? The image of the dot gets *larger* because we are no longer at the confluence of the rays of light as concentrated by the lens. If we do this only slightly, no one may notice. We say that this is still *acceptable focus*. If we shift a lot, most people would then perceive it as out of focus, but as we have pointed out, this is subjective. Taking into account the various factors, imaging scientists have quantified how much bigger that dot can get and still be deemed acceptable focus for most purposes.

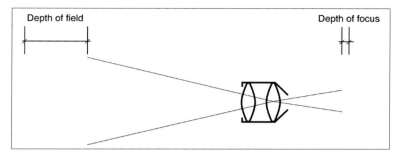

Circle of Confusion

The term for this is *circle of confusion*. Circle of confusion is defined as the largest blurred point of light that will still be perceived as a point by the human eye. The circle of confusion is basically a measure of how large the projected image of a true point source can be before it is considered to be unacceptably out of focus. Theoretically, of course, the point of light projected onto the film plane should be the same size as the infinitely small point of light it is seeing, but due to the nature of optics, it can never be perfect. For film work in 16mm, the circle of confusion varies from 1/2000" (.0005") for critical applications to 1/1000" (.0001"). For 35mm it ranges from 1/700" (.00014") to 1/500" (.002"). The circle of confusion is an important part of defining the depth-of-field at a given f/stop; it is part of the calculation.

The circle of confusion is smaller for 16mm because 16mm has to be blown up more to achieve the same image size on the screen or monitor. The circle of confusion is most important in the calculation of depth-of-field. Whenever you look at a depth-of-field chart, you will see listed the circle of confusion used in the calculations. It is important to remember that the end use of the footage is an important consideration in making these judgments: theatrical, DVD, broadcast — all these may have different requirements for format and other criteria.

DEPTH-OF-FIELD

Back to our model of a three-dimensional projected image. The portion of this image that falls on the image plane and is within the circle of confusion is called the depth-of-field. It has a near and far limit, but these fall off gradually. A number of factors affect depth-of-field:

- Focal length of the lens. The shorter the focal length, the more the depth-of-field.
- The aperture of the lens. The smaller the aperture, the greater the depth-of-field.
- Image magnification (object distance). The closer the subject is to the image plane, the less the depth-of-field.
- The format: larger formats (35mm or Imax) have less depth of field than smaller formats (such as 16mm or 2/3" CCD.)
- The circle of confusion selected for the situation.
- Indirectly: the resolving power of lens and film, end use, diffusion, fog, smoke, the type of subject.

With faster films, faster lenses, and less lighting, the depth-of-field becomes incredibly small. With a 150mm lens doing a tight close-up of a face, it is not unusual for your focus puller to ask, "Which eye do you want in focus?" Depth-of-field is not evenly distributed in front of and in back of the plane of critical focus. It is one-third

Figure 14.8. Deep focus (extreme depth-of-field) is a key component of the storytelling in *Citizen Kane*.

in front and two-thirds behind. This is because behind the plane of focus is, of course, farther away. This may be crucial when composing shots with very limited depth-of-field, particularly *table top* shots — close shots of small objects, particularly in commercials.

Depth-of-Field Calculations

There is no need to memorize optical or focus formulas, because you will almost certainly never need to do actual calculations based on them; however, it is useful to understand how these principals work. It will give you a better understanding of how your lens is working and what your charts or software are telling you. Most camera assistants carry physical or digital calculators for depth-of-field and other optical information they need quickly on the set. Depth-of-field is a plane of focus perpendicular to the optical axis where objects are focused to acceptable sharpness. The near and far planes of sharpness are calculated:

$$ND = \frac{H \times S}{H + (S - F)}$$

$$FD = \frac{H \times S}{H - (S - F)}$$

ND = Near distance

FD = Far distance

H = Hyperfocal distance

S = Distance from camera to object

F = Focal length of the lens

How Not to Get More Depth-of-Field

As a result of the basic principles of physics, wide-angle lenses will have more depth-of-field at a given f/stop. Here we must dispel one of the most persistent myths of filmmaking. Many people still believe that if you are having trouble getting the important elements in focus, the answer is to put on a wider-angle lens and you will have greater depth-of-field. This is technically true, but in actual practice, they then move the camera forward so they have the same frame size. The actual result? You end up with exactly the same depth-of-field you started with! This is because you have moved the camera forward and end up with same image magnification. It is image magnification that is the critical factor. You are decreasing *subject distance* and increasing *image magnification*, which decreases depth-of-field.

Hyperfocal Distance

For every focal length and f/stop there is a particular focus distance that is special: the *hyperfocal distance*. This is the closest focus distance at which *both objects are at infinity and closer objects are in focus*. When a lens is set at the hyperfocal distance, everything from 1/2 of the hyperfocal distance to infinity will be in focus.

The formula for hyperfocal distance is

$$H = \frac{F^2}{f \times Cc}$$

F   = focal length of lens
f   = f/stop number
Cc = circle of confusion

There are two ways of defining hyperfocal distance.

Figure 14.9. Before shooting *Citizen Kane*, cinematography Gregg Toland had used deep focus on other films, including *The Long Voyage Home*.

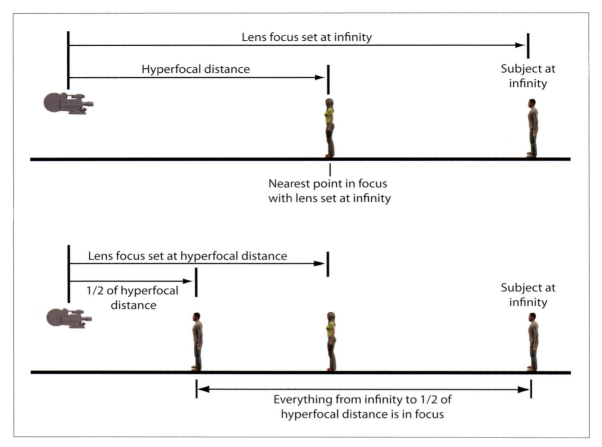

Figure 14.10. Two aspects of hyperfocal distance.

First: Hyperfocal distance is the focus setting of the lens when *objects at infinity and objects at the nearest point to the camera are both in acceptable focus.*

Second: If the lens is set at the hyperfocal distance, *both objects at infinity and at 1/2 of that hyperfocal distance will be in acceptable focus.* Most lens charts will list the hyperfocal distance for various lenses at any given f/stop. (Remember, f/stops are used for optical calculations and T-stops are used for setting the aperture.) For example, for a 50mm lens at f/8 with a circle of confusion of .0001", the hyperfocal distance is 40 feet. Thus, if you set the focus distance at 40 feet, everything from 20 feet to infinity will be in focus.

Opening up two stops (going to a lower f/stop, which admits more light) doubles the hyperfocal distance: it goes from 40 feet at f/8 to 80 feet at f/4. Conversely, closing down two stops decreases the hyperfocal distance by one-half. Another characteristic of hyperfocal distance is this. When the lens is set at the hyperfocal distance, depth-of-field extends from 1/2 HD to infinity. When the lens is set at 1/2 of HD, the depth-of-field is from 1/3 of hyperfocal distance to infinity and so on.

Nodal Points

Another enduring myth of depth-of-field is that all depth-of-field calculations are from the image plane. It's not true. Depth-of-field is calculated from the Front Nodal Point. This is accounted for in most depth-of-field charts. Each manufacturer determines their own method of calculating depth-of-field, so consulting the charts they provide may be the most reliable method in some critical cases.

"Nodal points" are the two points such that a light ray entering the front of the lens and headed straight toward the front nodal point will emerge going straight away from the rear nodal point at exactly the same angle to the lens axis as the entering ray had. The nodal points are identical to the principal points when the front and rear media are the same.

In simple double convex lenses the two principal points are somewhere inside the lens (actually 1/n the way from the surface to the center, where n is the index of refraction), but in a complex lens they can be almost anywhere, including outside the lens, or with the rear principal point in front of the front principal point. In a lens with elements that are fixed relative to each other, the principal points are fixed relative to the glass. Entrance pupil and exit pupils are not often where we think they should be — at the front and back of the lens (Figure 14.10). In fact, for some lens designs, it is possible for the front entrance pupil to actually be behind the film plane. An example: on a Zeiss 50mm lens at f/2.1 the FNP is 34.5mm back from the front vertex of the lens and the lens is a total of 77.9 millimeters from the front vertex to the focal plane.

This means that for this lens at this f/stop, focus and depth-of-field are measured starting at 34.5 millimeters back from the middle of the front element. Don't panic: in actual practice this is compensated for in depth-of-field charts, which add a fixed distance in front of the focal plane that varies for prime lenses and zooms. This also explains why there might be very slight differences between focus charts from different manufacturers.

For simplicity, all actual distance measurements in the field are from the focal plane. Most cameras have either a mark at the focal plane and usually also a protruding screw to which the camera assistant can attach a measuring tape. Some zooms designed for video measure focus from the front of the lens and will have a mark on the barrel.

The Rear Nodal Point and Special Effects Shots

The *Rear Nodal Point* is also important for lining up special effects shots through half silvered mirrors, certain types of panning shots where the camera must be panned or tilted without shifting the image and also in front projection.

If manufacturer's data are not available, the nodal point on which the camera must rotate can be determined in the field by mounting the camera on a head that has a slide plate. Then mount a cross on a C-stand in front of the camera. On the wall behind, mount a same-size cross so that the two are congruent — that is, the front cross perfectly covers the back one. Then experiment with sliding the camera back and forth until you find a position where you can pan the camera and the rear cross stays centered behind the front cross. You have found the nodal point of the lens and centered it over the pivot point of the panning head.

Zooms and Depth-of-Field

Zooms have some special characteristics when it comes to depth-of-field. As we discussed previously, depth-of-field is technically not measured from the film plane or video receptor. In fact, it is measured from the nodal point of the lens. Depth-of-field charts compensate for this in a general way by adding a fixed amount in front of the focal plane. This is why you may see different DOF charts for zooms and primes at equivalent focal lengths. The issue with variable focal length lenses is that as they are zoomed, the nodal point

Figure 14.11. (top) In both of these frames, the focal length and distance from camera to subject are the same but the F/stop changes. In the top frame, the lens is wide open and the depth-of-field is very small; only one card is sharp.

Figure 14.12. (bottom) The lens is stopped down to f/11 and almost all the cards are in *apparent focus* — meaning that they only appear to be in focus because they are within the depth-of-field. *Critical focus*, the point at which the lens is actually focused, is still on the red king.

may actually shift. With some zooms the nodal point actually ends up 5 inches behind the film plane at its long end. With the old Cooke 20-100 the range was about 10.5 inches in front of the film plane at 20mm, and 5 inches in front of the film plane at 100mm.

Motion control rigs that keep the nodal point over the pan center use a long worm gear that moves the camera/zoom back and forth over the center point as you zoom. There are nodal point camera heads for tripods, dollies, and cranes. In practical depth-of-field applications with zoom lenses, the only thing that is really of any consequence to us is at the wide end, where the nodal point is typically around 10 inches in front of the film plane. Thus, if you are shooting a close-up at the wide end of a zoom it's as if you were 10 inches closer to your subject matter, which also reduces your depth-of-field. Being closer you of course have less depth-of-field. This is one of the reasons that zooms are seldom used in macro, table-top, and other situations where critical focus is important. In average shooting situations, nodal point is not critical, but on more technical shoots, it is important to be aware of the implications.

Figure 14.13. (top) In this series, the f/stop remains the same but the focal length changes. With a wide lens (top) all the cards are in focus.

Figure 14.14. (bottom) With a very long lens at the same f/stop, the depth-of-field only covers one card. The camera is the same distance from the subject; only the f/stop has changed.

MACROPHOTOGRAPHY

For *extreme close-up* work, called *macrophotography*, it is more useful to think in terms of image magnification instead of depth-of-field. Macrophotography is any imaging where the image size is near to or greater than the actual size of the object (more than a 1:1 reproduction ratio). For example, photographing a postage stamp full frame is macro work.

Regular prime lenses can seldom focus closer than 9 or 10 inches; zooms generally have a minimum of around 2 to 3 feet. Extreme close-up photography has a set of problems all its own. The most critical aspect of macro work is the degree of magnification. A magnification of 1:1 means that the object will be reproduced on film actual size — that is, an object that is 1/2 inch in reality will produce an image on the negative (or video sensor) of 1/2 inch. 1:2 will be 1/2 size, 1:3 will be 1/3 size, and so on. In film, the 35mm academy frame is 16mm high and 22mm wide. Most lenses of ordinary design can focus no closer than a ratio of 1:8 or 1:10.

Figure 14.15. A *split diopter* gives focus both on the near objects (cards) and the far object (actor). Notice the fuzzy transition line, which is fairly well concealed here.

Exposure Compensation in Macrophotography

When a small image is being "spread" over a large piece of film, it naturally produces less exposure. With reproduction ratio's of greater than 1:10, exposure compensation is necessary. The formula for this is:

$$\text{Shooting f/stop} = \frac{\text{f/stop determined by meter}}{1 + \text{magnification ratio}}$$

Example: meter reading is f/8. Your reproduction ratio is 1:2 or 1/2 size. The calculation is 8/(1 + .5) = 5.3

Depth-of-Field in Close-Up Work

There are many misconceptions associated with macrophotography; perhaps the most basic is that "wide-angle lenses have more depth-of-field." Depth-of-field is a function of *image size*, not focal length. While it is true that wide-angle lenses have more depth-of-field, the problem is that once you have put a wider lens on, you still want the same image you had before, and in order to accomplish that, you must move the camera closer to the subject. Once you have done this, the depth-of-field is the same as it was before, since focus distance is also an determinant of depth-of-field. The important aspects are:

- Depth-of-field decreases as magnification increases.
- Depth-of-field decreases as focus distance decreases.
- Depth-of-field is doubled by closing down the lens two stops.

Calculating Depth-of-Field in Extreme Close-Up Work

Calculation of depth-of-field in extreme close-up work methods is different from normal situations. At magnifications greater than 1:10, the depth-of-field is extremely small and it is easier to calculate the total depth-of-field rather than a near and far limit of the zone of focus. Total depth-of-field is calculated by the following formula:

$$Dt = \frac{2C \times N (1 + M)}{m^2}$$

Dt = total depth-of-field
C = circle of confusion

N = f/number

m = magnification

Where magnification is calculated by the formula:

$$magnification = \frac{image\ size}{object\ size}$$

Lens Displacement When Focused Closer Than Infinity

When focused closer than infinity, front elements of the lens (or all the elements) are moved away from the focal plane. This is important in calculating exposure loss in extreme close-up work.

$$d = \frac{f^2}{a - f}$$

d = lens displacement from infinity position

f = focal length of lens in inches

a = distance focus in inches

CLOSE-UP TOOLS

Extreme close-up photography can be accomplished with a variety of tools; as with all optics, the basics are the same whether you are shooting film, digital, regular video, or High Def.

Diopters

Diopters are simple meniscus lenses that are placed in front of the camera lens and reduce the minimum focusing distance of the lens. The lenses are measured in diopters, which is the reciprocal of the focal length as measured in meters. A plus 1 diopter has a focal length of 1 meter, a plus 2 is 1/2 meter, and so on. Minimum focusing distance with the lens set at infinity is determined by dividing the diopter number into 100 cm. For example, a +2 diopter is 100/2 = 50 cm. This equals 19.68 inches. You will actually be able to focus a bit closer by changing the focus of the lens itself.

A diopter is defined as the reciprocal of the focus of this accessory lens in meters — that is, one divided by the focal length. Thus, a plus one is a magnifying lens of one meter's focus; a plus 1/2 is a milder magnifier that focuses at two meters. A plus two focuses at one-half meter, 500 millimeters. A plus three at 333 millimeters.

This spec shows you the farthest working distance you can work; put a plus one-half on your normal camera lens, set it on infinity, the farthest, and objects two meters away are in focus. Nothing farther could be shot sharp. Put on a plus one and the max working distance is one meter. Put on a plus two and stuff has to be 500 millimeters, or half a meter, or about 19 inches away (from the front of the diopter, not the film plane) to achieve sharpness. All those cases are with the main lens (prime or zoom) "set at infinity."

A split diopter is one of these magnifiers split in half, like a half-moon. It covers half your field, and the stuff seen through the glass is focused closer, and the other half, which is missing (just air), will be focused where the main lens is set. Put a plus one-half split on your camera. Focus the main lens at infinity. One-half of the field, through the diopter, is sharp at 2 meters. The rest of the field is focused at infinity. If you set the lens at 15 feet, the clear half is focused at 15 feet and the diopter half might focus at 1 1/3 meters.

The point is to fake extreme deep-focus effects. There's a fuzzy line at the edge of the split diopter in the middle of your picture, and this has to be hidden artfully in the composition, which is often done with a telephone pole, a shrub or some other object that is indistinct.

Diopter power	Focus distance of lens	Actual distance from diopter to subject
+1/2	Infinity	78-3/4"
	25'	62-1/2"
	15'	54-3/4"
	10'	47-1/2"
	6'	37-3/4"
	4'	29-3/4"
+1	Infinity	39-1/2"
	25'	34-3/4"
	15'	32-1/2"
	10'	29-3/4"
	6'	25-1/4"
	4'	21-3/4"
+2	Infinity	19-3/4"
	25'	18-1/2"
	15'	17-3/4"
	10'	16-3/4"
	6'	15-1/2"
	4'	14"
+3	Infinity	13-1/4"
	25'	12-1/2"
	15'	12-1/4"
	10'	11-3/4"
	6'	11-1/4"
	4'	10-1/2"

Diopter - Focus Conversion Chart (can be used with any focal length - any format)

Table 14.1. Focus with diopters.

Diopter recommendations include:

- Use the lowest power diopter you can, combined with a longer focal length lens, if necessary.
- Stop down as much as possible.
- There is no need for exposure compensation with diopters.
- When using two diopters together, add the diopter factors and always place the highest power closest to the lens.

Extension Tubes or Bellows

The advantage of extension tubes or bellows is that they do not alter the optics at all, so there is no degradation of the image. Extension tubes are rings that hold the lens farther away from the film plane than it normally sits, thus reducing the minimum focus distance.

A bellows unit is the same idea but is continuously variable with a rack and pinion. Either will give good results down to about 1:2. Extension tubes are generally incompatible with wide-angle or zoom lenses. Lenses with larger minimum apertures generally give better results than high-speed lenses. Optically, the best results at very high magnifications are obtained by reversing the lens (so that the back of the lens faces the subject) and mounting on a bellows unit. The simple rule is, to achieve 1:1 reproduction, the extension must equal the focal length of the lens. For 1:1 with a 50mm lens, for example, you would need a 50mm extension.

A variation of this is the *swing-and-tilt mount* (Figure 14.17), which gives the lens mount the same kind of controls used in a view camera. The lens cannot only be extended for macro work, but the plane of focus can also be tilted. This permits part of the image to be in focus and part of the image on the same plane to be out of focus.

Macro Lenses

Macro lenses are actually specially designed optics, optimized for close-up work. They are good in the 1:2 to 1:1 range. Some macros have barrel markings for magnification ratio as well as focus distance; this facilitates calculating the exposure compensation.

Snorkles and Innovision

Several types of *snorkle* lenses are available that are like periscopes. They generally allow for extremely close focus and for getting the lens into incredibly small spaces. Some of the units are immersible in water.

Innovision is a snorkle-type lens that can be fitted on both video and motion picture cameras for extreme close-up work. It has the advantage of an extremely narrow barrel that can reach inside very small areas, even inside flowers. The f/stop is fixed and is very high, around f/32 to f/45, depending on the application, however, a high f/stop is generally needed for extreme close-up work in any case.

Specialized Lenses

Specialized applications of the snorkle are the *Frazier* lens and the *Revolution* system (Figure 14.18). These have remarkable depth-of-field that seems to defy physics (it doesn't really) and also allows for the lens itself to rotate, pan, and tilt during a shot. It is possible to have objects that are actually touching the lens in focus and still maintain usable depth in the distance. They can be used in conjunction with perspective control lenses such as the tilt focus lens shown in Figure 14.17. The Frazier has a maximum stop of T/7; as a bonus it also minimizes the distortion normally associated with very wide-angle lenses. The *Kenworth* snorkle is similar to these.

Figure 14.16. (top) A snorkle system in use. (Photo courtesy of Mark Weingartner.)

Figure 14.17. (bottom) A full swing and tilt system. (Photo courtesy of Century Precision Optics.)

Figure 14.18. *The Revolution* snorkle lens system by Clairmont Camera. (Photo courtesy of Clairmont Camera.)

Lens Extenders and Filter Factors

Optical devices that increase the focal length of the lens have a corresponding effect on T-stop. To find the filter factor, square the extension factor. For example, a 2X optic will have a filter factor of 4, and a 3X extender will have a filter factor of 9. A factor of 4 translates to 2 stops, and 9 translates to approximately 3 stops, so a 2X extender will turn a 200mm f/4 lens into a 400mm f/8 lens. When combining extenders, the factors must be multiplied. For example, a 2X and 3X extender together would have a factor 36 (five stop increase in exposure).

LENS CARE

- Never clean a lens with dry lens tissue.
- Never put lens fluid on a lens; put it on the lens tissue.
- Brush or blow off loose grit before wiping with lens tissue.
- Never use eyeglass cleaning cloth; it may contain silicone.
- In dusty or sandy conditions, try to keep a filter on the lens. *Optical flats* are clear optical grade glass that can be used for this purpose.
- Never use rubber cement to attach a filter to a lens. Use Scotch ATG-924, otherwise known as *transfer tape* or *snot tape*.
- Be careful when mounting a net to the rear of the lens; it can get snagged or torn and this will affect the image.
- Always close at least one latch on a lens case.
- Protect all lenses from shock.

LENS ADAPTERS FOR VIDEO

As we have seen, video cameras with sensors smaller than a 35mm frame have more depth-of-field, which may not be desirable for artistic reasons. To deal with this, several companies have built adapters that allow film-style lenses to be mounted on video cameras. Contrary to a popular belief, it is not the lens itself that creates the depth-of-field look associated with 35mm film. The lenses generally are superior quality, but what gives the image that reduced depth-of-field is governed by another optical mechanism in the adapter itself. In most of these units, the image formed by the lens is projected onto a ground glass. It is this projected image that is then photographed by the video camera sensor. Since the image that is projected onto the ground glass has the depth-of-field characteristics of 35mm, this is what is recorded by the video camera. However, there are a couple of downsides to this. First, there is a loss of light with all of these systems; it can be a very substantial loss, as much as two stops — a heavy price to pay in terms of the need for lighting the scene to a higher stop.

Another disadvantage is that the texture of the ground glass will be apparent in the image. To counteract this, the manufacturers use different methods. Some have the ground glass rotate, and some have it vibrate, both of these keep the texture of the glass moving and thus far less visible. This adds an extra battery drain, and some of the units use a separate battery to power the motion of the ground glass. It is important to remember to switch this on with units that have a separate power switch for this.

Fortunately, more and more HD cameras are now available with mounts, such as *PL* (the *Arriflex* mount) or *PV* (the *Panavision* mount) that permit easy use of film-style lenses or lenses designed specifically for digital video cameras.

set operations

The director, the cinematographer, and the production designer are the three people directly responsible for all creative aspects of the film: how it looks, how it works, the "style," and the continuity.

The working relationship between the director and cinematographer is the key to getting a film made. Let's look at the responsibilities of everyone involved, first of all in a typical feature film. These procedures are general to most types of production including, commercials and music videos, and on small productions such as industrials and documentaries; many of these are omitted, but the essential functions are always the same.

In relation to the camera work, the director has a number of duties. It is the director who makes the decision as to what shots will be needed to complete a particular scene. He must specify where the camera will be placed and what the field of view needs to be. Some directors prefer to specify a specific lens, but most just indicate to the DP how much they want to see, and then the cameraman calls for the lens to be used, or in the case of a zoom, at what focal length it will be set.

The director must also specify what camera movement, zooms, or other effects will be needed. Most directors do all of this in consultation with the DP and ask for ideas and input. Problems most commonly arise when the director feels he must make every decision by himself without discussing it. Certainly it is their right to do so, but less experienced directors will sometimes call for specific lighting or even specific lights that are time-consuming and ineffective when there are more efficient ways of doing the same thing more quickly and effectively.

One of the most common situations is when directors ask for long complex dolly or Steadicam moves. It can be very effective and dramatic to shoot an entire scene in one shot, with the camera moving constantly with the characters even as they go from room to room or make other types of moves. However, these types of shots are generally difficult to set up, difficult to light (since you are so often forced to hide the lights), and usually very demanding for the focus puller.

They also require many rehearsals and many takes to get all the elements to work together: the timing of actors' moves, the timing of camera moves, changes in focus, and in some cases changes in T-stop. Lighting is much more complex because it is like lighting for multiple cameras with very different positions: it is very difficult to make the lighting work well for both cameras and hide all the equipment. As a result, the lighting often has to be compromised.

Long, complex shots are exciting to conceptualize and great fun when they are completed successfully. Also, it sounds so quick and convenient to just "go ahead and get the whole thing in one shot." The problem is that almost inevitably, the shot gets cut up into pieces anyway, with inserts, close-up, or other coverage. This means that time and effort spent to accomplish it were largely wasted.

Unless you absolutely know that the continuous take will be used, it is usually better to break it up into logical pieces. The director might also ask for special effects such as higher or lower shutter speeds, certain filtration effects and so on. Ideally, the director should arrive on the set with a complete shot list. This is a list of every shot and every piece of coverage needed for the scenes on that day's shooting. Some directors are extremely well prepared with this, and others let it slide after the first few days, which is a mistake. It is true that shot lists are often deviated from, but they still provide a starting point so that everyone in all departments is headed in the same direction.

Figure 15.1. (previous page) A typical working set. In the foreground is an *electrician* (*lighting technician*) with various colors of electrical tape for marking distribution cables.

THE SHOT LIST

The shot list serves a number of functions. It lets the DP and the assistant director better plan the day, including possibly sending off some electricians and grips to pre-rig another location. It also helps the DP in determining what film stock should be used, what additional equipment should be prepped, and how much time is reasonably allowable to light and set the shot within the constraints of what needs to be done that day. Even if the shot list doesn't get followed step by step, it will often at the very least provide a clue as to what style of shooting the director wants to employ: is it a few simple shots for each scene or detailed and elaborate coverage or perhaps a few "bravura" shots that emphasize style and movement?

In addition, it is very helpful in serving as a reminder for the director, the DP, the assistant director, and the continuity person so that no shots or special coverage are missed. One of the gravest production errors a director can make is to wrap a set or location without getting everything needed. Reshoots are expensive, and there is always the possibility that the location or the actors will not be available to correct this mistake. Although all these people assist in this, it is the director's fundamental responsibility to "get the shots." This is far more important than being stylish, doing fancy moves, and so on. None of these matter if scenes are not completed and usable. In HD, the absolute most basic rule is to never leave a location until you have checked the footage for problems, performance and continuity.

Even if not a formal shot list, some directors will charge the script supervisor with keeping a list of "must haves." This is especially useful for cutaways or inserts that might easily be forgotten. It is also helpful for "owed" shots. "We owe a POV shot from the window," is a way of saying that there is a shot that is part of this scene that we are not shooting now but we have to pick it up while at this location.

THE DIRECTOR OF PHOTOGRAPHY

The DP is primarily responsible for giving the director what she wants and also accomplishing the photographic style they have agreed on. Every director has a different style of working: some will be very specific about a certain look they want and exact framing, while others want to focus on working closely with the actors and staging the scenes and leave it to the DP to decide on exact framing, camera moves and the lighting style, filtration, and so on.

Figure 15.2. A crew working on a subway station set. A greenscreen has been rigged so that the background can be replaced in post. The crew also shot scenes in the actual subway station — see Figure 15.13. (Photo courtesy of Michael Gallart.)

Figure 15.3. DP Tom Denove using a spot meter on set. (Photo courtesy of Tom Denove).

Ultimately the director is the boss; he or she may work in whatever fashion they wish. A truly professional DP should have the flexibility to work with a director in whatever manner they choose. It is important to discuss this before shooting starts, and if the DP isn't comfortable with how a director wants to work, the time to bow out is as early as possible. Ultimately it is up to the DP to deliver for the director the kind of look and visual texture he or she is looking for and ensure that the director and editor have all the footage they need and that it is all editorially usable.

The DP's responsibilities are numerous. They include:

- The look of the scenes, in consultation with the director.
- Directing the lighting of the project.
- Communicating to the gaffer and key grip how the scene is to be lit: specific units to be used, gels, cuts with flags, silks, overheads, diffusion, and so on. Directing and supervising the lighting process.
- Coordinating with the production designer, wardrobe, makeup, and effects people concerning the overall look of the film.
- Filtration on the camera.
- Lenses: including whether to use a zoom or a prime lens (though this may sometimes be the director's call).
- If HMIs are used, ensuring that there are no flicker problems (see the chapter on *Lighting Sources*).
- Being constantly aware of and consulting on issues of continuity: crossing the line, screen direction, and so on. (see the chapter on *Cinematic Continuity*).
- Being a backstop on insuring that the director hasn't forgotten specific shots needed for good coverage of the scene.
- Supervising their team: camera operator, the camera assistants, the electricians, the grips, and any *second camera* or *second unit* camera crews; also the data wrangler and DIT.
- Watching out for mistakes in physical continuity: clothing, props, scenery, and so on. This is primarily the job of continuity and the department heads, but the eye looking through the lens is often the best way to spot problems.
- Specifying the specific motion picture film raw stock(s) or type of video camera to be used and any special processing or the workflow for video footage.
- Determining the exposure and informing the first AC what T-stop to use.
- Ensuring that all technical requirements are in order: correct film speed, shutter angle, and so on.

Typically, when starting to light and set up a new scene, the assistant director will ask for an estimate of how long it will take to be ready to shoot. This is not an idle question, and it is very important to give an accurate estimate. The AD is not just asking this to determine if the company is on schedule: there is another important consideration. He has to know when to start putting the actors *through the works*. This means sending them through makeup, wardrobe, and any special effects such as blood squibs.

Many actors do not appreciate being called to the set a long time before the crew is ready to shoot, and in addition, if they have to wait, their makeup might need to be redone, and so on. It may also affect the timing of rigging special effects.

THE TEAM

The DP has three groups of technicians who are directly responsible for: the camera crew, the electricians, and the grips. The DP also coordinates with the art department and of course the AD.

Camera Crew

Typically on a feature or commercial the camera crew will consist of the camera operator, the First AC (assistant camera), the second AC, and the third AC or loader. If multiple cameras are used, there will be more required, and on very small productions or industrials the crew might be as small as a first and a second. Producers often question the need for a loader, but it is always your responsibility to remind them that if the camera crew is not sufficiently staffed, the production will be slowed down because the second has to frequently leave the set to load magazines or download digital material.

Operator

The operator is the person who actually handles the camera: pans and tilts, zooms, coordinating with the dolly grip on moves. As she operates, she must always frame the shot as the director has called for, make the moves smooth, and also be looking for any problem that might ruin the shot. Typical problems include the microphone dipping into the frame, lens flares, a piece of equipment visible in the frame, reflections in windows or mirrors of the crew or equipment, missed focus, a bump in the dolly track, and so on. Almost everyone uses a *video tap* (*video assist* monitor) these days, but the image on the monitor is never good enough to see everything. In addition, the director will probably be so focused on the actor's performance that small problems will not be seen. The person actually looking through the lens has the ultimate responsibility for this.

It is essential that the operator immediately report any problems. For example, if the sound boom gets into the shot, the operator should immediately call out "*boom*" loudly enough for both the boom operator and the director to hear. Some directors want this and some don't; it is something that needs to be discussed at the beginning of the project. It is up to the director to decide whether to cut the shot or continue filming, knowing that most of the shot is still usable or there will be coverage. This practice will vary from set to set; some directors, especially on larger-budget projects, may want it reported only after the shot.

On smaller projects, there will be no operator and the DP will operate the camera. Although many DPs prefer to operate, it does take time and concentration away from the other duties. On union projects it is absolutely forbidden for the DP to operate. Under the English system (also used in a number of other countries) the distinction is even more dramatic. In this way of working the DP is only responsible for lighting the scene (they are occasionally listed in the credits as "lighting cameraman"). It is often the operator who receives orders from the director about camera moves, dolly moves, focal length, and so on. This applies to features only, of course.

First AC

The first AC is also known as the focus puller. The first is the crew member who directly works with the camera. Duties include:

- Loading film magazines on the camera or tape on a video camera with proper labeling.
- Ensuring that the camera operates properly.
- Checking for hairs in the gate before any scene is wrapped.

Figure 15.4. To create a loose hand-held feel for the shot, the camera the operator stabilized on a *sandbag* set on a short *C-stand*.

Figure 15.5. (top) Attaching a filter to a lens when there is no matte box or the filter won't fit the matte box can be accomplished by making a *daisy* out of *camera tape* (1 inch cloth tape).

Figure 15.6. (bottom) The filter attached to the tape. This is a last resort for when you don't have a matte box that will hold the filter. Be very careful; filters are expensive!

- Guarding against flares, light leaks, and any other problems.
- Setting the T-stop. Also, frame rate and shutter angle.
- Measuring the focus distances.
- Controlling focus so that the proper parts of the scene are sharp.
- In some cases operating the zoom control (this is often done by the operator using a zoom control mounted on the handle).
- Moving the camera to the next setup, with the help of the other AC's and sometimes the grips.
- Guarding the camera against damage or malfunction.
- Making sure the proper film stock is loaded.
- Calling out the footage so that the second AC can note it on the camera report.

Focus may be determined by measuring or by eye. Measuring is generally done in two ways. Most cameras have a mark on the side that identifies the exact position of the film plane. Positioned precisely above that is a stud that the AC can hook a cloth measuring tape onto and measure the exact distance to all the objects that will be focused on. Most ACs also carry a carpenter's metal measuring tape, either 1 inch or 3/4 inch wide. This is useful for quick checks before close in shots. The metal tape extends out quickly and the AC can make last-minute measurements in case something has moved.

The third method is eye focus. This can be done with either the operator and the ACs or by the first AC himself. Someone — either the actor, a stand-in or the second AC — goes to each of the key positions. The operator looks through the viewfinder and focuses. The first AC then marks it on the dial of the focus mechanism.

For critical focus it may be necessary for the second to take the top off a small flashlight (Maglight). The exposed bulb provides an accurate and fast focus point that can be used even in low-light situations. For complex dolly shots, the first may make tape marks alongside the dolly track, thus knowing that at a specific point he is x number of feet and inches away from the subject. The last component can only be described as *zen*. Good ACs are uncanny in their ability to visually judge distance and make adjustments on the fly. The first AC is also the one who goes to the *checkout*. Checkout is usually the day before shooting starts. At checkout the first:

- Checks that all equipment ordered is there.
- Checks every piece of equipment for proper operation.
- Tests the magazines for jamming or scratching.
- Tests the camera for jamming or scratching.
- Makes sure the proper ground glass is in the camera and that it is properly seated.
- Cleans anything that needs it: lenses, ground glass, the mirror shutter, and so on.
- Checks that all batteries are fully charged.
- If there are multiple cameras, labels each case appropriately (e.g., *A camera, B camera*, etc.). Usually, different colors of camera tape are used for this.
- Check that all menu settings and switches are properly set on a video camera.

Good ACs will always go through a mental ritual before every shot: is the T-stop properly set, is the focus prepared, is the camera set at the right speed, and are their any flares? It is best to do it in the same order every time for consistency. In previous times this checklist was

remembered as FAST: focus, aperture, speed, and tachometer. Most cameras no longer have tachometers, but they do have frame rate controls that must be checked regularly.

The first should also keep track of how much footage is used on the first take and then check to make sure there is enough stock left to get all the way through another take of the same shot. It can be very frustrating for the director and the actors to roll out in the middle of the take.

As soon as the director announces she is through with the scene, the first AC immediately checks the gate. This is to ensure that a hair or other piece of junk has not crept into the film gate and thus ruined the shot. Anything like this would not be visible through the eyepiece, and if something is in there, everyone must know immediately so that it can be reshot. There are three ways of doing it. One is to look into the lens from the front. This can be difficult with zooms because there is so much glass between your eye and the gate. The second is to open the camera and gently lift the film up and examine the gate. Many ACs don't like this method because there is a possibility that something was there, but lifting the film moved it. The most reliable method is to pull the lens and look at the gate.

Second AC

When the DP or first AC calls for a lens change, filter, or any other piece of equipment, it is the second who will bring it from the camera cart (Figure 15.19) or the truck. The *second assistant camera* is also sometimes referred to as the *clapper* or the *clapper/loader*. This is because one of her main duties is to operate the *slate* or *clapper,* as it is sometimes called. The slate serves several functions. First, it allows the editor or video transfer person to coordinate the visual image of the stick coming down with the audio of the *clap*, thus achieving sound sync.

The slate also identifies the scene number, the take number, and the roll number. It will also identify a scene as day-interior, night-exterior, and so on. The reason for this is that the timer at the lab or the video transfer person needs to know the general type of look the scene should have. It should also indicate whether a shot is sync

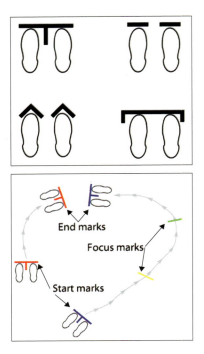

Figure 15.8. (top) Types of toe-marks.

Figure 15.9. (bottom) Different colored marks are used for each actor so there is no confusion. This is why the second AC always carries several colors of paper tape that are used for making marks.

sound or MOS. It should list the frame rate and any special filters being used. The slate will also indicate any effects such as different frame rates. In the case of multiple cameras, each one may be slated separately, or one slate might serve them all, which is called *common marker*. A variation on this is to *head slate* each camera with their individual roll number, frame rate, and other information and then use a simple clapper or timecode slate to clap all cameras together. This ensures the proper data for each camera but saves film by providing a single marker for all. The head slate need not be continuous; just a few frames and then turn off the camera. This is called *bumping* a slate.

This is not true with tapeless cameras — do a continuous roll. The reason for this is that with tapeless cameras, every time the camera rolls, a separate video file is created, which does not necessarily have any relation to the shot. This means you may end up with a hard drive or memory card that has dozens of slate shots that have no connection to anything else.

The second AC is also in charge of setting up monitors for the DP and director, cabling them and making sure they are operating properly. If there is a DIT on the job, they might handle this task.

Loader

The loader does exactly as the name implies: they load the film mags. In addition to keeping the mags loaded and ready to go, the loader also keeps track of the film stock received, the amount used, and excess recans or reloads kept in stock. To do this a film stock report is a standard form that they continually update.

Data Wrangler

Data Wrangler is an important position for digital crews. Essentially it replaces the *film loader*, who is no longer needed on a digital crew. The functions are similar: taking care of and keeping track of the recorded footage and preparing the medium for the next camera load. It's the same job but with different technology.

On tapeless jobs, the recording medium might be hard drives, *P2 cards, secure digital cards, compact flash cards* or direct to a laptop computer, such as the SI-2K HD camera. The data wrangler has three essential jobs: archive/backup, erasing/formatting for the next camera load and checking the footage for problems and data integrity. Some producers underestimate the job and just take the attitude that the second AC can do it on the side. This just means that the second will often not be available to perform their regular duties, which increases the opportunities for mistakes and stress on the part of the rest of the camera crew.

DIT

The *Digital Imaging Technician* is important on larger jobs but may not be needed (or affordable) on smaller jobs. The DIT is essentially a second pair of eyes for the DP. The DIT will generally have a station near the set with high-quality monitors and good viewing conditions (no stray light — often a light-proof tent for exteriors) and a waveform monitor and vectorscope. The DIT may also make camera adjustments and setup in accordance with the DPs instructions. In some cases, the DIT can remotely control exposure and other camera settings — this is especially useful on multi-camera shoots where it is important to keep the same look on all cameras.

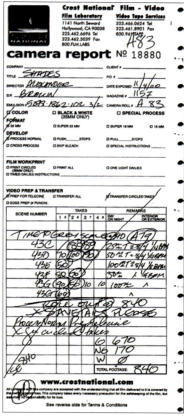

SLATING TECHNIQUE

At the time the AD calls *roll camera* and the AC announces *speed* (that the camera is up to sync speed), the second holds the slate where it is in focus and readable and announces the scene and take number so that it will be recorded on the audio track. She then says *marker* (so that the editor know that the next sound they will hear is the clapper) and slaps the clapper stick down sharply so that the clap is clearly audible on the audio. She then quickly gets out of the way. In case adjustments are necessary, such as changing focus from the slate to the scene, the operator will call out *set* and the director can then call for *action*. Learning proper slating technique is essential; bad slating can cause the editor real problem, frequently problems that end up costing the producer more money — and you can guess how they feel about that. In many cases, slating may be part of your first job in the camera department, so doing it badly can hamper your advancement.

Older slates could be written on with chalk. Most slates today are white plastic, and an erasable marker is used, or they are digital and the timecode and other information are displayed electronically. For erasable slates, the ACs tape a makeup powder puff to the end of the erasable marker; that way they will be conveniently together in one piece for both marking and erasing. This is referred to as the *mouse*. You can also buy erasers that fit on the end of a marker

In some cases, it is not desirable to slate before the shot. This might include filming with an infant where the clapper might frighten them. In such instances a *tail slate* can be used. A tail slate comes at the end of the shot and must be done before the camera is switched off or it can't be used for synchronization. For tail slates, the slate must be held upside down. The clapper is still used and a head ID should be shot as well, if at all possible.

Tail slates should be avoided if possible. It is time consuming and expensive for the telecine operator or editor to roll all the way to the end of the take, sync up, and then roll back to the beginning to lay the scene in. Another reason is that it is very easy to forget at the end of the take and switch off the camera before the slate comes in. It is also important to note the tail slate on the camera report. In the case of shooting without sync sound (*MOS*), everything is the same except that the clapper is not used. It may be necessary to open the clapper slightly on a timecode slate for the numbers to be visible, and running, but it is important not to clap it. If you do, the editor may spend time looking for an audio track that does not exist.

Figure 15.10. (above) A typical *camera report*.

Figure 15.11. (above, left) A properly done *MOS slate*. The fingers between the clappers make it absolutely clear to the editor that this is an MOS shot and the sticks are not going to be clapped.

Figure 15.12. Timecode slating with an iPhone. The camera being photographed is a 35mm Arri BL4. There are several excellent timecode slate apps for smart phones and notepad computers.

TIMECODE SLATES

Timecode slates include the usual information but also have a digital readout of the timecode that will match the timecode on the audio recorder; they are also called *smart slates*. Timecode slates make syncing up much quicker and cheaper and particular shots are more readily identified. The reason it is faster and cheaper in telecine is that the colorist rolls the film up to the frame that has the clapper sync on it. She then reads the timecode numbers that are displayed and types them in. The computer-controlled audio playback deck then automatically rolls up to the correct point to lay in sync. Having the deck find it automatically is significantly faster than manually searching — and telecine time is very expensive. If there is not sufficient preroll for the timecode on the audio tape or if the slate is unreadable, then this automation fails and sync must be set up manually. The clapper is still used on timecode slates. When the clap stick is up, the timecode will be displayed as it is running. When the clapper is brought down, the timecode freezes, thus indicating the exact timecode at the time of slating.

An additional feature of some timecode slates is that after the sync timecode freezes for a moment, today's date displays briefly.

The timecode is generated by the audio recorder, and the slate must be *jammed* at the beginning of every day and periodically throughout the day. Since there is a tendency for the code to drift, this must be redone throughout the day. Some slates will also display a message when they determine that jamming is necessary.

The second must be aware of the focal length of the lens and then estimate the proper distance at which to hold the slate. The slate must be readable and in focus; otherwise it will cause problems in syncing and for the editor who is trying to identify the shot.

Ideally, the slate must be as close to the focus distance as possible, thus eliminating the need to refocus after slating; however, this is not always possible. If the slate is held right in front of the actor's face, the clap should be as gentle as possible but still be audible.

One variation of this is used when multiple cameras are continuously shooting a big event such as a concert. In this case it is often wise to position a continuously running timecode slate (preferably hardwired to the recorder) where every camera can pan over and see it. Then, when a camera has to stop to reload, as soon as it starts up again, the operator pans over, shoots a few seconds of running timecode, and then pans back to the action.

Figure 15.13 A crew at work with a crane for low shots. This location was recreated full size for the green-screen shots — see Figure 15.2. (Photo by Michael Gallart.)

Camera Reports

In addition to slating, the second will also maintain the camera reports (Figure 15.10). The camera report will include some general information:

- Name of production company.
- Title of the project.
- In some cases the production number.
- Name of director.
- Name of DP.
- In some cases the purchase order number.
- Sometimes, as a courtesy, the film lab will pre-print this information on a batch of camera reports.

Then, the information gets more specific to this roll of film:

- Camera number or letter (A camera, B camera, etc.).
- The magazine number (very important if you are later trying to identify which of the mags is scratching or jamming).
- Roll number of the film stock loaded.
- Date exposed.
- Raw stock type used.
- Scene number.
- Take number.
- Footage used for each take, usually referred to as the "dial."
- Whether a shot was with sound or "MOS."
- Circle takes: the take number of shots the director wants to be printed are circled.
- Remarks.
- Inventory: the total amount good footage (G), no good (NG), and waste (W).
- The total amount shot when the mag is downloaded. For example, "Out at 970."

Camera reports are multi sheet, usually an original with two copies. Information written on the top sheet is transferred to the second two. The top sheet is folded and securely taped to the film can when

Figure 15.14. *SteadiCam* or *hand-held* can be difficult on a windy day. Trying to use a solid flag as a wind-block just creates an unmanageable and potentially dangerous sail. Here the grips are using a 4x4 double net; it cuts most of the wind but is more stable and easily controlled.

the roll is finished. The second sheet is usually yellow. It is given to the production manager, producer, or first AD, who then passes it on to the editor. The third sheet is retained by the production office or producer for reference in case there are any problems. In some cases there may be additional sheets for other departments such as the production coordinator.

Standard procedure is for the loader to fill in as much of the information as possible and then tape the camera report to the mag before it is delivered to the set. When the mag is loaded onto the camera, the second will usually then tape the report to the back of the slate for convenience; some assistants use a separate clipboard for writing on camera reports. This is helpful as they are multi-copy forms and you want to be sure that all the layers of the form are legible. After each take the second will then ask the first for the "dial," which is the cumulative footage shot as displayed on the counter. This is always rounded off to the nearest ten and only the first two numbers are given: for example, "97" rather than "970." The second then has to do some arithmetic to use the total cumulative number to determine the footage run on the last take. This is important in being able to predict when the magazine is about to "roll out." Having the camera roll out in the middle of a take can be very disturbing to the actors and the director — it is essential to warn the director when there is a possibility of rolling out on a shot. This is especially true if it is a shot that may be difficult or impossible to repeat.

The second AC is also responsible for providing the first with whatever he or she needs, most importantly the lens that is called for, fresh magazines, lens shades, charged batteries, and different tripods or other mounting equipment. Once the camera is set up on the dolly, on sticks or high-hat, the first AC or one of the other camera crew members should never be more than "two arms lengths away" from the camera.

Electricians

The electric crew carries out the DPs instructions on lighting. The crew consists of the *gaffer* (the head of the crew), the *second electric,* and other *electricians (lighting technicians).* As the job gets larger, the number of electricians must increase. An inadequate crew slows the entire production down. The gaffer is also sometimes referred to in the credits as *Chief Lighting Technician.* The DP gives his orders to the gaffer who then instructs the electricians what to do. It is important that the gaffer always be close to the DP for instant communication.

The gaffer's chief assistant is the second electric, also called the *best boy* electric, or *assistant chief lighting technician.* The second has three main duties: maintaining and overseeing all the equipment, supervising everything to do with electricity, and directly supervising the crew. On location, the second will spend a lot of time on the truck ordering, organizing, and maintaining the equipment.

The second designs the layout of the distribution — the location of the generator, the size of the cables to suit the total load, where distribution boxes will be placed, and so on. Important duties include checking that the cables and distribution equipment are not overloaded, that the generator is running properly and supplying the correct voltage. With HMIs it is also critical to check that the generator is running at the proper frequency (see *Technical Issues*). The second also supervises the crew to ensure they are being put to best use and working efficiently. The electricians do most of the actual work of bringing lights to the set, putting them in position, getting them to the height required by the DP, adjusting the barn doors, adding scrims if needed, and plugging them in after checking with the second to make sure they don't overload a circuit. If a gel is attached to the barn doors, the electricians do it. If it is in a frame and set separate from the light, the grips do it.

Figure 15.15. Rather than setting the dolly directly on the tracks, many grips use a *sled* that runs on skateboard wheels; it's fast to set up and more maneuverable. An *8x8 silk* is stored temporarily by laying it down and anchoring with sandbags at the corners.

Figure 15.16. When shooting out in the sun, the grips will provide a *courtesy flag* to protect the camera and operator. On the left is the *sound recordist*.

Grips

The grip crew is headed by the *key grip*. His assistant is the *best boy grip* or *second grip*. Then there is the *third grip* and whatever additional grips are needed. As with electricians, a three-person crew is the minimum for all except the smallest jobs.

The key grip may push the dolly, or there may also be a *dolly grip* whose sole responsibility is to lay dolly track (with help from other grips) and push the dolly. It sounds simple, but a good dolly grip is a real artist: timing the move exactly, hitting the marks, and keeping everything smooth. Experienced dolly grips are also excellent at consistency in the timing and speed of dolly moves; they can do it the same way take after take.

The grips have a wide range of duties:

- The grips handle all C-stands, high rollers, and so on, and whatever goes on them: nets, flags, frames, etc. This includes any form of lighting control or shadow making that is not attached to the light itself such as nets, flags, and silks.
- They also handle all types of mounting hardware, specialized clamps of all types that might be used to attach lights or almost anything else anywhere the DP needs them.
- They handle all *bagging* (securing lights and other equipment with sandbags). Once a light is set, the grips bring as many sandbags as are necessary to secure and stabilize it. They may also have to tie it off or secure it in another way in windy or unstable conditions.

- They deal with all issues of leveling, whether it be lights, ladders, or the camera. Their tools for this are apple boxes, cribbing, step blocks, and wedges.
- They handle all dollies, lay all dolly track, and level it. Also any cranes are theirs to set up and operate. This is especially critical when a crane is the type that the DP and first AC ride on. Once they are seated, the crane grip then balances the crane by adding weights in the back so that the whole rig can be easily moved in any direction. Once this has been done, it is absolutely critical that no one step off the crane until the grips readjust the balance. Stepping off would make the front too light and the crane would shoot up, possibly injuring someone or damaging the camera. Deaths from crane accidents are not uncommon; everyone must be on their toes and very focused when working with a crane.
- The grips are also in charge of rigging the camera if it's in an unusual spot, such as attached to the front of a roller coaster, up in a tree, and so on.
- The grips build any scaffolding, platforms, or other rigs necessary for camera rigs or other purposes. They may assist the stunt men in building platforms, for the airbags or mounts for stunt equipment. Any other small construction project that doesn't call for set builders is in their purview as well.
- The grip crew and the key grip in particular are in charge of safety on the set, outside of anything electrical.

This is the system in the United States; in other countries it is handled differently — the primary difference being that the electricians handle all lighting related issues such as nets and flags, and so on and the grips are primarily responsible for dollys and cranes.

Figure 15.17. Figuring out where to park the trucks is a big decision; you want it as close to the set as possible, but out of sight so that it doesn't have to be moved to accommodate an unexpected reverse angle.

The rolling carts for C-stands, 4x4s, and heads makes it possible to keep the key equipment mobile and as close to the set as possible.

Figure 15.18. Chief Lighting Technician Tony Nako (standing at left) setting muzz balls for a fire effect on *X-Men II*. (Photo courtesy of Tony Nako.)

Other Units

Three other types of teams will also be under the DPs control: second unit, additional cameras, and rigging crews. Second unit is an important function. Usually it is used for shots that do not include the principal actors. Typical second unit work includes establishing shots, crowd shots, stunts or special effects, and insert shots. Shots that include significant lighting are not generally considered for second unit, except in the case of special effects.

Second unit may be supervised by a second unit director, but often the team consists only of a second unit DP, one or two camera assistants, and possibly a grip. It is the duty of the second unit DP to deliver the shots the director asks for in accordance with the instructions and guidance of the director of photography. The shots must be in a style that is consistent with the principal photography. It will often be up to the DP to specify what lenses are used, film stock, and camera filtration. It is the DPs name that is listed on the credits as the person responsible for the photography of the film; the audience and the executives will not know that a bad shot or a mistake is due to the second unit. In light of this responsibility, it is standard practice for the DP to have a say in who the second unit cameraperson is.

In the case where additional cameras are used in principal photography, they are designated *B camera, C camera,* and so on. On a big stunt that cannot be repeated such as blowing up a building, it is not uncommon for a dozen or more cameras to be used. Some are used as a backup to the main camera in case of malfunction, some are just to get different angles, some run at different speeds, and some are "crash cams," small expendable cameras that can be placed in dangerous positions.

In slating with multiple cameras, there may be a separate slate for each camera, clearly marked as *A* or *B* slate. The slating AC then calls out "A marker" or "B marker" and claps the slate for that camera. Naturally, separate camera reports are kept for each camera. An alternative is to use a common marker. This is possible where all cameras are aimed at approximately the same part of the scene or where one camera can quickly pan over to catch the slate, then pan back to the opening frame. If this is the case, then the director must wait for all operators to call *set* before calling *action*. Calling out *set* should be standard procedure in any case where the slating can't be right where the camera is ready for the opening frame, if the first AC has to refocus or another adjustment needs to be made. In the case

Figure 15.19. *Video village* on a two-camera HD shoot. The monitors are mounted on the camera assistant's *Magliner Junior,* which makes moving them quick and easy.

of additional cameras, there is only one DP, and the rest of the cameras are run by additional operators. Ideally, each additional camera should have its own AC, and perhaps its own second AC.

In some cases, cameras are *locked off,* usually because it is simply too dangerous to have an operator in that position. In these cases the camera is mounted securely, the frame is set, and the focus and T-stop are set. They are then either operated by remote switch or as roll is called, and an AC switches on the camera and runs to safety. Protective metal housings, called "crash boxes," may be used if there is danger to the camera. Protective Lexan (bulletproof glass) or pieces of plywood with a small hole for the lens might also be used.

Coordinating with Other Departments

Besides his own crew, the DP must also coordinate with other crew members. The first is the production designer. If sets are being built or extensively dressed, it is essential that the DP look at them while they are still in plans or sketches, not after they are built. The DP will discuss with the designer what lighting opportunity will be part of the set. These include windows, skylights, doors, and other types of places to hide lights or bring light into the set.

Also to be discussed are the practicals — that is, working lights that are part of the set, and whether they are hanging lamps, wall sconces, or table lamps. A good set dresser will usually have a couple of spare table lamps or hanging lights on the truck. These can be invaluable either as a lighting source themselves or as a "motivator" of light. It may be up to the electricians to wire them up, however.

Figure 15.20. A common slating mistake: pulling the slate out while also clapping the sticks. This results in blurred frames that makes it difficult or impossible for the editor to read the numbers or see the frame where the sticks come together. See the DVD or website for more examples of slating mistakes, as well as video of proper slating procedure.

The situation may call for "wild walls," which are walls or other pieces of the set that can be easily removed to make room for the camera, dolly track, and other equipment. Finally, it is important to consider not only the set, but how it will be positioned on the stage. There might be a window or glass wall that would be a great lighting opportunity, but if it is only a few feet away from the wall of the stage, it may be difficult or impossible to use it. On the set, the DP is in constant communication with the assistant director concerning the schedule: how much time is left before the actors go into over-time, what scenes are left to do, and so on. Being the first AD is one of the most stressful jobs in the industry; a good one a real treasure.

Before the shooting begins the AD makes the schedule indicating what scenes will be shot on what days and a one liner, which is a one line description of each scene. The schedule also indicates whether scenes are day or night, interior or exterior, whether the day scenes are to be shot during the day or night and vice-versa. This is essential for the DP in planning what equipment and supplies will be needed.

At the beginning of each day, a production assistant or second AD will hand out *sides*. These are copies of the script pages to be shot that day that have been reduced to a quarter of a page, so that they can be easily slipped into a pocket. The sides are the "bible" for the day. Of all the principles of filmmaking perhaps the most important of all is that everyone must know what is going on and is working, as they say, "on the same page." Communication is the key — nothing can derail a production quicker than poor communication. This is why everyone should have a copy of the script pages for the day.

During shooting, the DP is under pressure and is thinking about a dozen things at the same time; complete focus and concentration are essential. One of the unwritten rules of filmmaking is that only certain people talk to the DP: the director, of course, the first AD, the first AC, the gaffer, and the grip. A working set is no place for idle chitchat, or as a great AD used to say, "Tell your stories walking."

Figures 15.21. The second AC slating on a day exterior HD shoot.

SET PROCEDURES

Generally the lighting for the scene will be *roughed in* based on a general understanding of the scene as described by the director. This may range from everything fully rigged and hot for a night exterior to only having the power run for a small interior.

Once the DP is ready to begin lighting seriously, the steps of production are reasonably formalized. They are as follows:

- The director describes to the DP what shot is wanted first. At this stage it is important to have at least a rough idea of all of the shots needed so there are no surprises later.
- The director blocks the scene and there is a blocking rehearsal.
- Marks are set for the actors. The first AC might choose to take some focus measurements at this time, if possible.
- The AD asks the DP for a time estimate on the next setup.
- The AD announces that the DP *has the set*.
- The DP huddles with the gaffer and key grip and tells them what is needed.
- The electrics and grips carry out the DPs orders.
- The DP supervises the placement of the camera.
- When all is set, the DP informs the AD that he is ready.
- The director takes over and stages final rehearsal with the actors in makeup and wardrobe. If needed, focus measurements are taken by the first AC, assisted by the second AC.
- If necessary, the DP may have to make a few minor adjustments (especially if the blocking or actions have changed),

Figure 15.22. (top) A 40 foot lighting truck *shelved out*. (Photo by Michael Gallart.)

Figure 15.23. (bottom) The truck fully loaded with gear. The 40-footer is the largest truck normally used by film crews; it is a semi-trailer. For features, there will generally be a 40-footer for grip and a separate one for lighting. (Photo by Michael Gallart.)

called *tweaking*. Of course, the less the better, but ultimately it is the DPs responsibility to get it right, even if there is some grumbling from the AD.

- The DP meters the scene and determines the lens aperture. When ready, he informs the AD.
- The AD calls *first team in* and actors are brought back to the set.
- The director may have a final word for the actors or camera operator, then announce that he or she is ready for a take.
- The AD calls for *last looks* and the makeup, hair, and wardrobe people to make sure the actors are ready in every detail.
- If there is smoke, rain, fire, or other physical effects, they are set in motion.
- When everything is set, the AD calls to *lock it up*: this is repeated by *second-second ADs* and production assistants to make sure that everyone around knows to stop working and be quiet for a take.
- The AD calls *roll sound*.
- The sound recordist calls *speed* (after allowing for pre-roll).
- The AD calls *roll camera*.
- The first AC switches on and calls *camera speed*. (If there are multiple cameras it is *A speed, B speed*, etc.)
- The first AC or operator says *mark it,* and the second AC slates, calling out the scene and take number.
- When the camera is in position and in focus, the operator calls out *set*.
- When applicable the AD may call *background action*, meaning the extras and atmosphere begin their activity.
- The director calls *action* and the scene begins.
- When the scene is over, the director calls *cut*.
- If there are any, the operator mentions problems he saw in the shot and any reasons why another take may be necessary or any adjustments that may make the physical action of the shot work more smoothly.
- If there is another take, the AD tells the actors and the operator tells the dolly grip *back to one*, meaning everyone resets to position one.
- The second AC calls for *dial* (amount of film shot on that take) and makes his notes on the camera report.
- If there is a need for adjustments, they are made and the process starts over.

Some directors prefer that they be the only ones to call cut. Others ask that if something is terribly wrong and the shot is becoming a waste of film, the DP or the operator may call cut and switch off the camera. The operator must be sure they know the director's preference on this point. The operator will call out problems as they occur, such as a boom in the shot, a bump in the dolly track, and so on. It is then up to the director to cut or to continue. If you as the operator are in a mode where you call out problems as they occur, you certainly want to do it between dialog, so that if the director does decide to live with it, the sound editor can cut out your comments.

Most directors prefer that no one talk to the principal actors except themselves. For purely technical adjustments about marks or timing, most directors don't mind if you just quickly mention it to the actor directly — but only if it will not disturb their concentration.

technical issues

FLICKER

As discussed in the chapter on *Lighting Sources*, there are two basic kinds of light sources. One is a filament (usually tungsten) that is heated by electrical current until it glows and emits light. The other type is a discharge source. These include fluorescents, HMIs, Xenons, mercury vapor, sodium vapor, and others. In all of these, an arc is established between a cathode and an anode. This arc then excites gases or a plasma cloud, inducing them to glow. All discharge sources run on alternating current.

Any arc-based bulb powered by alternating current has an output that rises and falls as the waveform varies. Alternating current rises and falls as it heats a tungsten filament as well, but the filament stays hot enough that the light it emits does not vary a great deal. There is some loss of output, but it is minimal, usually only about 10 to 15%, not enough to affect exposure. With discharge sources, the light output does rise and fall significantly throughout the AC cycle.

Although rarely perceptible to the eye, flicker appears on film as an uneven variation in exposure. This effect is a result of variations in exposure from frame to frame as a result of a mismatch in the output wave form of the light and the framing rate of the camera. Flicker can be bad enough to completely ruin the footage. The output of an AC power source is a sine wave. When the current flow is at the maximum (top of the wave) or minimum (bottom of the wave) the output of the light will be maximum: the light doesn't care whether the flow is positive or negative.

When the sine wave crosses the axis, the current flow drops to zero. When that happens, the bulb produces less output. Since the light is "on" for both the positive and negative side of the sine wave, it reaches its maximum at twice the rate of the AC: 120 cycles per second for 60-hertz current and 100 cycles per second for 50-hertz current. For an HMI with a magnetic ballast (a copper coil wound around a core), the output at the crossover point may be as low as 17% of total output.

With film there is another complication: the shutter is opening and closing at a rate that may be different than the rate at which the light output is varying. When the relationship of the shutter and the light output varies in relation to each other, each film frame is exposed to different amounts of the cycle. The result is exposure that varies enough to be noticeable.

There are two possibilities: the frame rate of the camera can be unsteady, or the frequency of the electrical supply can fluctuate or the frame rate of the shutter creates a mismatch in the synchronization of the shutter and the light output. The first two are obvious: if either the shutter rate or the light output are random, it is clear that there will be different amounts of exposure for each frame. The third is a bit more complex. Only certain combinations of shutter speed and power supply frequency can be considered acceptably safe. Deviations from these combinations always risk noticeable flicker. Four conditions are essential to prevent HMI or fluorescent flicker:

- Constant frequency in the AC power supply
- Constant framing rate in the camera
- Compatible shutter angle
- Compatible frame rate

The first two conditions are satisfied with either crystal controls on the generator and camera or by running one or both of them from the local AC mains, which are usually very reliable in frequency.

Figure 16.1. (previous page) A complex setup for a timeslicing shot. (Photo courtesy of PAWS, Inc.)

24FPS/50HZ POWER - SAFE FRAME RATES AT ANY SPEED				
1.000	4.000	6.315	10.000	**24.000**
1.500	4.800	6.666	10.909	30.000
1.875	5.000	7.058	12.000	40.000
2.000	5.217	7.500	13.333	60.000
2.500	5.454	8.000	15.000	120.00
3.000	5.714	8.571	17.143	
3.750	6.000	9.231	20.000	

25FPS/50HZ POWER - SAFE FRAME RATES AT ANY SPEED				
1.000	4.166	6.250	11.111	50.000
1.250	4.347	6.666	12.500	33.333
2.000	4.545	7.142	14.285	100.00
2.500	4.761	7.692	16.666	
3.125	5.000	8.333	20.000	
3.333	5.263	9.090	**25.000**	
4.00	5.882	10.00	33.333	

24 FPS	25 FPS
120	100
60	50
40	25
30	20
24	10
20	5
15	4
12	2
10	1
8	
6	
5	
4	
2	
1	

The shutter angle and frame rate are determined by consulting the appropriate charts. A fifth condition — relationship of AC frequency to shutter — is generally only crucial in high-speed cinematography and is usually not a factor in most filming situations.

At 24 fps camera speed, if the power supply is stable, shutter angle can vary from 90° to 200° with little risk. The ideal shutter angle is 144°, since this results in an exposure time of 1/60th of a second and so it matches the frequency of the mains power supply. In actual practice, there is little risk in using a 180° shutter if the camera is crystal controlled and the power supply is from the mains or a crystal-controlled generator (Tables 16.2 and 16.3).

With a 144° shutter opening, the camera is exposing 2-1/2 pulses per frame (rather than the exactly 2 pulses per frame as you would get with 144°) and so exposure can theoretically vary by as much as 9%. In other countries (especially in Europe), with a 50 cycle per second power supply, and shooting at 24 fps, the ideal shutter angle is 172.8°. Tables 16.1 through 16.3 list the acceptably safe frame rates for shooting at any shutter angle (with either 50 or 60 hertz electrical supplies) and the acceptably safe frame rates for specific shutter speeds.

A simple way to think about it is to divide 120 by a whole number — for example, 120/4 = 30, 120/8 = 15. For 50 hertz (Hz) power systems, divide 100 by a whole number. This results in a simplified series as shown in Table 16.1. Any variation in the frequency of the power supply will result in an exposure fluctuation of approximately .4 f/stop. The time for one cycle of fluctuation will depend on how far off the power supply is.

Any generator used must be a crystal controlled. Governor controls are never sufficient for the accuracy demanded. A frequency meter should be used to periodically monitor the generator. Most generators have a frequency readout, but it is often not precise enough for this purpose. For most purposes, plus or minus one-quarter of a cycle is considered acceptable. Flicker-free ballasts are available that minimize the possibility of flicker even under high-speed conditions. Flicker-free units use electronic ballasts instead of iron-core, wire-wound reactance ballasts. They utilize two basic principles: square-wave output and high frequency. Flicker-free ballasts modify the

Table 16.1. (above) Simplified safe frame rates with 24 Hz power supply and 25 Hz power supply.

Table 16.2. (left, top) Safe frame rates for any shutter speed with 24 Hz power supply.

Table 16.3. (left, bottom) Safe frame rates for any shutter speed with 25 Hz power supply.

wave form of the power supply by squaring it so that instead of the normal rounded sine wave, the output is angular. This means that the rising and falling sections of the wave are a much smaller portion of the total. As a result, the light output is off for less time.

Flicker-free ballasts also use increased frequency. The idea is that with 200 or 250 cycles per second it is less likely that there will be a mismatch from frame to frame. Since there is an increase in the noise from a ballast in flicker-free mode, some flicker-free units can be switched from normal to flicker-free operation. Flicker-free units are now available in every size of HMI, including the largest units; also, most HMI sunguns are flicker-free. With high-speed shooting, flicker can also sometimes be a problem with small tungsten bulbs, especially if they are on camera because the smaller filaments don't have the mass to stay heated through the cycle as do larger bulbs. Although not nearly as noticeable as with HMIs, it may still be distracting. At higher than normal camera speeds ordinary fluorescents may sometimes flicker because they are cycling on and off with the power supply.

FILMING PRACTICAL MONITORS

Because monitors may be a scanned image, most reflectance meters (spot meters) don't accurately read the exposure. They usually underestimate the exposure, often by a stop or more. Use tests and check with a digital still camera. You can use the brightness control on the monitor to turn it down to more closely match the scene. Also, most monitors run a little blue; you can either adjust the color towards orange or put some CTO over the screen to match your scene lighting. It will need to be flat enough so that wrinkles don't show.

If you are running your own source material through the monitor and you have the luxury of setting up to color bars, you can read the green band, (which correlates reasonably well to 18% gray) with a spot meter and open 2/3rd to 1 stop. Alternate method: read white and expose by placing that reading at between VI and VII. You will be surprised how dim you need to set the TV so it won't look washed out on the film later. The monitor will generally end up being set much dimmer than you would have it for normal viewing. You can't trust your eye or the meter; trust the tests done with a digital still camera or a waveform monitor. Because video runs at 29.97 frames per second, CRT televisions and monitors in a scene will exhibit a roll bar unless precautions are taken to prevent it. This includes non-LCD computer monitors, radar screens, and many other types of CRT (cathode ray tube) displays. The solution will depend on the nature of the monitor that appears in the frame and the requirements of the scene.

The frame rate of video is usually (not always) 29.97. Thus, each video field is *on* for approximately 1/60th of a second (actually 1/59.94). The frame rate of a motion picture camera with a 180° shutter is 1/48th of a second. It is the discrepancy between these two frame rates that results in the *roll bar* effect: a dark bar that appears across some part of the screen and may also move slowly up and down during the shot.

CRT monitors will be one of three types:

- Video from broadcast, cable, or prerecorded video on the set.
- A computer monitor, graphics workstation, radar screen, video game or other type CRT display.
- Specially prepared video to match a 24 fps or 25 fps frame rate on the camera.

There are four kinds of final results you will be aiming for:
- Film shot for theatrical projection with sync sound.
- Film shot for theatrical projection at 24 fps without sync sound.
- Film shot to be transferred directly to videotape, either with sync sound or without.
- Film that will be edited as film work print, then transferred to video. While film editors and video transfer houses can accommodate film shot at non-standard frame rates (even with lip-sync dialog) the inconvenience may be undesirable.

Unfortunately, it is impossible to lock a roll bar off the screen at the standard 24 fps camera speed. There are several methods available to achieve the desired result. The simplest case is film transferred directly to video. A crystal control is used to run the camera at 29.97 fps with a 180° shutter: this works only with a shutter angle of 180° or more. This works for both MOS and sync sound filming.

For theatrical projection (24 fps) that must be shot at sound sync speed (24 fps): use a 144° shutter and crystal-controlled camera at 23.976 fps. This works because a 144° shutter equals 1/60th of a second exposure, which approximates the video exposure time. A roll bar will still be visible but can be minimized and can be locked in place on the screen. There is a 1/3rd stop loss in closing down to 144° shutter angle.

This method can only be used with cameras that have adjustable shutters. Always discuss it with the rental house when you are going to be dealing with practical monitors so that they can ensure that all equipment is compatible.

Monitors and MOS Shooting

When the filming is MOS and is intended for projection at 24 fps, shooting can be at 29.97 fps with 180° shutter or at 23.976 with 144° shutter. At 29.97, there will be a noticeable slowing of the action when projected at 24 fps, if this is not acceptable, the 23.976 fps method should be used. If the film is to be transferred to video, either method may be used, but be sure to slate the film clearly and log the variation onto the camera reports so that the video transfer house will know how to deal with it. Without appropriate slating to alert them to this, all of the video dailies will be out of sync.

There is an alternate method that makes filming monitors very simple. Specialty video houses can transform the video source material to 24 fps video, which may then be filmed at normal camera speeds without a roll bar. This must be used in conjunction with a camera capable of supplying a framing pulse as output.

CRTs such as computer screens, radar screens, medical monitors, or video games have a wide variety of frame rates. In some cases they are raster scans (like a normal TV) or vector scans (where each line is traced separately). In many cases it is necessary to either determine the frame rate from manufacturer's specifications with a frequency checker or by observing the image through the viewfinder or gate while varying the frame rate of the camera with a crystal speed control. Several very accurate meters are available that will tell you the frame rate of a particular CRT. The simplest and most reliable method is to take a portion of the video signal and use it to drive the camera. This is accomplished with a synchronizer unit as described following. LCD monitors make all of this unnecessary because there is no roll bar problem.

SHOOTING PROCESS PHOTOGRAPHY

Greenscreen/Bluescreen

Chroma key, known as *bluescreen, greenscreen,* or *process photography,* is a method of producing *mattes* for *compositing.* The basic principle is the same for all processes and for both film and video: by including an area of a pure color in the scene, that color can then be made transparent and another image can be substituted for it. The people or objects you are shooting is called the *foreground plate,* and what you will eventually put in to replace the green or bluescreen is called the *background plate.*

Green and blue are the most common colors used, but in theory any color can be used. There is one fundamental principle that must be remembered: whatever color you are using to become transparent will be replaced for the entire scene. Thus, if the background is green and the actor has bright green eyes, his eyes will become transparent. The color chosen for the process background should be one that does not occur in the foreground.

If the foreground objects you are shooting contain blue or green, you can use another color for the background. What matters most is that the background color be different from any color in the foreground subjects.

If there is any camera movement in a matte shot, the post house will most likely request that you include *tracking mark*s (Figure 16.6). These can be as simple as crosses made of tape. They are placed on the background itself as a clue to the movement that will be required of the background element that is to be laid in.

The actors and props on the greenscreen set are called the *foreground plate*; what you shoot to be the background by replacing the green areas is called the *background plate.*

Another important safety practice is to shoot a *reference frame.* This is a shot of the same green or bluescreen background without the foreground element — just the screen itself. This is useful in case there is any problem with the matte. Other recommendations include:

- Use the lowest-grain film possible (low ISO). Grain introduces noise into the image. 35mm is preferred over 16mm.
- In video use the highest resolution format possible. For example, *DV (digital video)* is extremely difficult to composite.
- Do not use diffusion over the lens. Avoid heavy smoke effects. Keying software can deal with some smoke effects, but there are limits.
- Always shoot a grayscale lit with neutral light (3200K or 5500K) at the beginning of each roll when shooting on film.
- Try to avoid shooting with the lens wide open. The reason for this is that many camera lenses vignette slightly when wide open, which can create problems with the matte.
- In video, never compensate for low light levels by boosting the gain, which will increase noise. Never *push* film.
- To match the depth of focus of the foreground, shoot the background plate with the focus set at where it would be if the foreground object was actually there.
- The perspective of foreground and background plates must match. Use the same camera, or one with the same sensor size, the same lens, camera height and angle of tilt for both.
- Plan the lighting, screen direction, and perspective of the background plates; they must match the foreground plate.

Figure 16.2. Kinos used to light a large greenscreen in a water tank. (Photo courtesy of Kino Flo.)

Lighting for Bluescreen/Greenscreen

Optimum exposure levels depend on the nature of the subject and the setup. (Figures 16.2 through 16.8). In general, you want the exposure of the background to be about the same as the foreground. There is no general agreement on this. Some people set them to be exactly the same, some people underexpose the background by up to one stop, and some people light the background by as much as one stop hotter than the foreground.

The bottom line is simple: ask the person who will be doing the final composite — the *compositor* or *effects supervisor*. Different visual effects houses will have varying preferences that may be based on the hardware/software combination they use. Always consult with your effects people before shooting. This is the golden rule of shooting any type of effects: *always talk to the postproduction people who will be dealing with the footage*: ultimately they are the ones who are going to have to deal with any problems.

Lighting the background can be done in many ways using tungsten units, HMIs, or even daylight. Kino Flo makes special bulbs for lighting backgrounds; they are available in both green and blue (Figure 16.2). Figures 16.4 and 16.5 show Kino Flo's recommendations for using their units to light a background.

Set pieces (such as tables, boxes to sit on, etc.) that are painted to give the actor something to walk behind or interact with can present problems. The top of the piece will sometimes be hotter than the shadow side. This will definitely cause problems with the composite. Lighting can help, but it may create problems of its own. One trick is to use paints of different reflectances on the top and side surfaces.

Nothing will undermine the believability of a composite more than a mismatch of lighting in the foreground and background plate (the scene that will be inserted in place of the greenscreen). Careful attention must be made to recreating the look, direction, and quality of the lighting in the background plate.

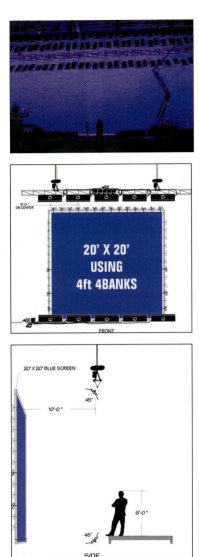

Figure 16.3. (top) A large bluescreen setup lit with Kino Flo units. (Photo courtesy of Kino Flo.)

Figure 16.4. (middle) Typical bluescreen (or greenscreen) lighting setup with Kino Flos. (Photo courtesy of Kino Flo.)

Figure 16.5. (bottom) Spacing is important for even illumination of the cyc, which is critical for a good process shot. (Photo courtesy of Kino Flo.)

When shooting greenscreen/bluescreen:
- Keep the actors as far away from the background as you can to guard against backsplash, 12 to 15 feet if possible.
- Light the background as evenly as possible: within 1/3 stop variation on any part of the screen is ideal.
- Don't include the matte color in the scene; for example, when shooting greenscreen, don't have green props or anybody wearing green wardrobe.
- Use a spot meter to read the greenscreen/bluescreen; use an incident meter to read the subject.
- In general, greenscreen is used for HD video and bluescreen is used for film. This is based on differences in how film and video react to colors with the least amount of noise.

The reason you use an incident meter to read the subject and a spot meter (reflectance meter) for the background is that greenscreen/bluescreen materials vary in their reflectivity. We are not concerned with how much light is *hitting* the background, only how much light it is *reflecting back* toward the camera. For the subjects (actors or whatever) being photographed, we read them as we normally would, with an incident meter. Using a spot meter on an actor can be tricky. What part of them do you read? Their forehead? Their shirt? Their hair? With a reflectance meter those are all likely to be different readings. Which one of them represents the actual exposure, the f/stop the lens should be set at? Yes, you can do it, if you have a good understanding of the Zone system, as discussed in the chapter *Exposure*. It is possible, but not usually necessary; an incident meter gives us an excellent reading when used properly as previously discussed: holding the meter so that it is receiving the same lighting as the subject, receptor aimed at the camera, and a hand shielding the meter from backlight, kickers or any other stray light that might not be relevant to the subject exposure.

When shooting video, a waveform monitor is useful in judging exposure and balance; a vectorscope can reveal any color problems.

Luminance Key
Luminance key is the same concept as chroma key except that the difference between light and dark objects is used as the key for producing a difference matte. If the subject is primarily light colored, then the background and all parts of the scene that you want to become transparent so that the composited background plate will show through should be black. The opposite is true if the subject is predominantly dark and shadowy.

DIMMERS
There are a number of ways we control the intensity of a light's output at the unit itself:
- Flood-spot
- Wire scrims
- Grip nets
- Diffusion
- Neutral density filters
- Aim (spilling the beam)
- Switching bulbs on and off in multi-bulb units (multi-PARs or soft lights)

The alternative is to control the power input into the light with dimmers. There are advantages and disadvantages.

Figures 16.6 and 16.7. An example of greenscreen used to fill in a window on a set. On the left, notice the *tracking marks* on the greenscreen, which are essential if there is any camera movement at all, including a tilt up or down. On the right is the final result after the *background plate* has been composited in.

The advantages are:

- Fine degree of control
- Ability to control inaccessible units
- Ability to quickly look at different combinations
- Ability to do cues
- Ability to preset scene combinations
- Ability to save energy and heat buildup by cooling down between take

The disadvantages are:

- Lights change color as they dim; see Table 16.4
- Some lights cannot be dimmed externally such as HMIs
- Necessity of additional cabling
- Cost

The first dimmers invented were *resistance* units. They operate by placing a variable resistance in the power line. The excess energy is burned off as heat. The major problem with resistance dimmers is that they must be loaded to at least 80% of their capacity in order to operate. If you put a 5K on a 10K dimmer, for example, the dimmer will only reduce the output a small amount; you won't be able to dim all the way down. This sometimes necessitates the use of a *dummy load* to operate.

The next generation of dimmers were *autotransformers*. They operate as variable transformers and alter the voltage. They do not have to be loaded to capacity, and they don't generate excessive heat, but they do operate only on AC. Known as *variacs* (for variable AC), they are used, particularly in the 1K and 2K sizes, although they are bulky and heavy.

For larger applications, silicon-controlled rectifiers are used. Known as *SCRs*, these are electronic devices that are small in size, quiet, and relatively low cost. They can be controlled remotely by dimmer boards, which means that the dimmer packs themselves can be near the lights, which saves cabling; only a small control cable needs to run from the board to the dimmer packs. The remote cable carries a control voltage of 0 to 10 volts and can be run up to 200 feet. The signal is multiplex and can run up to 192 dimmers.

SCR dimmers do not alter the voltage; they work by *clipping* the waveform so that the voltage is heating the filament for a shorter time. The result of this is that the output cannot be read with an ordinary voltage meter, only a *VOM* (*volt-ohm meter*), which reads *root mean square voltage* (*RMS*) such as the will work.

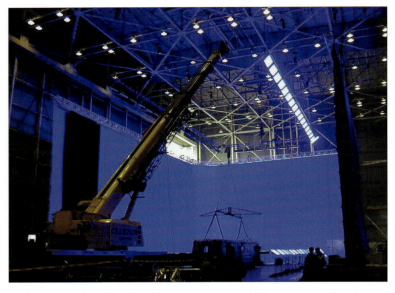

There must be a load on the circuit to read the output. The shorter rise time can sometimes cause filament *sing*. In most cases, with properly grounded audio systems, there should be no problem, but a portable radio can be used to test and find the source of any trouble. When using an SCR dimmer with a generator, the gennie must be frequency controlled, or the loss of sync will cause flicker; also, since most dimmers are voltage regulated, raising the voltage of the generator will not increase the output. An anomaly of these systems is that the neutral load can, in some cases, be higher than the hot line.

SCR dimmers are basically theatrical equipment, so their connectors will often not be compatible with the rest of your equipment. As a rule the outputs will be theatrical three-pin connectors, either 60 amp or 100 amp. It is important to order adapters to whatever plugging system your are using.

The input side of most dimmer packs are *Camlock* connectors. Frequently the neutral is reversed (male instead of female); the easiest way to run into trouble with dimmer orders is to forget to order feeder cable with the neutral reversed or "turnarounds": female to female connectors. Besides SCRs there are several types of electronic dimmers that work in various ways to reduce the ability of the electricity to make the tungsten filament produce light. These electronic dimmers are also used to control other types of sources such as HMI units, fluorescents, or neon lights.

Control panels vary in sophistication. Some are simply sets of slider switches, one for each circuit, and others include masters and submasters and may have separate banks for X and Y scenes, making it possible to do a cue from one preset to another. The next level is "soft patching," which allows for electronic routing of each line to a dimming circuit. The most advanced feature computer control, timed cues, and other sophisticated control features. Most control panels (dimmer boards) will run any set of dimmers. The standard for remotely controlling dimmers is called DMX; make sure that your control board and your dimmers match in terms of control standards and connectors. The effect of dimming on color temperature varies with the source, as is shown in Table 16.4. It is possible to use dimming to establish a warm color look for the scene.

TYPE	LAMP COLOR SHIFT	CCT DIRECTION	DEGREE OF SHIFT
Incandescent / Tungsten Halogen	Orange-red	Lower	Marked
Fluorescent	Not discernible	Negligible	Negligible
Metal Halide	Blue	Higher	Drastic
Mercury	Not discernible	Negligible	Negligible

Table 16.4. Most light sources shift in color when dimmed.

WORKING WITH STROBES

There are several types of strobe lighting for cinematography. The most widely known is *Unilux*; *Clairmont Camera* also makes strobe units. Strobes are generally used to create a different look for a shot. The fact that the strobe fires for a very short time means they have the ability to freeze motion. Several units can be controlled together for a greater number of heads. Frame rates of up to 500 fps are possible. The strobes are fired by a pulse from the camera that signals when the shutter is open. Any camera that provides such a pulse is compatible with the system. In some cases a pulse contact is added to a moving part of the camera, and this provides the sync signal to control the strobe.

Strobe lighting in film has three basic uses:

- To light cooler (strobes produce substantially less heat than tungsten heads), which can be a tremendous advantage when shooting ice cream, for example.
- To produce sharper images. The exposure duration for each flash can be as short as 1/100,000th of a second, and as a result, the image is "frozen" and appears sharper than if photographed on moving film at standard exposures.
- To provide sufficient exposure for high-speed photography with a small power input.

It is often used in spray shots of soft drink cans being opened: the strobe effect captures each droplet of spray crisply. In fact, it can be too sharp for some people. In shower scenes for shampoo commercials it can appear that the shower is a series of razor-sharp drops rather than a soft spray. As a result, for beauty applications, it is common practice to combine Unilux with tungsten lighting. In most cases, the Unilux light is balanced with an equal amount of tungsten within a range of plus or minus one stop. This presents an interesting exposure problem.

All strobes are daylight balance, and you will need to use gels or filters if you are combining them with incandescent lights, which are often used to avoid flicker. When mixing with tungsten, use CTO on the strobes to match color temperature.

Strobe Exposure

Consider this situation: you are shooting at 96 frames per second and the desired effect is equal amounts of tungsten and strobe lights. Every time you increase the frame rate of motion picture camera, you are decreasing the amount of time the shutter stays open: you are decreasing exposure. 96 fps is four times faster than normal, and the shutter speed is 1/200th of a second instead of the normal 1/50th (assuming a 180 shutter). This is an exposure loss of two stops.

This is simple enough to deal with; to achieve a f/5.6, for example, you light to an f/11. But the same is not true of the strobe lighting. The strobe is instantaneous: it fires for only a few thousandths of a second at some time while the shutter is open, and as a result, it is completely independent of the frame rate. It doesn't matter whether the film is moving at six frames a second or 600: the exposure will be the same.

Here's the problem. We read the tungsten and have to compensate, we then read the strobes with a meter and we don't have to compensate; not all light meters can do this — you need a meter that can read strobes. Clearly we can't read them at the same time. How do we arrive at a setting for the lens? The answer is intuitively obvious, but mathematically a bit complex: we read them separately and then add the two exposures. As it turns out, adding f/stops is not especially simple. Let's take the simplest case first. We read the Unilux by itself (and it is very important to turn off all tungsten lights when we do this) and find that they are an f/5.6. We have to balance the tungsten to do that. As we know, at 96 fps, we have to set the tungsten lights for f/11, which will be f/5.6 at 96 fps. The temptation might be to average them; that would result in a very incorrect exposure: we must *add* them.

What is f/5.6 plus f/5.6? No, it's not f/11.2. In effect we are doubling the amount of light: the tungsten is providing f/5.6 and the Unilux is supplying an entirely different illumination, which is also f/5.6. Twice as much light as f/5.6 is f/8. Recall that each f/stop represents a doubling of the amount of light. Now it gets a bit stickier. Let's say that the Unilux is f/8 and the tungsten is f/5.6. Think of it this way: if f/8 is a base of 100%, then the tungsten light is 50% (one stop less equals 1/2 the amount of light). We then have 150% of the base light. 150% of f/8 is 1/2 stop hotter than f/8 — f/8 and a half. If the one of the sources is f/8 and the other is f/4, the correct exposure is f/8 and 1/4. F/4 is only 25% the amount of light of f/8: 125%. Although a flash meter is the preferred method many ordinary electronic light meters can read high-speed strobes. The reason is that at 60 flashes per second, it is seen as continuous by some meters.

Typical Exposures

Unilux is switchable for four intensity levels. The Unilux H3000 System is switchable to 16 speed ranges, which gives 1/4 stop level control. The levels are determined by the speeds at which the lights are flashing. Remember that the flash rate is twice the camera speed because there is one flash for the shutter and one for the viewfinder. The lights only come up to full intensity when the camera goes to speed. If you want to take a reading, the lights must be running at speed. Other considerations:

- Shutter angle should be opened to the maximum.
- Check the synchronization frequently. This is done by removing the lens and looking at the shutter with camera running and strobes operating. The shutter will be "frozen" and it should appear open.
- For reflex viewing, the strobes can be run in *split sync* mode. In this case there are two flashes for each rotation of the shutter: one for the exposure and one for the viewfinder.
- Some types of strobe come with an operator and units are rented without operator, but be sure to check.
- Unilux requires 208v-240v 3-phase and a ground. Standard Unilux consumes 5 amps per light. The Unilux H3000 system requires 220 volt single-phase and 10 amps per light.
- Some cameras must be fitted with an additional pickup for synchronization.

HIGH-SPEED PHOTOGRAPHY

High-speed photography generally require specialized cameras such as in Figure 16.9. High-speed photography differs mainly in the amount of light needed and in the calculation of exposure. Variations in frame rate are covered in the chapter on *Exposure*. Video cameras are available that can shoot up to 1500 frames per second. A few formulae are also useful. (Thanks to Photo-Sonics, Inc., for the following calculations.)

- 1/Exposure Time = 360° ÷ shutter angle x frame rate.
  Example: 360° ÷ 120° x 360 fps = 1/1080 exposure time. Don't forget to compensate if there is a beam splitter in the camera — usually 1/2 stop.
- Times Normal Speed = Frame Rate ÷ Transfer Rate (e.g., 24 or 30 fps).
  Example: 360 ÷ 24 = 15 Times Normal Speed.
- Frames Exposed = Frame Rate x Event Duration.
  Example: 360 x .5 second = 180 Frames Exposed (for an event that lasts 1/2 second).
- Screen time = Frame Rate x Event Duration ÷ Transfer Rate.
  Example: 360 x .5 ÷ 24 = 7.5 Seconds Screen Time.
- Frame Rate Required = Screen Time ÷ Event Duration x Transfer Rate.
  Example: 7.5 Seconds ÷ .5 x 24 = 360 fps required.
- Run Time = Frames Per Foot x Footage ÷ Frame Rate.
  Example: 16 x 1000' ÷ 360 = 44.4 Seconds Run Time.
- Screen time for moving objects = Field of View ÷ Object Velocity x Frame Rate ÷ Transfer Rate. (Note: Field of view and object velocity must use the same units of measurement.)
  Example: 2' Field of View ÷ 20' per second x 360 fps ÷ 24 = 1.5 Seconds Screen time.

LIGHTING FOR EXTREME CLOSE-UP

There are two basic considerations in lighting for extreme close-up. The first is that due to extremely small depth-of-field (which is inherent in close focusing) and the need to stop down for improved optical performance, very high light levels are needed. Particularly with high-speed photography, an uncorrected stop of f/64 and higher is often called for. Since the area being lit is usually small, there is generally no problem with this, although in dealing with large units it can be quite a job just to get them close together. (Table 16.5).

The other problem is caused by the lens being so close to the subject. In some cases the front of the lens may be no more than an inch away from the subject. This makes it difficult to achieve any kind of front lighting or fill: the lens and the camera are in the way. It is more difficult when the subject is reflective. In this case no matter how much light is poured on the subject, what you will see in the reflective surface is a mirror image of the lens itself, which will appear as a large black circle.

There are two solutions: one is to cut a hole in a reflector card just large enough for the lens. Sometimes it is not even necessary for the hole to cover the entire front optic; with experimentation you will find that the hole can be smaller without interfering with the image.

The other solution is a half silver mirror. The mirror is placed between the lens and the object and angled slightly to reflect the image of the light source onto the subject in axis with the lens.

Figure 16.9. The Photo-Sonics 4B, capable of frame rates up to 3250 fps, 100 to 1000 fps in phase lock. (Photo courtesy of Photo-Sonics.)

UNDERWATER FILMING

Most professional cameras have underwater housings specially designed for them, and they are widely available for rental. Water, even fresh water, acts as a filter, absorbing the red wavelengths first, then on down the spectrum, until all frequencies are absorbed. This is why there is no light at all below a certain depth, which varies according to the clarity of the water. There are several underwater lighting units available, most of them smaller *sungun* battery-operated units. Observe the manufacturer's rated maximum depth carefully; exceeding it may lead to an implosion and short-circuit.

SeaPars

The *SeaPar®* by *HydroImage* is built around a 1200-watt Sylvania HMI PAR bulb, encased in a watertight container which can withstand depths of up to 220 feet in salt water (110 lbs/inch^2). The fresnel is permanently bonded to the front of the bulb to reduce the amount of glass, so instead of changing lenses, it is necessary to change lights. This is made easier by the inclusion of an underwater pluggable connector that can be detached underwater. It includes an aluminum retainer ring for gels and accessories and a bonded ground return line back to the ballast that operates above water and is equipped with a 20 amp ground fault interrupter. A flicker-free ballast is also available. *LTM* makes the *AquaPar,* which is similar.

Tungsten-halogen PAR 64s (1000 watts) and PAR 36s (650 watts) are also available in watertight housings. The PAR 36 can be configured for use with an underwater battery pack that can run two lights for an hour. In the tungsten units, the bulbs can be changed to alter the beam from wide-flood to narrow-spot and for daylight or tungsten color balance.

MEASURES OF IMAGE QUALITY

No matter what medium we are dealing with — video, film, still photos, computer monitors — we need ways to describe their ability to reproduce an image accurately. What we subjectively call "sharpness," whether in lenses, emulsions, or video tubes, is actually a combination of factors.

Modulation-Transfer Function

The modulation transfer function is a measure of an imaging system's ability to reproduce fine detail. Physically, the measurement evaluates the effect of the image of light diffusion within the emulsion. It is sometimes called the contrast transfer function. Modulation is an expression of the difference between lightest and darkest areas of a test pattern.

The film is exposed to a test pattern that consists of alternating black-and-white lines that become smaller and closer together. After development, the image is read with a micro-densitometer. Where the lines are large and far apart, the image system will have no trouble reproducing them as completely black or white, which is a modulation factor of one (the modulation of the reproduced image exactly matches the modulation of the test target), but where the lines get smaller and closer together, the image system will begin to blur them together until they eventually are reproduced as a uniform gray. The graph of the modulation transfer function shows the system's ability to accurately reproduce at all spatial frequencies (line pairs or cycles per millimeter).

The measurement shows the degree of loss in image contrast as the detail becomes finer (i.e., a higher frequency of modulation). The

Table 16.5. Magnification requires an increase in exposure.

Magnification ratio	Exposure increase in stops
1:10	1/3
1:6	1/2
1:4	2/3
1:3	1
1:2	1 1/3
1:1.4	1 1/2
1:1.2	1 2/3
1:1	2

rate of modulation is defined by the formula; where M is modulation and E is exposure:

$$M = \frac{E \max - E \min}{E \max + E \min}$$

The result is the ratio of modulation of the developed image to the modulation of the exposing pattern.

$$\frac{Mi}{fMo}$$

The ratio is plotted on the vertical axis as a percentage of response. The spatial frequency of the patterns is plotted on the horizontal axis as cycles per millimeter. When the detail is large, the film reproduces it accurately, as in the left-hand part of the curve. As the detail is finer and the lines closer together (the right-hand part of the curve), the film is less able to reproduce it accurately.

For most of us modulation-transfer functions are only useful in comparison to each other, but they can be useful in judging films, lens, imaging systems, and so on. The MTF of each component of a system (lens, emulsion, print stock or lens, video tube, tape, monitor) can be multiplied to arrive at an MTF for the entire system. When judged in a comprehensive manner such as this, film still has a clear superiority as a total imaging system over even high-definition video.

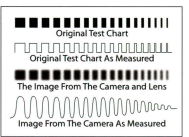

Figure 16.10 Modulation Transfer Function (MTF) is a measure of how much a camera, lens, or codec (or any combination of the above) degrades the sharp edges and contrast of the original test chart.

EFFECTS

Smoke

Many types of smoke are available for use on sets: incense in bee-smokers, smoke cookies, smoke powder and others. They have all been found to be hazardous to health except for cracker smoke. Cracker smoke is atomized oil: baby oil, cooking oil, and other types of lightweight oil are used. The oil is atomized by forcing compressed air or nitrogen through extremely small holes. Cracker smoke is very white, and fills an area with thick, billowing smoke very quickly. The smoke has the added advantage of hanging for an extremely long time ,which can be a tremendous time-saver in production. Other types of smoke required "smoking it up" before every take, followed by wafting it around, then waiting for it to settle. Smoke crackers are available in all sizes, from small hand-carry units up to big industrial-size crackers with compressors that are moved on dollies.

Fire

Real fire almost always needs help. It may deliver enough exposure itself, but if it is in the frame or even near the frame, it will flare the image badly and degrade the shot. The secret of fire shots is to use several sources on dimmers or flicker boxes. Fire jumps around; it doesn't just go up and down (Figure 16.13). One light or even two lights on dimmers that just get brighter and darker won't be convincing because the shadows don't flicker and jump like real flame. Fire is established by a low-key orange flickering effect. CTO can be used to warm the light, and the flicker can be accomplished in a variety of ways. Silver foil, waving hands and rotating mirror drums are used but are generally not very convincing; the simplest and most realistic effect is usually to place several lights on dimmers and have an electrician with an "eye" operate it. It may take two operators if you have three dimmers. It is important that the effect be random enough to not appear as a consistent pattern.

Figure 16.11. Without smoke and rain, this shot from *Nine and 1/2 Weeks* would be nowhere near as powerful.

A more high-tech method is the use of a flicker generator. Two kinds are available. One is a random generator that can be programmed for various rates of random flicker. The other uses an optical sensor to "read" the light of a candle or fire and drives a dimmer in sync with it. This is particularly effective for scenes where the dimmer or fire is the primary source and is visible in the scene. McIntire Enterprises makes several "magic boxes" that can drive up to 10K dimmers and a smaller unit that directly controls up to a 2K (Figure 16.13) — they all have adjustable settings.

Small handheld candles or oil lamps can be executed with an Inky socket and a small bulb. They can be AC powered with a wire running up the actor's sleeve or DC powered with a battery hidden on the actor's body. Flame bars, which are pipes with holes spaced along them through which gas is pumped, are far more reliable and controllable than real fire.

TV and Projector Effects

Like fire effects, the look of a flickering TV is best accomplished with dimmers. The source, which might be a fresnel or practical bulbs in porcelain sockets with some diffusion, are usually placed in a snoot box to confine the light in a realistic pattern. In general 1/2 or full CTB cools the light to simulate the blue look of black-and-white television. This is a convention even though most people watch color TV, which projects a variety of colors. Here again, it is important that the person operating the effect have some sensitivity to the mood of the scene and keep it random. Actual television flickers considerably less than is usually portrayed, but the activity helps sell the effect.

Projection effects can be accomplished the same way, with the addition of sometimes bouncing the light for a softer look: film projection is bounced off a large screen, while television is a smaller direct source. Projection can also be simulated by running actual film through a projector and aiming it at the audience. Obviously it is necessary to defocus the projector or remove the lens so the image won't appear on the faces. One drawback of this method is that most film projectors are far too noisy to be recording dialog; if it's an MOS scene, this won't be a problem. As an alternate, the projector can be confined behind glass to reduce the noise level.

Day-for-Night

Day-for-night was an important technique when it was very difficult to actually shoot at night on location. With the advent of high-speed film and HD video cameras which can operate at very high ISOs, high-speed lenses, high-efficiency HMIs, and sunguns, day-for-night is not done as often. In black-and-white, infrared film can be used for night effects, generally in conjunction with a filter such as a Wratten #25 (Figure 16.15).

Traditionally, day-for-night is done at mid-day, since long shadows will give away the fact that it is day. Of course, showing the sky is strictly forbidden. In color (both film and video), it is possible to achieve a reasonably convincing effect by underexposing from 1-1/2 to 2-1/2 stops. Moonlight blue can be simulated by removing the 85 filter with tungsten balance film or white balancing the video camera for tungsten (see Figure 9.43 in the chapter *HD Cinematography*).

Harrison and Harrison makes a series of day-for-night filters. The #1 is blue-red; the blue gives the night effect, while the red component helps hold the skin tones in balance. The #2 is the same color but also lowers the contrast, which can help maintain the night illusion; the #3 filter offers a greater degree of contrast control. They have an exposure factor of 2 stops. In other parts of the world, day-for-night is often named for the place where it was presumably invented and is known as *American nigh:* in fact, the original European title of Francois Truffaut's film known in the United States as *Day For Night* is *La Nuit Américaine*.

Moonlight Effect

As you recall from our discussion of the Purkinje effect, it is a widely accepted convention that moonlight is blue. The use of blue for moonlight varies from cinematographer to cinematographer — some feel it is simply unrealistic, and people purists insist on using no more than 1/2 CTB for the effect. More common is full CTB or double blue. Of course, these are all in addition to whatever blue is used to establish basic color balance. Some people also add just a touch of lavender for a romantic look that is slightly more pleasing to the skin tone of the actors. As we saw in Figure 12.18 in the chapter *Color*, some DPs use more extreme effects, such as cyan.

Figure 16.12. A Mole *Beam Projecter* creates the sharp shadows of the blinds, but you wouldn't be able to see them without the smoke effect.

Figure 16.13. A multifunction flicker box. (Photo courtesy of McIntire Enterprises.)

Figure 16.14. (above) The *Thundervoltz* from Lightning Strikes provides portable power for 70K lightning effects. Undersizing your lighting effects units can be a serious mistake. (Photo courtesy of Lightning Strikes.)

Figure 16.15. (above, right) Day-for-night, such as this shot from *Yojimbo*, is much easier to achieve realistically in black-and-white.

Water EFX

The dapple of light reflected on water can be a beautiful and subtle effect. It can be achieved in a number of ways. Some people use broken mirrors or crumpled aluminum foil to reflect a strong directional light (usually a fresnel or a PAR). These tend to be somewhat stilted and artificial and rarely result in a convincing illusion. The best effect is always achieved by using actual water. In a shallow pan with a black backing water itself can be highly reflective if you use a strong enough unit.

Rain

Rain is the province of the prop department, but it does have implications for lighting. To be visible, rain must be backlit (Figure 16.16). Front lighting will not work with anything but the most intense downpours, and even then the result will be anemic. Even with the most carefully controlled rain effect, water gets everywhere. Several precautions are necessary:

- Raise all connectors, especially distribution connectors, off the ground on apple boxes. Wrap them in plastic and seal with tape. Use electrical tape as gaffers tape won't withstand water.
- Ground everything you can.
- Put rain hats on all lights. Protect the lenses of all large lights; water on a hot lens will shatter it with the possibility of glass flying out.
- Cover equipment racks and other spare equipment with heavy plastic.
- Crew members should wear insulating shoes and stand on rubber mats whenever working with electrical equipment.
- Observe all electrical safety rules religiously.

Most rain conditions (which includes real rain as well as rain towers) call for a camera umbrella, which is a large sturdy beach or patio-type umbrella and perhaps an aluminized space blanket or rain cover for the camera. Many HD cameras have purpose-built rain covers. Be sure that the filters are protected as well; rain drops on the filter or lens are very noticeable. For heavier water conditions, a rain deflector may be necessary. A rain deflector is a spinning round glass in front of the mirror. It rotates fast enough to spin the water off and keep the lens area clear. One caution: when used with a Steadicam or other type of free-floating rig, the spinning glass acts as a gyro and tends to pull the camera off course. There are other devices that blow either compressed air or nitrogen toward a clear filter to keep water off. The air or nitrogen must be supplied from tanks or pumps which can be bulky and awkward to work with.

Figure 16.16. Rain can never be effective unless it is backlit, as in this shot from *Nine and 1/2 Weeks*.

Lightning

Because lightning must be extremely powerful to be effective, it generally calls for a specially built rig. Nearly universal now is the use of machines from *Lightning Strikes* (Figure 16.14), which are basically incredibly powerful strobes. Included with them are a controller that can vary the timing and intensity of strikes to very accurately reproduce actual lightning. For further realism, several units should be used. Except when a storm is far away, actually lightning comes from several different angles. If a storm is approaching in the scene, a skilled operator will increase the intensity and frequency as the storm nears.

Some older lightning rigs were based on carbon arc technology. They consist of an arc ballast and a set of carbons that can be pushed together, then rapidly withdrawn with a levered handle. The resulting arc produces a powerful and momentary blast of light that is very convincing. A brute arc itself can be used by reversing the polarity of the DC so that it is "wrong" and then throwing the striking lever. The carbons will produce a brief, powerful arc but won't strike because the polarity is wrong. This technique still works but is seldom used anymore.

Understandably, these effects can be very hard on a generator, so be sure you have plenty of headroom before attempting these effects. Sometimes flashbulb rigs are used for the effect. Small flashbulb effects may be appropriate where lightning is only needed for one shot and rental of a dedicated unit would be impractical. M type flashbulbs, which have a long burn time, are most effective for this purpose. Regular flashbulbs fire very quickly, and they might burn while the shutter is closed, resulting in no exposure. The same is true of electronic flashes.

Gunshots

Gunshots are flashes of short enough duration that they might occur while the shutter is closed. The standard procedure is for the operator to watch for the flashes. If the operator sees them, then they did not get recorded on film. If the operator saw them, it means the flashes occurred while the mirror was reflecting the image to the viewfinder. Depending on how critical they are, another take may be necessary to make sure all the shots are recorded.

Several things can be done to alleviate this problem. There are prop guns that do not use gunpowder but instead use an electrical pulse coupled with a chemical charge to produce a flash. This has the added bonus of being much safer. More safety in itself is good, but it also means much less need for safety rigging, which can be a time-consuming process. Also, a licensed pyrotechnician/armorer and fire safety officer are not needed. These electronic guns also produce a longer-duration flash, which means fewer retakes.

There are also some systems that time the gunfire to the shutter, thus ensuring a good take nearly every time. The Rolls-Royce of such systems is Aaton TCGun, which has a timecode generator on each gun, jam-synced to the camera. In addition to locking the firing of each gun to the shutter, it can be rigged with a timecode controlled limiter that automatically drops the record level of a digital audio recorder for the duration of the gunshot. Very loud sudden noises such as gunshots actually drop out on digital recorders: the recorder is so overloaded that it actually produces a momentary blank spot on the tape instead of a very loud noise.

Safety with Guns

Guns should only be handled by a licensed pyrotechnician/armorer; in most places this is a legal requirement. The same applies to bullet hits planted on people, props, or the set. Bullet hits are small black powder charges and can be dangerous. If the gun is not firing in the shot, the armorer should open each gun, verify that it is empty, then show it to the actors and camera crew with the action open.

If firing of blanks is anywhere near toward the camera, a shield should be set by the grips to cover the camera, the operator, and the focus puller. This is usually done with Lexan, a clear polycarbonate that is optically smooth enough to shoot through but strong enough to protect the people, the lens, and the camera. This shield needs to be secured and bagged so that it won't get knocked over by an errant diving stunt person or a chair that gets kicked in the action. Great care must be taken by the grips, since the disadvantage of Lexan is that it scratches very easily.

Explosions

The same type of shield is necessary for small explosions, rockets, shattering glass, and so on. For small explosions, the camera crew also need to be protected from objects that get blown into the air.

For larger explosions, the camera should be either locked down and switched on remotely, or operated with a remote-control head and video assist. In this case, either very heavy duty crash boxes are needed or expendable cameras. Explosions are usually filmed with multiple cameras at various frame rates; at least one or more of the cameras will be run a high frame rate — often up to 250 fps or more. HMI PARs are available in explosion-proof housings. This does not mean that they are completely impervious to explosions; it just means that they are sealed so that it will not cause an explosion.

TIME-LAPSE PHOTOGRAPHY

Time lapse is usually done with an intervalometer — an electronic device that controls the timing and duration of each exposure. The *Norris Intervalometer* starts at an exposure of 1/16 of a second and gets longer from there. There are also computer and iPhone/iPad apps that will drive a connected camera and function as an intervalometer. The interval between exposures can be anywhere from a fraction of a second up to several hours or even days apart.

With longer exposure you get not only a time-lapse effect but may also get blurring of the subject. This can be strongly visual with subjects such as car lights or moving clouds or a rushing stream. One issue with time-lapse shots is that the exposure may change radically during the shot, especially if it is night-into-day or day-into-

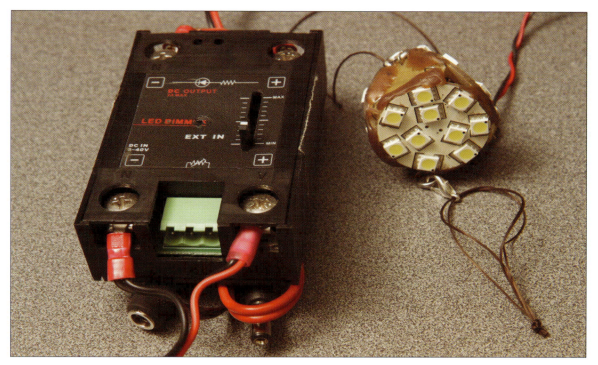

Figure 16.17. An on-the-set lighting effect (called a *gag*) such as this will often be executed by the lighting department. This one, a glowing ball of light for *The Sorcerer's Apprentice*, was designed by Michael Gallart and executed by the legendary Billmo. It consists of a three-faced cluster of LEDs powered from a 12 volt DC source, run through an LED dimmer. It is shown in use in Figure 16.18.

night, or if heavy clouds move in during the shot. This can be controlled with a timing device, or it may be necessary to stand by and do exposure changes manually. If you don't want the depth-of-field to change during the shot, you may want to add or subtract ND filters or alter the shutter setting. Also, with long intervals between exposures, it is possible for enough light to leak around the normal camera shutter to fog frames. An additional shutter, known as a capping shutter, is added to prevent this. Capping shutters are available from the same places that supply intervalometers. The *Steele Chart by Lance Steel Rieck* (Table 16.6) shows screen time versus event duration for time-lapse photography.

TIME SLICING

This is the effect that was popularized in a series of Gap ads and most famously in the film *The Matrix*. This is the effect where a character is suddenly frozen but the camera dollies around the figure or the object. This effect is accomplished with an array of 35mm still cameras arranged around the subject. A regular film camera is part of the array. At the moment of freezing the action, the entire circle of still cameras is fired. These still photos are then scanned and blended together to form a film shot (Figure 16.1).

Visualize it this way: imagine a film camera on a mount that can be dollied around the subject instantaneously, let's say 90°, with the film running at very high speed. Since the dolly is instant, it "sees" the subject from all points around that arc before the subject can move. This is what the still cameras do: they see the subject from as many points of view as you wish — all at the same time. In practice, the subject is often placed on greenscreen and then the green background is replaced with live-action footage of the original scene, usually matching the dolly action simulated by the still array. The result is a dolly around a live action scene with a frozen subject in the middle. The still cameras can be arranged in any type of move imaginable; the effect is not restricted to a dolly around.

Figure 16.18. The lighting effect shown in Figure 16.17. In use on the set, the wire will be hidden by wardrobe.

SUN LOCATION WITH A COMPASS

For shots involving the sun or the moon three things are necessary: the correct position of the celestial object at the time you want to shoot, a good compass and, geomagnetic declination information for the shooting locations.

First a word about compasses. You need a good one. Any compass will point to magnetic north, but you need one that is calibrated to at least 2° and that can be aligned precisely. This will usually mean either a compass with an optical sight or a military-style lensatic compass. Particularly for shooting sunrises, great precision is necessary. Perhaps the least-known fact about compasses is that they do not necessarily work equally well in all parts of the world. Compasses are manufactured with a certain amount of counterweighting and the proper amount of magnetizing to match certain locations, specifically north and south latitudes. A compass designed for the United States, as it nears the pole region, will increasingly begin to point into the earth. You'll have to hold the compass housing unevenly to get any kind of reading at all. All the needle wants to do is point into the ground, not to the horizon. So if you are going to locations significantly different in latitude from where you bought your compass, be sure to get a unit made for that area. Most compass manufacturers offer solutions to this problem. Silva, a Swedish manufacture of compasses, offers five varieties:

MN	Magnetic North
NME	North Magnetic Equatorial
ME	Magnetic Equatorial
SME	South Magnetic Equatorial
MS	Magnetic South

Suunto makes the *World Compass* that can be used anywhere in the world. The compass works by having the needle and the magnet pivot independently, thus allowing it to compensate for the changing vertical direction of magnetic north. Many GPS apps can also be used for north location. Be sure to distinguish whether a device is giving you true north or magnetic north, which needs correction for declination.

THE STEELE CHART
TIME COMPRESSION/INTERVALOMETER

SCREEN TIMES	1S	2S	5S	10S	15S	20S	30S	1M	2M	5M	10M	20M
FRAMES	24	48	120	240	360	480	720	1440	2880	7200	14400	28800
INTERVAL	EVENT DURATION											
12Frm/Sec	2S	4S	10S	20S	30S	40S	1M	2M	4M	10M	20M	40M
8Frm/Sec	3S	6S	15S	30S	45S	1M	90S	3M	6M	15M	30M	1H
6Frm/Sec	4S	8S	20S	40S	1M	80S	2M	4M	8M	20M	40M	80M
4Frm/Sec	6S	12S	30S	1M	90S	2M	3M	6M	12M	30M	1H	2H
3Frm/Sec	8S	16S	40S	80S	2M	2M 40S	4M	8M	16M	40M	80M	2H 40M
2Frm/Sec	12S	24S	1M	2M	3M	4M	6M	12M	24M	1H	2H	4M
1Frm/Sec	24S	48S	2M	4M	6M	8M	12M	24M	48M	2H	4H	8H
2Sec/Frm	48S	96S	4M	8M	12M	16M	24M	48M	96M	4H	8H	16H
3Sec/Frm	72S	2M 24S	6M	12M	18M	24M	36M	72M	2H 24M	6H	12H	24H
4Sec/Frm	96S	3M 12S	8M	16M	24M	32M	48M	96M	3H 12M	8H	16H	32H
5Sec/Frm	2M	4M	10M	20M	30M	40M	1H	2H	4H	10H	20H	40H
8Sec/Frm	3M 125	6M 24S	16M	32M	48M	64M	96M	3H 12M	6H 24M	16H	32H	2D 16H
10Sec/Frm	4M	8M	20M	40M	1H	80M	2H	4H	8H	20H	40H	3D 8H
15Sec/Frm	6M	12M	30M	1H	90M	2H	3H	6H	12H	30H	2D 12H	5D
20Sec/Frm	8M	16M	40M	80M	2H	2H 40M	4H	8H	16H	40H	3D 8H	6D 16H
30Sec/Frm	12M	24M	1H	2H	3H	4H	6H	12H	24H	2D 12H	5D	10D
1Min/Frm	24M	48M	2H	4H	6H	8H	12H	24H	2D	5D	10D	20D
2Min/Frm	48M	96M	4H	8H	12H	16H	24H	2D	4D	10D	20D	40D
5Min/Frm	2H	4H	10H	20H	30H	40H	2D 12H	5D	10D	25D	50D	100D

STEP 1: Decide how long you want the event to last on screen
STEP 2: Decide how long you want to film the event in real time.
STEP 3: Set interval according to data in the far left column.

NOTE: This chart is a guideline only. If the specific numbers you're looking for are not on the chart, you can use the chart to "guess-timate" by finding the closest corresponding numbers.

© The Steel Chart, Lance Steele Rieck, 1997

EXAMPLE: The DP wants 15 seconds time-lapse footage of clouds passing. You have six hours to film. First, look under SCREEN TIME for "15S". Follow column down till you find "6H" or six hours. Follow row to the far left INTERVAL column where you will find the interval: 1Min/Frm.

FORMULA: Event duration in seconds divided by screen time in frames equals the interval.

Declination

There is one more problem to be dealt with in using a compass. Only at 2 north/south lines in the northern hemisphere does the compass needle point to true north. One is through Russia, and the other goes through Wisconsin to Alabama and south. These are called the *agonic lines*. At all other places on the globe, the compass will either point slightly East or West of the actual geographical true north. The angle by which it is off is called *magnetic variation* or *declination*. Magnetic north is located about 1000 miles south of geographic north, near Bathurst Island, off the northern coast of Canada above Hudson Bay. In the continental United States, this angle of error varies from 25° east, to about 23° west of true north. Alaska's declination ranges from 15° east to 36° east. If you are west of the agonic line, you subtract the declination. If you are east of the agonic line you add the declination. For even more accurate and localized information, you can always call the local airport's flight control center, 24 hours a day. On remote locations, it may be necessary to obtain good-qual-

Table 16.6. The *Steele chart* for calculating time-lapse shots. (Courtesy of Lance Steele Rieck.)

Los Angeles, California

Latitude 34° 03' N
Longitude 118° 14' W
Magnetic Declination 14° E

N

Time Zone: 8 Pacific
Daylight Savings Time
(4/ 1/01 to 10/28/01)

Azimuth Bearings are given for MAGNETIC NORTH. DO NOT make a correction with your compass.
The Magnetic Declination has been used in the calculations.

	Date	Dawn	SUNRISE	Azimuth	Day Length	SUNSET	Azimuth	Dusk
Wed	10/24/01	6:48 AM	7:05 AM	90°	11:03	6:08 PM	242°	6:25 PM

———— **Wednesday, October 24, 2001** ————

15 minute intervals

AZ°- Azimuth ALT°- Altitude

	AZ°	ALT°	Sf°		AZ°	ALT°	Sf°		AZ°	ALT°	Sf°		AZ°	ALT°	Sf°		AZ°	ALT°	Sf°
7AM	89	-1	---		113	26	2.05	12PM	154	43	1.07		201	37	1.33	5PM	232	13	4.33
	91	1	57.3		117	28	1.88		159	44	1.04		205	35	1.43		234	10	5.67
	93	4	14.3	10AM	120	31	1.66		164	44	1.04	3PM	209	33	1.54		237	7	8.14
	95	7	8.14		123	33	1.54		169	44	1.04		212	31	1.66		239	4	14.3
8AM	98	10	5.67		127	35	1.43	1PM	174	44	1.04		216	28	1.88	6PM	241	1	57.3
	100	13	4.33		131	37	1.33		179	43	1.07		219	26	2.05		243	-1	---
	102	16	3.49	11AM	135	39	1.23		184	42	1.11	4PM	222	23	2.36		245	-4	---
	105	18	3.08		139	40	1.19		188	41	1.15		224	21	2.60				
9AM	108	21	2.60		144	41	1.15	2PM	193	40	1.19		227	18	3.08				
	111	24	2.25		149	42	1.11		197	38	1.28		230	15	3.73				

* Shadow Length = Object Height x Shadow Factor (Sf)

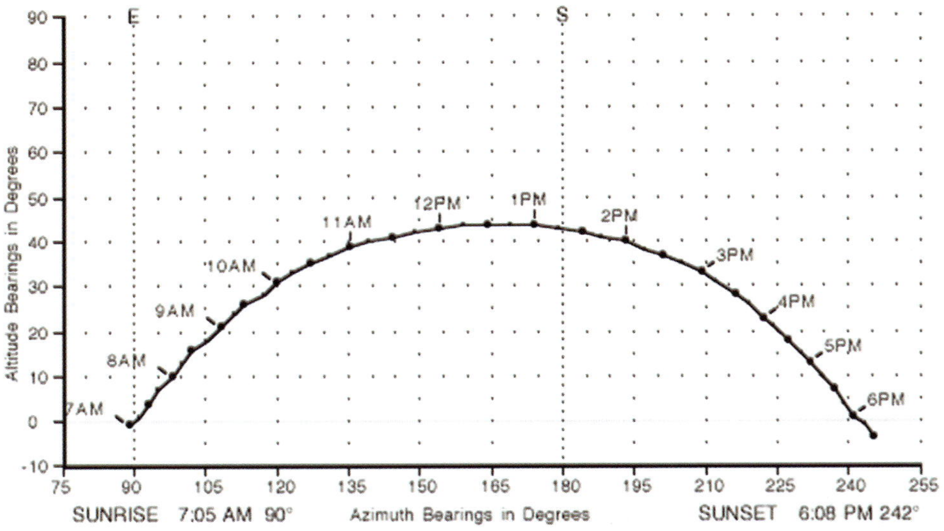

Altitude Bearings in Degrees

E S

12PM 1PM 11AM 2PM 3PM 10AM 4PM 9AM 5PM 8AM 6PM 7AM

SUNRISE 7:05 AM 90°   Azimuth Bearings in Degrees   SUNSET 6:08 PM 242°

sunPATH™ © 1995 David Parrish   Wide Screen Software™ USA: (818) 764-3639   Licensed to BLAIN BROWN

Figure 16.19. A sun path chart for a particular day produced by Sun-PATH® software; there are many smartphone and notepad apps that perform the same function.

ity maps for the area and to use a GPS locator to determine exact latitude and longitude. You now need the information for the sun or moon. You need to know its azimuth (compass direction) and altitude (angle above the horizon) at any particular point in time. The example in Figure 16.19 is from a sun location application; several smartphone apps will also provide more this information.

This type of software can also determine the length of shadows, where shadows will fall or as a guide in building a set or placing a window so that a particular sunlight effect will occur on a certain date. To do these calculations, you will also need an inclinometer, which measures vertical angles.

TRANSFERRING FILM TO VIDEO

When transferring 24 fps film to video at 29.97 fps, there is a mismatch of speed that must be corrected. Interlaced video has 60 fields/second (2 fields per frame), so five fields take 5/60 second = 1/12 second time, which is exactly the amount it takes for a film to show two frames. The solution to the problem is that each frame of film is not transferred to a corresponding frame of video.

The first film frame is transferred to 3 video fields. Next, the second film frame is transferred to 2 video fields. The total time for the original film should be 2/24s = 1/12s, which is exactly the same it took for NTSC to transfer the same frames (3/30s + 2/60s = 5/60s = 1/12s). This process alternates for successive frames.

This is called 3-to-2 pulldown, usually written as 3:2 pulldown. The problem with this is that every other film frame is shown for 1/20 of a second, while every other is shown for 1/30 of a second. This makes pans look less smooth than what they did in the movie theater. Film shot at 25 fps does not require this process.

Prepping for Telecine

A great deal of film that is shot now goes from the processing lab to a telecine house, where it is transferred directly to video. Transferring film to video is called telecine or film-to-tape transfer. At the same time it is being transferred, *color grading* (also called *color timing*) will usually occur, either preliminary grading for dailies or final grading for the release print. During the grading process, the colorist can adjust exposure, contrast, and both primary and secondary colors with a high degree of accuracy. They can also use what is called *power windows* to make adjustments only in a particular area of the picture; some systems are capable of many simultaneous power windows, which can also track with picture elements as they move.

Color grading for a DI (digital intermediate) is a similar process. Even features intended for theatrical release are telecined for non-linear editing and for video dailies. It is important to follow the correct steps to prepare for telecine. Failure to do so may cost the producer extra, which is not good for job security.

- For anything out of the ordinary: unusual color balances, off-speed shooting, and so on, confer with the telecine house first.
- Transfer rates other than 24-30 fps may not be available at all telecine houses — check before you shoot.
- Shoot a properly exposed gray card, especially for dailies where you will not be present for the transfer.
- Communicate with the telecine operator. A phone call or notes on the camera reports are important. Some DPs send a digital photo that they have manipulated in *Photoshop* or other imaging software.
- On the set grading software is available that allows the DP to send an actual color correction file for each scene and to create LUTs.
- Full and accurate camera reports. This is especially important if you are shooting at an off-speed frame rate, and want the footage transferred at that rate.
- Write it on the slate. Slates have spaces to record if the shot is day or night, interior or exterior, frame rate and other data.
- Make sure the slate is in focus and lit to be readable. This also applies to framing charts and any test or calibration charts.
- Mark the camera reports as *Prep for telecine*. When this is

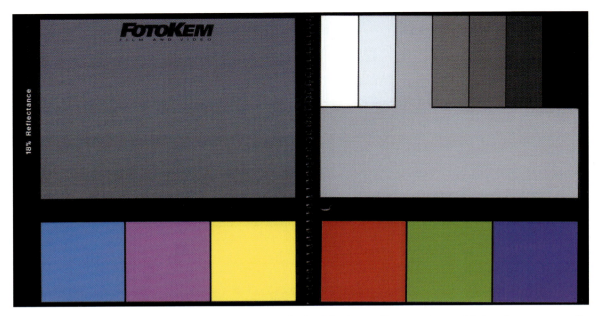

Figure 16.20. A grayscale and color chart and grayscale. (Photo courtesy of FotoKem Film and Video.)

requested, the lab cleans the negative and joins the camera rolls into lab rolls no larger than 1200 feet with 6 feet of leader on each end. Most transfer facilities can perform these functions, but at a much higher hourly rate.

- In some cases, editors may request hole punches at the head and tail of each camera roll and a *KeyKode* log. KeyKode is a written log recording the first and last KeyKode number for each camera roll within a lab roll. It is prepared by the lab during negative assembly to check the accuracy of the *Flex file* (a computer file database).
- Use correct slating procedures (see chapter on *Set Operations*).
- Shoot a framing chart and communicate to the colorist what framing you are shooting. This is especially important with formats such as Super 35. Be sure that the framing chart agrees with your ground glass and also that all the ground glasses on your shoot agree.

Shooting a Gray Card Reference

Using a *gray card* applies to both film finish and to film transferred to video. It is discussed here in relation to telecine and adjusting exposure on the waveform monitor and color on the vectorscope, but lighting and shooting are the same for both situations. In video, a gray card may be used as discussed in the chapter *HD Cinematography*; the gray card is useful in video for setting *color balance* (usually called *white balance*) because a photographic gray card is far more reliably neutral than a piece of white paper or a white wall or anything that *seems* white but has not been calibrated.

Getting What You Want in Telecine

You should always insist on being present for the film-to-tape or tape-to-tape transfer. It is really the cinematographers right to be present and have input for all transfers: it is their work and reputation that is at stake and they are mostly likely those with the knowledge and experience to make sure it gets done properly. This is where the real grading decisions will be made; just as they used to be made by sitting in a screening room with the film timer.

Kodak Gray Card Plus

Kodak makes the *Gray Card Plus*. In addition to a standard gray card, the dark patches reflect 3% and the light patches have 90% reflectance. Why 20 IRE instead of 7.5 for the dark patches and 80 IRE instead of 100 for the light patches, which are the actual standard values Kodak recommends for transfer?

The values that are used were chosen to be slightly above the toe and just below the shoulder of the contrast curve. This makes them less susceptible to variations in the film stock. Emulsions tend to differ more in the toe and shoulder areas than they do in the straight-line portion of the characteristic curve.

Also, a solid black and a pure white would narrow the threshold of adjustment on a wave-form monitor. It is difficult to set a pure black-and-white reference precisely at 7.5 and 100 IRE, respectively, when you're operating low on the toe and high on the shoulder. There's also the effect of lens flair to consider with only a solid black bottom reference. Even though the finish of the card (as is true of most high-quality gray cards) is as matte as possible, there is always going to be the possibility of some slight glare. The biggest problem with any gray card reference is the way it's shot. With uneven lighting or glare on the card it can't serve as an accurate reference.

A gray card should be lit specifically as a grading reference or as an exposure reference. For example, suppose you are lighting a scene with the key as moonlight blue — which you intend to be very dark and shadowy. If you then place the gray card in this moonlight blue and shoot it, the colorist or film timer would have no choice but to make the card *neutral gray* as it is supposed to be. This would be done by taking out all of the blue and raising the exposure to lighten it up: everything you have done with the lighting would be erased. This is a key point that crews sometimes don't understand or forget.

The ideal situation is to light the gray card (or gray scale or color chart) so that the exposure on it is exactly the same as the stop at which you are going to shoot the scene but this may not always be possible. If you are able to light the card it becomes a two-step procedure. Shoot the gray card as outlined above. Move the gray card and shoot a few seconds of the scene as you have it lit — color gels, camera filters back in, and so on. This gives the colorist not only a neutral reference, but it also shows the scene in relation to that neutral reference. It is mostly psychological — a way of showing the timer; "Yes, I really meant for it to look that way." This can sometimes be a struggle because telecine colorists for dailies (when you're not there) tend to make things neutral. There are advantages to making the transfer neutral: it gives you more flexibility for later corrections in the computer or in a tape-to-tape transfer of the final edited project; you may choose to transfer neutral if that suits your workflow. However, if you have decided to create your look in the camera, it is important that the dailies reflect what you are trying to do with the lighting, contrast, color balance, and effects.

The proper way to shoot a gray card reference is as follows. For a tungsten-lit scene, position the gray card so it fills all or most of the frame. Have your gaffer light it with a unit that is as near to pure 3200° Kelvin as possible. Make sure there are no filters on the light and it is not on a dimmer, which might change the color temperature. The light should cover the card as evenly as possible; this may be possible with a single light, but an ideal situation is to light it with two units, one on either side at roughly a 45° angle — the same distance from the card and at the same degree of flood/spot. No other

Figure 16.21. The *Kodak Gray Card Plus*. The light and dark patches are not pure black-and-white. The light patch is 90% reflectance and the dark patch is 3% reflectance. This assists the telecine colorist in setting the white and black points in the transfer.

Figure 16.22. Framing chart for video, film 1.85, and High Def.

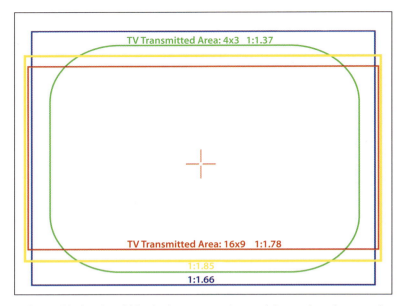

colors of light should be leaking onto the card from elsewhere in the scene. Remove any effects filters you have on the camera. Meter the gray card without regard to your metering of the scene; shooting the card is entirely separate from how you will shoot the scene. Be as precise as possible with your exposure of the card.

If you are shooting daylight balance, follow all of the above instructions, but make sure your grayscale lighting is 5500° Kelvin. When working with a less sophisticated director who doesn't fully understand the process, they can get the impression that they are not getting the look they were hoping for. Both for you and the director, it is important to be able to judge if everything is turning out like you had planned it would. This is similar to shooting RAW HD video: there is no *look* in RAW — it records only what hits the sensors, nothing else. This is the reason we use LUTs (*Lookup Tables*) to change the look of the picture on the monitors (see *Technical Issues*).

Framing Charts

Another part of your vision that you need to protect with references is the framing. Without a reference on the film, the telecine colorist has no way of knowing for certain what your exact framing is. Remember that the colorist can move the frame up/down, left/right, and zoom in or out over the entire area of the negative or positive frame. A framing chart is something the telecine colorist can copy to the frame store and quickly call it up. Figure 16.22 is a typical framing chart.

film formats

Figure 17.1. (previous page) An Imax frame from *The Dark Knight*.

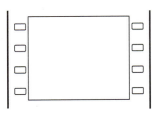

Figure 17.2. Full aperture
Aspect ratio: 1.319:1
.980" x 735"
.72 sq. in
25mm x 18.7mm
464.5 sq. mm

Figure 17.3. Academy aperture
Aspect ratio: 1.37:1
.864" x .63"
.544 sq. in
21.95mm x 18.6mm
351.2 sq. mm

Figure 17.4. Aspect ratio: 1:66:1
.864" x .63"
.544 sq. in.
21.95mm x 16mm
31.2 sq. mm

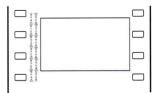

Figure 17.5. Aspect ratio: 1:85:1
.864" x .469"
.405 sq. in.
21.95mm x 16mm
351.2 sq. mm

ASPECT RATIOS

Before the introduction of sound, the entire width of the film was exposed. This is called full aperture or silent aperture. It is still used today for formats such as Super35 (see the following). The format is essentially what was developed in the Edison labs at the very invention of motion picture film, now called full aperture (Figure 17.2).

Academy Aperture

With the introduction of sync sound, the Academy aperture was created in 1932 to allow space for the optical soundtrack. With the introduction of sound, room had to be made for the optical track. To do this, the size of the aperture was reduced. This was called the Academy aperture (Figure 17.3).

1.66:1 and 1.85:1

The next step in the evolution was the wider *1.66* frame. After the wide-screen craze of the fifties, there was a need for a wider format that did not call for special cameras or wide-screen projection equipment. The response to this was the introduction of the *1.85:1* aspect ratio. In the United States this is still a very common format for anything going to theatrical projection. Anything wider is considered widescreen (Figure 17.4). When shot for television and standard video release, the 1.33 aspect ratio is used.

WIDE SCREEN

For true widescreen, anamorphic lenses *squeeze* the image onto 35mm film. In projection, the image is then *unsqueezed* to provide an image wider than standard 1.85. On the camera negative, the aspect ratio is 1.18:1. When unsqueezed, the aspect ratio in projection is generally 2.35:1.

Anamorphic

Anamorphic photography was invented in France in 1927. A special lens was suspended in front of the prime lens that compressed the image horizontally to one-half its width, then unsqueezed it again when projected. The horizontal compression was eventually engineered into the prime lens itself so an additional optic in front of the lens was no longer necessary. Several versions of this system are in use today, and most major lens manufacturers also make high-quality anamorphic lens sets (Figure 17.6).

Vistavision

VistaVision runs standard 35mm film horizontally (Figure 17.7). Each frame spans 8 perforations, twice the area of a regular frame. It is still in common use, especially for any kind of special effects or plate work. The reason it is used for this type of work is that something that is shot for a background plate or as part of a special effects piece will likely go through several stages of optical printing or perhaps digitizing. The larger format prevents the build up of excessive grain and loss of resolution. 70mm is also used for plate work on films for which the production format is 35mm.

IMAX

Currently the largest projection format is Imax, which is 70mm film run through the camera and projector sideways, similar to VistaVision. This results in a negative roughly the size of that produced by a 2-1/4 still camera (Figure 17.7). This extremely large negative allows for projection screens up to five stories high. Omnimax is a variation which employs a curved screen and anamorphic lens.

Alternatives to Anamorphic

There are many problems with anamorphic photography. First, anamorphic lenses are never as fast as standard spherical lenses. Secondly, because of the squeeze, the depth-of-field is 1/2 of that for the same image size. Both of these conditions mean that more lighting is required for anamorphic photography, which can be a problem in terms of time and budget.

All of the following formats are a response to the same problem: film is locked into a relatively square aspect ratio and has been since the days of Edison. On the other hand, film production has tended toward more rectangular wider aspect ratios. This means that the shooting aspect ratio is being shot on cameras that are not really suited for it. These adaptations are ways to address this problem.

Super35

One method to answer these problems is *Super35*. The basic concept of Super35 is to use the entire width of the negative: the aperture originally used in silent films (Figures 17.11 through 17.14).

From this full-width negative, a widescreen image is extracted. This is done with an optical print. This optical step is necessary to slightly reduce the image to leave room for the sound track and to squeeze it for anamorphic projection. Although the resulting image is not the full aperture, the original negative uses more of the available space. This is necessary because there is still a need for a sound track. Even though several alternatives have been developed to substitute for the sound track on film, including digital audio, because these systems are not universal, it is usually necessary to give back that audio track space on the side. The Univision format, discussed later, also relies on eliminating audio track.

Common Topline

For the DP, the director and especially for the operator, one of the greatest advantages of Super35 is that a common topline can be used. Because 4:3 video is more square, the top of video is always higher than the top of the widescreen format. As a result, it is necessary to frame for two formats at the same time. This is difficult at best and it is always a compromise. Since the Super35 format is extracted from the film in an optical process, there is the freedom to extract any part of the negative you like. Thus, the top of the video frame can be the same as top of the widescreen frame, thereby reducing the need to compromise the format.

Having a common top is most important, as the information in the upper part of the frame is nearly always more important than the lower part of the frame. Cutting a character off at the belt instead of across the chest usually makes no difference, whereas cutting off the top of the head can be very awkward. The fact that the sides of the frame are different is still inescapable and will remain so until widescreen TV becomes a standard.

The drawbacks of Super35 are the additional cost of the optical print and the slight increase in grain and contrast due to this extra step. However, with the recent improvements in film stock, these are now quite acceptable. Many major films have been shot in Super35. Nearly all cameras in use today have their optical axis centered on the Academy aperture. As a result they are not centered on the full negative. For Super35, the lens mount must be repositioned by 1mm to re-center it on the full aperture. Only lenses that cover the full area of the negative can be used. The ability to use standard spheri-

Figure 17.6. Anamorphic
Aspect ratio: 1.18:1
.864" x .732"
.633 sq. in.
21.95mm x 18.6 mm
408.27 sq. mm

Figure 17.7. Vistavision frame
Aspect ratio: 1.5:1
1.485" x .991"
1.472 sq. in.
37.72mm x 25.17mm
949.7 sq. mm

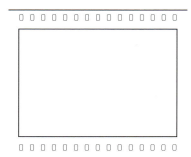

Figure 17.8. The Imax negative is a 15 perf image on 70mm film stock. It runs horizontally, like Vistavision.
Aspect ratio: 1.43:1
2.740" x 1.910"
5.24 sq. in.
70mm x 48.5mm
3430 sq. mm

Figure 17.9. A 2.20:1 widescreen aspect ratio on *Blade Runner*. The wide format allows for a graphic use of negative space and an off-balance frame.

cal lenses and the lessened requirement for lighting and schedule may offset the cost of the optical print.

Once the Super35 full aperture is shot, any number of formats can be extracted from it. Except in unusual cases, a hard matte would not be used to mask the negative. These illustrations demonstrate what would happen in the post-production process, not what happens in the camera. This is one of the beauties of this process: a single negative can be used for many different formats. See the ground glass chart for some of the combinations of Super35 and other formats (Figure 17.16).

If the film is going directly to video, there is no reason to waste film for an optical sound track. In this case, it is possible to use Super35 as it is. This is sometimes called *Super TV*.

3-PERF

All of the above methods are adaptations that deal with one basic built-in drawback of 35mm film; one that goes back to it's very invention. Since its inception, 35mm has been advanced by 4 perforations for each frame. Unlike the aperture gate, this is not something that is easily changed. Worldwide, there are tens of thousands of cameras, optical printers, lab equipment, telecines, and theater projectors that are based on this system (Figure 17.10). Some systems advance the film by three perforations for each frame. Specially modified cameras must be used for this process.

Since it would be impossible to change the entire world system to suit this, the 3-perf negative is converted at some stage to 4 perf. The original advantages in shooting remain. If the project is going directly to video, then it is not a problem, except that the telecine must be suited to this process. Arriflex can now make any of their cameras available in 3-perf formats. 3-perf systems have the advantage of using less film stock and longer running times out of each mag. Many television shows shot on film use 3-perf. It is also popular on features with a limited budget.

2-PERF TECHNISCOPE

Invented by Technicolor Rome, *Techniscope* is a 2-perf format for very wide screen but with half the film stock usage of normal 35mm. It was used on Sergio Leone on many of his films. This is a popular format again and with the greatly improved film stocks now available, excessive grain is not as much of a problem.

Figure 17.10. 65mm 5 Perf

Aspect ratio: 2.28:1

2.066″ x .906″ - 1.872 sq. in.

54.48mm x 23.01mm - 1207.58 sq. mm

UNIVISION

Another variation of 3-perf was developed by legendary cinematographer Vittorio Storaro in collaboration with his son. It is called *Univision* (sometimes spelled *Univisium*). Storaro's conclusion was that too much film is being wasted between frames; also, many soundtracks are not optical anymore. In his articles and interviews, Storaro makes a convincing argument for this format as more flexible and universal. Univision as he proposes it has a frame aspect ratio of 2:1.

The following are some of Storaro's observations on this format: in normal widescreen film for theatrical release filmed in 1:1.85, there is a lot of wastage in camera negative. With Univision's 1:2 aspect ratio and digital sound (the sound track not on the film itself), using

Figure 17.11. Super TV
Aspect ratio: 1.33:1
.945" x .709"
.67 sq. in.
24mm x18 mm
432 Sq. mm

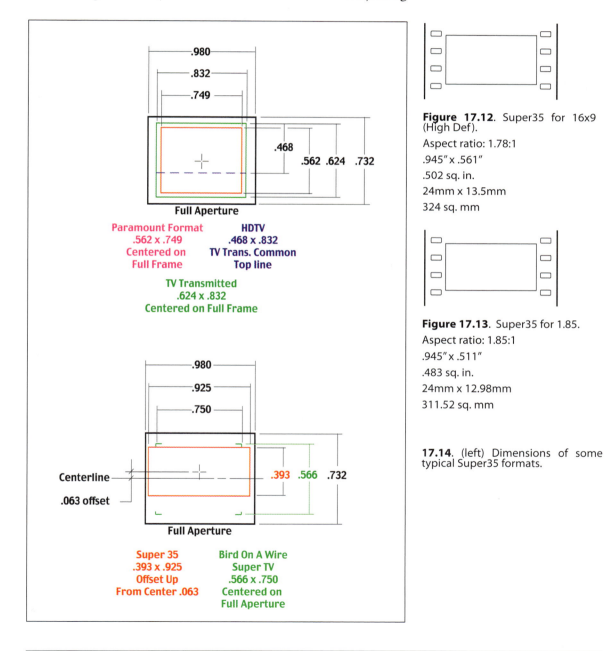

Figure 17.12. Super35 for 16x9 (High Def).
Aspect ratio: 1.78:1
.945" x .561"
.502 sq. in.
24mm x 13.5mm
324 sq. mm

Figure 17.13. Super35 for 1.85.
Aspect ratio: 1.85:1
.945" x .511"
.483 sq. in.
24mm x 12.98mm
311.52 sq. mm

17.14. (left) Dimensions of some typical Super35 formats.

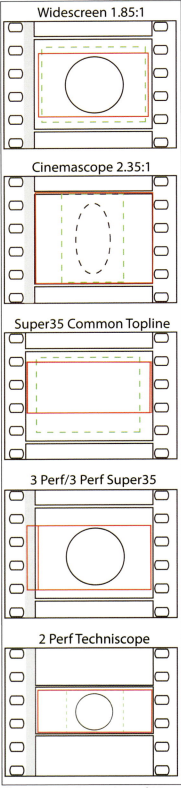

Widescreen 1.85:1

Cinemascope 2.35:1

Super35 Common Topline

3 Perf/3 Perf Super35

2 Perf Techniscope

Figure 17.15. Comparison of 35mm film frame formats. (Courtesy of Fotokem)

only three perforations per frame on the 35mm negative and the positive, it is possible to have:

- 25% saved on camera negative, with absolutely no compromise in the quality of the image. It actually increases the average quality of any panoramic and anamorphic picture.
- 25% more shooting time in the camera magazine; less frequent mag changes.
- Quieter running cameras because less film is moved through them.
- No need for anamorphic lenses on cameras and projectors.
- No distortion of horizontal and vertical lines due to the use of anamorphic lenses.
- Greater depth-of-field due to not using anamorphic lenses.
- Less lighting required because of spherical lenses.
- No use of anamorphic lenses.

16MM

16mm is considerably simpler; there are two basic formats — *regular 16* and *Super 16,* but it is possible to extract different aspect ratios in telecine. Super 16 currently enjoys enormous popularity. It can be easily blown up to a 35mm projection print and it transfers with little or no compromise to widescreen video such as High Def. Many companies are using Super 16mm as a way of protecting for future release of their production in widescreen HDTV — the aspect ratios are very similar, which makes transfer simple.

Standard 16 transfers easily to 4:3 video. With the improved film stocks and digital postproduction, the quality of a film originated on 16mm can be surprisingly good.

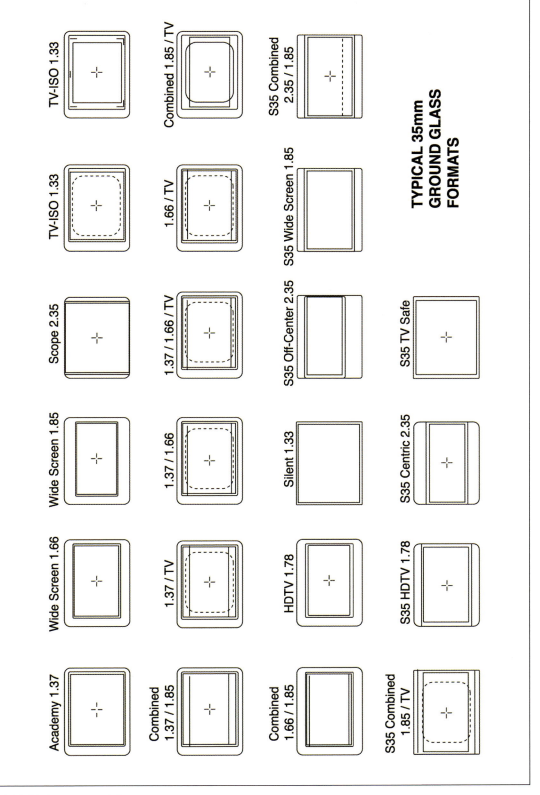

Figure 17.16. Various groundglass markings for 35mm film formats.

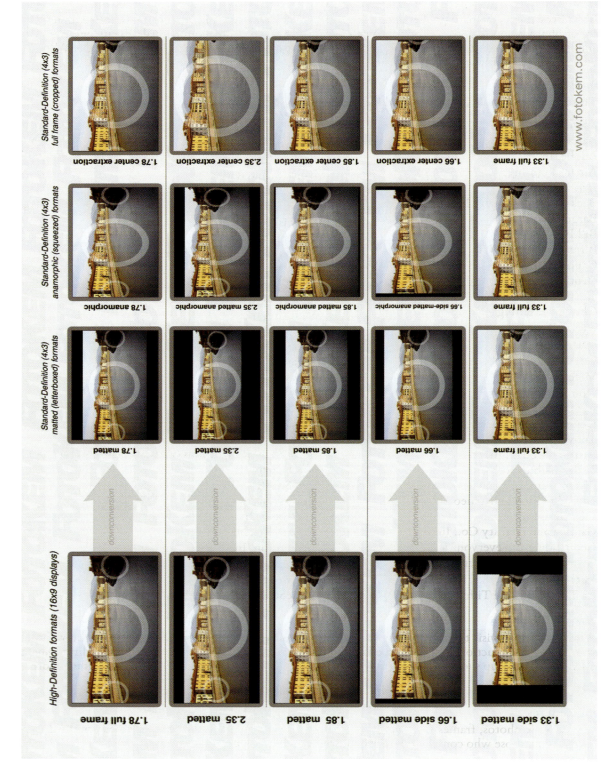

Figure 17.17. A graphic comparison of 35mm formats by Fotokem. The circles help illustrate if there is any anamorphic squeezing. (Courtesy of Fotokem.)

the author

Blain Brown is a cinematographer and writer/director based in Los Angeles. He has been the director of photography, director, producer, writer, and editor on features, commercials, documentaries, and music videos on all types of formats from 35mm and 16mm film to digital and High Def 24P video. He can be reached at www.BlainBrown.com.

dedication

This book is dedicated to my wife and inspiration, Ada Pullini Brown.

acknowledgments

Aaton, s.a.
Adobe, Inc.
Airstar Lighting, Inc.
Arri Group
Backstage Equipment, Inc.
Barger Bag Lights
Bill Burke
Birns and Sawyer, Inc.
Canon, USA
Century Precision Optics, Inc.
Chapman/Leonard Studio Equipment
Chimera Lighting
Harriet Cox
Tom Denove
Larry Engle
Michael Gallart
Don Lamasone
David Mullen
Derry Museum, Derry, England
Tony Nako
Eastman Kodak, Inc.
Fisher Light, Inc.
Flying Cam, Inc.
FotoKem Film and Video
Fuji Film, Ltd.
Gamma and Density Co., Inc.
Geoff Boyle and everyone at CML
Great American Market (GAM)
Michael Hofstein
Ira Tiffen and The Tiffen Company

Kino-Flo, Inc.
Keslow Camera
Lance Steele Rieck
Lee Filters
Brady Lewis
J.L. Fisher, Inc.
Lightning Strikes, Inc.
Lowell-Light Manufacturing, Inc.
Mark Weingartner
Mark Wood
Matthews Studio Equipment Corp.
McIntire, Inc.
Larry Mole Parker, Mole-Richardson Co., Inc.
Panasonic, Inc.
Panavision, Inc.
PAWS, Inc.
Photo-Sonics, Inc.
Rosco Laboratories, Inc.
San Luigi dei Francesi, Rome.
Schneider Optical, Inc.
Steve Shaw at Light Illusion (www.lightillusion.com)
Sony Corp.
Phil South
Sunray, Inc.
Tektronix, Inc.
Renato Tonelli
Ultravision, Inc.
Ultimatte, Inc.
Wade Ramsey
WideScreen Software, Inc.

about the website

Please be sure to visit the companion website for *Cinematography: Theory and Practice*. On the website, you will find instructional videos and examples of techniques discussed in this book, including camera essentials, setting up shots, scene shooting methods, lighting techniques, a day on set, and much more.

www.focalpress.com/9780240812090

illustrations

Illustrations, photos, frames from films and page design are by the author except where credited. My thanks to all those who contributed to the illustrations and instructional videos.

bibliography

Adams, Ansel. *The Negative*. Little, Brown & Co. 1983

ASC, Rod Ryan. *American Cinematographer Manual*. ASC Press, 2000.

Arnheim, Rudolf. *Art and Visual Perception*. University of California Press. 1954
    Film as Art. University of California Press. 1957
    Visual Thinking. University of California Press. 1969
    The Power of the Center. University of California Press. 1982

Barclay, Steven. *The Motion Picture Image: From Film to Digital*. Focal Press. 2000

Bellatoni, Patti. *If It's Purple, Someone's Gonna Die: the Power of Color in Visual Storytelling*.Focal Press. 2005

Bordwell, David and Kristen Thompson. *Film Art: An Introduction*. McGraw-Hill. 1997

Brown, Ada Pullini. *Basic Color Theory*. Unpublished ms. 2000

Brown, Blain. *Filmmaker's Pocket Reference*. Focal Press. 1995
    Motion Picture and Video Lighting. Focal Press. 1995

Campbell, Russell. *Photographic Theory for the Motion Picture Cameraman*. A.S. Barnes & Co. 1974
    Practical Motion Picture Photography. A.S. Barnes & Co. 1979

Carlson, Verne and Sylvia. *Professional Lighting Handbook*. Focal Press. 1985

Case, Dominic. *Film Technology In Post Production*. Focal Press. 1997
    Motion Picture Film Processing. Focal Press. 1990

Cook, David. *A History of Narrative Film*. W.W. Norton & Co. 1982

Davis, Phil. *Beyond The Zone System*. Van Nostrand Reinhold Co. 1981

Dmytryk, Edward. *Cinema: Concept and Practice*. Focal Press. 1998
    On Screen Directing. Focal Press. 1984

Eastman Kodak. *Professional Motion Picture Films* (H-1). Eastman Kodak Co. 1982
    Kodak *Filters For Scientific and Technical Uses* (B-3). Eastman Kodak Co. 1981

Ettedgui, Peter. *Cinematography: Screencraft*. Focal Press. 2000

Fauer, John. *The Arri 35 Book*. Arriflex Corp. 1989

Feldman, Edmund Burke. *Thinking About Art*. Prentice Hall. 1996

Fielding, Raymond. *Special Effects Cinematography*. 4th Edition. Focal Press. 1990

G.E. Lighting. *Stage and Studio Lamp Catalog*. General Electric. 1989

Grob, Bernard. *Basic Television and Video Systems*. McGraw-Hill. 1984

Happe, L. Bernard. *Your Film and the Lab*. Focal Press. 1989

Harrison, H.K. *The Mystery of Filters*. Harrison and Harrison. 1981

Harwig, Robert. *Basic TV Technology*. Focal Press. 1990

Hershey, Fritz Lynn. *Optics and Focus For Camera Assistants*. Focal Press. 1996

Higham, Charles . *Hollywood Cameramen: Sources of Light*. Garland Publishing. 1986

Hirschfeld, Gerald. *Image Control*. Focal Press. 1993

Hyypia, Jorma. *The Complete Tiffen Filter Manual*. Amphoto. 1981

Jacobs, Lewis. *The Emergence of Film Art*. Hopkinson and Blake. 1969

Janson, H.W. *The History of Art*. 6th Edition. Harry Abrams. 2001

Jones, et. al. *Film Into Video*. Focal Press. 2000

Kawin, Bruce. *Mindscreen: Bergman, Godard and First Person Film*. Princeton University Press. 1978

Maltin, Leonard. *The Art of The Cinematographer*. Dover Publications. 1978

Mascelli, Joseph. *The Five C's Of Cinematography*. Cine/Grafic Publications. 1956

McClain, Jerry. *The Influence of Stage Lighting on Early Cinema*. International Photographer. 1986

Millerson, Gerald. *Lighting For Television and Motion Pictures*. Focal Press. 1983

Nelson, Thomas. *Kubrick: Inside A Film Artist's Maze*. Indiana University Press . 1982

Perisic, Zoran. *Visual Effects Cinematography*. Focal Press. 2000

Rabiger, Michael. *Directing – Film Techniques and Aesthetics*. 2nd Edition. Focal Press. 1997

Ray, Sidney. *Applied Photographic Optics*. Focal Press. 1988
    The Lens In Action. Focal Press. 1976

Reisz, Karel and Gavin Millar. *The Technique of Film Editing*. 2nd Edition. Focal Press. 1983

Rogers, Pauline. *More Contemporary Cinematographers On Their Art*. Focal Press. 2000

Samuelson, David. *Motion Picture Camera Data*. Focal Press. 1979

Panaflex User's Manual. Focal Press. 1990

Sharff, Stephen. *The Elements of Cinema*. Columbia University Press. 1982

Shipman, David. *The Story of Cinema*. St. Martin's Press. 1984

St. John Marner, Terrence. *Directing Motion Pictures*. A.S. Barnes. 1972

Sterling, Anna Kate. *Cinematographers on the Art and Craft of Cinematography*. Scarecrow Press. 198t

Stroebel, Leslie. *Photographic Filters*. Morgan & Morgan. 1974

Sylvania. *Lighting Handbook,* 8th Edition. GTE Products. 1989

Thompson, Roy. *Grammar Of The Shot*. Focal Press. 1998

Truffaut, Francois. *Hitchcock/Truffaut*. Simon and Shuster. 1983

Ultimatte Corp. Ultimatte Technical Bulletin #3 "*Shooting Film For Ultimatte.*" Ultimatte Corp. 1992

Ultimatte Technical Bulletin #4 "*Lighting For Ultimatte.*" Ultimatte Corp. 1992

Walker, Alexander. *Stanley Kubrick Directs*. Harcourt Brace. 1969

Wilson, Anton. *Cinema Workshop*. ASC. 1983

index